FOURTH EDITION

MEETINGS, EXPOSITIONS, EVENTS, AND CONVENTIONS
An Introduction
to the Industry

George G. Fenich, Ph.D.

PEARSON

Boston   Columbus   Indianapolis   New York   San Francisco   Hoboken
Amsterdam   Cape Town   Dubai   London   Madrid   Milan   Munich   Paris   Montréal   Toronto
Delhi   Mexico City   São Paulo   Sydney   Hong Kong   Seoul   Singapore   Taipei   Tokyo

Executive Editor: Daryl Fox
Editorial Director: Andrew Gilfillan
Editorial Assistant: Lara Dimmick
Team Lead of Program Management, Workforce Readiness: Laura Weaver
Program Manager: Susan Watkins
SVP Field Marketing, NA: David Gesell
Executive Marketing Manager, Careers and Associations: Ramona Elmer
Senior Marketing Manager, Careers and Associations: Darcy Betts
Senior Marketing Coordinator: Alicia Wozniak
Marketing Coordinator: Les Roberts
Team Lead of Project Management, Workforce Readiness: JoEllen Gohr
Project Manager: Kris Roach
Digital Studio Team Lead, Careers: Rachel Collett
Digital Studio Project Manager, Careers: Leslie Brado
Multimedia Production Coordinator: April Cleland
Senior Art Director: Diane Y. Ernsberger
Cover Art: © Rune Hellestad/Corbis
Cover Designer: Studio Montage
Procurement Specialist: Deidra Skahill
Full-Service Project Management: Lumina Datamatics, Inc.
Composition: Lumina Datamatics, Inc.
Printer/Binder: RR Donnelley/Owensville
Cover Printer: Lehigh-Phoenix Color/Hagerstown
Text Font: 10/12 Minion Pro Regular

Library of Congress Cataloging-in-Publication Data

Fenich, George G.
   Meetings, expositions, events, and conventions : an introduction to the industry /
George G. Fenich, Ph.D. — Fourth edition.
      pages cm
   Includes index.
   ISBN 978-0-13-381524-5 — ISBN 0-13-381524-2 1. Hospitality industry.
   2. Congresses and conventions. 3. Meetings. I. Title.
   TX911.2.F455 2014
   338.4'791—dc23

                                        2014027133

10 9 8 7 6 5 4 3 2 1

ISBN-13: 978-0-13-381524-5
ISBN-10: 0-13-381524-2

Dedicated to Breast Cancer Survivors
Notably My Wife Kathryn

BRIEF CONTENTS

CONTENTS

PREFACE

The meetings, expositions, events, and conventions (MEEC, pronounced like *geese*) industry continues to grow and garner increasing attention from the hospitality industry, colleges and universities, and communities. This book gives a broad overview of this industry and is thus an introduction. It is not meant to provide a hands-on or step-by-step method for handling gatherings in the MEEC industry. The latter is addressed in two books by Fenich: *Planning and Management of Meetings, Expositions, Events, and Conventions* and *Production and Logistics in Meetings, Expositions, Events, and Conventions*. Both of the books are based on and aligned with the Meeting and Business Event Competency Standards (MBECS).

This book is being produced at this time for a number of reasons. One is the continued growth of this industry; in spite of the ebbs and flows of the economy, the MEEC segment of the hospitality industry remains resilient. Communities continue to build or expand MEEC venues unabated, and the private sector has also become a player in convention center construction and operation. People still find a need for face-to-face meetings. The MEEC industry appears to be on a growth curve and is of interest to many people.

Also, college faculties have indicated a need for a book such as this. The author has been teaching an introductory MEEC course for many years and has found himself having to continually supplement the existing books to make them both current and more complete in addressing the various segments of the MEEC industry. Therefore, he began to contemplate the development of a book on the subject. Then, at a meeting of the Convention Special Interest Group at the International Council on Hotel, Restaurant, and Institutional Education (ICHRIE) Convention in 2001, the need for a new text was discussed. The members of this group all noted the need, and the author/editor volunteered to spearhead an effort to put together a new book using faculty and industry experts to write various chapters. This book is a culmination of that effort. The result is a text where some of the best and most notable people in the MEEC industry have made contributions; as you will see, there is a fairly even balance between educators and practitioners among the chapter contributors.

The approach to deciding on topics was unusual. Rather than have a list of topics or chapters based on people's willingness to contribute, a more scientific method was used. The author/editor reviewed existing books, both theoretical and practical, to ascertain which topics to cover. Topics that appeared in more than one text were compiled into a list. Then a number of meetings were held with educators, and the relative importance of topics was discussed, which led to the development of a comprehensive list of topics. This list was sent to educators and practitioners, who were asked to rank the importance of each topic as critically important, important, or not important. Results were used to pare down the list, and this iterative voting procedure (Delphi technique) was used to reach the decision as to the topics to include in the book. This fourth edition not only has updated material and statistics but also has relied on feedback from adopters and reviewers to make improvements to the previous edition.

It should be noted that this industry is referred to in many ways: "Meetings and Events," "Events," "Meeting Planning," and others. A very common acronym, and one used extensively in Asia, is "MICE," which stands for "Meetings, Incentives, Conventions, Events" and is pronounced as the plural of mouse. That acronym was purposely *not* chosen for the title of this text. The reason is that most programs of study deal with the Incentives or Incentive Travel very little, if at all. Further, the Incentive Travel segment has evolved significantly in the past few years moving away from trips that were strictly for pleasure (as a reward for performance) and much more into trips that have notable education and training components. Thus, they are now much more like sales training meetings, motivational meetings, or team building exercises, but on a more grandiose scale. Thus, this book deals with meetings, expositions, events, and conventions.

New In This Edition

- All data has been updated
- Many new images
- The chapter on technology has been totally re-written and updated
- In chapter 2 on the topic of MEEC organizers and sponsors, a section has been added that discusses 'third party' entities
- In chapter 14 on international aspects of MEEC, additional regions of the globe are discussed
- The Glossary has been expanded to include all key terms found in the chapters

Meetings, Expositions, Events, and Conventions should be of interest to practitioners, educators, students, and the general public. It is the most up-to-date book on the MEEC industry and will provide users with an overview of the industry; it is also comprehensive and covers a wider range of MEEC topics than any other book available. It can easily serve as the basis for an introductory college course on the subject or for orientation sessions for new employees in the industry. It should meet the needs of anyone interested in knowing more about the MEEC industry.

George G. Fenich, Ph.D.

ACKNOWLEDGMENTS

I would like to thank Kathryn Hashimoto for her unabated support, patience, and encouragement; the chapter contributors for their work and insights; and students everywhere for their interest in the MEEC industry. Also, thank you to the educators in the MEEC field for helping develop the concept for this book and for continuing support through adoptions of this text.

I would also like to thank the reviewers of this edition for their thoughtful and insightful comments. They are Susan Alvarez, Indiana Purdue University Indianapolis; Pat Golden-Romero, Florida Gulf Coast University; Marla Harr, Arizona State University; Frank Lauterman, Daytona State University; Elizabeth Lewis, Florida State University; Cynthia Mayo, Delaware State University; and David Smiley, Indiana University Bloomington.

INSTRUCTOR'S RESOURCES

Online Supplements Accompanying the Text

An online Instructor's Manual, PowerPoint slides, and TestGen are available to Instructors at www.pearsonhighered.com. Instructors can search for a text by author, title, ISBN, or by selecting the appropriate discipline from the pull-down menu at the top of the catalog home page. To access supplementary materials online, Instructors need to request an instructor access code. Go to www.pearsonhighered.com, click the Instructor Resource Center link, and then click Register Today for an instructor access code. Within 48 hours after registering, you will receive a confirming e-mail including an Instructor access code. Once you have received your code, go to the site and log on for full instructions on downloading the materials you wish to use.

ABOUT THE AUTHOR

George G. Fenich, Ph.D., is a professor in the School of Hospitality Leadership at East Carolina University. Dr. Fenich worked in the hospitality industry for 15 years before joining academe. He teaches and researches in the area of conventions and meetings, has written over 60 academic articles, and has presented at over 150 conferences—including the International Council on Hotel Restaurant and Institutional Education, the Destination Marketing Association International, the Association for Convention Operations Management, the International Association of Assembly Managers, AHTMM in Istanbul, Taipei, and Mauritius, the International Conference on Meetings & Events held in Shanghai China, and the Professional Convention Management Association. He is on the editorial board of six academic journals—including editor-in-chief for the *Journal of Convention and Event Tourism*. He is also the principal of the consulting firm Fenich & Associates LLC.

CHAPTER 1

Introduction to the Meetings, Expositions, Events, and Conventions Industry (MEEC)

The Olympic Games are one of the many aspects of the meetings, expositions, events, and conventions industry. © Rommma/Fotolia

Chapter Objectives

This chapter provides the reader with an understanding of the following:

- The history of the Meetings, Expositions, Events, and Conventions (MEEC) industry
- Where MEEC fits in relation to the hospitality industry
- The magnitude and impact of MEEC
- Careers in MEEC
- Different types of gatherings

Prologue

The vignette that follows is meant to provide an example and insights into the field of meetings, expositions, events, and conventions (MEEC). The chapter concludes with the second half of this vignette. Readers are directed to the glossary at the end of this book and to the Convention Industry Council online glossary at http://glossary.conventionindustry.org for the definitions of any words or terms that they are not familiar with.

The Big Day

Picture this: The sun rises above the horizon, releasing rays of blue and pink light that whisk across the ocean and spill onto the beautifully manicured greens of the resort hotel's championship golf course. Against the backdrop of the crashing surf and pleas of hungry gulls, you can also hear the sounds of morning stirring at the resort hotel. Car doors slamming, muffled voices sharing greetings and farewells, china and silver clashing, and the squeaking wheels of fully laden carts, each heading off to its appointed area under the guiding hand of one of many hotel staff who have arrived before most guests are awake.

Today is a big day. The Association of Amalgamated Professionals (AAP) will open its 35th Annual Congress with an evening reception, and before the day is done, 1,900 guests and hundreds of vendors will have descended on this resort hotel. Since there are growing concerns about the image conveyed by using apparently "glitzy" venues, the venue eliminated the word "resort" from its name. This was done after the contract was signed.

Todd Cliver, Convention Services Manager (**CSM**) for the hotel, convenes a last-minute meeting for the hotel's team that is handling the Annual Congress. Todd has worked tirelessly for nearly nine months, when the account was turned over from the Sales and Marketing department of the hotel, coordinating all of the plans, wants, and needs of his client, the association's Senior Meeting Manager, Barbara Tain. Today represents the culmination of hundreds of e-mails, phone calls, videoconferences, and personal meetings between Todd and Barbara. Todd interacted with every department in the hotel. Barbara worked closely with AAP staff and volunteers, worked with other vendors, and supervised AAP support staff for the AAP's 35th Annual Congress.

Donna Miller, Director of Sales and Marketing, whose department was responsible for contracting this—the largest meeting the hotel will have ever managed—reports on her client's last-minute changes and concerns, all meticulously logged since her client, Barbara Tain, arrived two days ago. David Stern, Front Desk Manager, recaps the latest report on expected room occupancy and on the timing and numbers of anticipated arrivals. Throughout the day, he will continue to check with his staff to ensure that there will be adequate (and contracted!) numbers of front desk clerks to support the check-in flow, bell staff to manage the deluge of luggage and golf clubs, and

door staff, valet parkers, concierge and guest services staff, and housekeeping services.

David Fenner, Director of Catering, provides his final status report, commenting on the readiness of the kitchen and banquet staff to serve the equivalent of almost 12,000 meals and untold gallons of juice, milk, coffee, tea, soda, and alcoholic beverages over the next three days. In addition, the hotel's **outlets** (restaurants and lounges) expect a much higher than average volume and have planned for supplies and personnel accordingly.

Other hotel staff members report to the Director of Sales and the CSM. These include those involved with recreation (golf, tennis, health club, and pool), maintenance, security, and accounting. Even the animal handlers, who work with the parrots, an attraction for guests as they enter the property, want to ensure there are only healthy, well-behaved birds to greet the guests!

This one **convention** has already impacted and will impact every area of the hotel's operations. Armed with all this information, Todd leaves for his final preconference meeting (pre-con) with Barbara Tain, his client.

Meanwhile, on the other side of the country, Jane Lever steps onto Concourse B of the Philadelphia International Airport, her airline boarding pass, e-ticket receipt with its special "meeting discount" price, and government-issued photo ID firmly in her grasp. She has checked her luggage, making sure it is locked with only TSA-approved locks for a possible security search. She scans the bank of monitors for her flight information. Before her day ends, she will have touched down at two other airports, eaten one airline snack, grabbed a candy bar on her way through a change of planes at another airport, made numerous cell phone calls, bought a newspaper and a few magazines, and paid for a taxi to the hotel. Around the country, 1,899 other professionals just like Jane will do the same thing and travel to the same place for the same purpose—a **meeting**.

In the hotel's **destination** (city), Kathy Sykes, the Owner and President of Skylark Destination Management Company (**DMC**), is already at her office reviewing final arrangements for ground transportation for VIPs and off-site events, event theme preparations, and entertainment for the AAP meeting. Kathy has already received two complaints from the manager of the headliner rock star booked for tonight's reception: The entertainer wants only chilled glasses for his orange juice—which he expects to be freshly squeezed in his suite—and can only get dressed if he is provided with navy blue towels for his after-shower rubdown. Kathy, of course, will ensure compliance with these requests; she wants to avoid any problems before tonight's event.

With a thunderstorm threatening for tomorrow afternoon, Kathy's mind is also already racing about alternatives for the golf tournament. She knows the golfers can play in the rain, but a thunderstorm would endanger their safety.

Jack Ardulosky, a Senior Technical Engineer for an audiovisual company, pulls into the hotel's delivery area while completing his mental checklist for final site review, satellite link integrity, picture clarity, and sound quality. With three global broadcasts and webcasts, he will have little room for error. He sees the florist unloading the last of the fresh floral arrangements and makes a note to himself that leaves and petals can cause just as much of a viewing obstruction as meeting room columns. He scans the area around him for a parking spot since not much is available with all the trucks and vans unloading the trade show booths. Jack notices the rising ambient temperature and expects a long, hot day. He will feel better as long as he can find parking in the shade, even if he has to walk a greater distance.

Barbara Tain, the Senior Meeting Manager for the association, wipes the beginning of fatigue from her eyes—she has already been on site for two days, and her constant checking of details has not allowed her to sleep as well as she would have liked—and continues her walk-through of the registration area, information center, and cyber café, ensuring the meeting space will be appropriately set for delivery of the education critical to the meeting's objectives—en route to a meeting with Todd Cliver and David Fenner. Having eaten just a few bites of her breakfast during a meeting with association executives and key committee members, she will still be late to her meeting with Cliver and Fenner because of last-minute details and concerns from the meeting with association staff and volunteers.

Only half glancing at the space around her, she again reviews her lengthy checklists: speaker and trainer arrivals and needs, banquet event orders (**BEOs**), transportation schedules, badges, staffing, centerpiece design and delivery, phone and data lines, computers and printers, Wi-Fi bandwidth, exhibitor booth setup, VIP procedures, concerns about tomorrow's weather, special check-in processes, audiovisual equipment, opening production rehearsal times and needs, PowerPoint™ files, handouts, arrangements for participants with disabilities including those who have specified food allergies, and amenities for VIPs—her mind is crowded with details.

With all this and more going through her mind, her most dominant thought is, "What could go wrong over the next three days—weather? Delayed arrivals? Delayed departures? The illness, or worse, death, of a participant, vendor, or speaker? A natural disaster like an earthquake? How prepared am I, and is the hotel and our vendors and off-site venues ready to respond quickly and effectively?" The fact is, although it is almost never apparent to a meeting participant, some things may not proceed as planned. The meeting planner and CSM are never more important than at that moment when a crisis must be anticipated and then averted.

It is opening day at last, and everything is in motion.

INTRODUCTION

What a Difference a Day Makes

Planning for AAP's 35th Annual Congress began long before the previous year's program ended and before nine months ago when the file was turned over to Convention Services. The scenario in the opening of this chapter is only a brief glimpse of the multitude of complexities that support planning and management, and of the jobs that employ those who work in and around the meetings, expositions, events, and conventions (**MEEC**) industry, all of which contribute to a meeting's success. In some parts of the world, this industry is listed as meetings, incentives, conventions, events or MICE. MEEC and MICE are interchangeable.

By the time the AAP program is over, roughly 1,900 people (participants and exhibitors) will have flown on approximately 9 major airlines and regional carriers on 200 different flights; covered 4 million air miles; consumed 1,000 airline snacks and thousands of bags of candy or snacks grabbed on runs through airports; participated in 60,000 people hours of presentations, education, and social events; played 4,000 person hours of golf; and eaten approximately 12,000 catered meals. They will have made about 80,000 telephone calls, purchased and read

5,700 newspapers (both in hard copy and web based), transmitted and received more than 10,000 emails, and injected about $5,000,000 into the local economy. Their presence will generate about $500,000 in taxes toward state and local coffers. Countless local business owners will make sales in everything from clothing to artwork to souvenirs. Dry cleaners, cab drivers, restaurateurs, sports facilities, attractions, and hotels will all see jumps in their average weekly revenue. There may also be a significant boost to the local underground, cash-only economy, with contributions from the seamier side of this phenomenon such as gambling, drugs, and prostitution. In total, the convention-related activities for this single event will touch more than 250 local jobs.

Performing poorly at any of the hundreds of potential failure points or "moments of truth" of planning and executing a meeting or event, and especially not achieving the objectives and meeting the needs of the participants and vendors, can cause a dramatic immediate financial loss to the geographic area. In addition, the financial impact could result in positive or negative impacts for years to come: A good experience by each attendee will result in praise to many others; a negative experience will result in even more people hearing the results of the stay in that destination. Each of these people can bring or deny more business to the destination and the resort.

ACCEPTED PRACTICES EXCHANGE

Throughout this book, you will hear about the Convention Industry Council (**CIC**) and its Accepted Practices Exchange (APEX). The following is from http://www.conventionindustry. org/apex and is meant to provide early insight into this initiative.

The CIC is at the forefront of efforts to advance the meeting, convention, and exhibition industry. It represents a broad cross-section with 30 member organizations representing more than 103,500 individuals as well as more than 19,000 firms and properties involved in the meetings, conventions, and exhibitions industry. Formed in 1949 to provide a forum for member organizations seeking to enhance the industry, the CIC facilitates the exchange of information and develops programs to promote professionalism within the industry and educates the public on its profound economic impact. By its nature, the CIC provides an impartial and inclusive forum for APEX and the development of accepted practices for the industry.

APEX is an initiative of the CIC that has brought together all stakeholders in the development and implementation of industry-wide accepted practices to create and enhance efficiencies throughout the meetings, conventions, and exhibitions industry.

Some of the results of accepted practices implementation will be:

- Time & Cost Savings
- Eased Communication and Sharing of Data
- Enhanced Customer Service
- Streamlined Systems and Processes
- Less Duplication of Effort and Increased Operational Efficiencies
- Better Educated, More Professional Employees

WHAT IS A MEETING?

What are these things called "meetings," "exhibitions," "symposia," "congresses," "events," and "conventions?" In what ways do meetings contribute to furthering skills and knowledge for those who attend and participate? Why are they so important to the economy? Will virtual events take the place of face-to-face gatherings in the years ahead? Why hold meetings at all? In what ways can our specific events be designed better to meet our audience's needs? How do we differentiate what we do versus what the competition does so that we can improve market share? All of these questions are addressed in this chapter. Welcome to the fast-paced, tense, yet ultimately fulfilling world of MEEC.

The APEX initiative proposes the generic definition of *meeting*: An event where the primary activity of the participants is to attend educational sessions, participate in discussions social functions, or attend other organized events. There is no exhibit component. Compare with terms *Convention, Exhibition, Trade Show, Consumer Show*, which are explained in the following section "Industry Terminology and Practice."

Synonyms for "meeting" include the following:

affair, assemblage, assembly, assignation, audience, bunch, buzz session, call, cattle call, clambake, company, competition, conclave, concourse, concursion, confab, **conference**, conflict, confrontation, congregation, congress, contest, convention, convocation, date, encounter, engagement, gang, gathering, get-together, gig, huddle, introduction, meet, nooner, parley, powwow, quickie, rally, rap session, rendezvous, reunion, session, showdown, sit-in, talk, tryst, turnout

Industry Terminology and Practice

We have always, generically, referred to gatherings of two or more people as "meetings." This term clearly could encompass meetings that are also called "conventions," "congresses," "symposia," and so on, some of which could have tens of thousands of people in attendance. If one adds displays of materials or products to a meeting, the meeting then has a trade show or **exposition** or **exhibition** component. When sporting, social, or life cycle activities are added, then a generic term that encompasses them all is "events." Even broader and more generic is the term "gathering." One has to be conscious of how your stakeholders or target audience will interpret the name that is applied to a gathering.

The following list of terms is important for anyone involved in the MEEC industry to know. The terms were developed by the terminology panel of APEX, a part of the Convention Industry Council and are a small sample of the thousands of words that apply to this industry. The complete glossary of terms used in the MEEC industry can be found online at http://glossary.conventionindustry.org. The terms as well as other material from the CIC are used throughout this book and with their permission.

- **Meeting:** An event where the primary activity of the attendees is to attend educational sessions, participate in meetings/discussions, socialize, or attend other organized events. There is no exhibit component to this event. See also Convention, Exhibition, Trade Show, and Consumer Show explained in the following paragraphs.
- **Exposition:** See Exhibition.
- **Exhibition:** An event at which products, services, or promotional materials are displayed to attendees visiting exhibits on the show floor. These events focus primarily on business-to-business (B2B) relationships (same as Exposition or Trade Show). See Trade Show, Consumer Show, Gate Show, and Public Show.
- **Event:** An organized occasion such as a meeting, convention, exhibition, special event, gala dinner, and so on. An event is often composed of several different yet related FUNCTIONS.
- **Convention:** Gathering of delegates, representatives, and members of a membership or industry organization convened for a common purpose. Common features include educational sessions, committee meetings, social functions, and meetings to conduct the governance business of the organization. Conventions are typically recurring events with specific, established timing. See also: Meeting, Exhibition, Trade Show, and Consumer Show.
- **Trade Show:** An exhibition of products and/or services held for members of a common or related industry. Not open to the general public. If it is open to the public it is called a Consumer Show. See Exhibition. Compare with *Gate Show*, *Public Show*, and *Consumer Show*. See also: Exhibition, Gate Show, Public Show, and Consumer Show.
- **Seminar:** (1) A lecture and dialogue allowing participants to share experiences in a particular field under the guidance of an expert discussion leader. (2) A meeting or series of meetings of 10 to 50 specialists who have different specific skills but have a specific common interest and come together for training or learning purposes. The work schedule of a seminar has the specific object of enriching the skills of the participants.
- **Workshop:** (1) A meeting of several persons for intensive discussion. The workshop concept has been developed to compensate for diverging views in a particular discipline or on a particular subject. (2) An informal and public session of free discussion organized to take place between formal plenary sessions or commissions of a congress or of a conference, either on a subject chosen by the participants themselves or else on a special problem suggested by the organizers. (3) A training session in which participants, often through exercises, develop skills and knowledge in a given field.
- **Conference:** (1) A participatory meeting designed for discussion, fact-finding, problem solving, and consultation. (2) An event used by any organization to meet and exchange

views, convey a message, open a debate, or give publicity to some area of opinion on a specific issue. No tradition, continuity, or periodicity is required to convene a conference. Although not generally limited in time, conferences are usually of short duration with specific objectives. Conferences are generally on a smaller scale than congresses. See also Congress, Convention.

- *Clinic:* A workshop-type educational experience where attendees learn by doing.
- *Break-Out Sessions:* Small group sessions, panels, workshops, or presentations offered concurrently within the event, formed to focus on specific subjects. Break-out sessions are separate from the general session, but within the meeting format, and formed to focus on specific subjects. These sessions can be arranged by basic, intermediate, or advanced information, or divided by interest areas or industry segment.
- *Assembly:* (1) A general or formal meeting of an organization attended by representatives of its membership for the purpose of deciding legislative direction, policy matters, the election of internal committees, and approval of balance sheets, budgets, and so on. Consequently, an assembly usually observes certain rules of procedure for its meetings, mostly prescribed in its articles and bylaws. (2) The process of erecting display component parts into a complete exhibit.
- *Congress:* (1) The regular coming together of large groups of individuals, generally to discuss a particular subject. A congress will often last several days and have several simultaneous sessions. The length of time between congresses is usually established in advance of the implementation stage and can be either semiannual or annual. Most international or world congresses are of the former type, whereas national congresses are more frequently held annually. (2) A European term for convention. See also Conference, Convention.
- *Forum:* (1) An open discussion with an audience, panel, and moderator. A meeting or part of a meeting set aside for an open discussion by recognized participants on subjects of public interest.
- *Symposium:* A meeting of a number of experts in a particular field, at which papers are presented and discussed by specialists on particular subjects with a view to making recommendations concerning the problems under discussion.
- *Institute:* An in-depth instructional meeting providing intensive education on a particular subject.
- *Lecture:* An informative and instructional speech.
- *Panel Discussion:* Instructional technique using a group of people chosen to discuss a topic in the presence of an audience.

THE ORGANIZATIONAL STRUCTURE OF THE HOSPITALITY INDUSTRY: HOW MEEC FITS IN

MEEC is a part of and encompasses many elements of the hospitality and tourism industry. In order to understand how MEEC is related to the hospitality and service industry, one must understand the organization and structure of the tourism and hospitality industry itself.

There are six major divisions, or segments, of the tourism and hospitality industry: lodging, food and beverage, transportation, attractions, entertainment, and shopping.

1. *Lodging:* The lodging segment consists of all types of places where travelers may spend the night. These can include hotels, conference centers, resorts, motels, bed-and-breakfasts, cruise ships, trailer parks or campsites, condominiums, and college dormitories. The important characteristics of this segment are that they are available to the public and charge a fee for usage.
2. *Food and Beverage:* Obviously, this segment actually contains two sub-segments: food service operations and beverage operations. Food service operations can include the following: table service facilities that can be further broken down by price—high, medium, and low; by type of service—luxury, quick service, and so on; or by cuisine—American, East Asian, Italian, and others. Food service also embraces other types of operations including catering, chains, and institutional feeding. Beverage operations can also be broken down by price or type of service, and even whether they serve alcoholic beverages or not.

3. *Transportation:* This segment includes any means, or modality that people use to get from one place to another, including walking. The better-known elements include air, water, and ground transportation.

   Air transportation: This sub-segment includes regularly scheduled carriers such as Delta or Lufthansa and charter air service that can involve jets, propeller aircraft, and helicopters.

   Water transportation: This sub-segment includes cruise ships and paddle wheelers, charter operations, ferries, and water taxis.

   Ground transportation: This sub-segment includes private automobiles, taxis, limousines, jitneys, buses, trains, cog railways, cable cars, monorails, horse-drawn vehicles, and even elephants and camels.

4. *Attractions:* This segment of the hospitality and tourism industry includes anything that attracts people to a destination and can be further divided into natural and person-made attractions.

   Natural attractions: This sub-segment includes mountains, seashores, lakes, forests, swamps, climate, and rivers.

   Person-made attractions: This sub-segment consists of things made or constructed by human beings, including buildings such as monuments, museums, theme parks, zoos, aquariums, and some restaurants and shopping venues.

5. *Entertainment:* This includes anything that provides entertainment value for a guest such as movie theaters, playhouses, orchestras, bands, and festivals.

6. *Shopping:* This is an important segment of the hospitality and tourism industry, and an area in which people may spend considerable sums of money thus contributing to the local economy. Many attractions have developed products that carry their theme or logo and result in significant revenue streams for the operator. Probably the best known is Disney, whose products are sold not only at its attractions, but also in stand-alone retail centers.

As one can see, the hospitality and tourism industry is multifaceted. Furthermore, the framework offered in the preceding list is meant to help provide an understanding of the industry and is not intended to be a well-delineated typology. There are many overlaps between the categories: A hotel may be an attraction in itself, such as the CityCenter in Las Vegas; the same is true of some stores, such as FAO Schwarz in New York City or the Mall of America in Minneapolis. Hotels often have food and beverage outlets, retail stores, and even entertainment. Furthermore, some of the businesses mentioned above cater to both the tourist, meeting-goer and local resident, making it difficult to determine how much business is derived from each constituency.

It would seem then, that the MEEC industry is involved with all segments of the hospitality and tourism industry. Understanding the interactions and complexities of the hospitality and tourism industry, along with MEEC, helps explain why it is difficult to determine the size and scope of these industries. Until the late 1990s, the U.S. government, using its North American Industry Classification System (NAICS) codes, did not even track many elements of these industries. For example, the government did not even list "meeting planner" as a recognized profession until the late 1980s.

Background of the Industry

Gatherings, meetings, events, and conventions (of sorts) have been a part of people's lives since the earliest recorded history. Archeologists have found primitive ruins from ancient cultures that were used as meeting areas where citizens would gather to discuss common interests, such as government, war, hunting, or tribal celebrations. Once humans developed permanent settlements, each town or village had a public meeting area, often called a town square, where residents could meet, talk, and celebrate. Under the leadership of Alexander the Great, over half a million people traveled to what was then Ephesus (now Turkey) to see exhibitions that included acrobats, magicians, animal trainers, and jugglers. Andrew Young, the former U.S. ambassador to the United Nations, said at a Meeting Professionals International (MPI) meeting in Atlanta in the middle 1990s that he was sure there would have been a meeting planner for the Last Supper and certainly for the first Olympics. In Rome, the Forum was a type of organized meeting to discuss politics and decide the fate of the country. Ancient Rome had the Coliseum, which was the site of major sporting events such as gladiatorial contests—someone had to organize them! Through the use of excellent roadways, the Romans were able to establish trade markets to entice people to visit their cities. In Old England, there are stories of King Arthur's Round Table, another example of a meeting to discuss the trials and tribulations of the day. Religious gatherings of various faiths and pilgrimages to Mecca are examples of ancient religious meetings and festivals. The Olympics began as an ancient sporting event that was organized as similar events are today. World's fairs and expositions are still another piece of the MEEC industry.

The MEEC industry has also been a part of American culture and development. The white steeples surrounded by snow-covered ground seen in Currier and Ives prints actually depicted the town squares of New England cities. In one of the oldest communities in North America, Santa Fe, the square not only houses the seat of government but also has been traditionally used as a festival marketplace. Even today, Native Americans can be seen around the perimeter of the square displaying their handicrafts for sale.

The First Continental Congress in Philadelphia is an example of a "formal meeting," in this case to decide the governance of the 13 colonies. Political conventions have a long history in the United States and are part of the MEEC industry. Americans have also made festivals and celebrations of every sort, such as Mardi Gras in New Orleans, a part of their lives since the early days of this country, and events like these can also be part of the MEEC industry.

Today, structures supporting the MEEC industry are integral parts of major cities. It is a well-known fact that in order to be considered a *world class city*, a community must have a convention center and a stadium or arena for sports and events. All the largest cities have them, including New York, Washington, DC, Barcelona, Chicago, London, Moscow, Pretoria, and Hong Kong. The hope is that these public facilities will attract out-of-town attendees for conventions and events who will spend money in the community.

In spite of its long history, meeting planning as a recognized profession did not develop until 1972, when **MPI** was founded. Only 120 planners and suppliers attended its first convention. The first board of directors was headed by "Buzz" Bartow and led to the development of the first academic meeting planning program. This program, approved by the state of Colorado in September of 1976, was implemented by Metropolitan State College (now University) in Denver. This initiative was closely followed by the meeting planning program at Northeastern Oklahoma

Mardi Gras in New Orleans.
© *Wendy Kaveney/Fotolia*

University in Tahlequah. In 1979, Patti Shock started the convention service management (hotel perspective) and meeting planning classes at Georgia State University (GSU). In 1983, trade show classes were added with the financial support of the National Association of Exposition Managers (NAEM) (now the International Association of Exhibitions and Events, IAEE) and IAFE (International Association of Fairs and Expositions). GSU was the first to implement trade show classes, and therefore the first to cover the whole convention industry.

There were two factors that contributed to the rapid development of both industry workshops and academic programs during the 1980s. The first was the development and implementation of the Certified Meeting Professional (CMP) examination and designation by the Convention Liaison Council (CLC now CIC). This certification gives both status and credence to the person who achieves it. Additional certificate programs have followed, including Certified Meeting Manager (CMM), Certified Destination Marketing Executive (CDME), and others.

Since its founding in New York in 1949 by four organizations—the American Society of Association Executives (ASAE), American Hotel and Motel Association (AH&MA, now the American Hotel Lodging Association), Hospitality (then Hotel) Sales and Marketing Association International (HSMAI), and International Association of Convention and Visitor Bureaus (IACVB) (now Destination Marketing Association International or **DMAI**)—the CIC (then, the Convention Liaison Council) has traditionally followed the lead of its constituent organizations.

In 1895, the basis of today's destination marketing organizations (DMO) that are also called convention & visitor bureaus (CVBs) was put forth when journalist Milton Carmichael wrote in *The Detroit Journal* that local businessmen get together to promote the city as a convention destination, as well as represent the city and its many hotels to bid for that business. Shortly thereafter the Detroit Convention and Businessmen's League was conceived to do just that. Carmichael was the head of the group, that later evolved into the Detroit Metro CVB that is now labeled *VisitDetroit*.

The role of CVB's (now referred to as Destination Marketing Organizations or DMOs) has changed over time. As in Detroit, most began by trying to attract only conventions and business meetings to their community. Later, they realized leisure visitors were an important source of business and added the "V" for visitors to their name. Today, virtually every city in the United States and Canada, and many cities throughout the world, has a DMO or convention and visitors association (CVA). The DMO (CVB, CVA) is a membership organization that helps promote tourism, meetings, and related business for their cities. In some international destinations, the DMO is a division of government. Most recently, the term "DMO" is being used in place of CVB. In this text, the terms are synonymous and interchangeable.

Economic Impact

The MEEC industry is diverse. As a result, it is hard to estimate the size, magnitude, and impact of MEEC. According to recent reports there were 1.87 million meetings held in the United States that were attended by 225 million people and contributed $115 billion to the GDP of the country. In the United Kingdom, the contribution to the economy was $92 billion. The total economic output of U.S. meetings was pegged at $770.4 billion and generated $88 billion in federal, state, and local taxes. Most of the participants traveled more than the requisite 50 miles that makes them tourists and obviously spent money in the destination on hotel rooms, meals, and so on. The MEEC industry supports 1.78 million jobs in the United States alone. It is estimated that 1 in every 86 individuals is employed in some aspect of the industry. These numbers are estimated to grow every year as many individuals, corporations, and many countries start to understand the importance of the MEEC industry. This made the MEEC industry one of the largest contributors to the gross national product, larger than the motion picture industry ($113 billion), performing arts/museums/spectator sports ($87 billion) and data processing and information services ($80 billion). This should give great hope for anyone with a career in the MEEC industry because the MEEC industry is very important to the economy and jobs will always be needed. According to the U.S. Bureau of Labor Statistics, conventions and events are expected to expand by 44% from 2010 to 2020, far beyond the average projected growth of other industries.

The tough conditions facing meeting professionals during the recession are slowly fading. The hiring picture is also improving, with overall employment in the meeting and event industry ticking up a bit. Not surprisingly, economic uncertainty is still a worry for many meeting and event professionals.

Why Have Meetings and Events?

In the early to mid-1980s, there were discussions, (as there was immediately after September 11, 2001) and again during the economic crisis that begin in 2008, that face-to-face meetings would be things of the past—that virtual meetings (teleconferencing, webinars, etc.) would supplant face-to-face gatherings. The Foundation of MPI conducted studies in the mid-1990s that focused on what made meetings work for associations and corporations. These studies showed that people preferred meeting face-to-face, and that one of the most important values of gatherings is the ability to meet with and learn from peers. "Virtual" meetings in all forms (audio and video conferences, webinars, podcasts, online learning, and exchanges) do not yet create the desired effect, although various companies such as CISCO and other platforms are working to improve the future of virtual meetings. The debate rages on. The trend today is to add a "virtual" component to face-to-face meetings, thus expanding the potential market of participants. These are sometimes called "hybrid events."

Face-to-face meetings have the benefit of including all forms of communication, including verbal and nonverbal. For example, what does the strength and style of a handshake tell you about people in some cultures? How do their facial expressions support their words, or are they sending mixed messages? How do you feel if the people to whom you are speaking never look you "straight in the eye?" Nonverbal communication is a very important part of meeting with people. Others cite the importance of face-to-face versus virtual meetings in "closing deals."

When we meet, we build "communities of practice." Today, we use social media to develop communities of practice, which then often want to meet face to face. What we more often see is "blended learning" that is often used to define blending the use of technology and face-to-face interactions to deliver content and build communities of practice.

Virtually or face to face, through these communities of practice, we are able to strengthen skills (at sales or association educational meetings, or symposia), impact change (at political conventions or governance meetings), observe accomplishments (at incentive meetings and celebrations), renew acquaintances (at reunions), and learn about new products in our field (at exhibitions and trade shows).

Today, we participate, virtually, in many events and interactions: attending classes; viewing live streaming of sporting events and meetings; and even attending community, religious, or spiritual events. In 1999, *High Tech-High Touch*, written by John Naisbitt and others, was first

Shaking hand is a form of nonverbal communication.
© *albertobogo/Fotolia*

published. In this book the authors look at the impact of a technological society and the need for "unplugging" now and then. The need for experiential learning and participation, noted in Pine and Gilmore's *The Experience Economy*, continues to drive meetings and events: One attends the Super Bowl to participate in the excitement of the crowd and the experience of being there. One attends a wedding face-to-face to experience the joy of those gathered and to taste the cake and drink the champagne! Although there are sites, including islands in SecondLife™ (such as Virtualis™) that even offer virtual weddings, they are not yet in the mainstream.

Our jobs are to follow the trends and to find methods by which we can meet our objectives for meetings and events using the best methods possible for delivery for our demographic. In some cases, that will be face to face, and in others, virtual. In more cases, it will be blended.

EVOLUTION AND MATURATION OF THE MEEC INDUSTRY

(The following section is adapted from Fenich *Planning and Management of Meetings, Expositions, Events, and Conventions* 1st Edition)

It can be said that events and meetings have been around since the dawn of time. The Romans had the Forum where meetings took place and the Coliseum where events took place. Religious pilgrimages have taken place for thousands of years. In America, town hall forums were a type of meeting begun in the eighteenth century. While someone had to plan all of these events, there was neither formal training nor established sets of skills, standards, and abilities for MEEC professionals. However, like other industries, such as law and accounting, as an industry evolves and matures there is an increasing need among clients, employers, and governments to have a codified set of competency standards to which professionals must adhere. Until very recently no common set of knowledge, skills, and abilities (**KSAs**) existed for events professionals.

This dearth of standards changed in 2011 with the release of the Meetings and Business Events Competency Standards (**MBECS**). MBECS contains the KSAs required of meetings and events professionals.

MBECS

The MBECS are divided into 12 domains or blocks with 33 skills and almost 100 sub-skills or sub-segments. The domains and skills are listed below:

  A. STRATEGIC PLANNING
  1. Manage Strategic Plan for Meeting or Event
  2. Develop Sustainability Plan for Meeting or Event
  3. Measure Value of Meeting or Business Event

  B. PROJECT MANAGEMENT
  4. Plan Meeting or Event
  5. Manage Meeting or Event Project

  C. RISK MANAGEMENT
  6. Manage Risk Management Plan

  D. FINANCIAL MANAGEMENT
  7. Develop Financial Resources
  8. Manage Budget
  9. Manage Monetary Transactions

  E. ADMINISTRATION
  10. Perform Administrative Tasks

  F. HUMAN RESOURCES
  11. Manage Human Resource Plan
  12. Acquire Staff and Volunteers
  13. Train Staff and Volunteers
  14. Manage Workforce Relations

    G. STAKEHOLDER MANAGEMENT
        15. Manage Stakeholder Relationships

    H. MEETING OR EVENT DESIGN
        16. Design Program
        17. Engage Speakers and Performers
        18. Coordinate Food and Beverage
        19. Design Environment
        20. Manage Technical Production
        21. Develop Plan for Managing Movement of People

    I. SITE MANAGEMENT
        22. Select Site
        23. Design Site Layout
        24. Manage Meeting or Event Site
        25. Manage On-site Communications

    J. MARKETING
        26. Manage Marketing Plan
        27. Manage Marketing Materials
        28. Manage Meeting or Event Merchandise
        29. Promote Meeting or Event
        30. Contribute to Public Relations Activities
        31. Manage Sales Activities

    K. PROFESSIONALISM
        32. Exhibit Professional Behavior

    L. COMMUNICATIONS
        33. Conduct Business Communications

The list above represents all the KSAs an event professional needs to acquire, and be proficient in, during the course of their career. That these are, in fact, those KSAs needed by event professionals was validated when the CIC adopted MBECS as the primary basis for their new Certified Meeting Professional International Standards (CMP-IS) and for the CMP Exam. The development of these standards marks a milestone in the MEEC industry. For the first time all players in this industry have a common benchmark or point of reference.

USES OF THE STANDARDS The standards synopsized above represent the first time that the base of knowledge in the meetings/events arena has been codified. Thus, moving forward, the industry profession, academics, students, professionals, human resources staff, and so on can work from the same base.

USES FOR MEETINGS/EVENTS PROFESSIONALS The MBECS represent the KSAs a practitioner must possess in order to be successful in the field. Industry professionals can perform a personal "skills assessment" of those standards and skills at which they are adept and those that they are not. The resulting "gap analysis" can help guide their professional and personal development. MBECS can also help plot career paths. Being able to provide an assessment that shows a broad mastery of the subject will enhance employability and mobility across sectors and countries. This also allows an industry professional to promote their KSAs to employers or clients.

The MBECS is of great value to employers and managers. The standards can aid in the development of job descriptions and job specifications. This leads to improvements in determining workforce requirements and producing worker solicitations. The standards can also help in developing a sequence of training for employees as well as a basis for performance assessment and feedback.

USES FOR THE ACADEMIC COMMUNITY The MBECS provides the internationally accepted basis for developing courses of study and their requisite content. It is up to a given program or institution to determine how the content is delivered: in meetings/events specific courses, in business courses, in general education, or a combination. The significant advantage of using MBECS is that it is not prescriptive: one size does not fit all. Existing programs can "benchmark" themselves against the standards with resulting global recognition. The MBECS also provide a platform for dealing with governmental authorities and accrediting bodies. Using MBECS, a program can show the relevance of their course offerings and justify the content based on an international body of knowledge. Students can use the standards to develop their educational pathways and to validate their "employability" to recruiters. They could also use the standards to determine which educational programs best meet their learning needs. For academics, the standards can help delineate areas or topics in the meetings/events world that are in need of research.

USES FOR ASSOCIATIONS First and foremost the MBECS provides recognition of the KSAs required by the industry. This can then help guide the development of program content and delivery that is consistent with international standards. MBECS can also be used by the members of an association to determine their educational or professional development needs and how the association can best fulfill those needs (Fenich, 2012b).

THIS BOOK: MEETINGS, EXPOSITIONS, EVENTS, AND CONVENTIONS: AN INTRODUCTION TO THE INDUSTRY

This content of this book is meant to provide an introduction and an overview of the MEEC industry. Thus, only a few of the chapters deal with KSAs. However, those chapters that do such as "legal issues', "technology', and so on. are based on MBECS. In the chapter summary at the end of those chapters is found a list of the specific standards, skills, and sub-skills from MBECS that have been covered in the chapter. Thus, readers can cross-check those MBECS KSAs covered in the chapter against the full set of MBECS standards thus creating a personal "skills assessment." After completing this book, readers can progress to two additional texts "Planning and Management of MEEC" and "Production and Logistics in MEEC." After gaining the knowledge in these three books, the reader will have the knowledge base the MEEC industry expects of "manager level" employees. Further, the reader will be well positioned to be successful in pursuing the CMP certification.

EMPLOYMENT IN AND AROUND THE MEEC INDUSTRY

The MEEC industry is a sub-segment of the hospitality industry, which itself is part of the larger services industry. It encompasses many areas of the hospitality industry. Thus, readers are challenged to conceptualize their personal ideal job and then determine how and where in the MEEC industry they could be employed doing what they dream of.

Some of the careers in MEEC include the following:

- *Event Planner:* Puts together special events like the Olympics, the Super Bowl in football, the Final Four in basketball, festivals, and celebrations.
- *Meeting Planner:* Organizes meetings and other gatherings for companies, corporations, and associations. These gatherings can include a small board of directors meeting, a stockholders meeting, new product introductions and training, educational seminars, and regional or national conventions.
- *Wedding Planner:* A wedding planner assists the parties in selecting the site, décor, photographer, and other needed vendors and is often there on the day of the event to ensure smooth operations.
- *Hotel or Conference Center Sales:* The majority of sales and convention or catering services positions in hotels and conference centers deal with groups, and MEEC covers most of those groups.
- *Restaurant Sales:* While most people think of restaurants attracting walk-in clientele, many rely heavily on the MEEC industry for business. Food and beverage (F&B) venues employ significant numbers of people on their group sales staff. In New Orleans, Arnaud's and Emeril's, for example, have group or convention sales teams.

- *Entertainment/Sporting Venue Sales & Services:* Although these places primarily attract individual patrons, most also devote much time and effort to selling, providing space for, and producing events for groups. These off-site venues are often good alternatives for experiential learning.
- *Destination Management:* Destination Management Companies (DMCs) function as the "local experts" for companies and associations in organizing gatherings and events, arranging and supervising transportation, and securing entertainers. People employed for DMCs usually work in either sales or production.
- *Hotels:* Hotels are one of the primary locations where MEEC events are held, using ballrooms, meeting rooms, breakout rooms, and so on, for their gatherings along with sleeping rooms and F&B for their attendees. The hotel departments that deal with the MEEC industry are sales, catering, and convention services.
- *Convention Centers:* These venues include dedicated facilities such as McCormick Place in Chicago, the Jacob K. Javits Convention Center in New York, and the Mandalay Bay Hotel and Convention Center in Las Vegas. Also included in this category are multipurpose venues like the Superdome in New Orleans or the Astrodome in Houston. With these venues, careers are found in either sales or operations.
- *Exposition Services Contractors:* If you like to build things or have thought about being an engineer or architect, you should consider being an exposition services contractor (ESC). ESCs design and erect the booths, backdrops, staging, and so on for meetings and conventions. The decorations and backdrops for your school prom may have been done by an ESC. Again, career paths exist in sales and production and increasingly in design of sustainable/"green" products and services.
- *Destination Marketing Organizations (Convention and Visitor Bureaus):* DMOs serve to represent a wide range of MEEC companies and to market the destination to business and leisure travelers. DMOs have many departments and careers, including convention sales, tourism sales, housing bureaus, convention services, marketing, research, and member services.

As you can see, the MEEC industry is a vibrant, dynamic, and exciting part of the hospitality industry. Many careers in MEEC involve multiple aspects of the hospitality industry. For example, someone who works in convention or group sales in a facility must interface with, be knowledgeable about, and manage people who work with guest rooms, front desk, food and beverage, catering, and all of the meeting facilities. Some of the most important aspects of working in MEEC are business acumen (financial and people management, legalities and risk management, **sales and marketing**, ethical practices), visioning (what can be) and execution of ideas into concepts, and knowledge of adult learning techniques. In addition to knowledge and ability for preparing and delivering virtual and face-to-face meetings, industry professionals must know more about sustainability and "green" for meetings and events.

It is often said that MEEC is a "relationship industry," that is, one built on who you know and with whom you do business. As in many industries, we depend on those we know to help us learn and grow and to provide accurate information. These relationships are built over time and always with the understanding that first and foremost, ethical business practices will be the most important aspect of how we relate.

Think for just a moment about all the lives and jobs that could impact one of the meeting participants and the meeting organizers involved in the scenario for the Association of Amalgamated Professionals. They include the following:

The Meeting Sponsor

- The Association of Amalgamated Professionals
- Meeting planner
- Executive director or chief executive officer
- Staff specialists in departments that include marketing, governance and government affairs, education/professional development/training, membership, information technology, and accreditation
- Others who staff call centers, copy materials, process registrations, manage human resources, control purchasing, and more
- Board of directors

- Committees
- Sponsors

The Facility

- Owners
- Executive staff, including but not limited to: general manager, revenue manager, resident or hotel manager, directors of sales, marketing, convention services, catering, housekeeping, engineering, maintenance, purchasing, human resources, food and beverage, front office operations, social responsibility, and security.
- The thousands of other full- and part-time, year-round, and seasonal staff: groundskeepers, animal handlers, housekeepers, food servers (for banquets, room service, and the outlets), maintenance, security, and engineering.

The Destination

- DMO/CVB (president, directors of sales, marketing, convention services, membership, registration, social responsibility, and all support staff)
- Restaurants
- Attractions
- Off-site venues
- Theaters (movie and legitimate)
- Copy and printing companies
- Transportation (buses, airport shuttles, taxicabs, limousines)
- Airport concessions
- Doctors, medical personnel, and emergency workers
- Pharmacies
- Florists
- Department and other stores
- Destination management companies
- Audiovisual suppliers
- General services contractors
- Specialty services contractors
- Dry cleaners and tailors
- City, county, and state employees
- IT division and telecommunications department

All Others Who Provide Services for Meetings

- Talent (entertainers, disc jockeys, bands, magicians)
- Education (speakers, trainers, facilitators)
- Sound and lighting
- Transportation (air, rail, car, boat, and travel agencies)
- Printing
- Shipping
- Promotional products
- Off-property food and beverage
- Translators for those who speak American Sign Language and other languages
- Americans with Disabilities Act equipment
- Carpentry
- National sales (hotels, conference centers)
- "Third-party" or independent meeting planners

Is there anyone who does not have some influence on the MEEC industry? A case can be made that every person has an impact, in some way, on each and every meeting—even those meetings of two or three that take place in an office or restaurant. Take a few minutes and add to the jobs or functions above that might affect a meeting. Then think again. Even the president of the United States and Congress impact our industry by determining trade regulations, security issues, and whether or not our country goes to war.

What Does a Meeting or Event Professional Do?

When asked about a "typical day," there are few if any meeting/event professionals, whether they work in an organization or operate an external planning company, who could say that any day is "typical." The job of a planner is ideal for those who love to multitask, who have broad interests, who enjoy problem solving, and who care passionately about building community through meetings.

Doug Heath, Certified Association Executive (CAE) and CMP, who was the second executive director of MPI, said many years ago that meeting planners have to be more than coffee-cup counters. When Heath said that, it was a time when most meeting planners were concerned only with logistics—ensuring room sets, coffee and refreshment breaks, meals, and audiovisual setup.

Today, the jobs of an event professional are strategic. Planners are charged with supporting the work toward an organization's bottom line. To do that, and in the course of planning a meeting or event, a planner may do any or all of the following, and more:

- Define meeting/event goals and objectives and develop session content and design.
- Develop a request for proposal (RFP) based on the meeting/event objectives, audience profile, budget, and program (see Appendix A of this book for examples).
- Send the RFP to national sales offices of hotel and conference center companies, to DMOs, and to external meeting planning companies.
- Prepare and manage a budget and expenditures that can range from a few hundred dollars into the hundreds of millions.
- Negotiate contracts with a facility or multiple facilities, transportation providers, decorators, speakers, entertainers, and all the vendors and venues that will support a meeting/event.
- Market the meeting/event electronically and in print, and track results.
- Invite and manage needs (travel, lodging, registration, room setup, and audiovisual) for all speakers, trainers, and facilitators involved in delivery of information and knowledge for the meeting/event.
- Invite and manage contracts and needs for entertainers.
- Design food and beverage events, and negotiate contracts for these events. To do so, an event professional must know the audience (age of participants, gender, abilities, allergies, geographic location, and more) and timing for the programs, and the budget and prices including labor costs and taxes.
- Prepare a crisis management plan in conjunction with other staff, facilities, vendors, and emergency personnel.
- Register participants, or manage a registration company, ensuring data are accurately entered and processed securely.
- Manage the multitude of changes that happen from first conceptualizing a meeting/event to the execution and follow-up.
- Monitor industry and business publications for changes in hotel ownership or management company, hotel foreclosures, facility and other strikes, and other issues.
- Calm others' nerves and remain calm.

The following are some of the questions you might ask yourself to determine if this may be the right profession for you:

- Do you like to plan parties, work schedules, your day, and ensure that the details are locked in?
- Do you have and regularly update a date book or personal digital assistant (PDA) or smart phone that includes everything you need to do for weeks or months into the future?
- Have you discovered your strengths and do you see how those strengths fit into this profession?
- Do you ask good questions, rarely taken anything as a given? If you answered "yes" to at least three-fourths of those questions, you may just have the aptitude to be a good meeting professional.

To be prepared for short- and long-term change, *meeting/event professionals*—a term that encompasses those who plan and execute meetings/events, those who work for and in facilities in which meetings are held, and the many vendors who supply services for meetings—must begin to anticipate changes that will occur as the nature of meetings changes. In the scenario at the beginning of the chapter, there is a designated vendor to work with satellite and other e-communication tools. Still, the meeting/event professional needs to know enough to contract with and manage that vendor.

FUTURE TRENDS

The following are ten trends for the MEEC industry of the future

1. **Meetings Are Experiences**
   Meetings and events today aren't just face-to-face gatherings for the sole purpose of exchanging business information. Rather, they're enriching, one-of-a-kind experiences that attendees will treasure forever. Event professionals are increasingly creating these distinctive experiences in a variety of ways, oftentimes simply by choosing unique or unexpected venues that offer a "WOW factor." Another way to create memorable experiences is by engaging all five senses in what are referred to as "multi-sensory events." Meals are also part of the attendee experience, and in the years ahead, food and beverage offerings will be increasingly tailored either to reflect the event theme or to serve as special events in and of themselves.

2. **Content Will Condense**
   With attendees' attention spans ever shrinking, meeting and event content will become more engaging and entertaining = "edutainment."

3. **Attendees Want a Sense of Place**
   There is the growing popularity of incorporating local elements into the meeting or event—giving attendees a taste of the locale they're in such as offering attendees samples of the regional cuisine. Another way for attendees to experience a destination is to engage in local volunteer efforts or *voluntourism*, which can be included as part of the meetings program (inclusion) and also plays into the growing interest in and importance of sustainability.

4. **Attention to Diversity Will Become Even More Important**
   With various generations—all with different work ethics and characteristics—working alongside each other, and issues related to gender equity and racial diversity still being addressed, companies will continue to examine their recruitment and talent development strategies, approaching them with more awareness and creative solutions.

5. **Mobile Technology Is Here to Stay**
   Having an event Web site, app, and social media presence used to be nice-to-haves. Today, they're table stakes. At a recent annual convention of MPI, there were no printed materials: All had to be accessed electronically either through an "app" or the MPI Web site. How are you engaging the attendee before, during, and after the event? Mobile technology allows event professional to not only to push information out to attendees but also to get information from attendees to help them craft their programs on the front end and to make adjustments during the event to provide more value. Access to reliable, universal Wi-Fi will be increasingly expected with sufficient band width.

6. **Technology Will Get More Connected**
   The MEEC industry will continue to work toward greater connectivity, with the boundaries between online and offline further blurring the term "hybrid," as every event moves toward such multifaceted experiences.

7. **Social media's Dominance Will Deepen**
   Social media will play a more measurable part in marketing and communications strategies all across the MEEC industry.

8. **It's a Seller's Market**
   Hotels are going to be in a stronger position to negotiate. Event professionals will have to start thinking differently in terms of dates, rates, space and location.

9. **Meetings' Financial Importance Will Get Noticed**

Watch for meetings to get proper attention as they're the important economic indicators. Economic impact studies are now de rigueur in at least five big markets, and they have been executed with exacting standards.

10. **Face-to-Face Is Here to Stay**

Some prognosticators have predicted that technology and virtual gatherings will spell the demise of face-to-face, that is not the case. Human beings are social animals—they have an innate need to physically interact with one another. As an example: How many people do you know who have chosen to have a "virtual wedding" and "virtual first night" of being married? Technology is, and will continue, to be used to enhance and supplement face-to-face gatherings, especially before and after the event.

For meeting/event professionals, meetings/events never truly end. No matter how we define an "event," each is a matter of intense planning and execution, evaluation, follow-up, and starting over. The role of a MEEC professional is critical in ensuring outcomes, and from those outcomes, they contribute to a sound economy.

The success of the industry to individuals who currently work in or who choose to work in MEEC depends on what we do now and how we anticipate and plan for the future. Those who choose to stay in or join this industry must have critical thinking skills and the willingness to consider the impact of all local and worldwide events on one's own meetings and events. Event professionals will need to know more about changing demographics in order to accommodate the needs of broader audiences; adult learning techniques to incorporate experiential learning and technology into face-to-face or virtual presentations or for blended learning; nutrition and food allergies to ensure healthy and safe participants; climate change to understand its impact on sustainability and availability of food and water and the bottom line; current events and projections about world population shifts; and the worldwide economy and its impact on availability of products and services, including safety and security. The list is even lengthier than those stated; additions and further explanations would be a chapter in itself.

Those who succeed will look beyond the jobs of yesterday and today to jobs that use many of the skills for which you are preparing today: jobs in eldercare, community organizing, music and arts, politics, and more. Those who succeed in the future will begin now to impact how people learn at meetings by remembering the lessons from Pine and Gilmore and "The Experience Economy." They will change how spaces are used in facilities; how content is derived and

End of the First Day

It is the end of the first day of the AAP's 35th Annual Congress that Barbara Tain, the AAP Meeting Planner, refers to as the "Annual" or "Annual Meeting," and so far all has gone well.

Barbara will have had formal, prescheduled meetings with Todd Cliver, the hotel's CSM. Barbara will also have spoken with Todd and many others who work for the hotel via radio (sometimes referred to as a "walkie-talkie") and/or mobile device, and through chance and scheduled meetings. These talks include a review of banquet checks with various departments, one of which will include accounting. Barbara will have talked with those on the AAP staff and in volunteer leadership and with outside vendors. She will also check the weather many times on her smart phone, television, radio, and, if there is one, the newspaper. Barbara will have eaten on the run, tried to find a few minutes to check office voice mail and e-mail, and, through it all, kept a smile on her face, even while her feet hurt!

At the end of the day, she will review her notes and check room sets for the next morning's sessions and crawl into bed for a few hours of sleep before it all begins again.

When the final curtain closes on the AAP's 35th Annual Congress, Barbara Tain will be one of the last to leave the hotel. Before leaving for the airport to fly home, she will review all the master account charges, conduct a post-convention (post-con) meeting with the property staff and her vendors, and make notes for next year's meeting. Once back in the office, she'll work with the vendor companies that conducted the evaluations, review all the bills and ensure timely payment, and write thank you notes.

delivered; how participants are engaged. Those who succeed will enhance what they learn in classes and sessions by looking outside the industry for information.

Face-to-face meetings will continue because there is a need for human interaction. These meetings and events will succeed because they are enhanced by virtual audiences who add to the energy and diversity prior to, during, and after the meeting or event. (Think Twitter and the hashtags being used now for meetings; envision even greater involvement in the future.)

You've thus far decided to read this text and to learn about this dynamic industry. YOU are the future; you bring to it your experiences and insights. Observe, learn, and take action to keep MEEC moving forward.

Summary

In this chapter, you have been introduced to the world of MEEC. As we have seen, MEEC is multifaceted and exciting, and offers diverse career opportunities. MEEC is also very large and incorporates many facets of the hospitality industry. It has tremendous economic impact. You are now prepared to continue with the remaining chapters in this book. They expand on and provide more details about the concepts and practices of MEEC that this first chapter only touches on.

Key Words and Terms

For definitions, see GLOSSARY, or http://glossary.conventionindustry.org

APEX	CSM	exposition	MPI
BEO	destination	KSAs	outlet
CIC	DMAI	MBECS	sales and marketing
conference	DMC	MEEC	
convention	exhibition	meeting	

Review and Discussion Questions

1. What are meetings?
2. Describe some events from the past that were "meetings."
3. Describe some current aspects of MEEC industry jobs.
4. Who attends meetings?
5. What can be accomplished by convening or attending a meeting?
6. What are five key jobs in a facility (hotel, resort, conference center) that contribute to the successful outcome of a meeting?
7. What is the CIC?
8. What is APEX, and what is its impact?
9. What is the impact of meetings on the U.S. economy?
10. What is MBECS?
11. What is the future of electronic meetings?

About the Chapter Contributor

Kathryn Hashimoto, Ph.D., is a faculty member in the School of Hospitality Leadership at East Carolina University. She has theoretical expertise in marketing and consumer behavior with operational expertise in meetings/events and casino management.

Previous Edition Chapter Contributor

Joan L. Eisenstodt, president of Washington, DC-based Eisenstodt Associates, LLC, a company she founded in 1981.

CHAPTER 2

Meeting, Exhibition, Event, and Convention Organizers and Sponsors

Chapter Outline

Corporations organize a significant number of MEEC events, such as this Shaklee company meeting. *Pearson Education, Inc.*

Chapter Objectives

This chapter provides the reader with an understanding of the following:

- Major types of organizations that hold gatherings
- Types of meetings held by the different categories of organizations
- Typical lead times for planning the various types of gatherings
- Differences between the marketing strategies used to build attendance
- Associations that support the professional development of those responsible for producing gatherings

PURPOSE OF THIS CHAPTER

This chapter focuses on gaining an understanding of the entities that organize and sponsor different types of gatherings. Each segment of these entities creates gatherings to satisfy its unique needs and its constituent populations. Whether the organization is a nonprofit association or a corporation, a government agency or a private company that produces exhibitions, it has goals that may require a MEEC gathering to commemorate an event. Our purpose here is to identify who these organizing/sponsoring organizations are, the types of gatherings they hold, how much time they have to plan the event, who their attendees are, and how they build attendance. The people who play a major role in producing the gatherings are identified, as are the professional associations who provide them with support and professional development.

WHO HOLDS THE GATHERINGS

The three most significant entities that organize and sponsor MEEC gatherings are (1) corporations, (2) associations, and (3) the government.

Corporations

Virtually all businesses have needs that require them to plan and execute gatherings. Publicly held companies have a legal requirement to hold an annual meeting of shareholders. All companies have varying needs to hold a press conference or a ribbon-cutting ceremony. They also have continuing needs to train key personnel in matters of company policy and procedures, or to develop new policies and procedures and to improve their effectiveness. Client groups may be brought together to capture their opinions in a focus group or to introduce them to a new product or service. Incentive meetings are held in order to reward top producers within a corporation. Executive retreats may be held to improve communication or to develop long-term business plans. Gatherings are also held to honor employees (for promotion or retirement), to celebrate holidays, and to build overall morale within the organization. Companies may also be involved with a sporting event or entertaining clients in VIP areas at major sporting events such as the U.S. Open or Super Bowl.

DEFINITION Although there are numerous kinds of corporations, for the purposes of this chapter the term "corporations" will refer to legally chartered enterprises that conduct business on behalf of their owners with the purpose of making a profit and increasing its value. These include public corporations that sell stock on the open market and have a board of directors who oversee the affairs of the corporation on behalf of the shareholders (or owners) who elected them. Private corporations have the same fundamental purposes as public corporations, but their stock is not sold on the open market.

NUMBER AND VALUE OF CORPORATE MEETINGS When a corporation decides to hold a gathering, it determines what the budget will be, where the gathering will be held, and who will attend. Since the corporation typically pays for all expenses associated with attending the meeting, the corporation is in control. Attendance by corporate personnel is usually mandatory. Many corporate meetings are booked as needed, typically less than six months before the meeting will take place and are normally held at a hotel when exhibit space is not needed.

DECISION MAKERS The decision to hold a corporate meeting is typically made by persons in positions of key responsibility within the corporate hierarchy. Officers and senior managers in the sales and marketing area may call for a meeting of their regional sales managers to develop sales strategies for new product lines, or senior financial managers and controllers may call a meeting of their dispersed staffs to discuss budgets for next year.

TYPES OF CORPORATE GATHERINGS AND EVENTS—THEIR PURPOSES AND OBJECTIVES
Corporations have a variety of needs that can be satisfied by scheduling a gathering. What follows should not be viewed as a comprehensive list, but rather as an indication of the types of gatherings sponsored by corporations:

- *Stockholders Meeting:* Voting shareholders of a corporation are invited to attend the company's annual stockholders meeting. Attendees are presented with reports on the state of the corporation and have the opportunity to vote on issues of significance. While most stockholders do not attend this meeting, they do participate in the governance of the corporation by filing a proxy statement in which they identify how they want their shares voted. This is an annual meeting that is usually held in the city where the company is headquartered, although there is an emerging trend to move it to different locations to be more accessible to the stockholders.
- *Board Meeting:* The board of directors is the governing body of a corporation that typically meets several times a year, usually in the city where the corporation is located. While a board meeting may be held in the corporate headquarters, lodging, dinners, and related activities are often held at local hotels and other types of venues.
- *Management Meetings:* There are numerous reasons for a company to hold management meetings. Every major division of a corporation may have a need to bring its decision makers and other important personnel together to develop plans, review performance, or improve their processes. While some of these meetings may occur on a scheduled basis, others

may be called spontaneously to solve problems and address situations that require immediate attention.

- *Training Meetings:* As companies undergo change, it may be necessary to hold training meetings to bring their managers and key employees up-to-date on improved methods of job performance or to gain skills needed to operate new systems and equipment. Also, companies may use the training meeting to introduce new managers to corporate procedures and culture. Some of these meetings may be held on a regularly scheduled basis, while others may be held when conditions dictate.

- *Public Shows:* These types of gatherings are mainly tradeshows where exhibitors display their products that the general public living in the area where the event takes place will have an interest in and would be excited to attend. This is the reason they are called "public shows." There is normally a fee for each attendee to get into the event. Rarely are there educational sessions associated with these types of events. Corporations that sell the types of "goods" on display at a public show own and sponsor these events. In order to attract the public to attend, the organizers use social media, local radio and television stations, and many times local billboards to announce the event and encourage people to attend. Examples of these types of events are boat shows, car shows, winter sport shows, and art shows.

- *Incentive Trips:* Many corporations offer **incentive trips** to reward their top performers based on certain criteria. Those winning these trips may be employees, distributors, and/or customers. While these trips are often to exciting and glamorous destinations, an emerging trend is to schedule a number of activities for the participants to provide an added value to the sponsoring corporation. Companies may bring together these top performers with their corporate leadership to create a more synergistic organization. At these meetings, there is a large amount of time spent on "fun" activities that the employees see as rewarding them for a job well done, such as a golf tournament, sightseeing tours, and outdoor adventures.

- *Sales training and product launches:* These events are often held to upgrade the performance of the sales staff, distributors, and retailers, and to introduce new products and services to distribution networks and the general public. These events are designed to educate and motivate those who have a significant impact on the success of the corporation.

- *Professional and technical training:* These meetings may be held to bring managers and others up-to-date on issues relevant to their role within the company and to enhance the knowledge of their service providers. For example, a company may have a meeting of its unit and regional controllers to discuss changes in tax law and company policies.

ATTENDEES   Most of the attendees of a corporate gathering or event are members of the corporate family and persons who have a close business relationship with the company. In the United States, almost 1.3 million events are held annually with a total attendance of over 107 million.

NEED FOR MARKETING TO BUILD ATTENDANCE   While the purposes of corporate meetings should be carefully crafted, attendance at these meetings is mandatory for the majority of the attendees. Therefore, sending invitations or notices to those who will attend constitutes the majority of promotional activity. Company Web sites are normally updated with the information regarding the meeting, its theme, and objectives. Creating excitement prior to the meeting will help create enthusiasm ahead of time so attendees arrive eager to learn, listen, and enjoy their time out of the office. That it may be a command performance does not lessen the need to make the meeting informative, productive, and enjoyable for those attending.

DEPARTMENT AND/OR INDIVIDUAL RESPONSIBLE FOR ORGANIZING AND PLANNING   Corporate planners are really a hybrid group. Many of the people who plan corporate meetings have responsibilities beyond or in addition to the planning of meetings. Corporate planners spend about three-quarters of their time planning meetings. While about half of these meeting planners had meeting planner/convention management titles, the remaining majority had job titles that did not identify their meeting planning responsibilities (executive or management, 27%; general administration or management, 20%; sales and marketing, 14%; and other, 21%).

Therefore, at smaller corporations, since the typical meeting planner's job title does not specifically indicate "meetings" as part of their responsibilities, it should be no surprise that the majority do not work in a meeting planning department. They tend to work in the departments that hold the meetings (sales and marketing or finance) and have assumed meeting planning responsibility at the request of their supervisors. For larger corporations, like Microsoft, Coca-Cola, Exxon-Mobile, and Miller-Coors, meeting planning departments are large as these organizations have many large and small meetings throughout the year. These planners are members of meeting planning organizations so they can always be on the cutting edge of their profession and they are well respected within their organizations. Of the corporate meeting planners who have earned profession certifications, 32% were Certified Meeting Professionals (CMP) and 11% were Certified Meeting Managers (CMM).

PROFESSIONAL ASSOCIATIONS SUPPORTING THE CORPORATE MEEC INDUSTRY Many corporate meeting planners join associations to support their professional development. The associations that they most often join include Meeting Professionals International, 28%; the Society for Incentive & Travel Executives, 5%; the Society of Government Meeting Professionals, 3%; and the Association of Insurance and Financial Services Conference Planners, 3%.

Corporate Meeting Planning
Mary Jo Blythe, CMP
President, Masterplan, Inc.

Corporate meetings range from small VIP board of directors meetings to large sales meetings, customer incentive meetings, and lower tiered staff training meetings. One common thread between them is that they are always paid for (hosted) by the corporation. The funds come from a department or individual budget, thus creating a VIP(s) "host(s)" at the meeting. This VIP(s) usually expects special treatment, and it is the planner's job to ensure that the VIP(s) is taken care of well.

The planner must also embrace the corporate culture and ensure that it is depicted in all aspects of the meeting, from hotel selection to airport transportation, to menu choices and social activities. Flashy companies will have flashy meetings, and conservative companies will have conservative meetings. The planner is the ultimate controller of this element, and it is the planner's job to make sure that all entities hired to help execute the event are aware of this culture and what is expected from management and attendees.

The meeting objectives will typically include motivation, training, camaraderie, brainstorming, and reviewing goals. There is also quite often an emphasis on the social events at a corporate meeting. Although perceived as recreation, the opportunity for sidebar conversations and networking at non-meeting functions often will impact future corporate decisions. Social events should be strategically planned to ensure that the proper people are sitting together at dinner or assigned to the same foursome at the golf outing.

Corporate meetings, although a category of their own, can be as diverse as corporations themselves. Paying special attention to your VIPs, embracing the corporate culture, and knowing your objectives get the corporate meeting off to a successful start.

Associations

The name "association" implies the act of being associated for certain common purposes, whether for professional, industry, educational, scientific, or social reasons. Gatherings such as annual **conventions**, topical conferences, world congresses, and topical workshops and seminars are held for the benefit of the association's membership. Internal meetings need to be held for the betterment of the association. Examples of these include board of directors meetings, committee meetings, and leadership development workshops. Many **associations** have an affiliated exhibition held in conjunction with their annual convention at which products or services of interest to the attendees are displayed by the various vendors. Besides providing value to the members of the association and potential recognition for the association, these gatherings also generate a significant revenue stream for the organization. According to *PCMA Convene Magazine's* 22nd Annual Meetings Market Survey (March, 2013), associations derive 34% of their organization's income from conventions, exhibits, and meetings.

NUMBER AND VALUE OF ASSOCIATION MEETINGS A major difference between association and corporate gatherings is that attendance at association meetings is voluntary, not mandatory. Another difference is that many of the attendees are personally responsible for their own registration cost, transportation, hotel, and related expenses. In some instances, employers may fund the attendance of employees at industry and professional association events that are work related and are seen as having an educational value for the employee.

Association meetings, especially conventions, tend to be very large, ranging from several hundred to tens of thousands of attendees. This issue of size can eliminate many smaller cities and venues from being selected by the association to be the location for these events. This can also create increased demand by larger associations for prime big cities and venues for their meetings/events. It also creates increased competition among the larger destinations to capture the larger associations' business. This business means big dollars to the cities and venues and can have a big economic impact on the city as a whole.

To adjust to these supply and demand factors, larger associations typically book their major gatherings 5 to 10 years, or even more, ahead of the scheduled date to ensure that they have the space needed for their event. Small associations have a broader selection of locations that can accommodate their gatherings and therefore require less lead time to secure needed accommodations and facilities. However, unlike corporations, associations with smaller meetings still have a tendency to book their meeting locations at a minimum of one year out from the meeting date.

The top cities that hosted meetings in 2013 include:

International	United States
1. Singapore	1. Orlando
2. Vienna	2. Chicago
3. Barcelona	3. Las Vegas
4. Paris	4. Washington
5. Berlin	5. Atlanta

DECISION MAKERS The decision-making process for association meetings is rather complex and goes through several distinct stages. Once it is decided that a meeting will be held (usually by the board of directors or as stated in the association's constitution or bylaws), first the objectives of the meeting are established. No planning of any meeting should begin until these objectives are established. The next step is to decide on the location of where the meeting will be held. Some organizations rotate their meetings through their geographic regions, thereby dispersing hosting opportunities and responsibilities throughout their total membership. The specific city to host the meeting is sometimes decided by the association's board of directors and at other times is dictated by the executive director, based on the report of site visitations by the association's own meeting planner or by a contract meeting management provider. This report will give a summary of reasons why a particular city is being recommended: hotel prices, convention center prices, available **air lift** into the city, weather expected at the time of the meeting, availability of enough hotel rooms in the city, cost per attendee to attend in the city, history of the meeting being held in the same city in the past, labor rates in the city, and overall ease of doing business in the city.

Once the choice has been narrowed to a specific city, the meeting planner, based on site visits and inspections, will locate a venue (e.g., hotel and/or convention center) that is both available on the desired dates and well suited to the needs of the meeting. Typically, the meeting planner makes the recommendation to the association's board and leadership and, if approved, negotiates the financial and meeting details with the facility. This results in a contract that is eventually signed by both the venue and the association's senior staff person (usually the executive director or chief financial officer).

Types of Associations:

Local: Most members reside in the metropolitan area where the organization is located.

State: Most members are located within the state where the organization is located.

Regional: Most members are located within the region (e.g., New England) where the organization is located.

National: Most members are located with the same country as where the organization is located.

International: Membership is comprised of people from several different nations.

Professional: Membership is comprised of persons from the same industry.

Not-for-profits or nonprofits: These organizations have a special tax-exempt status granted by the Internal Revenue Service. Although they do not have a profit motive, these associations need to be run efficiently and must have their revenues exceed expenses. Since all revenues are used to support the mission of the organization, excess funds (similar to profits in the corporate world) are allowed to stay with the organization, tax-free.

SMERFs: These are not the little blue people from Saturday morning television. This term refers to small associations with members who join for **S**ocial, **M**ilitary, **E**ducational, **R**eligious, and **F**raternal reasons. Persons attending these meetings tend to pay their own expenses; accordingly, this category tends to be very price sensitive.

Types of Association Gatherings and Events—Their Purposes and Objectives

Conventions: These are assemblies of people for a common purpose. Depending on the type of association sponsoring the convention, it may attract attendees from state, regional, national, or international markets. Many conventions have an exhibition (or trade show) as an added feature. The exhibition may be a major source of revenue for the association. Exhibitors pay to participate in these events because these events offer them an opportunity to show their products and services to a well-targeted group of potential buyers at a much lower cost than it would if they had to make individual sales trips to meet with the association members individually.

Board meetings: The association's board of directors typically meets several times a year to provide collective advice and direction to the association. These meetings are usually the smallest association meetings held.

Committee meetings: Many association committees will hold their own smaller meetings to discuss the affairs related to their purpose (e.g., government relations, convention host committee, national conference program committee, and publications committee).

Regional conferences: Organizations with a regional structure often schedule one or more events each year to bring together members who are in the same geographic area.

Training meetings: Associations often offer their members opportunities to upgrade their professional skills and knowledge through meetings targeted to specific topics. Many professions require continuing education (e.g., continuing medical education for different medical specialties). Members will earn continuing education units/credits (**CEU**) by attending training meetings. Some associations offer training meetings to develop the leadership potential of the association's elected national and regional officers.

Educational seminars: Association meetings led by experts and allowing the participants to share their views and experiences.

ATTENDEES Since attendance at association meetings is voluntary, the meetings must offer appealing programs to draw members to the events. In the United States, 315,000 association meetings and events occur each year that are attended by 60 million people. Spending is anticipated to grow at about 4% per year.

NEED FOR MARKETING TO BUILD ATTENDANCE The marketing of association meetings is critical to the success of the gathering. All good association marketing should begin with an understanding of who the members are and their needs. This focus should be brought into the development of all meetings. In today's business world, attendees are reluctant to spend too much time out of the office in order to attend a meeting. It is the association's job to plan a robust program that entices the attendee and gives them a true and valuable reason to travel to a meeting. Many attendees have to prove the value of the meeting to their boss in order to get permission to attend. Good marketing material is crucial in order to demonstrate the value of the program to a prospective attendee.

If the meeting provides genuine opportunities for the members to satisfy their needs, the promotional aspect of marketing the meeting becomes much less intense. Since the primary group of attendees are members of the association, the key elements of the meeting promotion include providing advance notification of the date and location of the upcoming meeting along with information about the planned content, speakers, and special activities. Later, detailed registration information and a preliminary program will need to be provided.

The vehicle for communicating this information to the members has traditionally been through direct mail and notices or advertisements in the association newsletter and magazine. Technology and cost considerations have moved many associations toward the use of electronic media to communicate with their members. There has been a rapid growth in the use of e-mails and social media to promote a meeting that emphasizes that recipients visit the association's Web site to seek out the details. Promoting and marketing next year's meeting or convention at this year's event is also recommended so that attendees can block these dates on their calendars and can begin to create excitement one year in advance.

To expand the number of attendees at the gathering, many associations send promotional materials and notices to nonmembers who have been targeted as sharing an interest in the meeting's purpose. Since the nonmember fee to attend the meeting is usually higher than the member fee, this effort, if successful, could result in attracting new members to the organization and can raise additional revenue for the association

DEPARTMENT AND/OR INDIVIDUAL RESPONSIBLE FOR ORGANIZING AND PLANNING According to the *Meetings and Conventions* 22nd Annual Meetings Market Survey, with nearly half respondents working for associations, they were most likely (42%) to report to the Meetings and Events Department; 12% reported to the Marketing Department, and nearly half reported to entities or departments other than Meetings, Marketing, Finance, Travel, Procurement, or Sales.

Association Meeting Planning

Susan Reichbart, CMP
Director, Conferences and Meetings (Retired)
College and University Professional Association for Human Resources

Associations offer their members opportunities to enhance their professional development at conferences, seminars, and workshops. These events may combine structured educational sessions of several hours or days with informal networking events, such as receptions, golf tournaments, and dinners. These activities encourage collegiality and allow members to exchange information in a relaxed social setting.

Associations encourage their members to become involved so that meetings *for* members are planned with input *from* members. The meeting planner works with the member committees from the initial planning stage through the final production of the event. Committee members can suggest program topics and speakers that their colleagues will find appealing and, at best, compelling. Local committee members may suggest local venues for social events, tourist attractions and tours, entertainment options, and golf courses for a conference tournament. One particularly enterprising volunteer researched local options and put together a comprehensive notebook rivaling those found at hotel concierge desks. Working under the supervision of the meeting planner, volunteers perform a myriad of duties during the event, such as giving out badges to pre-registered attendees at registration, monitoring recreational events, and hosting social events—all duties that save the association the cost of

hiring temporary staff. Member assistance is a value-added and integral part of the planning that helps ensure an event's appeal and success.

Association events are a source of revenue for associations. The greater the number of paid attendees, the greater the revenue, and the more lucrative the event is to the association. However, since members must pay registration fees and spend additional funds for travel and lodging, the association must provide programs that its members will find too valuable to miss. The meeting planner develops a marketing strategy that promotes benefits to entice members and prospects to attend. The marketing plan may feature keynote speakers, concurrent session programs, an appealing location, and exciting social and recreational events. This information may be posted on the association's Web site, highlighted in newsletters, mailed in comprehensive preliminary programs, posted on social media, and sent as e-mail "blasts." In addition to promoting all facets of the event to members and prospects, additional marketing emphasis may be directed at targeted groups, such as past attendees.

Association meeting planners work with their member committees to develop worthwhile programs and then design effective marketing plans to maximize participation. The combined focus results in events that are beneficial to members and the association.

Most respondents held the position of Director (39%) followed by Manager (37%). CEOs or Vice Presidents represent 6% each. Eighty percent of respondents had at least 10 and more than a third had 20+ years of meetings management experience.

In another survey it was found that 26% of the planners possessed an industry certification (16% were CMP, 5% were Certified Association Executives (CAE), and 2% were CMM).

PROFESSIONAL ASSOCIATIONS SUPPORTING THE ASSOCIATION MEEC INDUSTRY Association meeting planners join professional associations in greater numbers than their corporate counterparts. Those associations include the American Society of Association Executives, the Center for Association Leadership, Meeting Professionals International, the Professional Convention Management Association, the Society of Government Meeting Professionals (SGMP), and the Religious Conference Management Association. There are also many local organizations of meeting planners that provide support and professional development opportunities for them.

Government

Governmental entities at all levels have continuing needs to hold gatherings, since they have continuing needs to communicate and interact with many constituent bodies. These meetings may involve the attendance of world leaders, with large groups of protestors and supporters, or a small group of elected local officials holding a legislative retreat. Government meetings are subject to many rules. The federal government and many state governments establish **per diem rates** (the amount of money a government attendee can spend per day on items like lodging and meals) that set limits on expenditures for lodging and meals. Facilities where federal meetings are held must be able to accommodate persons with certain physical limitations, as per the Americans with Disabilities Act, and they must meet fire safety certifications.

Since the list of per diem rate tables is so extensive, it is recommended that those in need of the current federal domestic per diem rates go to the General Services Administration Web site at http://www.gsa.gov/.

DECISION MAKERS Managers at government agencies are typically those who identify the need to hold a meeting and have the responsibility to provide funding through their departmental budget process or to locate other sources of funding. Meetings, like other parts of an agency's budget, are very dependent on funding provided through the legislative process. Accordingly, as political interest in an agency's mission grows or diminishes, the budget will increase or decrease, as will its ability to sponsor gatherings. The recent "sequestration" by the U.S. government severely curtailed off-site meetings by employees of government agencies.

TYPES OF GOVERNMENT GATHERINGS AND EVENTS AND THEIR PURPOSES AND OBJECTIVES The purpose of many government meetings is the training of government workers. On the federal level, many of these meetings will be replicated in several areas of the country to minimize travel expenses for the employees of an agency's branch offices.

Other government meetings may involve both agency employees and those in the general public who may have an interest in the topic of the meeting. Meetings such as those to discuss prescription drug proposals or the future of social security are likely to go on the road to gather input from the public. There has been some movement by government agencies to hold "virtual" meetings with the goal of reducing costs.

ATTENDEES Attendance by employees at government meetings would generally be mandatory, while attendance by the general public would be voluntary.

SECURITY There is no segment of the MEEC industry more attuned to safety and security than government. They work on a regular basis with the Department of Homeland Security in the United States since many of their attendees are high-profile leaders. The following are suggestions for implementing security:

• Plan and prepare
• Refine the pre-convention meeting to emphasize security issues

- Be sure there is coordination of all parties involved
- Establish a security team and its decision makers
- Provide education on security for attendees
- Be proactive rather than reactive
- Stay informed and alert to incidents

NEED FOR MARKETING TO BUILD ATTENDANCE Government meetings have characteristics typical of both corporate and association meetings. Mandatory attendance by government employees requires only that sufficient notice be provided so that participants can adjust their schedules in order to attend. Attracting voluntary attendees may require additional promotion.

DEPARTMENT AND/OR INDIVIDUAL RESPONSIBLE FOR ORGANIZING AND PLANNING Government meeting planners resemble their corporate counterparts, as they are located throughout their agencies. While some government meeting planners devote all their work time to planning meetings, others handle meetings as one of their extra assigned duties.

Many government agencies hire meeting management companies or independent meeting planners to handle meetings that fall beyond their internal capabilities. In the Washington, DC area, there are several meeting planning companies that specialize in managing government meetings. There are very strict guidelines within the government as to what a government meeting planner can provide to the attendees in terms of food and beverage and outside activities. It is imperative that the government meeting planner study these regulations and be prepared at any time to go through a financial audit at the conclusion of the meeting.

PROFESSIONAL ASSOCIATIONS SUPPORTING THE GOVERNMENT MEEC INDUSTRY Meeting planners who work for the government and/or independent meeting management companies are likely to join associations to support their professional development. These organizations will help the government meeting planner learn and understand the strict financial guidelines described earlier. Becoming active in these organizations will prove to be essential for the career growth of the government meeting planner. Regulations change yearly and staying on top of these changes is crucial for the planner's success. These associations include the SGMP and its local or regional chapters, the Professional Convention Management Association (PCMA) and Meeting Professionals International (MPI). Those who have responsibility for organizing exhibitions are likely to join the International Association of Exhibitions and Events (IAEE).

ENTITIES THAT HELP ORGANIZE GATHERINGS

There are a number of categories of organizations that are key players in aiding corporations, associations, and government in producing their meetings and events. They include exhibition management companies and meeting management companies.

Exhibition Management Companies

There are a number of companies that are in the business of owning and managing trade shows and expositions. These companies both develop and produce shows that profit their companies as well as produce events for a sponsoring corporation, association, or government client. While trade shows and expositions are both events at which products and services are displayed for potential buyers, the **trade show** or **exhibition** is generally not open to the public, while **expositions** are usually open to the public. The companies who operate these exhibitions are profit-making enterprises that have found areas of economic interest that attract, according to the purpose of the exhibition, either the general public (e.g., an auto, boat, home, or garden show) or members of a specific industry (e.g., high-technology communications networking). Exhibitions provide the opportunity for face-to-face marketing. Some associations hire **exhibition management companies** to manage all or part of their exhibitions. For their efforts, the companies are paid for the services they provide.

Among the largest exhibition management companies are Reed Exhibitions, which organizes over 500 events in 41 countries and Emerald Expositions (formerly Nielsen Expositions), which markets and produces over 20 shows. Their shows serve a wide variety

Government Meetings Are Different from a U.S. Perspective

Meetings for the government have characteristics that set them apart from other types of meetings. They are different from any other type of conference. Why is this so? Because these meetings are bound by government regulations and operating policies that do not apply to other types of meetings.

First, consider rates for sleeping rooms. In an effort to save the government money, the General Services Administration (GSA) Office of Government-wide Policy sets *per diem* rates for lodging, meals, and incidental expenses for individual travelers for all locations in the continental United States. In most cities, these rates are below those charged to conference groups, which take up a larger amount of a hotel's inventory of rooms than transient travelers. To offset this problem, GSA allows government meeting organizers to negotiate a rate up to 25% above the lodging allowance. Also, GSA's Federal Premier Lodging Program offers government travelers guaranteed rooms at guaranteed rates and enters into contractual relationships with hotels in the top 70 U.S. travel markets. Additionally, meetings may only be held in properties that comply with the Hotel Motel Fire Safety Act of 1990. Government regulations regarding travel are located at http://www.gsa.gov.

Federal procurement policies also distinguish the government meeting. Bids for meeting supplies and services must be obtained from *at least* three vendors for all but the smallest purchases. Additionally, government meeting planners usually are not the people who commit federal funds. All purchases must be approved and contracted for by a federal procurement official. In some cases, meeting planners have been trained by their agencies in procurement practices, so they are able to commit a limited amount of money (e.g., $2,500, $10,000, or $25,000). But private sector meeting suppliers should be forewarned to determine who has the authority to commit funds and sign contracts.

Hotel contracts are not considered "official" by the government. A hotel contract may be attached to the paperwork submitted to the procurement official, but in all cases, the government contract—not that of private sector—is the prevailing authority. This applies to all procurements for meeting services. Funds *must* be approved before the service is rendered, not after. In addition, the government *must* be able to cancel a contract without liquidated damages if funding for an event is withdrawn, if there are furloughs or closures of government facilities, or if other government actions make it inadvisable to hold the meeting. The government cannot pay for services not received. And the government cannot indemnify or hold harmless anyone who is not a government employee conducting official business.

Other characteristics that make government meetings unique include the following:

- *There is a short turn around time for planning government meetings.* While associations plan their conferences with many years of lead time, most government meetings are planned only months—or even weeks—before the event. This is true for large, multifaceted meetings as well as small gatherings.
- *Government meetings do not fit a particular mold.* They may be elaborate international conferences for high-ranking dignitaries or small scientific conclaves for 8 to 12 researchers. Some meetings may be held only once and therefore have no history.
- *Government meetings* often *require a disproportionately large amount of function space relative to the number of sleeping room nights booked.* This may be because only a small percentage of attendees are coming from out of town.
- *Policies for meetings can vary from agency to agency.* Some agencies collect registration fees to cover expenses. Others will not allow appropriated fees to pay for lunches; collections often have to be made on-site from attendees. In addition, as GSA allows each agency to implement the "up to 25%" allowance as they see fit, government lodging allowances may vary from agency to agency.
- *Government meetings frequently bring together representatives from the Uniformed Services and non–Department of Defense agencies.* Often, these groups share software applications designed for their *own* purposes, such as encrypted messaging and global directory systems that list only those with a "need to know" the information. Frequently, such meetings are classified and are required to be held in a "secure" facility, whether a government building or a public facility secured by trained personnel.

Government-sponsored meetings are far more complicated than most private-sector conferences that are often planned by people who are not full-time meeting planners. They may be budget analysts, public affairs officers, scientists, secretaries, or administrative officers. And as government meetings are perceived to provide less revenue for a hotel, they may be assigned to junior members of the hotel sales staff.

All government meeting organizers are bound by a code of ethics that prohibits them from accepting anything from a vendor that is valued at more than $50. Those who work with the government should realize this and not put the planner in a compromising position.

Thankfully, there is an organization that specializes in providing education and resources to government planners and suppliers—the SGMP.

of industries, domestically and globally, including aerospace, art and entertainment, electronics, hospitality, security, sport and health, and travel. Other exhibition management companies include International Gem and Jewelry Inc., Cygnus Expositions, and National Event Management Inc.

DECISION MAKERS The owners and senior managers of company-owned shows decide where, when, and how often they will produce their shows. The decision is driven by the profit motive—offering too many shows could lead to a cannibalization of the market. Offering too few shows creates an opportunity for the competition to enter the market with their own show.

TYPES OF GATHERINGS—THEIR PURPOSES AND OBJECTIVES

Exhibitions: Exhibits of products and services that are not open to the general public. They may be part of a convention or may stand alone. Exhibitions were previously referred to as trade shows.

Public shows: Exhibits of products and services that are open to the public and usually charge an admission fee.

ATTENDEES Depending on the nature of the exposition, the attendees vary greatly. For exhibitions, the market is well defined by the trade or profession. For **public shows**, the attendees are basically defined by their interests and geographic proximity to the show location.

NEED FOR MARKETING TO BUILD ATTENDANCE The exhibition management companies have a need to market to two distinctly different yet inexorably linked publics. One group that has to be targeted is exhibitors who need to reach potential buyers of their products and services. The others are members of the trade or general public who have a need or desire to view, discuss, and purchase the products and services presented by the exhibitors.

The trade group only needs to be informed of the dates and location of the exhibition/trade show. Direct mail, e-mail, and posting the tradeshow on social media outlets may be all that is needed for an established show. Shows appealing to the general public require extensive media advertising (newspaper, radio, social media, and television) to communicate the specifics within the geographic region. Promotional efforts like the distribution of discount coupons are common. In both cases, it is essential that the marketing effort results in a high volume of traffic at the exhibition to satisfy the needs of the exhibitors.

The exhibition management company really is a marketing company, since it is creating the environment in which need-satisfying exchanges can occur. Their focus is on selling exhibit space, producing an event that will keep the exhibitors happy and returning year after year, and building buyer attendance.

DEPARTMENT AND/OR INDIVIDUAL RESPONSIBLE FOR ORGANIZING AND PLANNING Larger exhibition management companies manage several exhibitions within a given year. They will divide their staff by the various shows so that their time can be dedicated to getting to know the event, growing it, marketing it, and eventually producing it on site. When the exhibition management company is smaller, all staff members most likely will work as one team on the exhibition.

PROFESSIONAL ASSOCIATIONS SUPPORTING THE EXPOSITION MANAGEMENT INDUSTRY The associations that support the exhibition management industry include the IAEE for the production side of the business. Other related associations include the Exhibit Designers and Producers Association, the Exposition Services and Contractors Association, and the Healthcare Convention and Exhibitor Association.

Association Management Companies

As the name of this category implies, this type of company is contracted by an association to assume full or partial responsibility for the management of the association, based on its needs. A designated person in the association management company is identified as the main contact (and many times assumes the title of Executive Director for the association) for the association and interacts with the board of directors and members to fulfill the association's mission. If the association is small and has limited financial resources, the contact person may serve in this capacity for two or more associations. Since they managed more than one association, association management companies were formerly known as multi-management companies. Confusion as to who they targeted their services to necessitated this change.

Other employees of the association management company support the main contact and provide services as contracted (such as membership, finance, publications, government relations, and meeting management services). With this type of arrangement, the association office is typically located within the offices of the association management company. Examples of these types of companies include SmithBucklin & Associates of Chicago, Illinois, and Washington, DC, and the Association Management Group of McLean, Virginia.

Meeting Management Companies

These companies, also known as **Third Parties**, operate on a contractual basis, like the association management company, but limit their services to providing either selected or comprehensive meeting management services. They may manage all aspects of the meeting or may be focused on meeting planning services (pre-meeting as well as on-site support), city and venue research (also called **Sourcing** in the industry), hotel negotiations and contracting, exhibit and sponsorship sales, on-site exhibit floor management, providing registration and housing services, providing lead retrieval equipment/platforms and meeting apps, marketing services, providing virtual meeting platforms, or any combination of these. In many instances, these types of companies make a big part of their money from collecting 10% commission from each hotel room night booked at the hotels in return for the bringing the booking to the property. A full-service third party will use some of these commissions to offset the fee charged to the client for other services provided. The meetings that these companies assist with may be held at convention centers, conference centers, special venue facilities, or hotels. Examples of meeting management companies include Conference Direct of Los Angeles, California, Meeting Management Group of McLean, Virginia, and Experient Inc. of Twinsburg, Ohio.

Independent Meeting Managers

Experienced meeting professionals often use their expertise and contacts to set up their own business of managing meetings, or parts of meetings, for an association or several associations. An independent meeting manager may be called in to run a golf tournament that is an integral part of a gathering, to provide on-site management, and in many instances, they act in a similar way to a full-service meeting management firm and handle all logistics for a meeting. There are also times when an independent is hired to handle crises in a meetings department at an organization. Personnel changes in the meetings department shortly before a meeting may require hiring a competent professional to pull the meeting together and bring it to a successful conclusion. The independent model works well for planners who have worked full time for an organization, gained significant knowledge and respect in the industry, and want to go out on their own and determine their own schedule. Independents are paid on a contract basis and can pick and choose for whom they want to work.

Professional Congress Organizers

Outside the United States, the term Professional Congress Organizer (PCO) is used to designate a meeting management company. In international destinations, a congress is defined as a conference or convention. According to the Convention Industry Council (CIC) APEX Glossary, it is a local supplier who can arrange, manage, and/or plan any function or service for an event. PCOs are very similar to destination management companies in the United States.

When sponsoring organizations from North America hold international events, they often engage the services of a PCO from the host region to assist them with local logistics. Some countries actually require that a domestic company be contracted to handle the meeting.

Professional Associations Supporting Independent Planners

The type of company that individuals are associated with will dictate the type of association that they would likely join to support their professional development. Many of them will join the PCMA or MPI. Others will choose to join organizations like the International Special Event Society, the National Association of Catering Executives, or the Association of Bridal Consultants.

Other Organizations Arranging Gatherings

There are a number of other entities that organize or sponsor gatherings or events. They include the following:

- Political Organizations
  - Republican or Democratic national parties
  - Local political organizations
- Labor Unions
  - The Teamsters
  - Service Employees International Union
  - Pipe Fitters Union
- Fraternal Groups
  - Kiwanis
  - Elks
  - University fraternities and sororities
- Military Reunion Groups
- Educational Groups
  - Universities
  - For-profit education groups (Associations)
  - Common interest groups
  - High schools

THE FUTURE OF MEETINGS, ORGANIZERS, AND SPONSORS

We find the world coming out of a global economic recession. Thus, it is uncertain whether emerging patterns are temporary responses to tight budgets or are evolutionary in nature. Experts believe that the face-to-face meeting business will never go out of "style." Although technology now allows people to join communities online and interact more frequently, human nature dictates that people enjoy and need to get together to exchange ideas and to network.

Meetings are also being influenced by emerging technologies and changing business needs. Some of those changing patterns are:

- *Budgetary constraints*: As the economy recovers, meetings/events must show value to those organizations that sponsor them and for the individual attendee. Meeting planners are being scrutinized and forced to rethink how they plan meetings and where they spend money.
- *Shortening meetings*: Some sponsoring organizations have clipped off a day or half day from their meetings to reduce lodging and meal expenses for their participants.
- *Changing frequency of annual meetings*: Some associations are considering holding their major meeting every other year and focusing on regional gatherings attendees can drive to at lower cost.
- *Creating more value for their members:* Some associations are streaming live video of keynote speakers to non-attending members, who in turn will see the enhanced value of their memberships.
- *Increasing the interactivity of meeting sessions*: Social media has been introduced to encourage greater involvement of attendees. The term **gamification** has emerged in the meetings industry, which involves the use of technology to help engage attendees during a meeting. Examples include the use of smartphones as voting devices in a meeting room or used to poll the attendees. Another example is having Twitter feeds on a large screen in the front of a meeting room, which gives instant feedback to the speaker and is highly interactive in today's meetings.
- *Merging of sponsoring organizations*: Organizations with compatible missions and goals and objectives as well as some overlapping members and exhibitors are combining their strengths into a single joint meeting. This helps reduce costs to the organizations as well as allows attendees to attend one single meeting instead of feeling obliged to attend two within one year. The educational track of joint meetings

in many instances brings a more robust program and a greater return on investment (ROI) to an attendee. Many attendees must justify to their employers why they want to attend a meeting, and the educational and networking value is one that attendees point to in many cases.

- *Virtual conferences*: Technology has evolved to allow meetings of all sizes to occur via the Internet, thereby eliminating the need for participants to get on a plane and check into a hotel. This type of event, often with limited objectives, will serve to complement more traditional face-to-face gatherings. Organizations also have a goal that if an attendee receives great value from attending a virtual meeting, they might get excited and think that the face-to-face meeting would also be a great personal benefit as well. This is one way to help an organization increase their attendance numbers at their face-to-face meetings.

- *Virtual trade shows*: A wider range of potential buyers can view innovations in their fields. There is very advanced technology today that allows a virtual attendee to feel like they are walking the aisles at the live tradeshow. Virtual tradeshows can also complement a live trade show where attendees and non-attendees can view the displays and communicate with representatives working the show.

- *Outsourcing*: Some organizations have downsized, or even eliminated their meeting planning departments as a cost-saving measure. The responsibilities are transferred to independent meeting planners or meeting management companies: entities to which the sponsor or organizer has no long-term commitment.

- *Focus on ROI*: Many organizations, whether they are corporations or associations, are increasingly concerned about the ROI of their meetings and events. They are taking a hard look at costs and benefits with the goal of decreasing the former and increasing the latter. Post-event evaluations are more and more important.

- *Limiting Government Meetings/Events:* The U.S. federal government has come out with laws that limit the number of meetings a government employee can attend in a year. This law is of great concern to associations because many of their members are government employees and they offer great value to these members. This is a trend that will be monitored over the years to come.

Summary

The types of organizations that sponsor gatherings are as diverse as the types of gatherings held and the people who attend them. Most of the U.S. population will participate in these gatherings at least once in their lives. For many of them, attending a meeting, convention, exhibition, or other event will be a regular occurrence. The gatherings they attend reflect the personal and professional interests of the attendees.

People seeking meeting planning career opportunities with sponsoring organizations will have to use targeting techniques to locate them, although these positions do exist throughout the nation. The greatest number of these positions can be found in locations where the organizations are headquartered. The metropolitan Washington, DC area is considered to be the "meetings capital" of the world, with several thousand associations located in and around the city. The federal government, also physically located in Washington, DC, also employs many people in the meetings professions as it too organizes and holds hundreds of meetings each year. State capitals are home to many state and regional associations, in addition to agencies of state government, all which have many meetings of their own that are held annually.

Major corporations tend to be located in large cities, although many may be located in smaller cities and towns. Their meetings are typically planned at corporate headquarters.

Employment opportunities with organizations and facilities that host gatherings are located in both major cities and small towns. The organization will select a location for its proximity to access by the attendees (near a major airport or the interstate highway) or for the purpose of the gathering.

With baby boomers (the largest age group in the U.S. population) approaching retirement age, it is anticipated that there will be an increasing number of employment opportunities in the coming years on both sides of the meeting, exposition, event, and convention industry.

Key Words and Terms

For definitions, see the GLOSSARY at the end of the text, http://glossary.conventionindustry.org or http://www.exhibitoronline.com/glossary/index.asp

air lift	exhibition management companies	SMERFs
associations	gamification	Sourcing
CEU	incentive trips	Third Parties
conventions	not-for-profits or nonprofits	trade shows
exhibition	per diem rates	
expositions	public shows	

Review and Discussion Questions

1. Identify the type of sponsoring organization that holds the greatest number of gatherings and the type that generates the greatest economic benefit.

2. Which type or types of sponsoring organizations have the greatest marketing challenges to ensure the success of their gatherings?

3. What changes are occurring with incentive trips to provide more value for the corporation sponsoring the gathering?

4. How do not-for-profit associations differ from for-profit organizations?

5. What type of organizations comprises the category of associations known as "SMERFs," and what similarities do they share with each other?

6. How do government procurement officers view meeting contracts from their hotel suppliers?

7. Distinguish between the trade show and the exposition.

8. What efficiencies do association management companies bring to the management and operation of small associations?

About the Chapter Contributor

Nancy DeBrosse, CMP
Senior Vice President, Sales and Account Management
Experient, Inc.

Nancy DeBrosse began her career in the meetings and events industry in 1986 working in sales for Projection, Inc., an audiovisual/production company based in the Washington, DC area. The majority of Nancy's career has been on the sales and marketing side of the business; however, she has also spent several years overseeing operations teams both pre-events and on-show site. She has experience working events for some of the largest associations in the country. Nancy is an active member of industry associations, including PCMA, ASAE, IAEE, and MPI. She has served on many local and national committees and boards and has been President of both the DC Chapters of PCMA and IAEE. Nancy was recognized in 2010 as PCMA's Outstanding Member to a Chapter. Nancy was elected to the PCMA National Board of Directors for a three-year term starting January 2014.

Nancy has worked for Experient since 2008 when she was hired as the VP in the Washington, DC office overseeing the Strategic Account Management team. After four years, Nancy was promoted to Senior Vice President, Sales and Account Management, overseeing sales and strategic account management. Together with her team of experts in the industry, the Event Management Division at Experient works with over 300 clients annually helping to produce some of the largest events in the association and government markets. Nancy has also been involved with Experient's global initiative to work with international meetings held in the United States as well as assisting Experient's clients wanting to meet overseas. Nancy has a great passion for the meetings industry as well as a passion for mentoring the younger generation entering the industry.

Contact information:
Experient
4401 Wilson Boulevard, Suite 500, Arlington, VA 22203
703-239-7412, www.experient-inc.com
Email: nancy.debrosse@experient-inc.com

Previous Edition Chapter Contributor

The contributor for previous editions of the chapter was Howard E. Reichbart, Emeritus from Northern Virginia Community College in Annandale, Virginia.

CHAPTER 3

Destination Marketing Organizations (DMOs)

DMOs exhibit at industry shows to promote their destination.   *Courtesy of Imex*

Chapter Objectives

This chapter provides the reader with an understanding of the following:

- The history of DMOs
- The role and functions of DMOs
- How DMOs can be organized and funded
- Marketing, Sales, and Services offered by DMOs
- DMOs Association—DMAI

INTRODUCTION

"If a destination were merely a place, a dot on a map, a bump in the road, or just another stop along the way, then the destination would not matter." Destinations matter. They are called destinations for a reason: People want or need to go there and visit. In many instances, people go to great lengths to get there. They are drawn to them. For a few, they may be the realization of some lifelong dream. By boat, car, plane, or train, they go. Why? Because contrary to the wise old proverb, it is not about the journey but about the destination. And the reasons for making the journey are as varied as the people traveling. Whether for business, convention/meeting, or leisure, they come because of the expectation of an enjoyable experience.

A desire for local flavor and fulfilling experiences is the force that centrifugally pulls visitors to destinations. This is the lure of a locale, and what a DMO is uniquely able to provide: an authentic exploration into the true heart of a destination.

Source: Michael Gehrisch, President and CEO of Destination Marketing Association International

THE ROLE AND FUNCTION OF DESTINATION MARKETING ORGANIZATIONS

What Is a Destination Marketing Organization?

Destination marketing organizations (DMOs), often called national tourism board, state or provincial tourism office, or convention and visitor bureau (CVB), are often not-for-profit organizations charged with representing a specific destination and helping the long-term development of communities through a travel and tourism strategy. The DMO in each city, county, state, region, or country has a responsibility to market their destination to visitors. This includes leisure and business travelers along with meeting/event planners who can hold meetings, conventions, and trade shows in their destination. DMOs also service those groups who hold a meeting in their destination with meeting preparations. DMOs entice and influence visitors to enjoy the historic, cultural, and recreational opportunities that the destination has to offer.

A DMO does not organize meetings, events, and conventions. However, it assists meeting planners in learning about the destination and area attractions, in order to make the best possible use of all the services and facilities the destination has to offer. The history of DMOs stretches back to 1895 when a group of businessmen in Detroit put a full-time salesman on the road to invite conventions to their city. His function expanded and the organization for which he worked was called a Convention Bureau. Today, DMOs operate throughout the world.

Initially, DMOs existed to sell and service conventions. As the years passed, more and more of these organizations became involved in the promotion of tourism. What were originally called Convention Bureaus expanded their scope to include tourism and were called CVBs. This evolution and expansion of roles and functions continues today. Many "CVBs" are interchangeably using Destination Marketing Organization or DMO to better reflect their activities in selling and promoting their destinations to their wide range of customers. DMOs are synonymous with CVBs.

The Purpose of a DMO

DMOs assist in the long-term economic development of their local communities. Some DMOs are membership based, bringing together local businesses that rely on tourism and meetings for revenue. DMOs serve as the "official" contact point for their destination. Some DMOs are departments of local government, not unlike the library or highway department. This structure is most common outside the United States where DMOs may be quasi-autonomous nongovernmental organizations (QUANGO) or may function as a division of local government called an authority. Many within the United States fall under the government tax structure of a not-for-profit organization and are classified as either "501(c)(3)" or "501(c)(6)."

For visitors, DMOs are like a key to the city. DMOs are an unbiased resource and are the experts about their destination. They are a one-stop shop for local tourism interests and save meeting professionals' time and energy. DMOs provide a full range of information about a destination, and they do not charge for their services.

For conventions, they are often the intermediary between the sponsoring organization and hospitality businesses. As such, the DMO may coordinate site visits, the dissemination and collection of **requests for proposals** (RFPs), and development of collateral material. Some DMOs will also find funding to help attract large conventions. DMOs offer unbiased and valuable information about a destination's services and facilities.

Association of Australian Convention Bureaux

The Association of Australian Convention Bureaux Inc. (AACB) consists of 17 city and regional bureaus and is dedicated to marketing each specific region as a convention destination. The destinations are marketed to local, national, and international markets. The bureaus also recognize their responsibility to promote Australia as a whole.

The role of the AACB is:

- To market its member destination as a leading locations for meetings and business events.
- To be the main vehicle in obtaining meetings and business event for destination.

- Incentive Travel Rewards Programs including corporate meetings, special events, and exhibitions.
- To derive the highest numbers of attendees by increasing marketing and promotions for events the destination has won.
- To exchange ideas, develop networking, and trade contracts.

The responsibilities of the AACB are to provide measurable benefits for its stakeholders through a range of sophisticated sales and destination marketing activities, and to coordinate advisory services.

AACB has its offices in South Wales, Australia.

If DMOs Do Not Charge for Their Services, How Do They Make Money?

DMOs do not charge their clients—the leisure visitor, the business traveler, and the meeting planner—for services rendered. Instead, most DMOs are funded through a combination of hotel occupancy taxes, membership dues, and sometimes through a tourism improvement district. In the United States, an improvement district is an area of a specifically designated area of the community where any incremental increase in property taxes generated is earmarked for a specific purpose, in this case the DMO. Thus, if hotels, restaurants, and other hospitality venues are added, expanded, or improved, the DMO benefits financially. The underlying concept is that these new facilities are a direct result of the marketing and promotion efforts of the DMO. If the DMO is a government agency, then funding comes from local government.

Why Are Meetings and Tourism Important?

Travel and tourism enhances the quality of life for a local community by providing jobs; bringing in tax dollars for the improvement of services and infrastructure; and attracting facilities, such as restaurants, shops, festivals, and cultural and sporting venues that cater to both tourists and locals. Tourism creates jobs at the local level.

WHAT A DMO CAN DO FOR MEETING PROFESSIONALS

What Meeting Planners Need to Know about DMOs

Many people are not aware of the existence of DMOs, and therefore, they do not realize the wealth of information and resources they provide.

A DMO has many responsibilities. Most important, it serves as *the* official point of contact for convention and meeting planners. It encourages groups to hold meetings in their destination and assists groups with meeting preparations. DMOs also provide promotional materials to encourage attendance and establish room blocks (hotel rooms set aside for a group), among other things.

Meeting planners can access a range of services, packages, and value-added extras through a DMO. Before going into the specifics of what a DMO can do for a meeting planner, let us examine a few common misconceptions about DMOs.

Misconception 1: DMOs solely book hotel rooms and convention space.

Fact: DMOs represent the gamut of visitor-related businesses, from restaurants and retail to rental cars and racetracks. Therefore, they are responsible for introducing planners to the range of meeting-related products and services the city has to offer.

Misconception 2: DMOs only work with large groups.

Fact: More than two-thirds of the average DMOs' efforts are devoted to meetings of fewer than 200 people. In fact, larger DMOs often have staff members specifically dedicated to small meetings, group tours, leisure tourists, and transient business travel.

Misconception 3: DMOs own and/or run the convention center.

Fact: Only 10% DMOs run the convention center in their locations, for example, The Las Vegas Convention and Visitor Authority. Nevertheless, DMOs work closely with local convention centers and can assist planners in obtaining what they need from convention center staff.

Misconception 4: Planners have to pay DMOs for their services.

Fact: In truth, most services of a DMO are free. Michael D. Gehrisch, President and CEO of Destination Marketing Association International points out, "DMOs are a hotel's best friend and a meeting planner's best friend. We don't charge either one. We book business for the hotel without a fee, and we provide the same service, for free, to the planner."

Some may question the need to work through a DMO when planning a meeting, particularly in cases where the bulk of an event takes place at one hotel or only at the convention center. However, the DMO can help a planner work with those entities and can help fill out the convention schedule (including spouse tours and pre- and post-tours) with off-site activities. Since the DMO is an objective resource, it can direct planners to the products and services that will work best to accommodate the needs and budgets of their attendees.

DMOs make planning and implementing a meeting less time-consuming and more streamlined. They give meeting planners access to a range of services, packages, and value-added extras. Before a meeting begins, DMO sales managers can help locate meeting space, check hotel availability, and arrange for site inspections. DMOs can also link planners with suppliers, from motor coach companies and caterers, to off-site entertainment venues that can help meet the prerequisites of any event. A DMO can act as a liaison between the planner and community officials, thus clearing the way for special permits, street closures, and so on. The DMO can offer suggestions about ways meeting attendees can maximize free time, along with helping to develop companion programs and pre- and post-convention tours.

 **2013 Profile of Destination Marketing Organizations**

The following is a profile of destination marketing organizations, as represented by a sample of 216 DMOs that participated in DMAI's *2013 DMO Organizational & Financial Profile Study. Note: Data were collected in mid-2013 and do not reflect any subsequent changes in DMO operations.*

The following is a DMO profile from DMAI's 2013 DMO Organizational & Financial Profile Study (218 participating U.S. and Canadian DMOs).

DESTINATION PROFILE AND INVESTMENT IN THE DMO

Average Tax Rates

- **Total** Tax on a Hotel Room (incl. hotel room tax, sales taxes, TIDs, etc.): 12.6%
- Average Hotel *Room* Tax: 10.4%
- Special Restaurant Tax: 3.0%
- Car Rental Tax : 12.5%

How Visitor Taxes Are Used

Hotel room/occupancy taxes are often allocated for tourism-related purposes. DMO investment, convention center operations, and the municipality's general fund are the most prominent use for city taxes as well as county taxes. Sports facilities also receive substantial support at the county level.

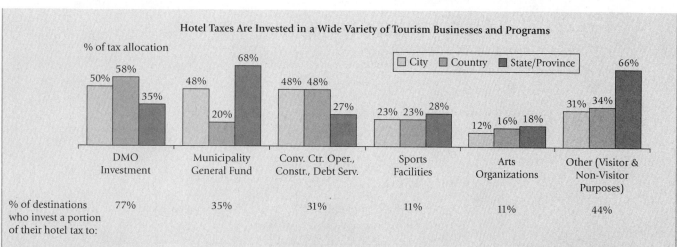

Hotel Taxes Are Invested in a Wide Variety of Tourism Businesses and Programs

% of tax allocation

Legend: City | Country | State/Province

	DMO Investment	Municipality General Fund	Conv. Ctr. Oper., Constr., Debt Serv.	Sports Facilities	Arts Organizations	Other (Visitor & Non-Visitor Purposes)
City	50%	48%	48%	23%	12%	31%
Country	58%	20%	48%	23%	16%	34%
State/Province	35%	68%	27%	28%	18%	66%

% of destinations who invest a portion of their hotel tax to:

DMO Investment	Municipality General Fund	Conv. Ctr. Oper., Constr., Debt Serv.	Sports Facilities	Arts Organizations	Other
77%	35%	31%	11%	11%	44%

Note: *The above allocations are for those destinations that reported the specific allocation. For example, for those destinations who invest a portion of the city room tax in the DMO, average allocation is 50%. As a result, the figures in the chart above do not add to 100%.*

Tourism Improvement District/Marketing District Assessment (MDA)/Voluntary Marketing Fee

Increasingly, destinations are looking to Tourism Improvement Districts (TIDs) and similar mechanisms to invest in their tourism industry. Currently, one out of seven destinations have developed a TID/MDA or established a marketing fee.

Three-fourths of destinations invest a portion of these fees in their DMO, with an average allocation of 85%.

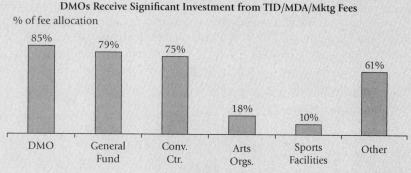

DMOs Receive Significant Investment from TID/MDA/Mktg Fees

% of fee allocation

DMO	General Fund	Conv. Ctr.	Arts Orgs.	Sports Facilities	Other
85%	79%	75%	18%	10%	61%

Note: *Above allocations are for those destinations that reported a specific allocation; e.g., for those that invest a portion of the TID/MDA mktg fee in the DMO, that average allocation was 85%. As a result, the figures in the chart above do not add to 100%.*

- Arts organizations are a distant second (9% of destinations).
- Convention centers and the municipality general fund tie as the third most common usage (6% of destinations); notably, they receive a very large allocation from those destinations.

Special Restaurant Taxes:

For destinations that have this tax (14%), the most common uses are convention center operations/construction/debt service and the municipal general fund.

Car Rental Taxes:

Revenues from this tax are typically used for airport operations/debt service, sport facilities as well as the municipal general fund.

DMO PROFILE

Revenues/Expenses

Destinations' investment in their DMOs continues to grow at strong, sustainable levels. 2013 saw the average DMO budget breaking the US$ 3.0 million mark, a 3% increase over 2012.

(continued)

DMO PROFILE (CONTINUED)

Investment in DMOs Rebound

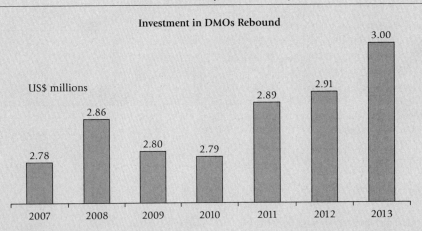

US$ millions

- *Public investment* grew 4% to US$ 2.4 million. *Private funding* remained flat at $356,000. *(Note: Among reporting DMOs).*
- More than three-fourths (79%) receive public investment in the form of hotel taxes, averaging 75% of all DMO revenue. 12% benefit from TID/MDA/ marketing fees, representing 60% of their revenue.
- In terms of *private* investment, 42% receive membership dues while 35% report partnership revenue. Other top private sources include: print and cooperative advertising programs, donated services, corporate sponsorships, event hosting, and publication sales.
- DMOs allocate half of their budget on sales and marketing efforts, with advertising the top activity (21% of total expenses). The remainder is spent on personnel (39%) and administration (11%).
- DMOs typically spend almost half (43%) of their *sales and marketing budget* on leisure marketing efforts (37% to consumers direct and 6% to the travel trade); 23% is allocated to the meetings and conventions marketplace and 6% to sports marketing. Communications/PR efforts comprise 11% of budget and Visitor Services (incl. visitor centers), 4%.

How DMOs Invest Their Sales & Marketing Dollars

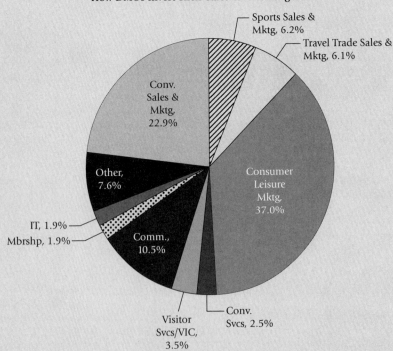

Structure: Almost three out of four are independent, not-for-profit organizations with 501(c)(6)s dominating in the United States (63%). Nineteen percent are government agencies (city, county, state/province, authority) and 5% are a chamber of commerce/a division of the chamber. Almost one-quarter of DMOs have an additional/affiliated corporation, the majority of which are 501(c)(3), or foundation.

Membership: Slightly fewer than half are membership organizations, averaging 559 members. The typical membership composition: 23% accommodations, 19% attractions/cultural institutions, 18% restaurants, 16% event services/suppliers, 9% retail, and 22% other. A growing number of DMOs (38%) have a partnership program with local tourism businesses.

Contract with Primary Funding Source: 59% have a contract. One out of ten is awarded through an RFP. Slightly more than one-third (39%) of the contracts are annual; the remainder are multiyear terms, averaging six years.

Quantifiable Goals in the Contract: Slightly more than half have quantifiable goals in their contract: room nights booked, 28%; ROI, 21%; visitor spending generated by the DMOs efforts, 17%.

DMO STAFF (AVERAGE):
13 full-time, 2 part-time, and 15 regular volunteers. Slightly more than one out of four DMOs increased their full-time staff levels in the current year. Staff for an additional 62% remained stable.

Figure 3-1 provides an example of the typical organizational structure for a DMO.

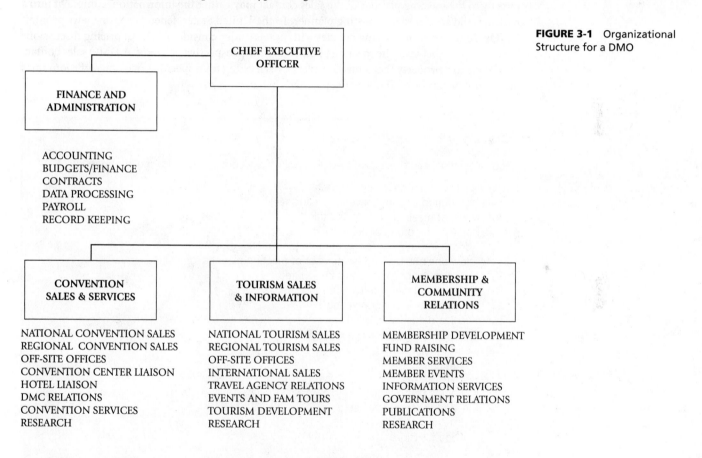

FIGURE 3-1 Organizational Structure for a DMO

Activities of DMOs Relative to Convention Marketing and Sales

Professionals who work in a DMO serve as the sales representative for their destination. There is an entire process that a DMO undertakes with a meeting professional to bring a meeting to its destination.

Site Review and Leads Process

Determining if a site or location can accommodate a meeting's requirements is critical. The DMO is the central information source for advice on-site selection, transportation, and available local services, all with no cost or obligation to the meeting or event manager. DMO representatives have the knowledge and information to provide up-to-date data about the area as well as future planned developments.

Regardless of the meeting size, the DMO can serve as the first stop in the site review process. When a meeting planner contacts a DMO, a DMO sales manager will be assigned to assist in securing the necessary information and facts to produce a successful meeting. The DMO sales contact will gather information about preferred dates for the event and find out what facilities are available, if there are adequate sleeping rooms and meeting rooms, and whether convention facilities are available for the entire time period, including time for exhibitors to move in and out.

In order to represent all their constituents, most DMOs have a "leads" process, wherein the sales contact circulates meeting specifications to facilities and lodging entities that can accommodate the requirements. Basic information required by the DMO is indicated on the convention lead sheet and distributed electronically.

The lead distribution may also be limited by establishing certain parameters, such as specifying a location downtown or near the airport. In cases as this, the lead would be forwarded only to properties that meet the requirements identified. If a meeting planner is familiar with the destination's properties, he or she may express interest in certain facilities by name. Then, only those facilities receive the lead.

The DMO sales contact will request that the receiving property send the information directly to the meeting planner or the sales contact may gather the information, compile it into a package, and send it to the meeting planner. In the United States, federal antitrust laws prohibit DMOs from discussing pricing policies with hotels under consideration. All pricing discussions must take place between the meeting planner and the prospective property. A DMO sales contact may relate to a property that a meeting planner is looking for a specific price range of room rates but cannot negotiate on the meeting planner's behalf.

Convention Lead Sheet

The convention lead sheet used by DMOs will usually contain the following information:

✓ Name of the DMO Sales Contact
✓ Distribution Date of convention lead sheet
✓ Name of meeting planner and title
✓ Name of the group or organization
✓ Address information for group or organization
✓ Telephone number and fax number of meeting planner
✓ Total number of room nights anticipated
✓ Peak room nights and day of peak
✓ Dates for the event or meeting
✓ Decision date
✓ Total anticipated attendance
✓ Occupancy pattern
  • Day
  • Date
  • Rooms
✓ Meeting space requirements
  • Exhibit space
  • Food functions
✓ History
✓ Competing cities
✓ Additional information
✓ Name of person who prepared the sheet and date of preparation

---

The "lead process" takes place in advance of the event. For an association, the average "horizon" or time between looking at a destination and the event taking place varies. However, with large groups and large cities, the horizon can be years and even decades in advance.

The DMO sales manager will communicate with the meeting planner and the facilities to ensure that all information is disseminated, received, and understood. Any additional questions will be answered, and the meeting planner will be encouraged to visit the city and visit venues/hotels being considered. The DMO can be of significant assistance during a personal site review by arranging site inspections.

Site Inspections

A site inspection is a physical review of proposed venues and services prior to the actual program. A site inspection may be required at any point in the sales process. A site inspection by the planner may occur prior to the proposal, after the proposal, or once contracted for space. A site inspection occurring prior to the proposal is a part of the information-gathering visit by the client. Often this is hosted by the DMO. A site inspection by the planner that occurs after the proposal has been submitted, yet prior to the customer's decision, is used to address questions regarding the execution of the submitted proposal. Finally, a site inspection visit by the planner occurring after the contract has been signed is often the first step in the finalization of a program or event. Site inspections can vary in time and detail.

These inspections must be carefully planned and orchestrated to show a customer the venues and services offered as well meet the destination team, which includes community contacts. The site inspection can often be the most critical step in winning a customer's business, as this is when the DMO has an opportunity to develop a relationship with the customer and gain their confidence. Many programs have been won or lost over a seemingly simple lunch conversation during a site inspection.

DMO SERVICES FOR MEETING PROFESSIONALS

The general services that DMOs provide meeting professionals include the following:

- DMOs can offer unbiased information about a wide range of destination services and facilities.
- DMOs serve as a vast information database and provide one-stop shopping, thus saving planners time, energy, and money in the development of a meeting.
- DMOs act as a liaison between the planner and the community. For example, DMOs are aware of community events with which a meeting may beneficially coincide (like festivals or sporting events). They can also work with city government to get special permits and to cut through red tape.
- DMOs can help meeting attendees maximize their free time through the creation of pre- and postconference activities, spouse tours, and special evening events.
- DMOs can provide hotel room counts and meeting space statistics as well as a central database of other meetings to help planners avoid conflicts and/or space shortages.
- DMOs can help with meeting facility availability—information on the availability of hotels, convention centers, and other meeting facilities.
- DMOs help connect planners to their local transportation network that offers shuttle service, ground transportation, and airline information.
- DMOs provide destination information—information on local events, activities, sights, attractions and restaurants, and assistance with tours and event planning.
- DMOs are a liaison in destination government and/or community relations—a local resource regarding legislative, regulatory, and municipal issues that may affect a meeting or the meetings industry.
- DMOs can provide access to special venues—as most DMOs have ties to city departments, personnel have the ear of local government officials. Whether an official letter of welcome from the mayor is needed or the blocking of a road for a street party, a DMO can pave the way.
- DMOs can assist in the creation of collateral material.
- DMOs can assist with on-site logistics and registration.
- DMOs can develop pre- and postconference activities, spouse tours, and special events.
- DMOs can assist with site inspections and familiarization tours as well as site selection.
- DMOs can provide speakers and local educational opportunities.
- DMOs can provide help in securing auxiliary services: production companies, catering, security, and so on.

A DMO wants clients to be happy and will work to match the meeting planner with the perfect setting and services for their meeting.

What Information Do DMOs Have about Hotels?

DMOs keep track of room counts as well as other meetings coming to the area. In this way, they can help planners avoid conflicts with other events. Moreover, as DMOs have firsthand familiarity with the hotels and with meeting space in the area. They can help planners match properties to specific meeting requirements and budgets.

Vienna Convention Bureau — About us

The Vienna Convention Bureau is your neutral partner. Our job is to promote Vienna as Central Europe's leading conference city. We offer our services free of charge to any national or international organizer of meetings, conventions, and incentives.

The Vienna Convention Bureau was set up in 1969 as a department of the Vienna Tourist Board with financial support from the Vienna City Council and the Vienna Chamber of Commerce. Additional funding comes from sponsors. In order to hold its corner in today's networked global markets, the Vienna Convention Bureau belongs to a number of international convention and meeting industry associations.

A team of 11 conference specialists, headed up by Christian Mutschlechner, acquire convention, meeting, and incentive business from around the globe and play a key role in maintaining Vienna's international reputation as a recognized destination.

Conferences, corporate meetings, and incentives play an important part in Vienna's tourist industry and account for 12.3% of all overnight stays. Outstanding conference facilities, excellent conference support services, and cultural appeal help ensure that Vienna ranks among the leading destinations for international meetings.

Courtesy of the Vienna Convention Bureau

DESTINATION MARKETING ASSOCIATION INTERNATIONAL

About the Destination Marketing Association International

As the global trade association for official destination marketing organizations (DMOs), **Destination Marketing Association International (DMAI)** protects and advances the success of destination marketing worldwide.

DMAI's membership includes over 600 official DMOs with more than 4,100 staff members in over 15 countries that command more than $2 billion in annual budgets. Membership is open to all official DMOs recognized by their respective governments from the smallest town to the largest country, including convention and visitor bureaus, regional tourism boards, state tourism offices and provincial tourism offices, and national tourism boards.

DMAI provides members with information, resources, research, networking opportunities, professional development, and certification programs.

Our Cause

DMAI protects and advances the success of destination marketing organizations worldwide.

Our Mission

DMAI advocates for the professionalism, effectiveness, and significance of destination marketing organizations worldwide.

Our Promise

DMAI is the passionate advocate and definitive resource for official destination marketing organizations and professionals worldwide.

Our Values

DMAI is committed to the following core values: Innovation, Transparency, Responsiveness, and Inclusiveness.

DMAI actively promotes DMOs worldwide, highlighting the value of using a DMO's services to the media and general public.

empowerMINT.com

The premier convention and meetings database, The Meeting Information Network (MINT) houses over 40,000 meetings from 20,000 organizations—including associations, corporations, military reunions, sporting events, and government institutions—in a Web-enabled format accessible from any location at any time. It represents a unique collaboration between 120+ DMOs that voluntarily report detailed meeting history information on the events held in their cities. This online database provides critical marketing and sales direction to thousands of DMOs, hotels, and other convention industry suppliers. Meeting professionals will find that accurate information in **empowerMINT.com** regarding their meetings will help in the negotiation process. The meeting information is entered into the system by participating DMOs—information they received from firsthand sources, including hotels, convention centers, and meeting professionals. This is one reason why it is important for planners to participate in post-convention meetings.

Once meetings are recorded into the database, meeting professionals can encourage suppliers and other interested parties to request a copy of the information in their post-convention reports. This report serves as an organization's meeting "credit report" to the industry. Making sure of the accuracy will reduce the number of unwanted sales calls a meeting planner receives and will make available more qualified information for the next round of negotiations—whether it is with a hotel or a destination management organization.

Destinations Showcase

Destinations Showcase is a fast-paced and productive one-day exhibition and conference, owned by the DMAI, where qualified meeting professionals attend valuable education sessions, network with industry leaders and peers, and explore a full range of destinations from throughout the world. *It is where meetings business gets done.*

Exhibitors are exclusively from DMOs and their exhibit facilities. Qualified meeting, convention, exposition, and destination planning professionals have the opportunity to meet face-to-face with professional staff representing destinations from around the world. A low planner-to-exhibitor ratio facilitates a meeting specifically for the purpose of site review and selection. Planners are encouraged to attend "with RFP in hand" and are encouraged to plan ahead with a pre-event exhibitor list.

Shows are held annually in Washington, DC, and Chicago. Full registration is complimentary, and attendance is restricted to qualified meeting professionals only. Meeting planners look for opportunities to earn credit toward the Certified Meeting Professional (CMP) certification at Destinations Showcase.

DMAI Professional Development Offerings

The DMAI provides professional development to DMOs and their employees via an annual convention, forums, summits, sales academy, and certification.

Certified Destination Management Executive

The DMAI has a certification program that is the equivalent of the CMP designation in the meeting professional community.

Recognized by the DMO industry as its highest educational achievement, the **Certified Destination Management Executive** (CDME) program is delivered under the auspices of Purdue University and the DMAI. The CDME program is an advanced educational program for veteran and career-minded DMO executives who are looking for senior-level professional development courses. The main goal of the CDME program is to prepare senior executives and managers of DMOs for increasing change and competition.

The focus of the program is on vision, leadership, productivity, and implementation of business strategies. Demonstrating the value of a destination team and improving personal performance through effective organizational and industry leadership are the outcomes.

PDM Program

Although Professional in Destination Management (PDM) is not a designation, like CDME, it is recognized throughout the industry as a highly valuable skills package needed for the destination management career journey. DMO professionals who participate in the PDM Certificate

Program acquire knowledge and skills necessary to be more effective and successful destination management professionals.

Accreditation

In fall 2006, DMAI launched the Destination Marketing Accreditation Program (DMAP), starting initially with a beta-test followed by a full program rollout. Currently utilized by the U.S. Chamber of Commerce, the healthcare industry, and institutions of higher education, accreditation programs are becoming increasingly popular with organizations that wish to define standards of performance for their member constituents and measure their compliance. DMAI research shows that 93% of DMO executives say their organization would seek accreditation if an acceptable program was developed by the association. DMAP aims to provide a good method to assure staff, volunteer leadership, and external stakeholders that their DMO is following proper practices and performing at an acceptable level for the industry. "This new accreditation program will provide a platform for official destination marketing organizations to assure their stakeholders that they have achieved the highest accepted standards," remarked DMAI President and CEO Michael D. Gehrisch.

DMAI Research

DMAI's research arm, the Destination & Travel Foundation, provides destination management professionals with access to insightful, comprehensive, and industry-specific information that they can use to enhance the effectiveness of their DMO's day-to-day operations and in their business planning. The DMAI offers a wealth of research and resources that provide statistical data and information essential for calculating economic impact, budgeting and strategic planning, marketing and promotion, and educating stakeholders.

> ***DMO Compensation and Benefits Survey*** This report, conducted biannually, provides a baseline for more than 45 job position compensation levels as well as for benefits packages offered to DMO employees in the United States and Canada.

> ***DMO Organizational and Financial Profile*** This survey, the most comprehensive of its type for DMOs, provides standards for a variety of operations while also allowing DMOs to compare their operations with their peers. Also conducted every two years, the report includes information on DMO funding sources, available facilities, tax rates, budgets, staff structure, expense categories, and reserves.

> ***MyDMAI*** This service was launched in 2008 and allows users to augment face-to-face interactions with fellow DMAI members. They can discuss topics of shared interest, provide solutions and best practices, upload documents, submit news, engage with committees, and more.

Destination & Travel Foundation

The DMAI Foundation was created in 1993 to enhance and complement the DMAI and the destination management profession through research, education, visioning, and developing resources and partnerships for those efforts. The DMAI Foundation integrated with U.S. Travel Association's Foundation in 2009 to become the Destination & Travel Foundation.

The foundation is classified as a charitable organization under Section 501(c)(3) of the Internal Revenue Service Code; therefore, donations to the foundation are tax deductible as charitable contributions.

FUTURE TRENDS

- The role and function of DMOs will continue to expand. Many are now involved in "managing" the destination. They are helping to guide the community in tourism development, tourism policy, building infrastructure, planning and expanding convention centers, attracting hotel developers, and more.
- Some consider DMO to stand for destination **marketing** organization, while others consider it to stand for destination **management** organization. Furthermore, some experts in the field have suggested that an even better and more descriptive term would be Destination Marketing and Management Organizations.

DMOs help visitors focus on aspects of the destination that will fulfill their wants and needs.
© Xuejun/Fotolia

- The trend of putting destination marketing, tourism services, and convention center operation under one umbrella is likely to continue. This helps to make sales and delivery of the tourism product, especially with large citywide conventions, more efficient and "seamless."
- DMOs will continue to educate the community and stakeholders about the importance and value of face-to-face meetings.
- DMOs are likely to see continued threats to their budgets. Politicians often try to divert funding away from DMOs and to "more visible" endeavors such as schools. Therefore, DMOs will look for ways in which to diversify their funding.
- The greatest increase in the number and scope of DMOs will likely take place in developing regions such as China and Africa.

HOW TO FIND OUT MORE ABOUT DMOS Visit http://www.destinationmarketing.org, the official Web site of the DMAI.

Summary

DMOs are an integral part of the meetings and convention industry. For over 100 years, DMOs have been working diligently to bring meetings and conventions to their destinations and to service these meetings with a variety of free services. Over the years, DMOs have gone from being destination marketers to destination managers, becoming involved in every aspect of their destinations and therefore enriching the experience for all visitors.

The DMAI is the professional association for DMO employees, and it has been providing a wealth of member services to DMOs since 1914.

Key Words and Terms

For definitions, see GLOSSARY and http://glossary.conventionindustry.org

Destination Marketing Association International (DMAI)
Destination Marketing Organization (DMO)

Destinations Showcase
empowerMINT.com

Review and Discussion Questions

1. Define the role and function of a destination marketing organization.
2. Name the different ways that DMOs can be funded.
3. Name two things that a DMO does for meeting professionals.
4. Name two things that the DMAI does for meeting professionals.
5. What can the DMAI do for DMOs?

Internet Sites for Reference

1. http://www.destinationmarketing.org
2. www.empowermint.com

Contact Information

Destination Marketing Association International (DMAI)
2025 M Street, NW, Suite 500
Washington, DC 20036
Phone: +1-202-296-7888

Fax: +1-202-296-7889
E-mail: info@destinationmarketing.org
Web address: http://www.destinationmarketing.org

About the Chapter Contributor

Karen M. Gonzales, CMP, is the Senior Vice President of Membership & Operations at DMAI.

Meeting and Convention Venues
An Examination of the Facilities Used by Meeting/Event Professionals

Cruise ships are sometimes used for meetings and conventions.   *George G. Fenich*

Chapter Objectives
The chapter provides the reader with an understanding of the following:

- The importance of the physical attributes of the meeting venue to the ability to use it for an event
- How the venue's financial structure impacts the ability to negotiate for the meeting
- The variations in service levels and service availability in different facilities
- Potential hazards often overlooked by novice event professionals
- What questions need to be asked of a facility in order to ensure the success of the event?

INTRODUCTION

Meeting planners and event professionals work in a variety of facilities (throughout this chapter the terms "meeting planner," "event professional," "planner," and "professional" are interchangeable). These facilities range in size from **hotel** suites that hold a handful of people to major convention centers and outdoor festival sites that accommodate tens of thousands. Any location where two or more people gather is a meeting site. Whether it is a multimillion-square-foot convention center or a street corner under a light pole, people will find a place to gather. The event professional's job is to match the meeting and the venue. Thus, the planner must determine two things about the group: (1) Who are they? and (2) Why are they here? Most events and meetings are appropriate only for a limited range of facilities. A national political convention would not work on a street corner nor would a board of directors' meeting work in an outdoor stadium. For an event to succeed, the characteristics of the event must be properly matched to the facility in which it is held. Whether the venue is the conference room at the end of a suite of offices, or the flight deck of an active aircraft carrier, the goal of the meeting must fit with the choice of venue for the meeting to work.

Thus, the planner must be sure to appropriately research the group and the facilities that may fit the group's needs, understand the needs and expectations of the group, communicate the benefits offered by a facility that meet the needs of the group, and verify the arrangements between the group and the venues. Before selecting a meeting venue, the planner must complete a **needs analysis**. A needs analysis is conducted to help guide the planner in formulating meeting objectives and in narrowing down the list of potential venues to those best suited for the event. By performing this important step, the planner can often immediately rule out certain venues, thus streamlining the site selection and planning process.

In order to properly exploit the tremendous range of available facilities, a meeting planner must be familiar with both the physical characteristics of the venue and its financial structure. The combined impact of these two factors determines a meeting planner's relationship with the facility management and both parties' relative negotiating positions. Many other features of a facility are relevant to the success or failure of any meeting/event, but an understanding of the significance of the facility's physical form and its financial structure is vital for a meeting planner to effectively use the facility to support the meeting.

The vast majority of meetings take place in conference rooms or offices on the meeting participants' property. Typically, one room in a suite of offices is designated as a conference room, and a handful of colleagues gather to address some current issue. Whether scheduled or impromptu, these meetings rarely involve a meeting planner. However, as these meetings become larger and involve more people, the person who has had the position of scheduling these on-property meetings frequently finds him- or herself planning meetings that take place off-property.

HOTELS

The second most common place for a meeting is a hotel. Hotels and their meeting spaces vary widely in size and quality. Virtually all hotels with any meeting space have at least one small **boardroom**. These boardrooms typically seat fewer than a dozen people, and the more elegant examples have permanent large tables and furniture that would be appropriate in the conference rooms of any major corporation. At the other end of the scale, hotel ballrooms tend to top out around 60,000 square feet. **Breakout rooms** vary from a little larger than boardrooms up to about half the size of a main ballroom. The whole facility, including breakout rooms, will likely not exceed 100,000 square feet of total meeting space, although a few are larger. Within the past few years there has been a surge in the expansion of hotel meeting space. Hotels with over 100,000 square feet of meeting space are no longer rare. Many privately funded hotels such as Gaylord, Sands, or Mandalay Bay are encroaching on the convention venue domains previously dominated by government-funded convention center facilities.

Hotels generally provide a variety of meeting spaces. They typically include a large carpeted ballroom with corresponding themed décor. These ballrooms are generally planned as part of the initial construction of the facility and are often divisible by the use of movable air walls. A common floor plan provides larger divisions flanked by smaller ones accessible from the side corridors. It is not uncommon for the ceiling to be lower in the smaller divisions than in the larger ones. This is not always obvious from printed floor plans. Breakout rooms tend to be decorated and equipped like smaller versions of the ballrooms and serve identical functions for smaller numbers of people.

Some hotels have been so successful at marketing their meeting space that they have found the need to add space. If the construction of additional permanent space is cost-prohibitive or the hotel is concerned the extra space won't be used on a regular basis, leveling out a parking lot to facilitate tents on an as-needed basis may be a useful alternative. The most common type of event held in a tent is a meal function or themed party. Public shows such as a garden show or horse show may also be held in tents. This space allows the hotel to maintain

Many hotels have magnificent pools that can be used for events and receptions. This one is at a Kremlin-style hotel in Antalya, Turkey.   *Slava296/Fotolia*

higher room occupancy levels by reducing the gap in the **shoulders** between meetings. Once the tent ceases to be a viable option, either due to weather or zoning issues, many hotels build spaces specifically designed for exhibits. These spaces have a rough, unfinished look to them and tend to be designed more for utility than beauty. These utilitarian facilities are less expensive to maintain and, due to their reduced cost structure, can be more profitable than the glamorous ballrooms.

In contrast to the stark exhibit facilities, many hotels have beautiful outdoor venues to support social and "networking" functions. Pools, patios, atriums, and gardens can all be used as meeting locations. Many of the resort hotels in Las Vegas have magnificent outdoor patios and pool areas that are regularly used for events. In addition to utilizing outdoor venues, the use of **prefunction space** such as corridors or lobbies adjacent to meeting rooms may provide a location for ancillary event needs. Refreshment breaks, registration desks, and Internet cafes may be situated in these prefunction areas to provide necessary services without compromising valuable meeting rooms. When first inspecting a meeting space, a planner should observe all of the physical attributes of the space. The facility's "hardware" has a significant impact on the delegates' comfort and their involvement in the proceedings.

Hotels tend to be owned by major hotel companies or are franchised by a hotel company to a local owner who manages the facility in accordance with corporate guidelines. Most hotels supporting meeting space are part of a larger corporate entity, which is likely publicly traded or a subsidiary of a publicly traded corporation. The Rosen Hotels in Orlando and the Atlantis in the Bahamas are notable exceptions. Hotels are rarely owned by individuals and almost never owned by local governments. Hotels are intended to be businesses and not charities, thus their mission is to generate profit for the parent company.

For most hotels meetings are rarely their primary business. The primary business of almost all hotels is the sale of sleeping room nights. The meeting space in a hotel business is often a **loss leader**, whose primary purpose is to fill what would otherwise be empty sleeping rooms. This single financial fact of life overshadows all other aspects of any negotiation between a meeting planner and a hotel. There are some hotels that derive significant revenue from their extensive meeting spaces, but these revenues are ancillary income and intended to drive their primary business, which remains sleeping room nights. While hotels derive the majority of their revenue from the rooms, many also generate significant income from the restaurants and bars frequented by convention attendees. A smaller percentage of revenue is the result of **concessionaires** at the pools, beach, or spa. This dynamic changes somewhat when the hotel is associated with a theme park or casino. Casinos can be moneymaking machines and may have a significant impact on a planner's ability to negotiate. Hotels associated with theme parks have a similar effect. There may be some exceptions such as the Gaylord properties: Their primary business is to host conventions, yet the primary source of revenue is still the hotel rooms and food and beverage (**F&B**).

Conventional wisdom states that planners do not pay for meeting space in hotels. However, meeting space costs the hotels money. The interest paid on the investment capital needed to build the hotel and the staff and materials to clean, maintain, and operate the meeting rooms are some of the most significant costs related to meeting space. These costs must be funded from somewhere. Most often these costs are covered by requiring a meeting to commit to using a minimum number of sleeping rooms for a minimum number of nights. The hotel's goal is to fill the rooms that would not be filled by its regular customers. The closer the hotel gets to 100% occupancy, the happier the owners and stockholders will be.

By linking sleeping room use with meeting space availability, hoteliers found they could induce meeting planners to use their facilities because the meeting space was free, at least to them. Unfortunately, after the system of financially linking sleeping rooms to meeting space became popular, many hotels discovered that some planners were consistently off in their projections of how many sleeping rooms their group would use.

Given the popularity of Internet travel booking sites, many planners are realizing that their delegates are finding cheaper rates at the same hotels as the meeting by booking outside the contracted room block. These rooms often wind up not being counted as related to the meeting. The planner can wind up paying **attrition** penalties even if the hotel is sold out due to the number of delegates at that convention. There are clauses that can be added to the contract that address this issue, but they should be discussed with an attorney familiar with these issues. The planner's ultimate goal in this process is to get credit for every room night the hotel sells that it would not have sold if the meeting were held somewhere else. This one issue may be the toughest part of any hotel negotiation. In order to avoid attrition, some associations (most notably PCMA) require their attendees to book in the room block or face paying a significantly higher registration fee.

Another significant source of revenue for most hotels is F&B. The hotel's restaurants and bars are generally designed to handle the hotel's "regular" traffic, which is likely a mix of business travelers or tourists. If the hotel has a nightclub, the probability is that its intended clientele is not the meeting delegate but rather locals or vacationers. The size and staffing levels of these outlets are rarely determined by the needs of the meeting attendees. Banquet catering is intended to fill that need. The scope and quality of hotels' banquet departments vary as much as the quality of the sleeping rooms. For example, at the Marriott Marquis in New York City, their catering department generates annual revenue in the tens of millions of dollars. In a reaction to the reluctance of some meeting planners to agree to elevated sleeping room rates in order to guarantee meeting space, some hotels have linked banquet revenue with meeting space. Thus, a meeting planner who meets a threshold of spending in the catering department gets a break in the meeting room cost.

Some events do not involve sleeping rooms, and many hotels are reluctant to deal with them. However, the demand for venues to hold the so-called "local social" event is great enough that hotels do market to them. In order for the planner of a **local event** to get "free" meeting space, he or she would have to guarantee a minimum amount of catering revenue. Events that do not involve sleeping rooms are generally a hotel's last attempt to derive some revenue out of vacant meeting space. What revenue it derives comes from food service and the commissions paid by other support vendors for the privilege of working in the hotel such as Exposition Service Contractors (ESC), **Destination Management Companies (DMCs)**, or Audiovisual (AV). Other vendors would include the disc jockey, the florist, limo service, and the entertainers, among others. If lighting or sound beyond the disc jockey's systems were needed, the in-house AV company would pay a commission back to the hotel. All of these revenue streams are calculated in the decision to accept a piece of social business once all other higher revenue opportunities have been exhausted. Since a planner of a social event is just as likely to fall short of his or her F&B projections as a planner of an event involving sleeping rooms, attrition on catering revenue projections is becoming more common.

Hotels derive revenue from a variety of other non-meeting services as well. Golf courses, spas, equestrian centers, and beaches all provide revenue to the hotel. Hotels often contract with exclusive vendors to provide services within the hotel. AV companies, DMCs, service contractors, musicians, disc jockeys, florists, and bus companies can all be contracted to the hotel as exclusive vendors of their specialized services. Commissions paid back to the hotel can be as high as 40%. Some hotels charge attrition on those services as well. The hotel's theory is that the hotel and the vendor have made an investment in the facility and equipment for the meeting planner's benefit. Should the planner elect not to use these services, the services should be paid for anyway because they were available. This is particularly common with AV services. Hotels often require planners to use the in-house AV department or an exclusive vendor. If a planner insists on using an outside company, they may have to pay a hefty fee. It is especially important to discuss these expectations early in the negotiating process to avoid confusion later. It is not always safe to assume that the hotel's exclusive vendor has that honor because it is the most qualified. The negotiated size of the projected commission may be the determining factor.

Hotels do pay some commissions, although the discussion to this point has focused on the commissions paid to them. Travel agents and destination management companies as well as site selection companies and third parties can be paid a commission for the business they bring to the hotel. One of the questions a planner must ask of every travel professional who recommends a facility is what his or her financial connection is to that facility.

Planners negotiating with hotels need to consider the entire financial package their business will bring to the facility. The more closely aligned the meeting's financial structure is to the needs of the hotel, the better deal the planner can get for his or her meeting/event. The entire financial package includes not just the revenue from the event itself but also the revenue from the sleeping rooms, restaurants, bars, and exclusive vendors. When negotiating with any convention facility, event professionals are negotiating not only on the basis of what they will use but also on the basis of what is available whether they use it or not. The availability of specific **amenities** often drives the delegates' expectations of the facility. It is important that planners match the level of their delegates' expectations with the level of service provided by the hotel at a cost the delegates feel is reasonable.

For instance, hotels attached to theme parks are a special case. It is not uncommon for a theme park–based hotel to include an estimate of how much money the delegates or their families will spend in the attached "entertainment" facilities when they decide whether or not to take a particular piece of business. Clauses relating the number of theme park passes purchased to the availability of meeting room space can appear in some contracts at these hotels. Meetings planned with sufficient free time to allow the delegates to avail themselves to visit the theme parks may have an easier time contracting their desired meeting space.

If the hotel is attached to a casino, it is possible for the hotel to derive more revenue from the casino than it does from the sleeping rooms. In recent years, casino hotels have come to realize that convention attendees are good business: They come during the week and thus are synergistic with the typical gambler who comes on the weekend; they do not need comps or other enticements to come as gamblers do; they will pay a higher price for their hotels rooms; and they often gamble as much when not in meetings as other casino patrons. All of the hotels constructed in gaming destinations over the past decade have included significant meeting and event space. The prices charged for the sleeping rooms are fixed in advance of the guests' arrival. The potential revenue derived from the casino is limited only by the availability of credit on the guests' accounts. Meetings then can become a means to bring guests to the casino, where they potentially spend more money gambling than they will on other activities. On the other hand, if a group fails to spend enough time and money in the casino during their meeting, the sales department may be told not to contract with the group again in the future.

Seasonality and fluctuating occupancy levels can have a significant impact on the cost of using a facility. A hotel with a severe seasonal variation can have an off-season price that is as little as half of its peak-season price. By paying attention to a facility's seasonal occupancy patterns, meeting planners can find some true bargains. A common misconception among meeting delegates is that the incredibly cheap rate that they pay to use an exclusive resort is due to their planner's negotiating prowess, when it is more likely that the great rate is because of the planner's choice of a venue with extreme seasonal variations.

Aside from the typical considerations when booking meeting space in hotels, such as the size of the space available, attrition penalties for sleeping rooms and/or catering, and seasonality, planners must be aware of move-in/move-out schedules and other groups that are in-house. Depending on the size and scope of an event, it may take anywhere from a few hours to a week to set up (or tear down) the physical aspect of an event, particularly if there is an exhibition component. This time is essentially a lost opportunity for the hotel because rather than booking another group, which could generate money, the space is unavailable. Hotels may charge a rental fee for the space itself to gain back some of that lost revenue, but there is no opportunity to make additional profit through catering or other revenue centers. Planners must keep this in mind and expect to negotiate move-in/move-out dates because hotels prefer to utilize their meeting space as efficiently as possible. In addition, hotels often host meetings for several different groups at any given time. In many cases this is a nonissue, but when a corporation is promoting a new product launch or discussing proprietary information, they generally prefer their competitors not be in the same facility. Coordinating space is also important when groups may have conflicting behavior. For instance, a significant conflict could arise if a professional organization giving a certification exam was placed in a meeting room adjacent to a daylong band rehearsal or if a convention alcohol provider is booked at the same time as a Mormon convention. These are considerations planners must be cognizant of during the negotiating and contracting process to ensure the planning and execution of their event is successful.

CONVENTION CENTERS

Conventional wisdom has it that convention centers are huge. Many are, and the biggest are getting even bigger. Convention centers are designed to handle larger events than could be supported in a hotel. Several convention centers feature over a million square feet of meeting and exhibit space. Their very size is both their strength and their weakness. Convention centers are meeting facilities without sleeping rooms and are often little more than large bare buildings with exposed roof beams. Others are mammoth architectural marvels involving magnificent feats of engineering and awe-inspiring vistas.

Compared to hotels, convention centers are more likely to devote the majority of their space to **exhibit halls** and utilitarian spaces than to plush ballrooms. While hotel lobbies are designed to be comfortable and inviting, convention center lobbies are designed to facilitate the uninterrupted flow of several thousand delegates. This difference in design philosophy is evident in every phase of a convention center's operation. Just as hotels have a variety of space sizes, convention centers also have a variety of spaces. In the typical hotel, the ballrooms are the largest meeting spaces, followed by the exhibit spaces. In a convention center, the exhibit halls tend to be the largest spaces, followed by the carpeted ballrooms followed by breakout and meeting rooms. It would not be unusual for the prefunction spaces in a convention center to be larger than the breakout rooms attached to them, unlike a typical hotel where the prefunction spaces tend to be smaller.

The Las Vegas Convention Center contains over 1.3 million square feet of exhibit space.
George G. Fenich

Increasingly, convention centers have rooms with built-in stage and even full-sized theaters, a characteristic relatively uncommon in hotels. They are also more likely than hotels to have "congress-style" permanent classrooms, although such rooms would not be as uncommon at conference centers. If we compare the facilities on the basis of the philosophy of their design, it would appear that hotels are designed by psychologists, while convention centers are designed by industrial engineers. Engineering considerations are relevant in both types of facilities, but the difference in scale significantly impacts how hotels and convention centers operate.

Convention centers are often described as utilitarian and occasionally "cold" when compared to hotels. Some newer convention centers have added more artistic design elements like sculptures and paintings. Unlike hotels, convention centers generally do not have spas or swimming pools, exercise rooms, or saunas, restaurants or bars. While a hotel is open around the clock, convention centers can, and do, lock the doors at night and the staff goes home when nothing is scheduled. In a hotel, someone is on duty at all times, whereas if someone is required to be available at odd hours in a convention center, that person must be scheduled in advance. This rigidity of structure and scheduling means that the planner who uses a convention center may need to plan in more detail than the planner who holds the same meeting in a hotel.

Unlike the hotel, which is most likely part of a major corporation, most convention centers are owned by government entities. Professional management is frequently contracted to a private company that specializes in managing such facilities. SMG and Global Spectrum are two such companies. Many convention centers are actively supported by the local DMO, and some DMOs/CVBs even operate centers. As with everything that concerns government, the managements of these facilities are ultimately responsible to the taxpayers. One controversial issue among convention center managers is whether the public-sector or the private-sector companies can do a better job of managing these facilities. There are strongly held opinions on both sides of the issue. Even with all the discussion, one thing is still true. The quality of a planner's event is as dependent on the planner's relationship with the individuals running the facility as it is with how well the event is planned. Especially in a convention center, the more thorough the planning, the more successful the event.

This management structure creates an environment in which the convention center can take a very long view but at the same time must think short term. Generally, the intent of the government that built the building is that the facility be an economic driver for the whole community. Therefore, the facility can take events that benefit the community as a whole with less concern for driving the demand for sleeping room nights in the surrounding hotels. This is part of the reason why convention centers, unlike hotels, will take events such as local consumer shows that generate no sleeping room nights. While the convention center may be funded in part by some kind of hotel sleeping room tax, in most cases it is not required to maintain a specific ratio between meeting space and sleeping rooms.

How does a convention center make money? In most cases they are not expected to make a profit, in the conventional sense. Their primary purpose is to drive spending by people from out of town—a benefit to the community. However, taxpayers will not support a big building forever if it revenue does not at least cover expenses. Convention centers charge for everything they provide on a pay-per-use basis. Every square foot of the building has a price attached to it. Room rental, by the square foot per day, is the center's biggest single revenue source. Every chair, every table, and every service provided by the convention center has a price. The center makes additional income from catering and the concessions. In a hotel, much of the real cost of holding the meeting is hidden in the sleeping room price; in the convention center, every cost is specifically itemized. This "nickel and dime" approach is the convention center's way of charging for services used and not charging for what is not needed.

One overlooked fact that sets convention centers apart from many other types of facilities concerns the portion of their budget spent on energy. It is not unusual for a convention center to spend more money on utilities than it does on its full-time staff. This is not a reflection of the staffing levels, but rather an indication of how expensive it is to keep a large facility properly climate controlled. Hotels have significant energy bills as well, but unlike a convention center, they are not trying to climate control huge spaces with high ceilings and massive doors that stay open all day. In newly constructed convention centers, the green movement is at the forefront. Ceilings are being made of transparent materials and windows are being included to let natural sunlight come in, thus reducing costs of lighting. Thermal heat pumps are being installed to reduce heating costs. Run of water and "brown water" is being recycled and used for irrigation. The list goes on.

Similar to a hotel, a convention center has relationships with vendors for services it does not provide internally. Such services might include parking, buses, audiovisual, power, data–telecom, and florists.

In a convention center, catering is often contracted to an outside vendor. Each of these vendors pays a commission to the center. This commission may not be in cash but may be in the form of equipment owned by the vendor installed in the building. For example, in many buildings, the facility does not own the soft drink vending equipment. The soft drink company with the exclusive rights in the facility owns and services the equipment in return for a specified level of product sales. Another debate in the convention center industry has to do with whether a facility should have "exclusive" or "preferred" vendors. It is no longer safe to assume that any vendor suggested by a facility is either exclusive or preferred unless the vendor is identified as such. Traditionally, catering was the only exclusive service, but in some facilities power, rigging, AV equipment, security, and telecom can be exclusive vendors to the facility. Some of these relationships are the result of governmental regulations, and others are an attempt to avoid liability lawsuits. In contrast, in some convention centers even the catering can be outsourced to vendors other than the ones who have the relationship with the facility. The relationships between the vendors and the facility are fluid and changing. Therefore, no planner should ever assume the nature of the relationships without asking specifically.

It is also not safe to assume that an exclusive vendor is somehow more or less competent than an outside vendor. Many convention industry salespeople have tried to paint their competition into a corner with broad-brush statements that may or may not be true. Determining the competence of the facility's preferred or exclusive vendors is one of the toughest jobs a planner must face, and while there are some guidelines, there are no absolutes. Unfortunately, the success or failure of any given meeting or event often depends on vendors with whom a planner has no experience.

Given the political climate in which most convention centers operate, combined with the size and scope of the events they support, they tend to be bureaucratic and inflexible. Negotiations can take longer than in a hotel, but a convention center is more likely to publish all its rate information either in print or on a Web site than is any other type of meeting facility. It is possible to go through many convention centers' documentation and know before talking to a salesperson what that event is likely to cost. This is difficult, if not impossible, to do in many other types of facility. With all this information readily available, it becomes the planner's responsibility to access the information, and not the facility's responsibility to guide a novice planner through the process. Figure 4-1 lists the ten largest convention centers in the United States.

FIGURE 4-1 Ten Largest Convention Centers in the United States.

Name	Size (1,000 square feet)
McCormick Place	2,600
Orange County Convention Center	2,100
Las Vegas Convention Center	1,900
Georgia World Congress	1,400
Sands Expo & Convention Center	1,300
Kentucky Exposition Center	1,100
New Orleans Morial CC	1,100
Reliant Park	1,056
International Exposition Center	1,050
Dallas Convention Center	1,019

NOTE: The Sands is the only privately owned and operated center on this list

CONFERENCE CENTERS

Much of the focus of the education of meeting planners has focused on the larger meeting. Many of the most critical meetings determining the future health of an organization involve fewer than 25 people. These meetings are often attended by people who understand the importance of the decisions they will make to the careers and livelihoods of the employees of entire corporations. One such meeting involves the review of pharmaceutical research. The people in the meeting will decide whether to continue to fund development of a potential new drug or abandon it. They will decide which drugs to prepare for regulatory review and which to send back for more tests. The success of these meetings is critical to the survival of the companies that hold them. Conference centers are the ideal venues for such meetings.

For the most part, conference centers are small, well-appointed facilities specifically designed to enhance classroom-style learning. The Convention Industry Council defines a conference center as a facility that provides a dedicated environment for events, especially small events. The International Association of Conference Centers (IACC) has developed a specific set of guidelines as to what constitutes a "conference center" as opposed to other types of meeting facilities. Adherence to these guidelines essentially guarantees the planner that the facility is well managed and well suited for intense, small group learning situations. Several major corporations run conference centers, including Aramark, Dolce, Sodexo, Marriott, and Hilton. Several smaller companies are also involved, including Conference Center Concepts and the Creative Dining Group.

A planner contemplating using an IACC conference center would be well advised to visit the IACC Web site and ensure that the scope and expectations of the meeting make it appropriate for a conference center in advance of meeting with the facility's salespeople. Conference centers can be either resident or nonresident. The biggest difference between the two is that resident facilities have sleeping rooms and nonresident facilities do not. While it is easy to draw the comparison between hotels and resident conference centers, the comparison would likely be misleading. One of the major differences concerns the conference centers' focus on teaching and learning instead of on elegant parties. This tends to translate into better furniture and a greater tendency toward permanently installed work surfaces as well as permanently installed projection and audio systems.

Many conference centers, whether resident or nonresident, employ a pricing strategy called the **complete meeting package**, which essentially means that whatever the facility owns, the planner may use at no additional charge. This puts the facility's entire inventory of easels, projectors, microphones, and sound systems at the planner's immediate disposal. For the planner, this is a flexible way to work, in that he or she is freed from the task of getting scheduled AV companies to provide their equipment requirements in advance.

Some conference centers are in remote locations. Some of the nonresident centers are part of large corporate office complexes and are offered to the public only when the parent company is not using the facility. The IACC guidelines have a distinctly "corporate" feel to them. The guidelines strictly control the inside of the meeting rooms. The impact in variations of location would be felt less inside the classroom than it would in the supplemental activities the delegates would partake of when not in meetings. Suburban and rural conference centers routinely feature high-quality golf courses, while the more urban centers would link to cultural and sporting activities located in the city centers. Some of the more rural facilities offer horseback riding or outdoor activities like hiking or skiing in season.

When choosing a conference center, a planner should review not only the facilities offered by the center but also the expectations of the delegates attending the event: Who are they? Why are they here? A nonresident facility might be better if all the delegates are local. A rural facility might be better if the delegates have a tendency to slip away at midday when they should be in classes. A review of the event's history is important in determining if a conference center will work for the event.

Like hotels, corporations generally own conference centers, although some are closely held family businesses. They are not government entities. Therefore, they operate more like hotels than like convention centers except that their meeting spaces are focused almost exclusively on classroom-style education. Conference centers can also have seasonal patterns much like hotels. A conference center located in the midst of several ski slopes will be much less expensive in the summer than it will be in the winter. A conference center located in an urban area may be the same price year-round. If the event dates are flexible, moving a week or a month could yield significant savings.

Conference centers using the complete meeting package tend to be entirely self-contained. If outside vendors are used, they will likely be transparent to the planner. By using the complete meeting package concept, the facility ties all its revenue into a single bundle of services. The only variable is the number of delegates who actually show up as opposed to those who register.

Attrition takes on a new meaning in a conference center. It is not unusual for a conference center to charge a planner a fixed price for up to a certain number of delegates. If some of the delegates do not come to the event, the planner is still responsible for the full amount of the contract. This fee is not based on the ability of the facility to resell the rooms. It is based on 100% of the negotiated facility fee regardless how much of the facility is used. Although the planner's tasks on-site are less intense than would be the case in a convention center, the planner's ability to predict room night use is very critical. A planner deciding whether to use the complete meeting package or buy their own equipment needs to look beyond the simple cost of the projector or microphone. They need to evaluate the proper use of their time. Is their time well spent hauling a large plastic case through airport security, or is it better spent making sure the coffee is refreshed and lunch is ready on time? Many planners see their jobs in terms of cost containment. While that is surely part of the job, it would seem that helping guarantee the success of the meeting is the more appropriate goal. Sometimes a penny saved is not a penny earned. Sometimes it is a pound lost in a missed opportunity. The planner's job is to know the difference.

RETREAT FACILITIES

Retreat facilities can be viewed as a special group, much like rural conference centers. They are more likely to be owned by a family or closely held corporation than the other facilities and focus on a smaller portion of the conference center market. Not-for-profit entities, charitable organizations, or religious groups own many of the retreat facilities. Several evangelical organizations run retreat facilities as part of their internal training programs. Other groups can rent these facilities when the parent organization is not using them. In addition to the classroom learning typical of a conference center, retreat facilities often specialize in some unique extracurricular learning opportunities. Some retreat facilities are at dude ranches; others are cabins in the woods where nature is part of the lesson plan, while some are attached to religious organizations where a spiritual message is incorporated into the program. Many planners, out of fear that their delegates may not appreciate the opportunities presented by the unique environment, can unjustly overlook retreat facilities.

These unique meeting environments can be used as a stimulus to energize a moribund group of delegates. The challenge of using these facilities derives from one of their greatest strengths—their relative isolation. Transportation and logistical issues become magnified due to the distance from airports and highways. These impediments can be overcome, and the result can be well worth the effort.

CRUISE SHIPS

In a sense, cruise ships are floating hybrids of hotels, conference centers, and full-service resorts. Cruise ships are often underrated as meeting venues, but with proper planning, they can provide a satisfying meeting experience.

The quality of the planning for a cruise event has a greater impact on the success of the meeting than it does with any other type of venue. A ship moves by its own schedule that could have more to do with the tides than it does the ability of a group of guests to be at the dock on time. Failure to properly accommodate the ship's schedule into the transportation plan can have disastrous results. Unlike a building, once the ship leaves port, latecomers are left behind.

Cruise ships have long been considered ideal venues for incentive trips. There are few options available to a planner that can provide as romantic an ambiance as a cruise ship. However, romantically inclined couples often have children attached. Many cruise lines have well-developed children's programs, which allow the adults to participate in their meetings without being concerned

Cruise ship meeting rooms are indistinguishable from those found in a hotel.
George G. Fenich

where their children are or what they are doing. In fact, the children's programs on many ships are better developed and provide more opportunities than in many major resorts.

The size and availability of meeting rooms varies widely among different ships. Meeting planners should not only look at the spaces identified as "meeting facilities" but also consider other creative alternatives. Many ships have extensive theaters and lounge facilities that, depending on the size of the group, can be reserved for the group's exclusive use. Theaters that are utilized in the evening for shipboard entertainment are often empty space during the day, thus the rental of these areas by meeting groups generates additional income for the cruise line. These spaces can provide the facilities needed for the business and educational components of the meeting.

In addition to finding creative uses for purpose-built facilities on existing ships, new ships are being designed and constructed with the MEEC industry in mind. Royal Caribbean's *Oasis of the Seas* boasts a dedicated convention center designed to accommodate up to 300 meeting attendees. Other areas on the ship, such as the ice rink and several nightclubs, were constructed in such a way to allow them to easily transform into meeting/event venues when needed. The increased popularity of destination weddings has also influenced cruises. Several lines have implemented shipboard wedding packages, thus resulting in the construction of wedding chapels and private reception areas.

Similar to conference centers, many cruise lines offer complete meeting packages. These packages routinely include everything except the bar tab and taxes. By carefully working with the ship's technical staff, it is possible for the entire meeting's technical needs to be accommodated with the on-board equipment. In many ways, this is no different from working with a conference center.

The relative isolation of many conference and retreat centers is one of their greatest strengths as meeting facilities. A ship at sea can be even more isolated. A meeting held while the ship is under way will have a different attendance pattern than the same meeting held when the ship is in port. Schedule planning coordinated with the ship's itinerary can have a significant impact on a meeting's attendance. One issue many planners face is keeping the delegates in the meetings. Hotels adjacent to casinos and theme parks are notorious for having low delegate attendance at sessions. On a ship at sea, out of range of cell phones and pagers, a meeting that requires perfect attendance could have a greater opportunity for success than in many competing facilities. Many planners frequently overlook ships as meeting facilities except for incentive trips, but that shortchanges the potential of these mobile meeting venues.

SPECIFIC USE FACILITIES

Theaters, **amphitheaters**, **arenas**, **stadiums**, and **sports facilities** tend to be underused as meeting facilities but, depending on the needs of the meeting, may support a variety of events. Spectacular and impressive events can be planned for any facility designed for public assembly. Entertainment venues range in size from huge outdoor stadiums to hole-in-the-wall nightclubs. Planners who wish to use these venues can be successful if they are careful to remember that entertainment, not meetings, is the venue's primary business, and services considered standard in a hotel or convention center may not exist in an entertainment venue.

Most of these facilities are focused on events for the general (ticket-buying) public, and a closed event for an invited audience can be a welcome change for their staff. Even though the front-office staff might welcome the meeting planner, the planner needs to carefully determine whether sufficient house and technical staff will be available to support the event. Entertainment events generally occur on evenings and weekends; therefore, staff is frequently composed of part-time employees, or, in the case of those who are available during the day, retirees. The availability and demographics of the staff may or may not be an issue for any given event, but it should be discussed with the facility management prior to signing a contract.

Like convention centers, these facilities are typically owned by government agencies or are public–private partnerships. Specific use facilities are similar to convention centers in the amount of planning required, but unlike convention centers in that while dealing with large numbers of people are their greatest asset, meetings are not their primary business. Depending on the facility's public event schedule, long rehearsal and setup times may not be feasible. If a facility has a resident sports team that might go into postseason play, management might be reluctant to confirm space availability more than a few weeks in advance.

Finances in a special use facility can be a hybrid between the practices of the convention center and those of a conference center. There is generally a fixed fee for the use of the facility and a specific subset of its equipment and services. "Normal" cleanup, comparable to a public event, would likely be included in the facility rental fee. The facility may require a minimum level of staff for which there would be an hourly charge based on a minimum number of hours. All other labor, equipment, and services would be exactly like a convention center on a bill-per-item system.

Among the specific use facilities, theaters can be ideal meeting facilities. They come equipped with comfortable chairs arranged in sweeping curved rows for maximum comfort. They have lighting positions and sound systems built-in, and staff members who know how to use them. If delegates are local, they probably know where the theater is and do not need directions. The stages are designed for acoustics and the seats arrayed to enhance visibility. One of the ironies of this industry relates to the amount of time and energy expended converting hotel ballrooms into theaters and how few meetings are actually held in theaters. However, this is beginning to change as theater companies have recognized the cross-promotional opportunities and now advertise their venues as event locations.

On the surface, it would seem that the better technically equipped a theater is, the more likely the meeting's support team would use it rather than bring it in. This, however, is not usually the case. In many theaters, any equipment that is moved must be restored to its original location. The economics of that policy works if the equipment's natural location is in a storeroom somewhere out of the way. Where the policy does not work is when the equipment's location is in an "in-use" position. The cost of putting the equipment back to its in-use location can be greater than merely removing the rental equipment and packing it in a truck for the run back to the warehouse. This is especially true of lighting and projection. If the theater has custom draperies for the stage, those will typically be used because finding replacement drapes in the correct size can be difficult.

Another issue with using the in-house equipment has to do with reliability. Many theaters, particularly educational and community theaters, are not funded to the point where their equipment can be considered properly maintained or reliable. A lighting designer, unsure of the condition of the installed equipment, would likely import his or her own rather than take a risk.

Catering in a specific use facility may require more planning than in some other venues. Given that the venue's primary revenue sources are based on ticketed events, they would probably have a well-developed concessions operation but may or may not have sufficient catering capabilities. Menu selection may be challenging, depending on the scope of the meeting. Kitchen equipment for a concessions environment may not be capable of supporting the menu needs of a meeting, therefore forcing the planner to contract with an off-site caterer.

COLLEGES AND UNIVERSITIES

It would seem that since colleges and universities devote all their energies to education and research, they should be ideal meeting facilities. Some are, but it is important for a planner to remember that while meetings bring much appreciated supplemental income to an educational institution, few colleges are well equipped for major meetings, and staff may not be as adept at responding to immediate meeting needs as expected at a full-time meeting facility. The planner using an academic facility needs to investigate and coordinate with multiple members of the institution's organizational structure. It is not sufficient to ask the person in alumni relations who booked the use of the faculty center after hours whether the lawn sprinklers have, in fact, been turned off for the evening. The planner must verify such details directly with the department responsible.

The impact of seasonality on hotels and other meeting facilities is moderate compared to the impact of seasonality on most academic facilities. During summer vacation, many college campuses become ghost towns. A vacant college campus could provide an effective meeting site as a result. The planner who wishes to use a college campus for a large meeting may have to make some extra logistical arrangements. College classrooms are generally open and airy with plenty of light, but they are not known for comfortable furniture. A student chair with a writing arm may be acceptable for a twenty-something but may not be ideal for a forty-year-old adult. Nevertheless, more and more college campuses are offering conference services to willing clients, particularly those looking for an economical or budget conscious option. Many large universities incorporate their meetings department into the university-wide hospitality services umbrella, while smaller colleges often operate a seasonal summer conference division. The increased demand for meetings at institutions of higher learning has prompted these organizations to make an effort to meet that need. Increasingly, special sporting events such as tournaments are turning to college campuses with their extensive, and usually top quality, athletic facilities.

College dorms have beds, and rooms are generally arranged along hallways like hotels, but that is where the similarities end. College dorm rooms have single beds instead of doubles or queens, and most of those are extra long so standard linen does not fit. It would probably be a good idea to contract with the college's linen service to provide bed linen and towels. While some dorm rooms are singles, the majority are double occupancy. The process of arranging and processing roommate assignments can be a full-time job. If the meeting is large, it might be a good idea to hire an intern for this task. Another issue sometimes overlooked is that dorms generally have bathrooms shared among several rooms. While that might be appropriate for groups of high school and college athletes, it would likely not be comfortable for a meeting of professionals such as doctors or stockbrokers. Newer and some recently renovated dorms have elevators, but many older dorms still do not have ADA-compatible access to upper floors. Considerable savings can be realized using college campuses, particularly if the college's athletic facilities are part of the meeting plan; however, not all meetings work well in this environment.

Many meeting planners have less-than-fond memories of college food. With the advent of professional food service management companies operating many college food service operations, the food quality on many campuses has improved considerably. Planners should be aware, however, that a college dining hall will never be elegant. Equally important is that the quality of the food served is a direct result of the budget available. Any poor quality college food is more likely a function of a small budget than a function of inadequate kitchen capabilities. With an adequate budget, the planner can provide high-quality meals in an academic environment.

College art museums and student centers may provide interesting and exciting locations for meetings. Art museums provide especially interesting opportunities for conversations that can enhance a "networking" event. All the delegates at the event will probably have opinions about the art, motivating strangers to converse. One common mistake planners make when using art centers is the tendency to redecorate them. Without spending a lot of money, it is unlikely that the planner can provide more impressive décor than what the museum's galleries already offer. If the planner feels the need to engage in a massive redecorating project, the art museum may not be the correct venue for the event.

The art centers and theaters at colleges and universities have a unique attribute that many planners and the general public frequently overlook. Unlike the staff in the majority of meeting and special event venues, the venue is not just a job. It is a passion. The people who run these facilities on a daily basis take great pride in and care deeply about the condition of the building and its contents. This is not to say that people in other venues do not care, but usually not with the intensity or even obsession that the academic theater and art directors demonstrate. Any planner who intends to use one of these facilities must understand the sensitivities involved. Equally important, they must convey this message to their own staff. The traveling staff (mere "transients" in the eyes of the permanent employees) must be sensitive to the fact that in spite of the large amount of money they will be spending on this event, they are visitors and not necessarily welcome guests. It is entirely likely that the budget for this one event is greater than the resident staff's monthly or even annual budget, and some jealousies may arise.

Some colleges have academic programs in hospitality, food service, or cuisine. They will usually have food labs with multiple cooking and preparation stations. These can be ideal places for food-oriented meetings, non-meeting activities, or team building.

UNUSUAL VENUES

Meeting planners continually insist on having meetings in places that were never designed for meetings. Airplane hangars, remote islands, nature preserves, city parks, open meadows, museums, and athletic fields are all unusual venues that are often used for meetings. Perhaps the most common of these unusual venues is a large tent in a parking lot. All of these venues have more in common with each other than they have differences.

None of these venues has support equipment. Virtually everything needed for the event must be brought in. These venues also have little or no staff. In addition to all the normal concerns a planner needs to deal with for an event, the planner using these facilities will need to provide all the support services normally considered the purview of the facility. Such services could include portable restrooms, parking, and trash removal. Weather is an issue in any outdoor venue, but that is no different than would be the case with a pool party at a hotel.

One challenge that frequently catches planners by surprise is obtaining permits. Many local governments require permits to use parks or even private property for special events. Failure to procure the proper permits can lead to an event being shut down at the last moment. Not only must the police and fire department be notified, but in many places the building code office must be notified as well. Tents must usually be inspected by the fire department. In some areas, generators are under the purview of the fire department; in others, there is a special office that deals with electrical issues. This office may be part of the Building and Zoning department or may be part of a designated special events office.

Airport facilities have the additional issue of heightened security. More stringent security measures have been implemented there than ever before. Failure to conform to these security procedures can be detrimental to the event. For those planners who need an aeronautical theme, an airplane museum would likely be a better choice than a working airport. Political rallies are sometimes held at airports just as they used to be held at railroad stations in previous elections. The constant noise of the aircraft in the background does give the impression of excitement, but it can also obscure important parts of a candidate's speech. The quality of the sound system, too often the last item considered, is vitally important to success of the event.

Tents routinely show up as meeting venues. Tents fall into three categories: pole, frame, and clear span. An open-sided pole or **frame tent** set up on the grass is one of the simplest of all meeting venues. It requires little advance planning beyond making sure the tent rental people can get set up in time. Permits are required in many jurisdictions. Weather is a factor, but adding tent sides and air-conditioning can reduce the impact of weather. The tent may require a floor so that rain drainage flows under the floor and not over the feet of the people in the tent. Lighting or decorating a tent can also be a challenge. To hang lighting in a **pole tent** requires special brackets to attach the lights to the poles if the poles are sturdy enough to support them; therefore, for a pole tent, supporting the lighting from the floor on boom stands or truss towers may be a better plan.

Clear span tents have a strong roof structure, and it is possible to hang lighting from its beams by using special clamps. Since the purpose of the tent is to create a meeting space where none previously existed, other support services such as power, water, and restrooms may also not exist and will have to be brought in. If lighting is to be hung in a clear span tent, the lighting should be hung before the floor is put in, since many of the tent floors will not support the scissor lifts used by the lighting and décor people during setup.

All unusual venues share a general lack of support and equipment. All of them have heightened challenges with security and logistics, but some venues have additional, unique challenges.

Access to the meeting site is an issue in some remote locations. One perfectly delightful special event venue in Park City, Utah, is only accessible via horse-drawn sleigh and then only in the winter. Another example was Disney's Discovery Island in Bay Lake. At this location the only access to the island is via a wooden bridge that is not strong enough to support a vehicle and its slatted wooden deck makes it impossible to roll catering carts. When the locale was still being used as a special event venue, the only way to bring material to the island was on a float barge. The water was too shallow for anything larger to dock. There are many stories about the "amp rack that almost got away" on the trip to the island. In fact, there are unconfirmed rumors that one amp rack *did* get away and still rests on the bottom of Bay Lake.

Access can also be an issue even if there are roads directly to the area. Some roads flood in the rainy season, while others are impassable in the winter. Even if the road is substantial enough to support the delivery trucks, it is necessary to determine if there is a dock where supplies can be unloaded or whether a forklift is needed. If a forklift is needed, the planner must determine who supplies the driver as well as any other pertinent logistical questions.

One would think that outdoor sports arenas with their large array of seats or bleachers would be easy venues in which to work, and while they are easier to deal with than many outdoor venues in that they come with restrooms, they also present their own challenges. The irrigation systems for the landscaping at professional or competition fields are fragile enough that driving heavy loads over them can break the piping beneath the surface. Some venues prohibit anything heavier than a golf cart. Forget building a stage on a soccer field unless it is properly padded with plywood sheeting. Pushing that cart of riser tops across the grass is not likely to pass muster with the facility's head of grounds either.

While the technicians have one set of challenges dealing with outdoor sports venues, caterers have another. It is not uncommon for caterers to dump the leftover ice out on the ground, a practice that will kill the patch of grass underneath. Ice should be dumped in a storm drain, on the pavement, or in a mulched area. Also, portable bars are heavy and can damage the ground underneath. They must be placed on pavement or have a sheet of plywood underneath. That plywood should only be in place a few hours, or the grass underneath will die. There are plastic flooring

Busch Stadium was an unusual venue for a hospitality event: a reception for the MPI Annual Convention.   *George G. Fenich/ Meeting Professionals International*

pieces that will distribute the weight and still allow the grass to breathe. These are preferable to plywood if they are available. Portable bars also leak. If the water was clean, that would not be a problem. However, while most of the runoff from the bars is melted ice, some of it is excess from the soft drink dispensers. This excess contains sugar, which attracts ants. The ants then dig up the grass in search of more sugar, and soon there is an anthill behind third base. The partially melted ice from the shrimp buffet must also be disposed of properly; otherwise, the smell from the shrimp will last long after the event is over.

Public parks can be beautiful venues except that they are open to the public. If the event is a public event like an art show, a public park with its regular traffic can be an ideal location. But if the event is more private, especially if it involves alcohol, a public park may not be such a good idea.

When planning an outdoor convention function, an indoor backup plan is vital to the success of the event. For an outdoor arts festival, for example, an indoor plan is simply not feasible. However, a professional planner should always recognize the potential for weather to have an impact on the event.

In recent years, unique venues have become more and more utilized for the purposes of holding MEEC gatherings. Companies want their meetings to stand out from competitors; private parties have the desire to host events that are larger than life and feature unusual aspects, and in the wedding business where couples regularly insist on a one-of-a-kind ceremony, unique venues are frequently incorporated to provide the additional "wow" factor. Some venues unaccustomed to this kind of business are now courting groups based upon increased interest and demand. For instance, the Ngala Private Animal Reserve in Naples, Florida, and the Maryland Zoo were both originally intended to house animals and related exhibits. But as a result of interest from group business, both facilities have constructed venues on their properties for the specific meeting and events rentals. The PCMA annual convention has rented out and taken over Seaworld in Orlando, including the Shamu show, Universal Orlando, an aircraft carrier in San Diego, the entire Gaslamp District in San Diego, and Faneuil Hall in Boston: for the exclusive use of their convention attendees.

In addition to utilizing unusual venues for meetings and receptions, these locations have become increasingly popular with weddings. Destination weddings occur when a couple chooses to hold their wedding in a location where neither individual resides. For instance, a couple living in Chicago may elect to hold their wedding in Hawaii, as opposed to their hometown. In many cases these destination weddings take place in an unusual venue. Beaches, botanical gardens, castles, sailboats, or theme parks are some of the many facilities that may be used for a destination wedding. Walt Disney World in Florida plays host to more than 2,500 weddings each year, some of which actually take place in Cinderella's castle in the Magic Kingdom (yes there is a career opportunity to be a princess and be paid for it). In short, almost any venue may be used to host an event if the planner is willing to be a little creative.

COMMON ISSUES

Regardless of where an event is held, there are some issues that all events have in common. Many of these issues are logistic, such as transporting delegates from the airport. The following issues are common to most, if not all, meeting venues, and most, if not all, meetings.

For information on "common issues" in producing and logistics in meetings and events, see text *Production and Logistics in Meeting, Expositions, Events, and Conventions* by Fenich.

Obstacles

Perhaps a planner's greatest challenge is to overcome the obstacles in the way of the delegates' ability to be successful as a result of the meeting. The facility can present many obstacles that a planner will need to overcome. An example of such an obstacle would be an understaffed or undersized registration desk. Another would be inadequate parking space for the delegates who drive. Yet another would be a noise ordinance that prohibits loading out between the hours of 10:00 PM and 6:00 AM. Physical obstacles are not limited to disability considerations. There are also questions of how the delegates will get from their rooms to the gala dinner in their formal gowns if it is raining, and whether the busses transporting guests to the off-site venue can get to the actual door of the venue.

Power

Most outdoor special events and many events in smaller indoor venues have power requirements that exceed the power available. A generator usually provides this power, and generators are expensive. Properly anticipating the power needs is even more important in this type of event than one in a traditional meeting venue. With a generator, the planner will pay not only the daily cost to rent the generator but a fuel charge as well. The fuel consumption is determined by two factors: how long the generator runs and how much power is actually drawn from it. The fuel cost will be a multiple of the cost per gallon of the fuel, the time the generator runs, and the power consumption. The planner has control over two of the three elements in this equation.

For any meeting or special event using video or name entertainment, more than a few trade show booths or large scenic units will have special power requirements. Power is expensive. The power to run the sound system can be more expensive than the rental of the equipment. Many convention centers offer a discount if the power is requested early. The technical vendors can calculate power requirements fairly easily. If the discount for requesting power early is 30%, which is a fairly common discount, it would make sense to order 10% to 15% more power than estimated. In this way, ample power is available for less than it would have cost to place the power order after all the detailed requirements had been calculated.

Power charges are not based on consumption but rather on the maximum amount of power deliverable at any one time. To meter the actual power consumption and charge accordingly is illegal in many states. This would make the facility a utility company and subject to rate regulations. It would appear that generator use is charged based on power consumption, but it is actually based on fuel consumption. A generator that is idling uses fuel even if it is supplying no power. Turning a generator off when it is not needed will save money.

Event professionals involved in events around the globe must be very conscious of local differences. The base voltage may vary: 110 volts in North America versus 220 volts in much of the rest of the world. The style of electrical outlet and corresponding plugs vary widely with over 10 different configurations.

Rigging

Plaster ceilings are a production rigger's worst nightmare. Precast concrete roofs with no steel underneath run a close second. Any event involving more than a few hundred people or video image magnification should involve lighting suspended from the ceiling. Unless the facility is unusually well equipped for lighting from ceiling positions, lighting must be accomplished by hanging trusses, and hanging trusses involves rigging. Theaters are generally adequately equipped for lighting without hanging trusses, but not necessarily hotels.

A lighting grid suspended from the ceiling. *George G. Fenich*

The hotel's contracted rigging company will require access to all floor plans not less than two weeks in advance of the event. While it would seem that two weeks' lead time on a floor plan should be simple for an event contracted a year in advance, generating an accurate floor plan turns out to be a challenge many planners cannot accommodate. In some jurisdictions, the fire marshal, building code inspector, or safety officer can refuse to allow a show to be hung without a detailed hanging plan. Having to cancel a show at the last minute due to failure to submit paperwork can be a career-ending mistake.

Most facilities contract rigging to an outside company for liability protection. This is in addition to the normal reasons one would outsource any task that the facility management may not have enough experience to properly supervise. Given that the rigger's normal job description involves hanging "live loads" over the heads of the general public, they take their work seriously. This sometimes obstructionist attitude is intended to keep people safe and is not meant to impede the event. Adequate advance notification of schedules and requirements can help ensure that the event venue is hung properly and on schedule.

Floors

It is not safe to assume that just because the building has a ground level loading door big enough to drive a tractor-trailer through, that once it fits through the door, the floor will support it. Even though the floor may be made of four inches of steel-reinforced concrete on the ground, the utility boxes in the floor may not be so well designed. One Orlando area facility dug up and re-poured the concrete around several floor pockets because the constant forklift traffic drove them into the ground. It is also not safe to assume that a certain size scissor lift can be brought into the ballroom. For events where these issues are relevant, as part of the site inspection, the planner must ask about the floor load because the information is rarely readily available.

Ballrooms are carpeted, and many hotels insist that plastic sheeting be placed over the ballroom carpet during the move-in and move-out process. If the facility has such a requirement, it is important that the **ESC** and all technical vendors know about it in advance. The requirement to cover the floor with "Polytack" or one of several similar products is becoming more common. Failure to submit a proper floor plan to the people who apply the floor covering or failure to properly schedule the installation can result in expensive delays.

Many academic theaters have polished wood floors on the stages. Nailing or screwing into them is not recommended and is generally a fast way to be refused the use of the venue in the future. These floors are not designed for heavy loads such as scissor lifts or forklifts. Staffing and equipment requirements may need to be adjusted to compensate.

Access

Not only must the delegates be able to find the venue and its entrance, but the technical support and catering people need to gain access as well. The design of the loading access can have a significant impact on an event's finances. There is a facility in South Florida where the only loading access to the ballroom is to back a truck along a sea wall for a hundred yards. A 21-foot truck will not make the corner; a 17-foot truck will. The closest a tractor-trailer can park is a quarter mile away. An event here whose technical support equipment is shipped on a tractor-trailer would need to be unloaded off-site and the equipment trucked into the loading dock using a smaller truck at considerable additional expense. There is another facility on Florida's west coast where the loading access to the ballrooms is via an open-sided elevator with no top attached at the outside of the building. In this part of Florida, it rains almost every afternoon in the summer. A load scheduled for 4:00 PM in July stands an excellent likelihood of having a problem.

The presence of truck height docks is not enough to guarantee smooth loading. Some facilities, including the WDW Dolphin and the Gaylord Palms, have elevators from the docks to the ballroom. Access to the theater at the Orange County Convention Center involves two elevators and a push down the hall between them. The number and location of the docks is significant. The Morial Convention Center in New Orleans is all on one level, with loading docks lining one entire side of the building.

FUNCTION ROOMS AND SETUPS

Most meetings are held in boardrooms, breakout rooms, or ballrooms. Exhibit halls are considerably larger and most typically are used for large events such as tradeshows or concerts, while prefunction spaces are the hallways and foyers outside meeting rooms often used for refreshment breaks or registration areas.

There are a number of factors that must be considered when planners are booking meeting space. Aside from the actual accommodation of meeting attendees and/or exhibitors, it is important to consider other setup aspects such as AV needs, refreshment break areas, and stages and podiums for speakers and panels, among other things. But the most basic layout refers to the type of seating used. The way seating is determined is again directly related to the needs of the group. A meeting where attendees will need to interact with one another during a session will require a different type of setup than one where individuals will be hearing a lecture from a speaker at the head of the room.

In the MEEC industry there are endless potential types and designs in which rooms may be set up. Since this book is meant to provide an overview of the industry, the three basic room sets are explained here.

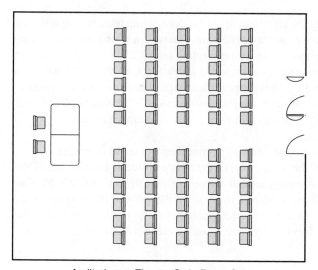

Auditorium or Theater Style Room Set

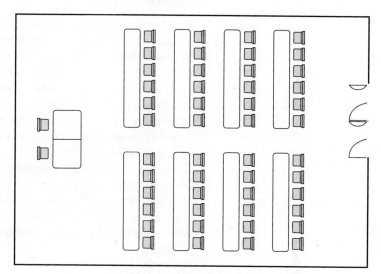

Classroom Style Room Set

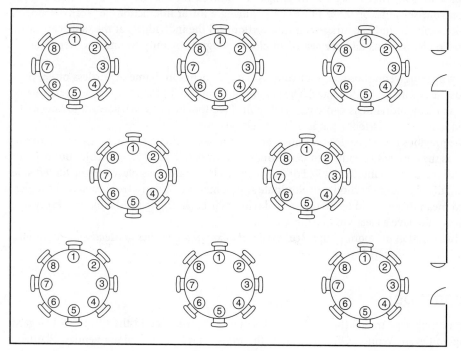

Rounds of Eight

Different meeting rooms setups or layouts *George G. Fenich*

Auditorium or Theater Style

Probably the most common seating arrangement in meetings is an auditorium or theater design. An **auditorium style** room setup is particularly useful when there is no need for attendees to interact with one another during the course of the session. In this instance, chairs are arranged in rows facing the same direction. Most commonly those rows will face the head of the room, which may be designated by a stage, head table, lectern, or screen. A speaker or panel will generally run the meeting, often lecturing to attendees who may be taking notes based on the information the speaker is conveying.

As shown in the image above, all the chairs are arranged in rows while facing the head table and the two panelists stationed there. Depending on the number of seats required for the meeting, the auditorium style may be altered slightly. For instance, an auditorium room set with 8,000 seats would have several aisles to allow attendees to move freely as needed. The chairs may also be set up in a V-shaped pattern or semicircle to allow those individuals on the far ends of the rows a better line of sight.

Classroom Style

Sometimes meetings may require tables for attendees to use for completing tests, taking notes, or interacting with other attendees to solve presented problems. **Classroom style** is the most common setup used for these types of meetings. In classroom meeting setups, chairs are arranged in a similar manner as in an auditorium but with tables provided for each row of chairs. These tables are generally six or eight feet long and 18 inches deep. If the design is intended for attendees to be sitting on each side of the table, then 30-inch-deep tables (or two 18-inch tables placed back to back) are used to allow sufficient space. In this room setup, the tables are draped, with pads of paper and pencils/pens at each place setting.

Similar to auditorium room sets, classrooms may be modified as needed. Sometimes classrooms are arranged diagonally toward the head table, or even perpendicular to the front of the room. Perpendicular room sets are challenging because it often necessitates a significant number of attendees to have their backs toward the speaker at the front of the room. If the purpose of the session is to work with table partners, this may not be problematic, but a perpendicular classroom setup is seldom wise when attendees need to be focused on the individual on stage.

Rounds

Round tables are sometimes used for meetings but utilized most often for food functions. In smaller breakout sessions, or those meetings requiring a lot of interaction between attendees, round tables facilitate and encourage communication. All the individuals at the table can easily see their table companions and are seated in close enough proximity to one another to allow collaboration.

Many meeting venues use six-foot rounds (i.e., 72 inches in diameter) or less often, five-foot rounds (i.e., 60 inches in diameter).The size of the rounds is important because the diameter dictates how many individuals can comfortably fit. Five-foot rounds can accommodate six to eight individuals, while six-foot rounds may seat eight to ten.

In the previous image, six-foot rounds were used to seat eight guests each. An alternative to full rounds is the crescent rounds. **Crescent rounds** may use full-sized round tables but will not have seats all the way around the table. For instance, if a head table was placed at the far left side of the room, the planner may choose to eliminate seat numbers 6, 7, and 8 from each of the tables. This would mean there would be no one seated with their backs to the head table and every one at the table would have a clear view of the speaker.

For information on room setups, see text *Production and Logistics in Meeting, Expositions, Events, and Conventions* by Fenich.

FUTURE TRENDS

There are a number of trends that will likely become commonplace in the future with regard to meeting and event venues. One of those is the mass utilization of unique venues. Planners are always looking for the newest and freshest ideas to make their events stand out from the competition, and the choice of venue is perhaps the most obvious method for accomplishing that. Attendees also expect to be "wowed" and not see the same cookie-cutter event format year after year. Rather than holding an opening reception for attendees in a convention center hall, the planner can use unexpected venues to keep the attendees guessing and prevent them from getting bored. One year the opening event could be held at Mardi Gras World in New Orleans, the next year at the Cowboys Stadium in Dallas, and the following year at the Seattle Space Needle. In each location the attendees will have a different experience and leave feeling that their event was one of a kind.

The size and composition of convention centers may also see some significant changes in the next few years. Over the last decade convention center space in the United States has continued to increase with many second- and third-tier cities building new centers and/or building additions to current facilities. Despite the fact that the MEEC industry is continually growing, the mass construction of convention centers will likely slow down because demand has not caught up to the available supply yet. However, some centers have moved toward adding space, which can easily double as business and entertainment venues. This trend may see more growth in lieu of building larger facilities.

Summary

RECOMMENDATIONS FOR DEALING WITH ALL VENUES

Obtaining accurate information is essential to planning successful meetings. Detailed and thorough research is the first step in the process. This first step is much easier now than it has been and promises to become even easier, as the Internet and World Wide Web provide planners powerful resources with which to plan their events. Many of the best meeting facilities have extensive Web sites with volumes of available information. Some venues have 360-degree visual imaging that allows a planner to remotely view the facility. This technology is becoming more and more affordable and common. Before calling a sales representative, a planner should visit the facility's Web site and print out everything that might be of interest. Once having studied the material and determined that the facility may be appropriate for the event, then, and only then, should the planner call the facility's salespeople to open the dialogue.

The most important component of dealing with any facility is the development of an open, honest, and trusting relationship with all parties involved. Unfortunately, there are facilities that will take advantage of that relationship, just as there are planners who do not deal honestly with their suppliers. In spite of the risks involved, the attempt must be made, because the success of every event depends on the interaction between the planner and all the other parties. This relationship begins with understanding what each of the participants brings to the relationship and what each needs.

Communication begins with a set of requirements. The more accurate the requirements are, the better. It is important to note, however, that "accurate" and "detailed" are not the same thing. In a contract, the hotel needs to know how many people are coming, but they do not need the names until relatively close to the event. Accurate and timely listings of requirements are the first step in developing a successful relationship. Verification of the documentation returned by the venue is the other half of this communication. Not only should the planner provide requirements, but the venue should also reply and acknowledge that it understands the requirements and how it will fulfill each requirement as appropriate.

The key to working with any venue is fourfold: research, understand, communicate, and verify. Research, understand, communicate, and verify. Repeat until done! This chapter provides information that can be used by meeting planners in the first two steps of the process. The rest is what separates the best planners from the rest.

Key Words and Terms

For definitions, see GLOSSARY, or http://glossary.conventionindustry.org

amenities	classroom style	ESC	pole tent
amphitheater	clear span tent	exhibit hall	prefunction space
arena	complete meeting package	frame tent	seasonality
attrition	concessionaire	hotel	shoulder
auditorium style	crescent rounds	local event	sports facilities
boardroom	destination management	loss leader	stadium
breakout room	company (DMC)	needs analysis	theater

Review and Discussion Questions

1. What is the single most important thing a planner can provide a venue to ensure the effective and cost-efficient execution of a meeting?
2. What is attrition, and why should a planner care?
3. What is the most significant single difference between a hotel's meeting space and a convention center's meeting space?
4. What is the most important single activity that facility personnel depend on the meeting planner to provide?
5. How is the financial structure of a hotel different from that of other facilities? What is a hotel's biggest source of revenue? A convention center's?
6. Why is seasonality important to a planner?
7. Why is ceiling height significant?
8. Why should a meeting planner care about copyright laws?
9. What should be a planner's greatest concern on an outdoor event? What should a planner do about it?

About the Chapter Contributor

Kathryn Hashimoto is a faculty member in the School of Hospitality Leadership at East Carolina University. She has theoretical expertise in marketing and consumer behavior. Her operational expertise is in meetings/conventions, the Meeting and Business Events Competency Standards, and casinos. She has authored many books and articles.

Previous Edition Chapter Contributor

Kelly Virginia Phelan from Texas Tech University
Bob Cherny, Paradise Light and Sound

Exhibitions

Trade shows are used throughout the world to promote products and companies. This one takes place in Chang Rai, Thailand.   *George G. Fenich*

Chapter Objectives

After reading Chapter 5, the reader should be able to:

- Define the different types of exhibitions
- Identify the key players of exhibition management
- Categorize the components of exhibition planning
- Identify the role of the exhibitor and fundamentals of exhibit planning
- Recognize trends in the exhibition industry

INTRODUCTION

With more than approximately 14,000 exhibitions annually in North America alone, the long history of exhibitions has turned into a thriving, ever-changing industry. This chapter provides an overview of the exhibition industry and looks at it from the perspective of the show organizer and the exhibit manager.

HISTORY

Trade fairs began in biblical times and became popular in Medieval Europe and in the Middle East. These fairs served as an opportunity for craftsmen and farmers to bring their products to the center of the town or city to sell their goods as a means of survival. These were the beginnings of the "public" trade fair and featured handmade crafts, agricultural products, and other specialties. Germany and France have the first recorded history of organizing the earliest organized fairs. Some examples include the Leipzig Fair in 1165, the 1215 Dublin Fair, Cologne's biannual fair starting in 1259, and Frankfurt's Book Fair in 1445. These types of trade fair continued through the Renaissance period until the beginning of the Industrial Revolution when goods began being mass produced.

The poster announcing the Dublin Fair in the year 1215 AD.
George G. Fenich

This pie stall from the Dublin Fair of 1215 is not so different than food vendors at festivals today.
George G. Fenich

Eventually, the businesses realized the value of meeting, sharing information, and providing previews of their products to potential customers. This part of the industry blossomed in the late 1800s, with many facilities being built strictly for world-class exhibitions. This buyer–seller format was termed an **exhibition** and typically took place in a large city at a facility built specifically for the exhibition. For example, the Crystal Palace in London was opened for the "Great Industrial Exhibition of All Nations" featuring 13,000 exhibits from all over the world and attracted more than 6 million attendees. In the United States, facilities were opened in Chicago and Philadelphia to commemorate "world's fairs" that, in reality, were exhibitions highlighting the industrial advances of participating countries. In 1895, Detroit started the first joint effort to attract exhibition business, and in 1914 the National Association of Convention Bureaus (now Destination Marketing Association International—DMAI) was formed.

In the early and mid-twentieth century, trade associations grew and saw the potential of exhibitions being held in conjunction with their annual meetings as a way to stimulate communication in the industry and expand their revenues gained from the annual meeting. The twentieth century brought exciting and trying times to the exhibition industry, with notable pauses in progress during World War I, World War II, and the Great Depression. To increase the awareness and value to exhibitions, a group of industry professionals created the National Association of Exposition Managers (which is now named the International Association of Exhibitions and Events [IAEE]) in 1978 and has members sponsoring, hosting, and organizing exhibits worldwide.

The State of the Exhibition Industry

The exhibitions industry continues to be resilient and its growth always slightly trails economic recoveries of global sectors. Exhibitions are an integral part of the overall sales and marketing budgets and strategies for corporations and associations. Face-to-face interaction definitely enhances and augments the availability of information via the Internet and other valuable resources. Significant progress has been made as the exhibitions and meetings industry focuses on demonstrating its value, measuring return on investments, and justifying participation and attendance at trade and consumer shows.

According to the Center for Exhibition Industry Research (CEIR), the exhibition industry's independent research organization, forecasts for 2014 and beyond call for a steady growth of 2.5 to 5.0% and that will tie directly into the global economic growth realities. CEIR measures the four metrics of net square feet sold, attendance, exhibitor participation, and overall growth. The estimated direct spending for the global exhibitions industry is over $100 billion. The aggressive expansion of exhibition and convention centers around the world will initially create increased over supply of inventory. It will take many years to grow the demand for new exhibitions and that will be directly tied to the vitality and growth of the global economy. Additional information is available via two Websites. The International Association of Exhibitions and Event, www.iaee.com and The Center for Exhibition Industry Research, www.ceir.org.

Authored by: David DuBois, CMP, CAE, FASAE, CTA, President and CEO

International Association of Exhibitions and Events, Dallas, Texas, USA

TYPES OF EXHIBITIONS

Business-to-Business (B2B)

Business-to-business **(B2B)** exhibitions are a private event and not open to the public. The definition of a trade fair has become close enough to that of a trade show that the terms are used interchangeably. The term "trade fair" is more often used outside the United States than "trade show." Trade fairs are discussed in more detail in Chapter 14, "International Perspectives in MEEC." Although the historical definition of exhibition is quite different from today, this term has also evolved to mean a trade show or trade fair. The term "**exposition**" has also evolved to be similar in meaning to trade show. An association meeting may include an exposition, or expo, as the trade show segment of the association's annual gathering. In this chapter, we refer to trade shows, expositions, and exhibitions interchangeably.

The exhibitor is usually a manufacturer or distributor of products or services specific or complementary to those industries represented by the sponsor or organizer. Often, attendance is restricted to buyers from the industry, and business credentials are required for registration. Educational programs may or may not be a part of the exhibition program; although in recent years, educational programs have expanded as a method of attracting attendees. Sponsorship or management of the exhibition is usually either under the auspices of a trade association or has evolved to come under the sponsorship of a management company. Some exhibitions are the result of initiatives by companies and are fully intended to be profit-making ventures. Usually, exhibitions are annual events, although some occur more frequently, and others less frequently. Major organizations may also have regional exhibitions that are smaller than their standard national or international event. Attendees and exhibitors may come from all over the country or world; therefore, hotel rooms and transportation may be considered in selecting the show's location.

Many organizations are considering moving to a **hosted buyer** exhibition format. At these events, attendees are pre-qualified as having the buying influence and/or have the authority to make a purchasing decision. These attendees have all or most of their travel expenses covered by the show management company or exhibitors/sponsors. The exhibition organizer, in return, schedules meetings between these attendees and suppliers to conduct business.

Ray Bloom, the founder of IMEX. *Courtesy of Imex*

In 1988 when Ray Bloom, now the Chairman of the IMEX Group, had booked space in Geneva's PalExpo for his first non-U.K. trade show, he became concerned that his target audience of incentive travel buyers might not make the cross-border trip. He turned uneasiness into positive action, however, when he decided to ask industry trade publications whether they would like to host the top buyers from their readership, paying for their travel and hotel costs. Every publication he approached (whom he had built former relationships with) agreed to the proposal, and suddenly there was a whole new momentum for his event and a brand new way to make a trade show work.

What started with a handful of trade media intermediaries in Europe has grown to include a global list of over 400 intermediaries for IMEX in Frankfurt and 300 intermediaries for IMEX America. Intermediaries can include hotel chains, representation and destination marketing companies, airlines, trade publications, trade associations, and more.

Not only does this three-pronged relationship create a unique experience for the hosted buyer, but the intermediaries are also able to expand their networks, develop new or strengthened business relationships, bring new value to their top clients and prospects, and explore new business opportunities and partnerships. "As a business model, once you can guarantee that the very best buyers are going to be at your show, then you have a compelling proposition for exhibitors. One follows the other," says Bloom.

Hosted buyers meeting with suppliers. *Courtesy of Imex*

Now on its 12th year, IMEX in Frankfurt 2013 featured 3,962 hosted buyers from 75 countries and 4,800 exhibitors from 83 countries. The newer addition to the family, going into its 4th year, IMEX America posted 2013 numbers of 2,600+ hosted buyers representing over 40 countries and nearly 2,700 exhibitors from 150 countries—double-digit growth from the previous year. Success has clearly been strong around the hosted buyer model for Bloom and his now global team, but it didn't happen overnight and requires immense amounts of work to manage intermediary and hosted buyer relationships to ensure quality.

To qualify for a place on the IMEX hosted programs, buyers must be responsible for planning, organizing, recommending, or making financial decisions for corporate meetings, conferences, seminars, exhibitions, road shows, association meetings, or incentive travel programs. In terms of reach to qualify, buyers need to place business outside their home country with two "global" events in 12 months being the ideal. Given the immense size of the U.S. home market, however, IMEX America also reserves a few hosted buyer places for high-level buyers who place business outside their home state but not necessarily internationally.

In return, from IMEX hosted buyers receive complimentary travel and accommodations, one-stop shopping to domestic and global destinations and suppliers, and world-class education and networking. Hosted buyers are asked to schedule up to eight appointments per day using the exclusive IMEX online scheduling tool, which gives them full freedom of choice of who they choose to meet with. Further, these meetings can be individual appointments, open-stand presentations, or group appointments, which give hosted buyers even more freedom. This is a win-win for all as many hosted buyers report getting a full year's worth of business done during the three day IMEX shows.

IMEX Frankfurt statistics. *Courtesy of Imex*

A common form of marketing to potential B2B exhibitors is advertising in trade publications or targeted electronic communication. Until recently, well-established exhibitions had little trouble marketing to potential exhibitors. The exhibit halls were full, and waiting lists of exhibitors were commonplace. However, the past few years have seen many companies downsizing their exhibit space or opting to exhibit at fewer shows. Management companies have now placed a renewed focus on marketing to potential exhibitors. Exhibitions are now in competition for exhibitors, and exhibition management companies are working hard to retain existing exhibitors and attract new ones.

Examples of U.S.-based exhibitions include the following:

- *National Restaurant Show: The International Foodservice Market* is held annually at McCormick Center in Chicago, Illinois, each May. The show typically attracts almost 40,000 attendees and 15,000 exhibitors.
- *The International Consumer Electronic Show*, or simply known as CES, is held each January in Las Vegas, Nevada. It attracts over 3,000 exhibitors and over 150,000 attendees who come to see the latest technology innovations being introduced into the market.
- *International Builders Show*, the largest building industry exhibition in the country, is held in January in Las Vegas, Nevada.
- *American Society for Cell Biology Annual Meeting and Exposition* was held in New Orleans in 2013. Attendees included scientists and students in academia, industry, government, and higher education. More than 350 commercial and nonprofit exhibits offering new products and services participated in the exhibition. Over 100 scientific sessions along with 2,500 poster sessions were presented.

Business-to-Consumer (B2C)

Business-to-Consumer (**B2C**) **public shows** are exhibitions that are open to the public and offer a wide variety of products for sale. This type of show is used by a consumer-based industry to bring their goods directly to their market's end user. Show management may or may not charge an admission fee, and shows open to the public are typically held on the weekend. Consumer shows are often regional in nature, with exhibitors traveling from city to city with their displays and products. They also provide excellent opportunities for companies to brand or test market new products.

Summary of Characteristics—B2B and B2C

Show Type	Attendee	Registration or Admission	Marketing	Show Days	Location
B2B Show	International and national	Preregistration, qualified buyers	Targeted Electronic Communications	Business Week (Monday–Friday)	Large markets with significant meeting space, hotel, and transportation
B2C Show	Regional or local	Ticket purchase on-site, general public	Newspaper, regional magazines, billboards, social media, and TV advertising	Weekends (Friday–Sunday)	Large or secondary markets with large parking areas

Public exhibitions also require promotion to be successful. Typically, public shows are marketed through advertisements in trade or local public media. Advertisements may offer discounts for purchasing early tickets or may promote special events or speakers that will attract the largest number of attendees. Promoting public exhibitions is a daunting task because the potential attending audience is so large that it requires a significant expense to reach them through print, radio, social media, and television advertising. Producers must be confident that their investment in promotion will result in reaching the attendance objectives. Producers must also be attentive to other events that may be occurring during the exhibition time period that can affect attendance. Many B2C shows feature local and national celebrities to draw additional attention to the exhibition.

Common types of consumer shows include home and garden, travel-related, and sports-specific shows. Some examples include:

- *The Central Florida Home and Garden Show* hosted each spring features hundreds of exhibitors showcasing remodeling, home improvement, and outdoor gardening ideas.

- *The Kansas Sports, Boat & Travel Show* has been one of the most popular shows in the Heartland. It features exhibits in ATV, hunting, fishing, camping, or the freedom of traveling in an RV. Tickets for the February event cost $7 for adults.
- *The Michigan Golf Show* hosts more than 400 exhibitors with great deals on every aspect of the golf game. This weekend show will cost adult golf lovers around $10.

Consolidation Shows (Also Called Combined or Mixed Show)

Consolidation shows are open to both industry buyers and the general public. Exhibitors are manufactures or distributors. Hours may differ based on the type of attendee, allowing the trade professionals to preview the show prior to the consumer buyers. Consumer electronics and the automobile industries, which have diverse audience needs, use this format to accommodate the varied industry buyers and retail consumers.

EXHIBITION MANAGEMENT: KEY PLAYERS

Regardless of the exhibition type, there are three key players that ensure that the components of the show come together to accomplish the objectives of each stakeholder—the exhibition organizer, the facility manager, and the general service contractor.

Exhibition Organizer

The exhibition management company (organizer) may be a trade association, a company subcontracted to the trade association, or a separate company organizing the show as a profit-making venture. The exhibition management staff member in charge of the entire exhibit area is called the exhibit manager and is responsible for all aspects of managing the show. Think of exhibition management as the "systems integrator" responsible for implementing the show, marketing it to buyers and sellers, and gathering together all the resources needed for success.

The exhibition management company must also consider the types of programs offered in addition to the event itself. Exhibition programs have evolved to encompass additional programs that serve to boost attendance. Additional programs to consider include:

- Educational programs
- Entertainment programs
- Availability of exhibitor demonstrations and educational/training programs
- Special sections on the show floor for emerging companies, new exhibitors, or new technologies
- Celebrity or industry-leader speakers
- Meal programs
- Continuing education units or certifications for educational programs
- Spouse and children programs
- Internet access and e-mail centers

Facility Manager

Facilities are also needed to conduct the exhibition. Facilities range from small hotels with limited meeting space to large convention centers. Facilities also include adjacent lodging and entertainment facilities that are used by the exhibitors and visitors. The facility manager, typically known as a convention service manager or event manager, will assist the show manager in arranging the show's logistical details. Exhibition organizers consider a number of variables when selecting facilities, including the size of the facility, services available at the venue (telecommunications, dining, setup, and teardown times), cost, availability of service contractors, preferences of exhibitors and attendees, logistical considerations (airline services, local transportation, parking), and lodging and entertainment in the area.

Meeting and convention facilities have kept pace with the growth of the industry. From small, regional facilities to mega convention centers located in major cities, destinations have understood the benefits of attracting exhibitions and conventions to their

Key players. *Chart produced by George G. Fenich, Ph.D.*

area. Hotels and nontraditional venues are also investing in larger exhibit areas and expanding their meeting space. Many fair grounds, sports centers, and large parking lots or museums, nightclubs, and community centers are being used for expositions. These options must be considered as alternatives to convention centers and large hotels for smaller exhibitions.

The chart that follows shows a range of convention center space available to show organizers.

Convention Center Size

Center	Square Feet of Exhibit Space	Meeting Rooms
McCormick Place (Chicago)	2.6 Million	114
Orange County Convention Center (Orlando, FL)	2.1 million	94
Las Vegas Convention Center	2.0 million	103
Indiana Convention Center (Indianapolis, IN)	66,600	48
Austin Convention Center (Austin, TX)	371,000	54

Source: George G. Fenich

General Service Contractor

The general service contractor, also known as an official exhibit service contractor or decorator, provides products and services to the **exhibition management company** and the show's exhibitors. Their services are often key to the success of a show. Once selected, the general service contractor will provide the exhibition management and exhibitors with a list of services supplied by the contractor or other subcontractors. Types of services the general service contractors provide include:

- Floor plan development and design
- Aisle carpet and signage
- Custom and modular booths
- Freight handling and shipping
- Storage and warehousing
- Installation, maintenance, and dismantling labor
- Lighting, electronics, and plumbing
- Telecommunication and computer requests
- Sound and audio visual
- Coordination with specialty contractors

Arranging and managing these services for a large show can be quite complex for the exhibition management company and exhibitors. Convention centers, management companies, and even exhibitors have become accustomed to working with various arrangements and companies.

Because the service contractors operate in a very competitive environment, they have learned that customer service, fair pricing, and responsiveness to customer needs are important. This enables organizers and exhibitors a level of comfort in relying on service contractors to take care of the problems that arise with organizing a successful show.

The general service contractor, in conjunction with the exhibition management company, usually develops an exhibitor service manual that encompasses all details that an exhibitor needs to plan and implement an exhibit program for the show. It also includes the forms needed to order services from the service contractors and the rules and regulations of the exhibition management company, convention center or hotel, and the local government.

Despite the controls and organization put in place by the exhibition management company and service contractors, disputes arise. When this occurs, it is important to get all concerned parties involved in achieving a successful resolution. The show manager is responsible for compliance of exhibitors, attendees, and service contractors to the show rules. See Chapter 6 for more information on service contractors.

CONSIDERATIONS IN PLANNING THE SHOW

Location

Exhibition planners consider a number of variables when deciding on the location of the show. It is no secret that the city and venue selected to host the exhibition has a major effect on attendance. Thus, a balance must be attained between location, cost, and the ideal attendance level. Many organizations that conduct annual meetings and expositions stay in the same city year after year, and thus they can negotiate the best agreements with the local convention center and hotels and still retain the optimum attendance levels. Typically, these are association meetings that have strong educational programs and are held at a desirable site.

However, other organizations or exhibition management companies prefer to move their exhibition from city to city each year. This strategy may help attract additional visitors. Not only is a different local attendance base able to attend inexpensively, but out-of-town visitors may be attracted by local tourist offerings as well.

Organizations and exhibition management companies often survey their membership or potential attendees to assess their preferences on location. The success of convention centers in cities like Las Vegas, Orlando, and Chicago is indicative of organizations paying attention to the needs and desires of their members and potential audience. Expansion of the convention facilities in each of these cities indicates that these destinations value the revenue generated by large B2B and B2C shows.

Hotel facilities are also a factor to be considered when determining the location of the exhibition. Are the local facilities adequate for the projected attendance? Are the negotiated room rates within the budget of the typical attendee or exhibitor? What is the proximity to the exhibition site, and will local transportation need to be provided? What is the potential for labor problems to arise in the host city or at host hotels? Do the convention center and local hotels comply with ADA requirements or other government requirements?

In addition, the largest exhibitions often require dedicated local ground transportation to assist visitors and exhibitors in getting from their hotels to the show site. Planners are now looking at a variety of public transportation options for their ground transportation needs, such as trolleys, subways, or even bicycles, as they select meeting sites and venues. With increasing concerns about sustainability, ground transportation is being a key factor in the decision to select or not select a city for an event.

When determining whether dedicated ground transportation is required, consider that safety is often the key decision point. Even if hotels are within walking distance from the convention center, the conditions of the city between the hotels and the center may dictate that it is in your best interests to provide transportation. For example, in New Orleans there are many hotels within walking distance of the convention center, but in the summer when temperature and humidity are both in the 90s, the meeting organizer is better off to provide transportation. When choosing ground transportation providers, be sure to take into account experience, availability, special services, insurance, condition of vehicles, labor contracts, and cost.

Housing and transportation are essential elements to success for any B2B exhibition that attracts a national or international audience. A large part of any organizer's time is spent negotiating room blocks in the host city and airline and car rental discounts for attendees and exhibitors. Recently, the trend has moved toward outsourcing housing and transportation arrangements to local convention and visitor bureaus or third-party housing vendors. Regardless of how housing and transportation issues are handled, the expectation is that they will be "transparent" to the attendee or exhibitor.

Another selection factor is weather. Unlike B2B exhibitions with many people coming from outside the city, B2C exhibitions rely on the local and regional population for attendance. Locals and regional tourists will not venture out to a public show in the midst of a serious snowstorm or rainstorm. Thus, one episode of bad weather can drastically affect the bottom line of a show producer. The National Western Stock Show, held in Denver each January, is a good example of this. Years with extreme cold and snow greatly reduced the event's attendance. During years of unseasonably mild weather, attendance skyrockets. The solution for the National Western Stock Show has been to extend the show to a sixteen-day period, ensuring that there will be "good days" and "bad days." This has led to a more consistent overall attendance figure from year to year.

Shipping and Storage

Once the location is chosen, the booths and other show materials need to be transported to the site. While air freight may sometimes be used, over-the-road freight by truck is the most common method. Charges are typically per hundred pounds and are based on the distance the freight must travel.

Since an exhibitor cannot afford for the freight shipment to arrive late for an exhibition, extra time is allowed for transit. Thus, the exhibitor must arrange for temporary storage of the materials at the destination, but prior to the move-in date for the exhibition. One must also consider storage of the freight containers while the show is open. When the show closes, the whole process is reversed. Some exposition services contractors such as GES of Freeman have separate divisions of their company that deal with shipping and storage.

Marketing and Promotion

Without exhibitors, the exhibition will not be successful, and in turn without attendees, exhibitors will not participate or return. Exhibition planners focus their attention to marketing and promotion programs that will fill the exhibition hall with both exhibitors and attendees. Regardless of the type of exhibition, attendance is the key to success. It is primarily the responsibility of the exhibition management company to target and market to the right audience. This is typically done through direct mail, advertising in trade publications, social media, the show management Web site, and e-marketing.

Exhibition management companies and service companies also offer additional marketing opportunities for exhibitors to consider. Exhibitors want to invest in a show because their potential customers are in attendance. Based on their objectives for the show, exhibitors can choose to invest in a number of programs:

- *General Sponsorships:* These programs usually involve the company's name or logo being included or printed in the show's promotional materials or being posted in a prominent place in the exhibit hall.
- *Special Event Sponsorship:* Special events are often conducted during the exhibition, such as receptions, press conferences, or entertainment. Companies who sponsor these events have their name or logo mentioned prominently in promotional materials and throughout the event.
- *Advertising in the Show Daily:* Large shows usually have a daily newspaper available to all exhibitors and attendees each morning. It reviews the previous day's events and previews what is coming up. Exhibitors have the opportunity to advertise in the show daily.
- *Advertising in the Show Directory:* Almost all exhibitions provide attendees with a show directory containing information about the show and exhibitors. Advertising opportunities also exist for this show directory.
- *Promotional Items Sponsorship:* Management companies may offer sponsorship opportunities to companies for badge holders, tote bags, and other promotional items given to registered attendees.

Management companies (for B2B shows) must provide a convention program that has additional information beyond the exhibit hall to help attract visitors. Often, educational programs are provided as an incentive, or prominent industry leaders are hired to give keynote addresses that attract visitors. Contests, gifts, discount programs, and other tools to attract visitors have been commonplace. Exhibitors are also involved in helping boost attendance at shows. Usually, they are given a number of free passes to the show that can be passed on to their best customers. Exhibitors are also encouraged to sponsor or conduct special events and to promote them to their customer base.

Technology

Advances in technology have made managing the show, as well as exhibition itself, easier and more productive (for more information, see Chapter 12 on technology).

- The Internet has had a great impact on how exhibitions are marketed to potential visitors. Most shows have sites that allow attendees to register online (B2B shows) and purchase tickets in advance (B2C shows). Attendees can view exhibitor lists, review educational programs, and even make their travel arrangements online. They can also view interactive floor plans and select educational programs and/or special events to efficiently plan their time.
- Lead retrieval systems are a great benefit to exhibitors. Systems are in place that enable the exhibit staff to "swipe" an attendee's card or bar-coded badge and capture all of that individual's contact information, saving many hours of entering business card data.
- The use of **radio frequency identification (RFID)** is now being used by convention and exhibition managers to track attendees' movement and behavior. This advanced technology is beneficial for data acquisition, lead retrieval, and reporting, but raise many issues regarding privacy and use of personal information.
- Many organizations are now introducing the option to participate at an exhibition virtually to save attendees travel time and costs.
- Technology is also used in promoting a company's products. Many companies now give visitors inexpensive flash drives or provide Web site links instead of bulky brochures. The electronic format can contain much more information and more elaborate presentations that the potential customer can view at his or her leisure.

Risk and Crisis Management

Organizing and exhibiting at a show can be a risky business. If things are not done correctly, the show can quickly become a colossal failure. Both exhibition organizers and exhibitors need to have a risk management program. A risk management plan does the following:

- Identifies all potential risks for the exhibition management and the exhibitors.
- Quantifies each risk to determine the effect it would have if it occurs.
- Provides an assessment of each risk to determine which risks to ignore, which to avoid, and which to mitigate.
- Provides risk avoidance steps to prevent the risk from occurring.
- Provides risk mitigation steps to minimize potential costs if the risk occurs.

Always keep in mind that an exhibition is a business venture that should be given every chance to succeed. Knowing how to apply risk management principles will help ensure success.

Crisis management has also become critical to exhibition organizers. A crisis is different from a risk in that it poses a critical situation that may cause danger to visitors or exhibitors. Examples of recent crises include the tsunami in Japan, the flooding in Nashville, or volcanic ash cloud that paralyzed travel to Europe. Exhibitions that were scheduled during these incidents were either canceled or curtailed midway through the schedule. Organizing companies suffered deep losses for these events.

Every exhibition organizer should have a crisis management plan that addresses the prevention, control, and reporting of emergency situations. The plan should address the more likely types of emergencies, such as fire, food-borne illness, demonstrations, bomb threats, terrorism, and natural disasters. It should contain all procedures to be followed in the event of an emergency situation.

Consider having a crisis management team who is well versed in assessing the potential for a crisis, taking actions to prevent emergencies, and taking control should a situation occur. The crisis management team should be represented in the site selection process.

EXHIBITOR PERSPECTIVE

If exhibitors were not successful from a business perspective, exhibitions would not exist. Exhibiting at shows is often a key part of a company's integrated marketing strategy. Companies invest a significant portion of their marketing budget into exhibitions appearances and must see a positive return on their investment. This section of the chapter looks at the issues that face the exhibiting companies.

Why Exhibit?

An exhibit booth is constructed to showcase products/services and to convey a message. It is important for a company to understand and analyze the benefits of exhibiting at a show prior to beginning the planning. Exhibiting is the only marketing medium that allows the potential buyer to experience a product or service, and therefore, more money is spent on participating in exhibits than on traditional advertising or individual sales travel.

Additional reasons that companies participate in an exhibition include the following:

- Branding of their name in the industry
- Annual presentation of products to industry analysts
- New product rollout
- Opportunities to meet with potential and existing customers
- Opportunities to learn about customer needs
- Opportunities to meet with trade media
- Opportunities to learn about changes in industry trends and competitor products

Exhibit Design Principles

Although exhibit design may be limited by the rules established by the exhibit management company, the constraints of the facility, or the business culture of the host country, there are some general principles that can be discussed. These principles include selecting the right layout of the exhibit to meet your purposes, selecting the right size for your company's budget and purposes, and making proper use of signage, lighting, and personnel. Exhibits and the space they occupy are a significant corporate investment, and attention must be given to each of these factors.

Exhibit size is a major consideration, if only because of cost. The cost of a standard booth can vary greatly based on the industry, show location, and venue. The more space an exhibit occupies, the more it costs in space rental, materials, labor for setup, additional staff, and maintenance. Therefore, be sure to balance the costs with the benefits of having a larger exhibit. A larger exhibit typically means being noticed by visitors, and it creates a better impression if done well. It gives the impression that the company is in a solid financial situation and is a leader in the industry. However, the space must be used well and convey the messages that the company desires to impart to potential customers.

Top Reasons Exhibitors Fail

1. Do not understand that every show is different
2. No SMART objectives were set for the show
3. Failure to differentiate your company from your competitors
4. No formal marketing or promotional plan created or shared
5. Logical planning is poor
6. Do not give attendees any reason to visit your booth space
7. Staff is not trained to sell your product or service
8. Exhibiting for all the wrong reasons—did not ensure the "right" buyers would be there
9. Do not know how to measure return on investment
10. Do not do any post-show follow-up with leads generated at the show

Companies that participate in a large number of shows will have exhibits that range in size from very small (for less important or more specialized shows) to very large (for their most important exhibitions). For example, Xerox, a company that exhibits at a variety of shows each year, has very large exhibits for information technology shows but also smaller peninsular or in-line exhibits for specialized shows or smaller, regional shows. Some companies even have two or three exhibits at the same show: a large one promoting the main theme and message they want to communicate and smaller exhibits in other halls to promote specialized products or services.

Space assignments are often based on a priority points system in which the exhibition management company awards points based on desired space size, total dollars spent in exhibit space, number of years involved, and participation in sponsorship and advertising programs. From the organizer's perspective, this type of arrangement helps retain exhibitors and gives favor to the loyal, highest-paying exhibitors.

When selecting space, the company's exhibit manager should consider the following:

- Traffic patterns within the exhibit hall
- Location of entrances
- Location of food facilities and restrooms
- Location of industry leaders
- Location of competitors

Exhibit layout is also linked to the objectives a company establishes for the exhibition. If a company's main objective is to meet as many people as possible and establish its brand in the industry, a large open exhibit is appropriate. This type of layout encourages people to enter the exhibit, and it facilitates a large amount of traffic flow. There will be a few parts of the exhibit that require visitors to stay for a period of time, such as product demonstrations. It is the responsibility of the exhibit manager to notify the show management company if the company is hosting any celebrities, giving a loud presentation from a stage, or is hosting any special events in the booth that would draw an unusually large crowd.

Another type of layout may even purposely discourage people from entering, and parts of the exhibit may be "by invitation only." Why would a company do this? If their purpose during the show is to only meet with serious buyers or existing customers, it is important to limit visitors to only those falling in these categories. Therefore, this exhibit layout is set up to minimize traffic through the exhibit. Another strategy is to create a "closing room" within the booth space to meet with prospective buyers privately.

Most exhibition floor plans in the United States are based on a 10-foot by 10-foot grid or an 8-foot by 10-foot grid. This is known as the **standard booth**.

Typically, standard booths are set up side-by-side and back-to-back with an aisle running in front of the booth. Standard booths may also be used to line the inside walls of the exhibit area. Companies may combine standard booths to create an **in-line exhibit** using multiple standard booths to give greater length to the exhibit.

Island booths are created by grouping standard booths together into blocks of four, nine, or larger configurations. Island booths have aisles on four sides and can be an excellent format for medium-sized companies. **Peninsula booths** are made up of four or more standard booths back-to-back with aisles on only three sides.

Multilevel exhibits are often used by large companies to expand their exhibit space without taking up more floor space. The upper floor may be used for special purposes, such as meeting areas, private demonstration areas, or hospitality stations. Exhibitors using multilevel exhibits must be aware of each convention center's unique regulations for this type of exhibit.

As mentioned earlier, exhibitors must be aware of the location of food facilities, restrooms, entrances, and other special event areas. Each of these factors affects the traffic flow in the aisles and can either hinder or help an exhibit. Although many companies strive to be directly in front of an entrance for exposure, it may create more problems than expected because of the large amount of traffic. The exhibit staff may have difficulty discerning between serious visitors to the exhibit and those just trying to get in or out of the exhibit hall. Food service areas may create unexpected lines at meal times that spill into an exhibit area, essentially making that area useless for that time.

A standard trade show booth.
George G. Fenich

Small exhibitors face a different set of problems. If they have an in-line exhibit, their options are limited in how the exhibit is organized. If they want to maximize interactions with visitors, they may "open" the exhibit by ensuring that there are no tables or other obstructions between the aisle and their staff. If, on the other hand, they want to focus interaction on serious potential customers, their approach may be to block off the inside of the exhibit as much as possible and have meeting areas within the exhibit.

Many people who pass by or through an exhibit only read the signs that the company is displaying. Signage, therefore, is important in planning the exhibit. Signs must communicate the messages that the company wants to convey clearly and quickly to visitors. Detailed itemizations of equipment specifications on signs are almost always ignored. Signs should instead focus on selling points and benefits to the user.

Lighting technology has come a long way in the past twenty years. Today, many companies use pinpoint lighting to focus visitors' attention on their products and signage. Color lighting is often used to accentuate certain parts of an exhibit to communicate a mood for the visitor. Lighting is also important for areas that will be used for discussions or meetings with potential customers.

Staffing the Exhibit

The most important part of any exhibit is the staff. A company may have an attractive, open, inviting, and informative exhibit space, but if the staff members are untrained, communicate poorly, and do not dress professionally, the exhibit will communicate the wrong message to an attendee about the company and its products or services. Therefore, it is important that, whether for a large or small exhibit, the staff is well prepared and trained to promote the company and represent the product or service professionally.

Staff must be trained to "meet and greet." It is important that visitors are greeted warmly and made to feel welcome to the exhibit. Staff must also "qualify" visitors to determine if they are potential customers or not. By asking the right questions and listening to visitors, they can easily determine whether to spend more time with them, pass them to another staff member, or politely move them through the exhibit. Time is important, especially during the busy times at a show. Qualifying visitors is an important step in focusing your staff's time.

Many companies provide product demonstrations or even elaborate productions about their products or services at the booth. This aspect must be well managed and focus the visitors' attention on the main messages the company wants to communicate.

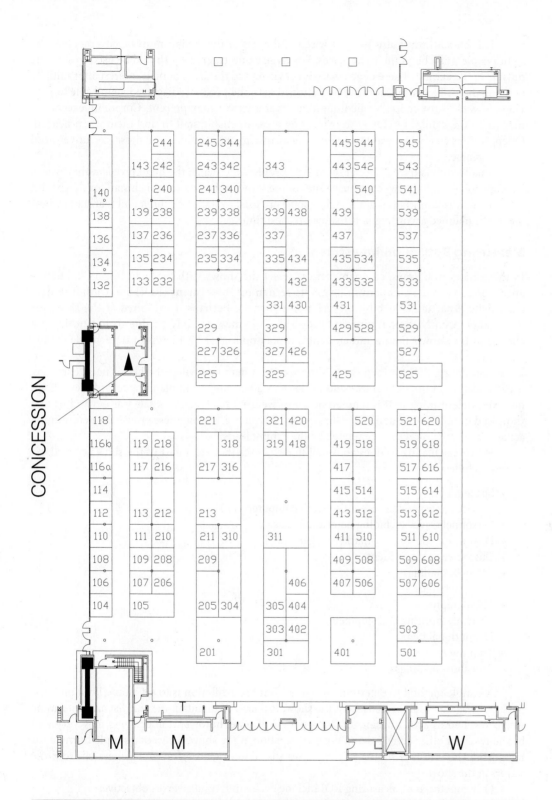

Key for Floor plan

103-Standard, perimeter booth   301-End cap booth

201-Peninsula booth   401-Island booth

Floor plan. *Courtesy of George Fern & Co.*

Exhibit staff must also be used wisely. All areas of the exhibit must be covered, and the right people must be in the right places. For large exhibits, greeters should be used to staff the outside of the exhibit. These people will direct visitors to the areas of their interest after initially greeting them. Technical staff may be stationed with the products displayed, being able to provide answers to the more detailed questions that a visitor may present. Corporate executives may roam the exhibit or cluster near meeting areas to enable staff to find them when needed. Often, serious customers want to be introduced to senior executives, and those executives need to be available.

Small exhibits have a special set of staff problems. Usually, the main problem they face is having enough staff to cover the busy times of the show, or having too much staff for the exhibit size. Again, it is important that the right people are used to staff the exhibit and that staff assignments are planned according to the show's busiest times.

Measuring Return on Investment

In these economic times, companies must select the shows with the right buyers in attendance. Far too often a company analyzes its **return on investment** (ROI) and cannot understand why a particular exhibition was not a success. Perhaps it exhibited at the show for years, and recently their return has dropped. This may possibly be due to not noticing a change in the show's theme and audience; it may no longer be an appropriate venue for the company.

Calculating ROI for each show is more critical than justifying whether or not a company is participating in the right shows and using the right strategy and planning techniques. Often, however, determining ROI is ignored because "we can't tell whether a sale was derived from a show lead or not" or "we don't have the data to be accurate." Avoid these excuses by determining actual expenses and revenue generated by the exhibit leads.

When calculating ROI, establish all the expenses that are a part of the show. Typical expenses include:

- Space rental
- Service contractor services (electrical, computer, etc.)
- Personnel travel, including hotel and meals
- Personnel time for non-marketing personnel
- Customer entertainment
- Preshow mailings
- Freight charges
- Photography
- Brochure printing and shipment
- Promotional items
- Training
- Post show mailings

A simple method to determine revenue from the exhibition is to set a time limit on business that was the result of leads from the show. It is easy to maintain the lead list and determine which resulted in actual business; after a period of time, however, the business may very well be the result of other activities and not participation at the show. Thus, one simple formula for measuring show ROI is subtracting expenses (listed above) from revenue generated from the buyers at the show.

Other methods of measuring ROI include evaluating results versus objectives:

- Cost per lead (total investment divided by the total number of leads)
- Percentage of the sales goal achieved (leads gathered divided by the leads identified in objectives)
- Percentage of leads converted to sales (number of sales divided by the leads generated)

Therefore, it is important that an exhibitor continually evaluate its show program and ensure that it is exhibiting at the right shows in order to meet its potential customers. Exhibitors can use a variety of tools to measure success. Examples of these include lead retrieval data, in-booth and post-event surveys, media clips, and RFID sales tracking.

A company exhibited at a show and collected 400 qualified leads and spent a total of $75,000 to exhibit. In the next six months, the company tracked its sales from the show and found it generated 100 new sales totaling $175,000 in new business. Below are the calculations of ROI based on the company's objectives for participation in the show.

Leads generated = 400 qualified leads

Total cost to exhibit = $75,000

Sales resulting from the show = 100 new sales

Revenue resulting in show sales = $175,000

Target number of leads to gather from show = 700 qualified leads

ROI Calculations

Revenue − Expenses = $175,000 − $75,000 =$100,000

Total cost per lead = $75,000/400 leads = $187.50 per lead

Percentage of goal achieved = 700/400 = 57%

Percentage of leads converted to sales = 100/400 = 25%

FUTURE TRENDS

Exhibitions have been around and will continue to be around for many decades to come. However, as times and economic conditions change, the exhibition industry must adapt in order to both survive and thrive.

- Attendance at future shows may be reduced, but it appears that the buying power of the attendee is greater. Many companies and organizations are not sending multiple representatives to shows and conferences, but are sending the decision makers.
- Technology will continue to push the exhibition industry to explore new ways of conducting business. Virtual shows will advance and continue to be a supplement to, not a replacement of, the face-to-face event. The human factor is still important in business. However, there is now significant information available online, and attendees are researching companies and their products and services, prior to attending the exhibition.
- With information readily available for attendees, exhibitors will have to be creative in their booth design and activities to draw attendees into their space. The use of the booth space, décor, signage, and displays will become even more important as attendees select vendors to engage with at the show site.
- Like associations, organizations and private media firms may be forced to merge shows or events as exhibitors may only be able to participate in a limited number of B2B and B2C exhibitions during this tough economic time. This trend allows for creative business agreements, bigger and better shows, and the opportunity to be innovative in event planning.
- Some exhibitions are being downsized or even phased out and replaced with hosted buyer. This is an attractive format for both exhibition attendees and exhibitors. More and more show management organizations are seriously considering this hosted buyer format in place of the traditional tradeshow program.

Summary

Exhibitions provide businesses the opportunity to sell products and services to other businesses (B2B) or directly to the consumer (B2C). The exhibition organizer, the facility manager, the general contractor, and other suppliers must communicate and work together to service the show's exhibitors. Coordinating an exhibition requires the exhibition organizer to select a show venue and appropriate suppliers, to promote and market the show, to consider risks to the event, and to organize all logistics, including move in/out, shipping, technology, and many others.

Each individual booth also requires significant coordination. Exhibitors should carefully select the exhibitions they choose to participate in and establish clear goals and objectives for each show. Planning for the exhibit operation includes staffing the booth appropriately, determining the physical layout of the space, and designing strategies to engage with booth visitors. These exhibiting opportunities are business ventures and companies need to collect qualified leads. Following the show, the sales team should follow up with sales prospects, and the company should evaluate its ROI from each exhibition.

Key Words and Terms

For definitions, see GLOSSARY, or http://glossary.conventionindustry.org

B2B	exposition	peninsula booth	standard booth
B2C	hosted buyer	public show	trade fair
exhibition	in-line exhibit	radio frequency identification	
exhibition management	island booth	(RFID)	
company	multilevel exhibit	return on investment	

Review and Discussion Questions

1. What is the difference between a B2B and B2C exhibition?
2. Give some examples of services that exhibition service contractors provide to exhibitors.
3. What attributes of an exhibit layout would a company want if its major objective is branding?
4. Describe the layout of a peninsula exhibit.
5. What kinds of additional marketing opportunities do management companies typically offer?
6. Why is risk management important to an exhibition management company? To an exhibitor?
7. What factors are considered by an exhibition management company when determining the location of an exhibition?
8. What are the three phases of planning that a company exhibit manager must address?

References

TRADE PUBLICATIONS

Convene

Exhibit Builder

Exhibitor Magazine

EXPO

Facility Manager

IdEAs

Meetings and Conventions

About the Chapter Contributor

Amanda Cecil, Ph.D., CMP, is an associate professor at Indiana University's Department of Tourism, Conventions and Event Management in Indianapolis, Indiana, and teaches several courses in meeting and exhibition management. Prior to joining the faculty at IUPUI, Dr. Cecil was an exposition manager for Host Communications, Inc., an association and event management association.

Previous Edition Chapter Contributor

Ben McDonald, Vice President of BenchMark Learning, Inc.

CHAPTER 6

Service Contractors

One of the services provided by exhibition service contractors is booth design and construction. © Ayhan168585/Fotolia

Chapter Objectives

This chapter provides the reader with an understanding of the following:

- Service contractors and their role in MEEC
- General services contractors compared with specialty contractors
- Exhibitor-appointed contractors
- Associations in service contracting

INTRODUCTION

An event producer or show manager (or show organizer) may have all the tools at his or her fingertips to promote, sell, and execute a show or conference, but there are many pieces of knowledge, human resources, and equipment that he or she does not have. For example, while you might be a great cook, you do not make the frying pan or the spatula—you turn to experts for that. For exhibitions and events to be produced smoothly and efficiently, the producers and managers must rely on professional service contractors to give the event/show manager and the exhibitors the tools necessary to be successful. These are called **service contractors**. This chapter discusses their various roles in the process, their relationship with the organizer, and their relationship with each other.

DEFINITION OF THE SERVICE CONTRACTOR

Depending on where you are in the world, a person who manages a tradeshow is known as a service contractor, show manager, or an event manager or an event producer. It should also be noted that not all events and conferences have an exhibitor component. If you are going to be doing events/conferences/tradeshows outside of the United States or Canada, be sure to use your network to find the appropriate company that will help you wade through the changes in the meanings of positions, cultural and business changes, language barriers, and so much more. Remember, only the United States uses feet and inches. In Canada, because much of the business is from the United States, dimensions will be given in feet and inches as well as in metric dimensions. Elsewhere in the world, be prepared for dimensions to be metric only.

A service contractor is anyone who provides a product or service for the exhibitor or show/event management during the actual show or conference. Service contractors can be the florist, the electrical company, the registration company, staffing agency, and just about every service you can think of. Some service contractors are hired by the show organizers to assist with their needs, and others are hired directly by the exhibitor.

A service contractor is an outside company used by clients to provide specific products or services (e.g., pipe and drape, exhibitor manuals, floor plans, dance floors or flags). MEEC service contractors and their roles have evolved over time. Historically, they were referred to as *"decorators."* This is based on their earliest primary function as service contractors, which was to "decorate" the empty space of a convention center or hotel ballroom. This decorating function included pipe and drape, carpets, backdrops, booths, and furnishings.

SERVICE CONTRACTORS RESPONSIBILITIES

Over the years, service contractors have expanded the scope of their activities to match the growing sophistication of MEEC. Today, service contractors can be, and likely are, involved in every aspect of the event from move in, to running the show, to tear down, and move out. As a result, the service contractor provides an important interface between the event organizer and other MEEC suppliers such as hotel convention services, the convention center, exhibitors, local labor, and unions. Service contractors work with the organizer to lay out trade show floors, after taking careful measurements. Service contractors are also involved before the setup of the show by sending out exhibitor kits and other information, generally electronically.

General Service Contractors

The **general service contractor** (also called the official show contractor or exposition services contractor) is hired by the show manager to handle the general duties necessary to produce the show on-site.

> *General Service Contractor* (GSC) An organization that provides event management and exhibitors with a wide range of services, sometimes including, but not limited to, installation and dismantling, creating and hanging signage and banners, laying carpet, drayage, and providing booth/stand furniture.

The show may have a contractor appointed by show management whose definition is

- *Official Contractor* Organization appointed by show management to provide services such as setup and teardown of exhibit booths and to oversee labor, drayage, and loading dock procedures. Also known as general service contractor.

GCSs are responsible for assisting the show organizer with graphic treatments for the entrance and all signage, putting up the pipe and drape or hard wall exhibits, placing aisle carpet, and creating all the official booths, such as association centers, registration, food and beverage areas, lounges, and special areas. More importantly, the GSC offers the show organizer a valuable service by hiring and managing the labor for a particular show. They have standing contracts with unions and tradespeople. They know how to hire enough labor to move a show in and out based on the requirements of the show. It is their responsibility to move the freight in and out of the facility, manage the flow of the trucks coming in and out of the facility, and the storage of the

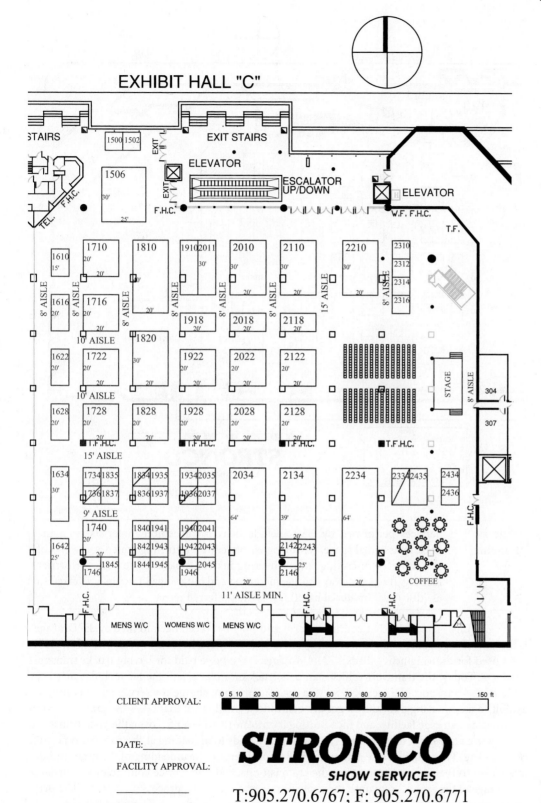

EXHIBIT HALL "C"

Trade show floor layout, metric measurements.
Stronco Show Services

CLIENT APPROVAL:

DATE:

FACILITY APPROVAL:

DATE:

STRONCO
SHOW SERVICES
T:905.270.6767; F: 905.270.6771

crates and boxes during the show. This is called **material handling** or **drayage** ("drayage" is an outdated term; however, the reader may still see it from time to time. It is the same as "material handling," the more common term).

It is important to understand that material handling may be a separate services contract, or included with the general services contract for the show/exhibition.

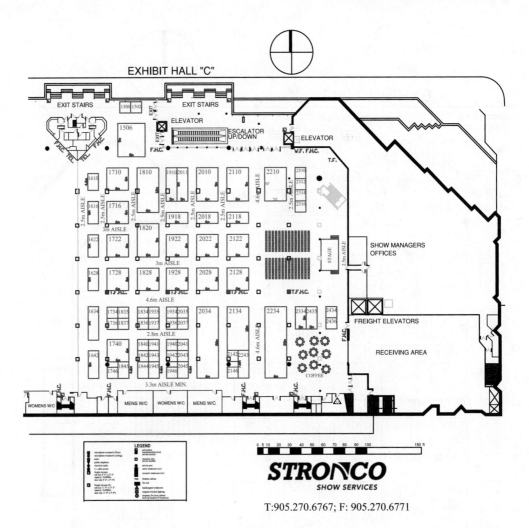

EXHIBIT HALL "C"

Trade show floor layout, metric measurements.
Stronco Show Services

STRONCO
SHOW SERVICES

T:905.270.6767; F: 905.270.6771

Material Handling	Services performed by GSC include delivery of exhibit materials from the dock to assigned space, removing empty crates, returning crates at the end of the event for re-crating, and delivering materials back to the dock for carrier loading. It is a two-way charge, incoming and outgoing. Sometimes referred to as "drayage," "material handling" is the preferred term.

"Drayage" is a somewhat confusing term and may be traced back to medieval. "Drayage" is the sum charge paid for the use of a dray or drays (a *dray* is a low, strong cart with detachable sides used for drawing heavy loads). Thus, *drayage* is the price paid for having trucks transport products. Today, the transport vehicle can be a truck or a plane, and the fee includes many aspects of the transportation service. Service contractors may charge for services like crating an exhibit in a box, using a forklift to get the box onto a small truck that takes the crate to a local warehouse or storage facility, and then putting it onto an 18-wheeler for over-the-road transport. The reverse happens at the other end and ultimately leads to unloading at the convention center or event site. There, the service contractor will also supervise the unloading of the crate and delivery of it to the proper booth. After the crate is unpacked, the service contractor will arrange for storage of the empty crate until the show is over and the whole process is reversed. The price for drayage is based on the weight, not the size of the materials or crate. The fee is based on each one hundred pounds of weight, and thus is called *hundredweight*. A "bill of lading" is completed by the shipper and delineates what the package contains, who owns it, where it is going, and any special instructions. This is the official shipping document, and authorities at checkpoints like state or provincial borders and especially national borders may insist on examining it.

Many GSCs have expanded into specialty areas. Thus, GSCs today may provide audiovisual equipment, security, cleaning, and more. This is done for a number of reasons. One is that the GSCs are building on the relationship they have established with show organizers over years of interaction and rely on the marketing concept of "relationship marketing." Provision of a wide range of services also gives the show organizer the advantage of "one-stop shopping." By using a GSC that provides general and specialty services, the show/event organizer does not have to deal with a multitude of companies to produce the show. Also, providing an array of services allows the GSC to increase revenues and, it is hoped, profitability.

A note of caution if you are the show organizer—you must compare pricing for individual contractors versus putting all your eggs in one basket as described earlier. What is most cost/time efficient for your event/show?

GSCs not only serve the show organizer but also are the official service contractor for exhibitors. Exhibitors can rent everything they need for their exhibit from the GSC, from a simple chair to a complete exhibit. Some GSCs will build a booth for exhibitors, store it, and ship it to other shows on behalf of the exhibitor.

The GSC adds value to his or her services by creating the **exhibitor service manual** (exhibitor services kit) along with the show organizer. This manual is a compilation of all the show information, such as dates, times, rules, and regulations for both the show manager and the city. Also included are all the forms necessary for an exhibitor to have a successful show. These forms typically include orders for carpet, furniture, utilities, setup and dismantling, and material handling. Some show organizers also include promotional opportunities to help exhibitors do preshow and on-site promotion. The service manuals can be printed and mailed, though most today would be in electronic format, included on a Web site, cloud technology or as an application, allowing exhibitors to order services and products from wherever they are.

On-site, the GSC works with both the show organizer and exhibitor to ensure a smooth move in and move out. He or she is often the conduit to a facility to make sure that the rules and regulations are observed. Many times, he or she solves the problems of the exhibitors by finding lost freight, repairing damaged booths or crates, and cleaning the carpets and booths in the evenings.

The services provided can include the following:

To Show/Event Organizers:

- Account Management
- On-site coordination of the event
- Pipe and drape
- Entry areas
- Offices
- Registration areas
- Setup and dismantling of booths

Signage is an important service.
Goodluz/Fotolia

- Planning, layout, and design of exhibit area
- Carpet
- Furniture
- Signs
- Graphics
- Backdrops
- Interface with labor and unions
- Cleaning
- Transportation services
- Material handling
- Customer Service

To Exhibitors:

- Exhibit design and construction
- Booth setup and dismantling
- Carpet
- Furniture and accessories
- Signs/signage
- Interface with labor and unions
- Rigging
- Material handling
- Exhibitor kit
- Customs brokerage when dealing internationally

Trade Unions

Exhibition service managers as well as show/event organizers will make use of tradespeople in the community to help set up and tear down the show. Many of these tradespeople will be members of a trade union. Everyone involved in a show should be aware of the local laws and policies in the city, state/province, country that your show/event is being held regarding the use of unionized personnel. The primary issue is whether the community is located in a "right to work" state/province. In these states/provinces, an individual working in a specific trade is NOT required to join the trade union representing that skill. Thus, show/event organizers and participants are free to hire whom they please, regardless of whether they are a union member. However, if the community is not in a right-to-work state/province, then people working in the trades such as electricians, plumbers, riggers, and porters

This simple example of rigging was used to attract attention to a booth selling chairs.
George G. Fenich

must belong to the union. In these communities, there can be significant repercussions if the proper union members are not used. In some locales, an exhibitor cannot even carry their own materials from their automobile to the trade show booth: They must use a member of the porters union. Prior to signing a contract, you should find out when union contracts are due for negotiations and learn whether past negotiations have been friendly or not. If a strike happened, how long before it was resolved? And should a strike be in process, who manages the work that must be done to ensure your conference/tradeshow setup and/or teardown is not jeopardized.

The Case of Exhibiting in a Unionized City

Service contractors can play a pivotal role in dealing with unionized labor. This is especially problematic since (1) the unions and rules vary throughout the United States and other countries, and (2) local labor is essential for putting together an event or trade show. The following portrays one exhibitor's interaction with unionized labor in a city in the northeastern United States. The exhibit, in its crate, was transported to the convention center in a tractor-trailer; and according to local rules, the trailer had to be driven by a member of the Teamsters Union. On arrival at the convention center, the driver opened the back of the trailer but could do no more to facilitate removal of the crate. That required a forklift, and the forklift is considered a piece of heavy equipment, not a truck, and thus had to be operated by a member of the Heavy Equipment Operators Union. So they waited for the forklift operator, who then moved the crate to the exhibit booth and placed it on the ground. At that point, the exhibitor was eager to get set up but could do nothing until a member of the Carpenters Union arrived to take the nails out of the crate: Wood and nails are a job for a union carpenter. The crate was opened, but the exhibitor was restricted from doing anything himself that a union member should do. Thus, he waited for a member of the Porters Union to come to take the exhibit contents out of the crate. That was followed by a string of different union members who each did a separate but distinct job and would not infringe on the responsibilities or activities of a different union. So the exhibit frame that was made from pipes had to be assembled by someone from the Plumbers Union: Only plumbers handle pipes. The products and cloth were assembled and laid out by a member of the Stage Hands Union: After all, an exhibit is part of a "show." The sign over the booth required someone from the Heavy Equipment Operators Union to drive a bucket lift, while a member of the Riggers Union occupied the bucket to "rig" the sign. The exhibitor could not even plug his computer into the electrical outlet provided by show management—that had to be done by a member of the Electricians Union. The Internet and Wi-Fi had to be set up by a member of the Communications Workers Union, and the flowers had to be "arranged" by a member of the Agricultural Union. Of course, the cleaning people, security, and other service personnel had to be members of the appropriate union. Furthermore, part of a supervisor's pay in each these unions had to be paid by the exhibitor in proportion to the amount of time that union spent at his booth. Further complicating matters is that, unless special fees are paid, there can be significant time lapses between when one union member finishes one particular job and when the next arrives. And—oh yes—if any union rule is violated or the exhibitor tries to do something himself, all the unions will boycott that booth and refuse to work. Obviously, a service contractor who is knowledgeable about local union rules and has established an ongoing relationship with local labor can be worth his or her weight in gold to an exhibitor or show organizer

However, unions do serve a number of laudable purposes. They represent a class of workers such as electricians when negotiating with management over pay scales and working conditions. Thus, they carry more clout than any single worker could possibly have. Unions also set very specific guidelines regarding termination of an employee and will provide a union member with legal counsel if necessary. In addition, they help ensure that working conditions are safe and comfortable. Lastly, they work with government agencies to help establish guidelines for the construction trades.

EVOLUTION OF SERVICE CONTRACTORS

Today, GSCs are evolving and changing to meet the needs of the client and the environment. One of the major changes has been increasing the scope of their work to center on meeting the needs of exhibitors. As is the case with the organizers of events, GSCs have come to the conclusion that it is the exhibitors who are the driving force of the trade show segment of MEEC. Furthermore, they have come to understand that exhibitors have more trade shows and vendors than ever to choose from, along with increased numbers of marketing channels through which to promote and distribute their products. Thus, both GSCs and show/event organizers are directing their attention to the needs of the exhibitor. Exhibitors are reacting to this effort by getting much more specific about their wants and needs, and they are also becoming much more discreet and selective when choosing a service contractor. Exhibitors spend huge amounts of money to participate in a trade show and thus want the best ROI they can get. In today's economic environment, exhibiting companies have to justify the expense of a trade show and are looking to service contractors to help with that justification and to show the value added by participating in a face-to-face show.

In the long run, service contractors must deliver quality service and products to the user, whether it is the organizer or the exhibitor. Otherwise, both constituents will seek other marketing avenues and strategies, with organizers left out in the cold. The status quo does not hold true any longer, and some companies have decided to forego trade shows in which they have participated for years. The COMDEX Show faced exactly this type of problem, and has resurfaced as the Interop Show. In lieu of exhibiting at an alternative trade show, some companies are developing their own private trade shows targeted to specific target markets or customers. Many are designing social media campaigns that eliminate some of the need to be face to face with customers.

Still another change for GSCs is that many facilities are now offering to do in-house what used to be the exclusive domain of GSCs. For example, many convention centers are now offering to provide utilities like electricity, water, steam, and gas, and may no longer allow GSCs to do this. These services are exclusive to the venue, and the show organizer must use the in-house services. Venues are also offering services like cleaning, security, audiovisual, Internet services, and room setups. This approach is cutting into the business and revenues of service contractors. The venues are creating exclusivity of product versus suggested contractors, leaving the show/event organizer with no choice of service contractor for specific services as listed earlier.

The advent of **exhibitor-appointed contractors** (EACs, which are discussed later in this chapter) has cannibalized the business of the GSC. This trend began in the mid-1980s, when the U.S. courts ruled that service contractors could not have exclusive right to control and negotiate with organized labor. Thus, an EAC from out of the area had the legal right to compete with GSCs and set up a booth for an exhibitor. EACs are a subset of GSCs that, rather than work from one city or location, work for the exhibiting company and travel throughout the country setting up and dismantling their booths. Their success is based on the long-term relationship they have built with the client company and is known as "relationship marketing." Because the EAC works for the same company over many trade shows and events, the EAC is more knowledgeable about the client company's needs and can provide better service than the broader GSC.

This competition between GSCs and EACs has encouraged the GSCs to provide more specialized, streamlined, and efficient service to exhibiting companies. For example, one GSC now provides exhibiting companies with the same service representative before the trade show opens, during the show, and after the show for reconciliation and billing. This lets the customer deal with one source for ordering of all services and products, a one-stop service desk, and a single master bill representing every product and service used. This is analogous to an individual who gets a different credit card receipt for each transaction but a single, cumulative bill at the end of the month. Several service contractors have special programs for their best customers that can provide a special customer service representative who is available twenty-four hours a day, seven days a week, and a private service center that has a lounge, fax, phone, copy services, and so forth. Many sales representatives of service contractors are equipped with cell phones, tablets, and so on so that they can go to a booth and provide on-the-spot service. Business transactions happen in real time, on the spot. A client uses their own tablet or smartphone and transacts most

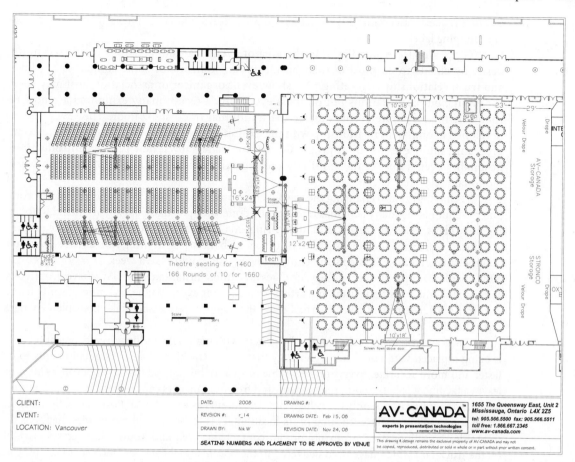

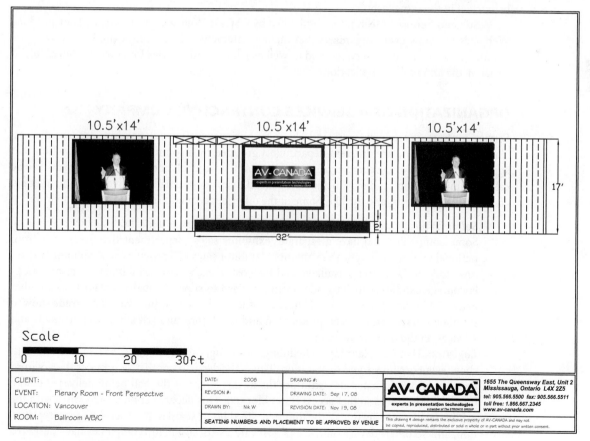

Floor plan for Vancouver Convention Center. *Produced by AV-CANADA: floor plan of Vancouver Convention Centre*

business requests, ascertains freight status, and prints forms like order forms, invoice summaries, and shipping labels.

GSCs are also expanding into the area of event marketing. This too is based on the desire by clients to do most of their business with someone or some company they know and trust: relationship marketing. The show/event organizer or association host may sponsor events, but corporations put on most events. As a result, many exhibitors are now responsible for corporate events outside the traditional trade show floor. The GSCs, having developed a long-term relationship with the exhibitor, are now developing corporate events programs, multi-event exhibit programs, private trade shows, new product introductions, hospitality events for clients, multi-city touring exhibitions, and more nontraditional promotional materials.

Technology is also changing the way GSCs do business. As with many businesses, the computer is eliminating many activities traditionally done with pen and paper. This includes updating floor plans, tracking freight, and monitoring small package deliveries. For example, as little as a dozen years ago, floor plans had to be drawn by hand using drafting instruments. A simple booth change, because it affects the entire show layout, could take a week or more to redraft. Now, thanks to computer technology, changes are almost instantaneous. GSCs have proprietary software that includes floor plans and artists' drawings for every major convention facility in the country. Thus, clients can take a "virtual tour" through the venue and make floor plan changes immediately.

GSCs are also using technology to help them with material handling. Again, pen and paper is being replaced with computer technology that allows tracking of all sizes of shipments to be faster and more accurate. Everything is online or in a mobile app so that when a truck enters or leaves a facility, it is in the computer system, and freight managers can go to the central computer to check the status of not only the vehicle but its contents as well. Global Positioning Systems on many trucks allow satellite tracking of its location. This technological monitoring happens on the trade show floor, too. An exhibitor can contact the GSC and know which crates are still on the truck and which have been delivered to the booth. Small packages such as brochures can be tracked in the same fashion.

Still another use of technology embraced by GSCs is Web site development. They produce Web sites for show/event organizers that include interactive floor plans, exhibitor show information, booth reservation services, and as well as personal itineraries for show attendees, using social media and mobile applications

ORGANIZATION OF A SERVICES CONTRACTING COMPANY

Service contractors are businesses, and like most businesses are organized into functional areas. This means that there are different departments grouped by a common activity or function that support the mission of the company. The department that controls and directs the company can be called "administration" and may include the general manager or chief executive officer, marketing, assistants, receptionists, and the like. Some of the other departments or divisions are as follows:

- *Sales:* Typically divided or broken up into national sales and local sales or special events. Some companies also have a separate "exhibitor sales" department that takes over from national sales in dealing with exhibitors. Exhibitor sales will provide each exhibitor with an inventory of the supplies available and the cost of each item. Exhibitor sales also work to encourage exhibitors to "upgrade" from standard to superior quality products at a higher price. Exhibitor sales typically will have an office and full-time presence at the trade show to facilitate interaction between production and exhibitors, and sell additional products and services on the trade show floor.
- *Logistics:* Handles planning, scheduling, shipping, labor relations, site inspection with show/event organizer, and preparation. This is the department that determines the flow and delivery of booth materials—with booths in the center of the hall being delivered before booths by the doors so that access is not blocked. This department may also work with the exhibit facility and lay out all the different-sized booths, aisles, food service areas, registration, and so on. Today a multitude of software exists and many companies have designed their own proprietary software to design exhibit floors and conference stages.

- *Material Handling and Warehousing:* This includes transportation of materials, booths, exhibits, and so on, along with their temporary storage in the host city. Drayage may include air transport, over-the-road tractor-trailer, and local transportation.
- *Event Technology:* This includes technology, special effects, reports, and so on. This department oversees the planning and subsequent installation of the output of the production department.
- *Event Services:* Exhibitor kits, on-site coordination, registration. The exhibitor kit tells exhibitors everything they need to know about the facility, capacities, rules, regulations, labor, and move-in and move-out times, along with the array of services provided by the service contractor. Today, this is largely handled using technology and saved electronically so changes can be made quickly and everyone who needs to has access.
- *Production:* Woodworking, props, backdrops, signs, electrical, lighting, metal work, and so on. For example, at Freeman Decorating in New Orleans, clients regularly request backdrops that look like the French Quarter or a swamp. They are produced on large boards like those used in theater productions
- *Accounting and Finance:* Accounts receivable, accounts payable, payroll, and financial analysis.

Two of the largest U.S. GSCs are Freeman Decorating and GES—Global Experience Specialists. You can learn more about these companies by using a search engine and viewing their Websites.

The Freeman Companies are headquartered in Dallas, Texas, and they have offices in the United States, Canada, and the United Kingdom. Begun in 1927, they are a full-service contractor for expositions, conventions, special events, and corporate meetings. The company is privately held and owned by the Freeman family and company employees.

GES is headquartered in Las Vegas, and they have offices in 60 countries worldwide including the United States, Canada, and the United Kingdom. GES is a wholly owned subsidiary of Viad Corp. In Canada, The Stronco Group of Companies is an all-Canadian, privately owned company that was established in 1952. For more than 50 years, it has put on everything from trade shows and conventions to special performances, sporting events and conferences. Stronco has grown to be the largest privately owned full-service contractor in the trade show and convention services industry in Canada.

AV-Canada is a division of the Stronco Group of Companies, specializing in audiovisual, lighting, and staging. Both bring their expertise across Canada and the United States. They are headquartered in Toronto, Canada.

SPECIALTY SERVICE CONTRACTORS

To this point in the chapter, discussion has been about GSCs and how they interact with the individual exhibitor and the show/event manager. Now, the focus will broaden to all the potential service contractors that help to create a successful event. **Specialty service contractors** deal with a specific area of show/event production, whereas the GSC tends to be broad and generic. Specialty service contractors can either be official contractors (appointed by show/event management) or EACs (see below). They handle all the services to complete the production, whether a special event/tradeshow/conference or general meeting, including:

- *Audiovisual:* Services and supplies to enhance the exhibit/conference/special event through audiovisual technologies, possibly before and after the exhibit/conference/special event.
- *Business Services:* Copying, printing, faxing, and other business services.
- *Catering:* Food and beverage for show/event organizers at the conference/special event and for individual exhibitors who may want to include food and beverage in their booth or at a private client event.
- *Cleaning Services:* Cleaning of public areas of the conference/event, especially carpet along with booths, offices, and nonpublic areas.
- *Communications:* Providing the tablets, cell phones, and wired and wireless services.
- *Computers:* Rental of computers and monitors.
- *Consulting:* This can include pre-event planning, coordination, facilitation, layout and design of the tradeshow/event/conference, and booth design. Often called third-party planners or independent consultants.

- **Décor:** Basic décor company that can enhance staging, general décor theme. Can also provide florals and entertainment.
- **Electrical:** Brings electrical power to the exhibits and any other areas that power may be required.
- **Entertainment Agency:** Provides entertainment and acts as liaison between entertainer and show/event organizer.
- **Floral:** Rental of plants, flowers, and props.
- **Freight:** Shipping of exhibit materials from the company to the show and back. There are various kinds of shippers—common carrier, van lines, and airfreight.
- **Furniture:** Rental of furniture for exhibit, often fancier than in your home!
- **Internet Access and Telephones:** Rental of equipment and lines on the show floor or any other area required for the event/conference, including Wi-Fi and wired Internet access, ensuring enough bandwidth as required.
- **Labor Planning and Supervision:** Expertise on local rules and regulations regarding what tradespeople to work with, union requirements, and supervision of workers on-site.
- **Lighting:** Design and rental and lighting operators. Could be included with audiovisual supplier.
- **Material Handling:** This includes over-the-road transportation of materials for the show, transfers, and delivery of materials from a local warehouse or depot to the show site, airfreight, and returns.
- **Moderator:** A specialist who manages the dialogue between virtual attendees, on-site attendees, and the presenter. Can be a part of the audiovisual team
- **Producer:** A specialist who acts as a producer for the event, ensuring all production is designed and delivered without any errors or omissions. Can be a part of the audiovisual team
- **Social Media Expert:** A team or person who is adapt at social media to enhance the reach of the exhibits/conference or special event before, during, and after.
- **Staffing:** Temporary hiring of exhibit personnel or demonstration personnel, or registration.
- **Utilities:** Plumbing, air, gas, steam, and water for technical exhibits.
- **Photography:** For show/event organizers to provide publicity and to individual exhibitors.
- **Postal and Package Services:** For both organizers and exhibitors.
- **Registration Company:** A company outsourced to manage the entire registration process for an event/conference or tradeshow. They manage all registration processes, including database, payment, badges, and often on-site staffing.
- **Security:** Security to watch the booth during closed hours and to control the entrances when the show is open or general security for an event/conference.
- **Speaker Bureaus:** Work with show/event organizer to find ideal keynote speakers to open/close conference.
- **Translators:** Work with the show/event organizer to do simultaneous translation of speeches and presentations. They also work with exhibitors to provide communication between sales representatives and foreign attendees.

The Translator Who Knew Too Much

A small American company decided that it wanted to exhibit at a trade show in Europe. One of the things it determined was that none of the sales managers who were going to staff their booth spoke any language except English. So it was decided that a translator fluent in Spanish, Italian, and German would be hired. The translator worked so well that she was hired to provide services at another trade show a year later. At this second show, attendees asked many of the same questions asked at the first trade show. Since the questions were repetitive, the translator had learned the answers and would simply answer the attendee without translating and asking the sales managers. Response at this show was low, in spite of high attendance, and reactions to the products being displayed at the booth were poor. When the company manager did a post show assessment, he uncovered the reason. The attendees got the impression that since a mere translator knew about the products, they must be very simplistic and not cutting edge. So at all future trade shows, the translator was told to always translate, ask the sales managers, and never answer on her own!

Besides the standard needs listed earlier, each show has its own needs. A show in the food and beverage industry will have a contractor for ice and cold storage, while a show in the automotive industry might have a contractor who cleans cars.

EXHIBITOR-APPOINTED SERVICE CONTRACTORS

As companies do more and more shows, their exhibits become more involved, and they often want one service supplier working with them throughout the year. Or, they have a favorite vendor who they have worked with in a city where they do many shows. This is particularly true with regard to the installation and dismantling of the exhibit. Most times, show/event organizers will allow this, assuming that a company meets the qualifications for insurance and licensing. This company is called an **exhibitor-appointed contractor (EAC)**. As an EAC, they perform the same duties as a specialty contractor but only for that exhibitor, not the show manager.

Some services may be provided only by the official service contractor and are called **exclusive services**. This decision is left up to the show/event manager who makes that decision based on the needs of the show and rules and regulations of the facility or to ensure the smooth move in and teardown of the show. Can you imagine what would happen if every freight company and installation company tried to move its exhibitors' freight in all at once? It would be chaos! So material handling (drayage) is a service that is often handled as an exclusive. Many facilities have very specific guidelines regarding the use of EACs. In some cases, the exhibitor must apply to the facility to use one.

RELATIONSHIP BETWEEN CONTRACTORS AND EVENT ORGANIZERS

One of the first actions that show/event organizers take when developing an event is to hire the GSC. This partnership develops as the show develops. GSCs will often recommend cities where a show should be held, the times of the year, and the facilities that fit the event. It is important to hire this company early on.

The process for hiring service contractors is through an **RFP (Request for Proposal)**. The show organizer creates a list of questions and specifications for each show. Other areas of concern include knowledge of the industry, knowledge of the facility, other shows being handled in the same industry, size of the organization, and budget.

As the show is developed, GSCs watch closely to suggest how marketing themes and association logos can be used in entrance treatments and signage so that when a show comes alive, it looks and feels the way the show organizer wants it. Color schemes, visual treatments, and types of materials all come from the mind of the GSC.

Specialty service contractors work with show organizers to help exhibitors save time and money. Reviewing the past history of a show can tell a service contractor what types of furniture, floral, and electrical needs the exhibitors have used. This permits the specialty contractors to offer money and time-saving tips to the show organizer and pass those savings on to exhibitors. All of this creates a feeling of goodwill among exhibitors who will continue to exhibit at the show.

After a time, the service contractor knows the show as well as the show organizer. This can be added value to the show organizer because as staff changes occur, the service contractor becomes a living historian of the show and its particular nuances.

RESOURCES IN THE SERVICE CONTRACTOR INDUSTRY

There are several associations for individuals and companies in the service contractor industry. They can help the reader find a services contractor in the city where the exhibit/conference/special event is taking place. To learn more about each association's mission, ethical principles, member responsibilities, contact information, and so on, go to their individual Websites using a search engine. The following is a partial listing.

EIC: Exhibit Industry Council was formed in late 2009 to address the concerns from trade show exhibitors and to promote best practices for serving exhibitors at trade shows, exhibitions, and events. The associations forming the council are: Corporate Event Marketing Association (CEMA), Exhibit Designers & Producers Association (EDPA), Exhibitor-Appointed Contractor Association (EACA), Healthcare Convention and Exhibitors Association (HCEA), and Trade Show Exhibitors Association (TSEA).

CEMA: Corporate Events Marketing Association

HCEA: Healthcare Convention and Exhibitors Association

ESCA: Exhibition Services & Contractors Association. Organization serving general and specialty contractors.

EDPA: Exhibit Designers & Producers Association. Organization serving companies engaged in the design, manufacture, transport, installation, and service of displays and exhibits primarily for the trade show industry.

EACA: Exhibitor-Appointed Contractors Association. Representing EACs and other individual show-floor professionals that provide exhibit services on the trade show floor.

IAEE: International Association for Exhibits and Events. An association of show organizers and the people who work for service contractors.

CAEM: Canadian Association of Exposition Management. Canadian association of show organizers and the people who work for service contractors.

NACS: National Association of Consumer Shows Association of public (consumer) show organizers and the suppliers who support them.

EEAA: Exhibition and Event Association of Australia

CEIR: Center for Exhibition Industry Research

TSEA: Trade Show Exhibitors Association

The example of ESCA indicates the professionalism that the various associations strive for. When looking for a show services contractor (or any contractor), be sure to check out the associations they belong to.

FUTURE TRENDS

- Healthy relationships between service contractors and planners will continue to be crucial to achieve mutual success.
- To build lasting relationship with suppliers, planners look for two main ingredients:
  - competitive pricing
  - flexible contracts
- Sustainability and corporate social responsibility are increasing. Venues play a lead role in this by designing specific policies and procedures to ensure end users and service contractors meet requirements. Contractors can play a key role in the sustainability of exhibits/conferences/special events by:
  - Reducing carbon footprint
  - Embracing use of recyclable materials
  - Using products that are locally produced
  - Working with the venues to meet the venue's guidelines with respect to low lighting usage when full lighting is not required
  - Working with the venues to ensure waste management policies are met
- Service contractors will develop relationships with organizers, planners, and sponsors and help produce meetings and event in multiple locations.
- As technology improves, the hybridmeeting will take more focus when a hybrid helps to meet the objectives of the exhibit/conference/special event. To that end, there will be more specialized needs from the audiovisual and/or technical service contractors. A producer and a moderator will be specialized consultants to ensure the meeting is successful, that whether an attendee is online, face to face, or views the event after, the attendee will be engaged
- As technology continues to evolve, the use of social media platforms will have a larger focus for the success of an exhibit/tradeshow/special event. Consultants in this field will become one of the service contractors

SO HOW DOES IT ALL WORK?

Take a look at the organizational chart that follows (Figure 6-1), and you can see how the GSC interacts with the show/event organizer, the facility, the exhibitors, and the other contractors. Remember, exhibitions are like small cities, and the show organizer must provide everything

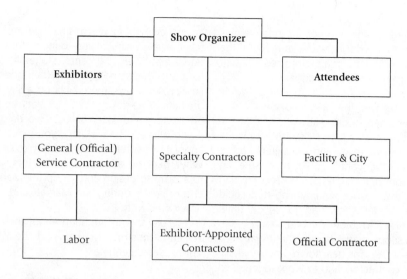

FIGURE 6-1 Relationship between show organizer and service contractors
Source: Sandy Biback

a city does—from safety (security and registration) to a place to work (think of the exhibits as offices), electricity and water, and transportation (shuttle buses). It has to be done in a very short period of time, sometimes less than a week. Communication between everyone always must be functioning properly, and often it is the GSC who provides that conduit. The coordination of all the contractors likely is the responsibility of the GSC, who is acting as the right hand of the show organizer.

When you read this Case Study as it relates to The Lowe's Toronto Christmas Market, keep in mind the need to have contingency plans in place. Also, keep in mind the need to ensure that all your contractors become a part of your team and are brought in as early in the process as possible. Each contractor understands its specialty and can add to the success. Each contractor will also have contingency and risk plans in place that the event organizer can add to the overall plans of the particular event/conference.

A Case Study of the Relationship between Service Contractors and Show Organizers

Each year, since 2011, in a historic section of Toronto known as The Distillery, the two-week Lowe's Toronto Christmas Market takes place. Recently, 240,000 people came to enjoy food and beverage; caroling; stage performances by well-known artists; the ability to purchase unusual gifts and to enjoy the outdoor festival. In a short period of time, the Market has become a tourist destination and has a substantial economic impact on the shops of The Distillery and the City of Toronto.

When the public come, they see the Market in full swing. Most don't comprehend the two weeks prior to opening it took to build the Market. Working with The Distillery Special Events staff, general contractors had to work as a team to ensure it all ran smoothly. Before any of this could happen, The Distillery Special Events staff had to contract the vendors who would sell their products and contract the variety of service contractors to ensure success.

There were the builders of the huts that would sell goods, food and beverages. There were electrical contractors required to add electricity to each hut. There were skyjacks brought in to put up the 40-foot Christmas tree and decorate it. The lighting people put up thousands of lights above the buildings. The vendors set up their wares. The entertainers had to be contracted and scheduled, both on the stage and off. The established restaurants had to ensure they were staffed appropriately and purchase enough food to handle the extra diners. The cobblestone streets had to be checked to ensure no cobblestones were loose. Extra security had to be hired. Porta potties had to be brought in. Valet parking and parking attendants had to be hired to manage the increased car traffic. Firewood had to be delivered for the outdoor fire pits. Permits had to be obtained for the use of much of the equipment. When the market opened, 80% of the work had already been done!

Now it was time for the 10%—while guests came over the next two weeks. Any on-site crisis had to be dealt with so that the guests didn't know. A snow storm meant the plows had to be ready and the salters had to quickly salt the cobblestones to ensure no one fell and injured themselves. Security had to be on the lookout for anything that could go wrong. Entertainers had to be on time. Outdoor fires had to be watched.

No sooner had it begun and it was over. Now the 10% for teardown and analysis. Again, all contractors had to work together to ensure everything was dismantled and safely taken away. Electrical and sound systems come down first. Then the center stage. As all this happens, the vendors remove their goods. Security is, as always, there 24 hours a day. Lastly, the huts come down; the wood slats are stored on tractors and taken away. Two days later, if you walked The Distillery, you would never know a two week Market had just taken place. Why? Because all service contractors worked as a team to design and set up the Market, to ensure safety during the Market, and to tear down efficiently.

For more information about the Lowe's Toronto Christmas Market, find the Website using a search engine.

Summary

Service contractors are the backbone of the exhibition/event/conference industry. Their support structure, like the backbone, allows the show/event organizers and exhibitors to create an atmosphere that is smooth and efficient. Understanding the responsibilities of each contractor will allow a show/event organizer to offer the exhibitors the best possible service as well as creating a successful environment for buyers and sellers to do business in the exhibition format.

Key Words and Terms

For definitions, see GLOSSARY, or http://www.conventionindustry.org/glossary

drayage	exhibitor-appointed contractor	material handling	service contractor
exclusive service	general service contractor	RFP	specialty service contractor
exhibitor service manual			

Review and Discussion Questions

1. What types of services do specialty contractors provide?
2. What are some of the questions that should be asked in an RFP?
3. Describe the difference between a general (official service contractor) and an exhibitor-appointed contractor.
4. How can the GSC assist the show/event organizer as it prepares for the exhibition/event/conference?

5. You are the event manager of a large conference that includes a tradeshow component. The trucks are ready to move and the weather sets in. Winter storms are everywhere on the route. Who do you contact? What alternative plans can you make? What if the trucks can't get there in time to set up?

About the Chapter Contributor

Sandy Biback, CMP, CMM, has been involved in the design and implementation of business events/conferences/tradeshows for over 30 years. Biback currently teaches a variety of courses related to meetings and conventions in a postgraduate program at Centennial College in Toronto. She has previously taught online for the University of Nevada, Las Vegas, and George Brown College in Toronto. She is a member of Professional Convention Management Association (PCMA) and Canadian Society of Professional Event Planners (CanSPEP).

Previous Edition Chapter Contributor

Susan L. Schwartz, CEM.

CHAPTER 7

Destination Management Companies

DMCs arrange ground transportation. In Thailand that includes elephant transport.
George G. Fenich

Chapter Objectives

After reading this chapter, the reader will be able to:

- Identify the needs that destination management companies meet for their clients.
- Explain how destination management companies interact with meeting professionals, local hotels, event participants, and various suppliers within a destination.
- Describe how destination management business is conducted.
- List the competitive factors at work in the business process used by destination management companies.
- Evaluate what projects destination management companies should pursue.
- Detail how destination management companies deliver their contracted services to clients.

INTRODUCTION

One of the many career opportunities that exist within the MEEC industry is providing local destination management services. These services include being a liaison with suppliers such as on-site meeting management, hotel services, convention centers and bureaus, airlines, and catering. Typically, when thinking about careers in the MEEC industry, one may not always consider working in the supplier side of the business.

However, services provided at the event destination play a key role in the successful planning and execution of meetings, conventions, and events. This chapter will discuss the business and services provided by destination management companies (DMCs).

DEFINITION OF DESTINATION MANAGEMENT COMPANY

A **Destination Management Company (DMC)** is a professional services business that possesses extensive local knowledge, expertise, and resources. It specializes in the design and implementation of events, activities, tours, transportation, and program logistics. Depending on the company and the staff specialists in the company, they offer, but are not limited to, the following: creative proposals for special events within the meeting; guest tours; VIP amenities and transportation; shuttle services; staffing within convention centers and hotels; team-building, golf outings and other activities; entertainment, including sound and lighting; décor and theme development; ancillary meetings and management professionals; and advance meetings and on-site registration services and housing.

Destination management companies may also go by the title of professional congress organizer (a predominantly international term) or ground operator (a term originally used for DMCs before their services as role in the industry expanded to what it is today).

Destination management companies offer a critical layer of services and are hired by meeting and event professionals to provide local knowledge, experience, and resources for corporate and association gatherings. DMCs work cooperatively with airlines, hotels and resorts, convention centers, and other service suppliers in the delivery and implementation of MEEC activities. Successful MEEC events require comprehensive local knowledge of destination infrastructure, local laws and statutes, and regulations. Meeting and event professionals must work with local professionals who have verified and often first hand information about supplier availability, capabilities, and capacities, gained through actual project work to ensure a successful event.

When discussing DMCs and their services, the industry denotes this as the **client project**, which, be it a meeting, exhibition, event, or convention, is typically referred to as a **program**. A program will include all activities and services provided by the DMC to the client while visiting a destination over a specified time.

SERVICES PROVIDED BY DESTINATION MANAGEMENT COMPANIES

Meeting and event professionals work closely with DMCs to provide recommendations for local destination resources that will best fit and satisfy the goals for a gathering. After these services are determined, a contract is written for the DMC to plan, set up, and deliver those services. Services typically offered by DMCs include:

- Budgeting and resource management
- Creative itineraries
- Creative theme design
- Dining programs
- Entertainers
- Event production
- Event venue selection
- Hotel selection
- Incentive Travel
- Meeting support services
- Sightseeing and tour options
- Speakers
- Special event concepts
- Staffing services
- Team-building activities
- Transportation planning and delivery
- VIP services

DMC services facilitate networking among attendees, celebrating accomplishments, or the introduction of new ideas and/or products. In today's competitive environment, where the impact and return on investment of meetings and events are expected to be measured, professionals rely on DMCs to provide unique and creative event concepts that will accomplish the specific goals of the event, be consistent with other activities carried out in the client's program, and stay within the client's budget. Full-service DMCs provide both meeting management support services, such as arrangements for transportation, and all aspects of event production, such as staging, sound, and lights. DMCs often are a reliable resource for entertainment solutions, from a small trio for background music at an intimate cocktail party to the headline entertainment for large **special events**. Familiarity and access to local musicians and entertainers is an important criterion when selecting a DMC. In addition, DMCs often suggest and supply décor such as props, floral designs, and decorations to enhance event spaces and venues.

Transportation logistics are often a key service provided by DMCs. These services include airport "**meet and greet**" services, hotel transfers and baggage management, and shuttles. Moving groups of participants—large or small—is an important component of most events that require precise timing and execution, local expertise, and management responsibility. This is best provided by a professional DMC to ensure attendee comfort, convenience, and safety. In addition, many DMCs will provide customized sightseeing tours and recreational activities, such as golf and tennis tournaments.

Because of the creative element associated with meetings and events and the variety of each group's needs and expectations, the list of services that are provided by DMCs is almost limitless. It is important to note that while one client may require a DMC to manage and execute the entire event, another client may contract a DMC to provide only one or two components of the event.

DESTINATION MANAGEMENT COMPANY VERSUS DESTINATION MARKETING ORGANIZATION

The DMC business process has been compared to, and often confused with, the services provided by a **destination marketing organization (DMO)**. Although they are very different organizations, there are some similarities between their services. DMOs optimize the exposure of a destination, leading it to develop innovative experiences for tourists, enabling the community to develop a sustainable infrastructure to ensure positive returns on investments.

Today's consumers expect a destination to offer customized product and service offerings that match their expectations. The destinations that manage to maximize the satisfaction levels of customers' expectations, and support consumers throughout the buying process, will be the ones to survive and yield maximum benefits. Therefore, DMOs work with the interests of both the community at large and the private companies that provide many of these services.

DMCs will often get leads on new accounts through requests by meeting and event professionals that have gone through a DMO. Once the lead has been passed on by the DMO, the DMC will communicate through direct and electronic communications and presentations. These presentations almost always exhibit the DMC's competence using examples of their past successful programs. Once it has been established that the DMC has the expertise to meet the client's needs, it will respond to the client's **request for proposal (RFP)**.

Typically, potential DMC customers will request that two or more DMCs bid on its program, based on a set of specifications in their RFP. Each DMC will then provide detailed, creative proposals for services, which will best satisfy the client's specifications. These proposals are almost always delivered free, intended to win the customer's favor, which is a major issue.

Responding to a client's RFPs often incurs a considerable cost and requires staff time to formulate a customized proposal; therefore, DMCs must choose wisely when determining what potential business to pursue. Today, the cost for collecting and submitting bids to client's RFPs is controlled by the development of standards for submitting these RFPs electronically. The Convention Industry Council has been a leader in the development of these standards, and templates for the electronic formats can be found and retrieved under the APEX guidelines.

Business Structure of DMCs

Some prerequisites are essential to the destination management process:

- Staff
- Temporary "field staff"

- Office
- Technology
- Licenses and insurance
- Community contacts
- Customer contacts
- History
- Destination resources

A strategically located office is a basic necessity for a DMC. Convenient proximity to major hotels, convention facilities, tourist attractions, and event venues is a must. In today's competitive environment, DMCs must have access to the best possible technology. DMC clients are usually associations and major corporations that are accustomed to technology and expect to work with DMCs that are also proficient in using electronic communications. Communications equipment, office computer capabilities (including database management), imaging software, and high-speed Internet are all expected to be standard tools in today's DMC. The quick processing of information and the ability to make on-the-spot changes and produce professional documents and graphics are becoming an industry standard and a necessity for DMCs.

Given the nature of the services provided by DMCs, they must be legally insured for business liability as well as other standard coverage such as workers' compensation and automobile insurance. Each destination will have unique laws and licensing requirements for the DMC's services. Meeting and event professionals must ensure that their chosen business partners are adequately insured and knowledgeable about local ordinances that could affect the successful operation and production of their events.

As with many businesses in the service sector, DMCs compete in a relationship-driven industry. Customers and professionals will literally put their reputations and jobs on the line when selecting a DMC. DMC management and staff should have extensive community contacts among hotels, attractions, convention bureaus, airports, law enforcement, and the supplier community, and must articulate their commitment to building and sustaining positive relationships with their clients. It is through the cooperation from these business partnerships, gained through repeated work experiences, that a DMC can properly service the diverse needs of its clients.

Reputation outside of the destination community, that is, in the client community, is very important to the long-term success of a DMC. The most valuable asset a DMC has is its history of success, which is the best verification a professional can rely on when choosing a DMC partner.

Finally, the destination community must have the necessary resources to support the DMC in the execution of a well-run program or event. It must have a competitive service environment, with many suppliers that have good reputations.

THE DESTINATION MANAGEMENT COMPANY ORGANIZATION

Destination management companies come in a variety of sizes and organizational structures. Given the nature of the services that they provide, it is possible to get started in this business with little start-up funding. This section will discuss the range of organizations that operate as DMCs.

Independent Operator

Independent destination management companies are locally owned and operated by small businesses who often got their start as a "ground operator." For many years, these DMCs were the backbone of destination management and provided a limited array of targeted services such as transportation operator, tour organizer, staffing, or special event management. Today, independent DMCs are still a major factor in the industry and many have expanded their services to compete with the larger national DMCs. The long-term success of independent DMCs is largely predicated on the ability of the owner to develop lasting relationships and goodwill by exceeding clients' expectations. Although it is relatively easy to start this business, the hours and challenges can be long and arduous.

Multi-Services Operator

Destination management companies that offer multi-services are typically larger organizations rather than independent operators. Over time, these organizations establish large networks of service offerings. These multi-services suppliers have to be staffed with well-trained professionals who can put together complex, diverse client programs. Often the larger multi-services operator has staff and offices in multiple destinations and can offer its clients a significant advantage in securing high-quality services at a lower cost than can typically be found with an independent operator.

Destination Management Networks

Because local "one-destination DMCs" do not enjoy the same economy of scale that a national or international DMC such as Hosts Global Alliance would, networks of DMCs have been formed. An example of this is "The DMC Network." This group was formed in order to pool resources from individual one-city DMCs for sales and marketing purposes. Other such "DMC groups" exist primarily for the sharing of mutual sales and marketing efforts and expenses.

Destination management networks are a collection of independent destination management companies that pay a fee or commission to be affiliated with a national or regionally based organization. Destination management networks allow meeting and event professionals the peace of mind when dealing with DMCs in unfamiliar locations. This arrangement allows for smaller, independent DMCs to remain autonomous while gaining significant advantages typically afforded to the larger multi-services, multi-destination DMCs.

In some cases, particularly with DMC networks, it makes sense to employ professional representation firms to call on particular market segments. Usually, this representation is contracted for a particular geographic location, such as New York, Chicago, or London. These companies typically call on potential and existing customers in the geographic area on behalf of a DMC network. They will seek to familiarize professionals about the DMC network while uncovering leads for future business. When appropriate, these representation firms will sometimes also serve as a local liaison between the customer and a DMC partner.

BUSINESS MODEL OF DESTINATION MANAGEMENT COMPANIES

DMC clients are those who plan meetings, exhibitions, events, conventions, and **incentive travel programs**. When describing the business model of DMCs, the terms "customer," "client," and "professional" are used to describe the person, organization, or company for which the DMC is providing services. In some instances, the customer, client, and professional can be three separate entities or the same. The customer is the organization that will be securing and paying for the services provided by the DMC. The client is the representative of the organization who is in a leadership role when making the decision to purchase DMC services. The professional, representing the customer organization, is the person (or persons) whom the DMC works directly with planning and coordinating programs and events.

It is important to note that those who participate in the planning of the services provided by a DMC are almost always staff of the DMC, such as a corporate sales force. It is common for DMCs to service the leisure traveler or tour groups that partner outside of the DMC organization. Increasingly, the value of DMC services is being recognized by large tour operators, and they are often contracted to assist with transportation and/or tours for large groups. A good example of this is a cruise ship that employs a DMC to manage land tours, transportation, and excursions.

A DMC may be contracted directly with an organization whose employees or members will be participating in the program, or it may contract with a third party or independent professional meeting professional who is offering their meeting services to the participating organization (customer) (see the flow chart in Figure 7-1).

Most meeting and event professionals consider the DMC as a local extension of their own office and staff while in the destination. They expect the DMC to be their "eyes and ears" in the destination, always acting on their behalf, offering unbiased, experience-based suggestions on logistics, venues, event concepts, and social program content. Professionals depend on DMCs to help them design event programs that meet their specific needs, which can vary in size, budget, length, and purpose. For example:

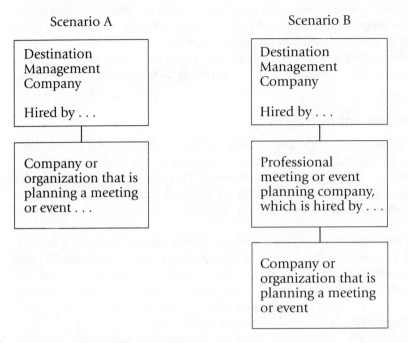

FIGURE 7-1 Sample DMC Flow Chart

Clients

Destination management companies receive business from several categories of customers. Their contracted programs may come from corporate, association, incentive-based, or special event clients.

CORPORATE ACCOUNTS   Given the recent challenges facing the world economy, corporate clients organizing meetings are receiving greater scrutiny. In the past, **corporate meetings** holding a half-day of meetings while spending the remainder of their day on the golf course would not generate much attention. Today, just the location where the corporate meeting is being held can generate negative publicity. DMCs must be very sensitive to the constraints and attention that are facing corporate clients when planning and organizing meetings.

In addition, corporate clients are reassessing the value of holding face-to-face meetings. It is very important that DMCs focus on working with their clients to ensure that the meetings and events have a higher level of value than could be achieved by not hosting a face-to-face or "virtual" event.

The following is a list of sample event programs that DMCs work on with corporate clients:

- National sales meetings
- Training meetings
- Product introductions
- Dealer and/or customer meetings

ASSOCIATION ACCOUNTS   Associations are organizations that are created to support an industry, common interest, or activity. Associations can range from local, state, regional, national, and international groups. Most associations exist to provide networking and educational opportunities to their membership. In carrying out these activities, associations will hold a variety of meetings, conventions, and conferences.

In today's competitive environment, potential conference/convention attendees are being more selective as to which meetings they will attend. Attending a meeting out of town is costly in time and money. The factors involved include the return on investment that individuals believe they will receive by attending the event. DMCs can provide considerable resources and support to help clients create events that will be offered to their membership with the highest impact. The following is a list of sample event programs that DMCs work on with association clients:

- Industry trade shows (food, construction, aircraft, etc.)
- Professional trade shows and conferences (for architects, doctors, teachers, etc.)
- Fraternal organizations (VFW, Lions, etc.)
- Educational conferences (medical symposia, other professional groups)
- Political conventions

INCENTIVE-BASED ORGANIZATIONS   Incentive-based meetings and events are organized to recognize and reward employees who have reached or exceeded company targets. This segment of the meetings and event market continues to experience rapid growth. Today's organizations are recognizing the value of providing rewards and recognition for employees' outstanding performance. These events can typically last between three and six days in length and can range from a modest to extravagant getaway for employees and their partners. DMCs can provide the organizing client a range of services that are customized based on the budget of the organization and the desires of the employee. The following is a list of sample event programs that DMCs work on with incentive-based clients:

- Sales incentives
- Dealer incentives
- Service manager incentives

DESTINATION MANAGEMENT COMPANY PROCESS

Unlike hotels, resorts, convention centers, and restaurants, a DMC does not require an extensive capital investment to start up and operate its business. The DMC office is usually located in office space somewhere near the location where most meetings and events take place. Proximity to major airports can be an advantage, since so many program services involve group arrivals and departures.

Primary responsibilities and job titles for a DMC vary from company to company. Many DMCs are small, stand-alone, single-office companies that are locally owned. Other larger companies may have offices in multiple destinations with local staff fulfilling management responsibilities on all levels. (See Table 7-1 with categories of job responsibilities that follows.)

To be successful, a DMC's job tasks include finding business leads, proposing appropriate services, contracting services, organizing the group's arrival, delivering the contracted services, and following up with billing and program reconciliation. These task areas are carried out by contracting with supplier companies, hiring **field staff**, and assigning program staff. Field staff,

Table 7-1   Categories of DMC Job Responsibilities, with Sample Job Titles

Management and Administration
- General Manager
- Office Manager
- Accounting Manager
- Executive Assistant
- Administrative Assistant
- Receptionist
- Research Assistant

Sales and Marketing
- Director of Sales
- Director of Marketing
- Director of Special Events
- Sales Manager
- Sales Coordinator
- Proposal Writer
- Research Analyst

Operations and Production
- Director of Operations
- Director of Special Events
- Operations Manager
- Production Manager
- Transportation Manager
- Staffing Manager

Field Staff
- Meet and Greet Staff
- Tour Guide
- Transportation Manager
- Event Supervisor
- Field Supervisor
- Equipment Manager

who carry out such functions as tour guides, hospitality desk staff, and airport "meet and greet" staff, are usually temporarily contracted employees who are hired by a DMC only for the term of the program. It is common for field staff in a destination to work for more than one DMC as the needs arise for their services.

The job titles listed earlier are examples and will vary from company to company. However, sales and promotion responsibilities, operations and production responsibilities, and management and administrative responsibilities are the basic responsibilities of all DMCs. As in most companies, the levels of authority and reporting lines do vary and are usually based on the size of the company and the qualifications of its staff. For example, a "Director of Special Events" title may appear under both the sales and marketing function and the **operations and production** function. The position can be either or both, depending on the company and the individual executive's area of expertise.

In many cases, DMCs do not own transportation equipment, props, décor, or other supplies that the DMC packages and sells to its customers. It is common for DMCs to buy or rent from selected suppliers and manage these products and services in the context of the larger event program. As such, the DMC becomes a "contractor" for the services of a myriad of local supplier companies.

A critical characteristic for the long-term success of DMCs is the ability to objectively recommend and select suppliers for the services contracted. A DMC's value proposition to meeting professionals depends on their ability to select the best provider for the services that meet the client's budget and program specifications. Clients must feel confident that the DMC is earning its money for the management services provided and not from some inflated financial "arrangement" made with the supplier companies.

The Sales Process

For DMCs to be successful, new business projects must be continually found and secured for the company. Business opportunities may present themselves in a variety of ways. Not all DMCs service all the clients listed earlier in the chapter. Some DMCs have created successful businesses by specializing in associations' convention business, corporate meetings, or international travel groups. Some DMCs may work with individual travelers, while others focus heavily on the domestic incentive market. However, most DMCs operate in multiple markets, which are usually determined by the nature of their destination.

In other words, the infrastructure and appeal of the destination will often dictate which of the above market segments DMCs will do business with. A destination's infrastructure such as its convention centers, convention hotels, resorts, and airport facilities all play into the equation. Other destination assets such as natural and man-made attractions play heavily into whether or not corporations will plan important meetings and/or incentive travel rewards in a location. Beaches, forests, weather, recreational facilities, fishing, arts, gambling, and theme parks all can enhance a destination's appeal.

Identifying New Business Opportunities

The first stage of the sales process is to discover new business opportunities and pursue those leads. Almost all new business opportunities involve going where the customers are or where the customers do business, such as attending industry trade shows or conferences. Some examples of these trade shows are the American Society of Association Executives (ASAE) Annual Meeting and Exposition, IMEX America (held in Las Vegas), Springtime in the Park (held in Washington, DC), and Holiday Showcase (held in Chicago).Sales executives representing DMCs must carefully research these trade shows to maximize their sales and marketing resources. Knowing in advance which potential customers will attend and knowing what business opportunities they represent will ensure an increase in the DMC's prospects for creating new client relationships.

Some customers, particularly corporate customers, incentive companies, and meeting management companies, will designate a "preferred" DMC in selected destinations. For DMCs, this is known as a "house account." Whenever house account planners require services, the chosen DMC can help without going through the often-onerous competitive bidding process. These accounts are very important and require careful maintenance. There is considerable competition for them, and competing DMCs are always active in their attempts to take over these accounts.

Periodic visits to these customers and open lines of communication are vital in maintaining these relationships. In addition to continued good service, part of the successful "maintenance" of these relationships may include membership in the same industry organizations as the professionals. Attending these organizations' conferences and meetings allows DMC representatives to visit and network among existing and potential planner clients.

Sales efforts at the destination level are considered by most DMCs to be an important part of the sales plan. Creating relationships with local industry representatives who are conducting business with the same customers and planners is an efficient way for DMCs to identify new business opportunities. For example, networking at local hospitality industry functions, such as local Hospitality Sales and Management Association International (HSMAI) monthly meetings or convention bureau "mixers," is a common practice among successful DMCs. In addition, staying abreast of industry news, people who work in the industry, and knowing changes in services and staffing within the local industry make for a well-informed DMC.

Collateral materials are essential to a comprehensive sales and marketing plan. Collateral materials include brochures, letterheads, business cards, proposal shells, and fact sheets for the various activities and services offered by the DMC. In addition to these materials, a DMC will often produce a company newsletter to enhance the company's image and recognition in the industry.

Request for Proposal

Destination management companies will prepare detailed proposals for services, which are based on the planner's specifications and budget. A meetings and events professional will provide the DMC with information so that the DMCs' proposed itinerary can be designed to best suit the group's purpose, demographics, and expectations. Initial proposals will often include more than one suggested itinerary, providing the client with several options, costs, and details about proposed services.

Once a DMC has secured the sales lead, contacted the customer, and convinced that client to consider the DMC, the DMC will be asked to provide a proposal of services. The following items must be considered and addressed in this proposal stage:

- Project specifications
- Research and development
- Creativity and innovation
- Budgets
- Response time
- Competition

As a DMC begins to determine exactly what to offer a customer, the client's project specifications become a valuable tool. A great deal of detailed information is usually included in these specifications, such as:

- Group size
- Choice of hotel, resort type
- Meeting space allotments
- Dates of service
- Types of services required
- Demographic information about the attendees
- Management's goals for the meeting or event
- Approximate budget
- History regarding past successes and challenges
- Deadlines for completion and proposal submission

Armed with the client's specifications and other information, the DMC will determine what items to offer in the proposal of services that will best fit the client's expectations. The first step is often a series of creative meetings among DMC staff to discuss what might best satisfy the client specifications. After these meetings, research and development should begin. Availability of suppliers, venues, transportation, and entertainers, plus bids for services like catering, transportation equipment, and venue costs, are all reviewed and incorporated into the proposal. Costs for all items must be identified for accurate budgeting.

Creativity and innovation are usually highly valued in winning proposals. Selected programs will reflect the customer company; therefore, creativity and innovation along with a thorough and well-designed program tends to win. Response time is critical when responding to clients' proposals; however, there is a trade-off as creativity takes time, and a proposal that does not meet the clients' deadline will rarely receive the business.

A final and critical step in the proposal process is pricing. Several factors must be considered when pricing the proposal, such as:

- Total estimated costs for delivering the proposed services
- Staff time and involvement necessary before, during, and after the program
- Amount of DMC resources necessary to operate the program
- Unknown costs, which are factored into the planning stages
- Factors surrounding supplier choice and availability
- Time of the year and local business activity during a particular season
- Costs of taking staff and company capacity off the market for this customer
- Factors regarding competitive bids on the project

The following questions are the type that a DMC should ask itself prior to making a final decision on how much effort to dedicate to a given opportunity. The answers may show that ultimately the best decision is for a DMC to choose not to bid on a client's RFP.

- What is the revenue potential of the business opportunity?
- What is the value of a future relationship with the customer?
- How much proposal work will be involved in the bid?
- How many companies are bidding?
- Which competitors are bidding?
- What success rate does your company have on similar projects?
- What success rate do your competitors have?
- What time of year will the program be operating?
- What are the approximate odds of winning the program?
- How profitable will the program be?

Given the variety among proposal elements offered by the competing DMCs, a client may not choose a winning bid based solely on price. The client, in awarding the bid, may consider other important factors, such as:

- Is the proposal feasible?
- What is the perceived value of services offered?
- Will the participants appreciate the suggested program?
- Will the quality be sufficient to make the program or event a success?
- Is the DMC capable of producing the program or event in an acceptable manner?

Site Inspections

While DMCs may be involved in **site inspections**, they do not usually organize nor sponsor them. That responsibility lies with the DMO in the locale (see Chapter 3, on DMOs, for more information).

Program Development

The execution and civility of business transactions are supported through contractual agreements and are essential in all aspects of the meetings and events industry. Hotels, convention centers, cruise ships, airlines, and DMCs all produce contracts with their clients, which precisely spell out the details of the purchase and the obligation for both parties. Depending on the size and complexity of the program and the services provided by the DMC, contracts can vary in size.

After a program is contracted, a transition begins, moving from the active selling of the program to the operations and production of the program. At this time, all suppliers contracted by the DMC are notified that the program is definite and their services are confirmed. The operations staff, which typically is different from the sales staff in larger DMCs, meets with the sales representatives to review the customer's needs, program goals, and any details that will be a factor in the successful delivery of the program.

During this phase of the business process, the participants that are actively engaged can fluctuate, requiring the DMC management to constantly monitor costs and other details. With the active involvement by the client, activities and services may be added or removed from the program during this phase. It is important that the DMC representatives are available, responsive, and note these changes. As a contracted member of the customer's team, the DMC is responsible for the destination management portion of the larger, overall customer event—therefore, the DMC must be fully cooperative and flexible. The program's project manager, either an operations or events manager, will assume primary responsibility for the entire program or event. During the setup period, each activity and service for the program is reviewed and confirmed in detail. Full-time and part-time professional program managers, supervisors, tour guides, and escorts are scheduled well in advance.

Program Execution

Destination management companies require the coordination of staff and suppliers into one cohesive program of products and services. After finding the opportunity, creating proposals, earning the professional's confidence, contracting the program, and careful preparations, it is up to the operations and production staff to successfully deliver the program. At this point, everything is "on the line": The image of the customer organization, the reputation of the planner, future prospects for the DMC with the planner, the DMC's reputation in the destination, and the opportunity to profit from the contract are all at risk.

The successful execution of the client's program is very important. If the program is for a large association's convention, the members' perception of the organization is at stake. The American Medical Association, the American Bar Association, and the National Automobile Dealers Association are examples of associations that employ a DMC. Meeting and event professionals for these associations are orchestrating major events with thousands of participants on an ongoing basis. The participant's perception of the convention can easily be affected by the quality of the shuttle transportation to and from the convention hall, the quality of the networking events, cocktail parties, meal service, and activities like the annual golf tournament and optional sightseeing tours. All of these services are potentially the DMC's responsibility. The events must live up to the participants' expectations. The activities and tours must be entertaining and well run. The participants are the association planner's customers, and membership renewals and future convention attendance will be affected by the quality of the program delivery.

Similar dynamics are in effect with corporate programs. Exhibiting at a trade shows gives the exhibiting corporation an opportunity to entertain their customer through special event programs developed by their contracted DMC. Insurance companies reward top sales producers with incentive programs that effectively show the best of their workforce how the company's top executives value their contributions. Computer companies and software companies produce new product introduction events either as stand-alone events or in conjunction with industry conventions. Often the success of these events has the future of the sponsoring companies at stake.

Through these examples, one can clearly see the tremendous pressure of running a logistically sound and high-quality program. These pressures are riding on the shoulders of the meeting and event professionals and the DMCs. The DMC's operations and production staff have one chance to deliver the program. When mistakes or missteps occur, the event cannot be rescheduled for the next day. If the bus and limousine suppliers do not provide equipment as ordered, the departure time cannot be changed. It is the reliability of execution that is the most important issue in the success of a program; price runs a distant second to reliability. However, all DMCs are not equal, and choosing the best fit for a particular program is essential. A close working relationship that fosters confidence, easy communication, and mutual understanding requires that the planner's DMC contact be readily available. Likewise, the planner must be immediately available to the DMC's operation manager throughout the course of the program.

Transportation Services

Transportation management is often a major part of a DMC's business. It encompasses routing, vehicle use, staff requirements, special venue considerations, equipment staging areas, staff

DMCs may arrange outdoor performances. *Tony/Fotolia*

scheduling and briefings, maps, and signage. Transportation scenarios and requirements are usually scattered throughout the program itinerary.

Corporate programs usually begin with airport transfers. Airport transportation services customarily include "meet and greet" service and luggage management. Management of the arrival manifest by the airport transportation manager is a key component of the service. The arrival manifest is a detailed list of each guest's name, arrival flight, and time. The manager schedules with the arrival manifest as a guide. People change flights, miss flights, fail to accurately supply flight information, and flights can be delayed or canceled. Because of the inaccuracies common to arrival manifests, the transportation manager must not only expect surprises, but plan for them. Constant communication is necessary between the DMC and the airlines, the transportation equipment suppliers, and the airport "meet and greet" staff. Equally important is the need to keep open communication with the hotel(s) to which the participants are being transferred and the meeting professional, who may be receiving information about individual participants' changes in travel plans.

When airport transfers are run properly, the participants receive a friendly welcome by someone who knows their name, after which they are directed to the proper baggage belt to identify their luggage. Motor coaches, minibuses, vans, sedans, and limousines could all be used. A DMC must proactively manage the changes and challenges of airport transportation. The first impression made on a participant is the arrival transfer, and the last impression is the departure transfer.

Transportation requirements of clients often include shuttle services between event venues and the participating hotel(s). Shuttle supervisors, dispatchers, and directional staff, sometimes referred to as "human arrows" or "way finders," manage this personalized service. Whatever the transportation requirement, the DMC is expected to plan, prepare, and deliver the service in a timely and efficient manner.

Production of Events

Event production is also typically a major part of a DMC's services. Events can be large or small, on a hotel property, or in a remote location. Some examples of events are:

- Cocktail receptions and networking events
- Breakfasts, luncheons, and dinners
- Dining events at unique venues
- Gala dinner events
- Extravagant theme parties
- Outdoor and indoor team-building events
- Guest and children's programs

Operational staff must be familiar with all the necessary municipal regulations regarding insurance, fire safety codes, crowd control, and police requirements. When considering all these issues, there is no substitute for experience, and working with a DMC that has a known track record of success is very important.

Whether planning and operating sightseeing tours, a scavenger hunt, a golf tournament, or running a hospitality desk, strong organizational skills, sound preparation, and a sense of commitment and responsibility are essential traits for a professional DMC operations manager. When everything is riding on the performance of the firms, planners will often bond with the managers and become dependent on them to be their on-site consultants in the community.

Meeting and event professionals will often have to deal with on-site questions and requests for VIP arrangements with little advance notice, and the DMC staff will support them in securing appropriate arrangements. Some examples of last minute requests that DMCs are asked to take care of are:

"Where can I send my VP of marketing and her husband for a romantic dinner? She just realized that today's their wedding anniversary!"

"My company president is arriving early in the corporate jet. Can we get a limo to the executive airport in forty-five minutes?"

"The boss just decided he wants a rose for all of the ladies at tonight's party."

"Can we get Aretha Franklin to sing 'Happy Birthday' to one of our dealers during her performance at the party tonight?"

A wise person once said, "It is often the little things, the details that separate great events from ordinary ones." Knowing someone's favorite wine, song, or dessert can turn an ordinary event into one that will be remembered forever. These are things that are not included in the contract, but add special touches to an event and are great opportunities for the production staff to demonstrate their passion of service to the client. A production manager who has developed strong relationships with suppliers can often count on their suppliers to be swept up in the process and suggest ideas for program improvement on their own. Suppliers will do this because they want the event to be the best to establish an ongoing relationship with the DMC for possible future events. Planners are often pleased to be presented with options. Examples include being offered confetti cannons for the dance floor area, additional accent lighting, or separate martini bars are all on-site event upgrades.

Much of an operations or production manager's day is spent confirming and reconfirming services. Constant communication with vendors and suppliers is critical to ensure that final participant counts and timing are accurate. One common task to ensure success of events is the "advancing" of a venue, which is when DMC staff arrives well ahead of a group to make sure that the service staff and the event location are prepared and properly set up. Details such as the number of seats, room temperature, serving instructions, menu inclusions, and beverage service are all examples of items that should be verified when advancing a dinner event.

Throughout each event, operations and production managers must carefully monitor the original contracted services and all changes that occur after the original itinerary and contracts. Every addition to the program, such as changes in participant counts, times of service, and additional services, must be documented. Accurate, up-to-the-minute data on the actual services delivered must be kept for billing purposes. To avoid billing disputes, it is also important to identify that an authorized representative for the client has accepted the change or addition. Ideally, these authorizations are in writing and approved in advance by the client.

Wrap-Up and Billing

The final invoice for a program should mirror the contract of services agreed upon prior to the execution of the program. Actual services delivered should be outlined along with the number of participants that each charged item is based on. In most cases, items are billed either on "lot" costs or on a per-person basis. Lot costs are fixed and independent of the number of participants, such as bus hours, the price of an entertainer, or a décor package for a ballroom. Per-person pricing is based on the actual number of participants, such as food and beverage at a luncheon that is billed at a fixed price per person, plus tax and gratuities.

All additions or deletions to the originally contracted services should appear on the invoice. The "grand total" for the program should be reflected along with all deposits and payments received prior to the final billing. When possible, final billing details should be reviewed and approved by the planner or representative on-site at the completion of the program, while details about the program's operation, additions, and changes are still fresh in everyone's mind. The more time that elapses between the time the program is completed and receipt of the final invoice, the more likely there will be disputes about program details, such as participant counts, times, and items that were approved to be added to the program.

FINDING AND SELECTING A DESTINATION MANAGEMENT COMPANY

When the time comes that meeting and event professionals need to find and select a DMC, there are several steps and guidelines that are helpful in ensuring a successful outcome. When searching for DMC candidates, it is best to begin with contacting industry professionals that are managing and executing meetings and events on a regular basis. One of the best benefits of networking is to have contacts that can be called on to provide advice and guidance when searching for suppliers. If the meeting and event professional is lacking suitable connections, contacting industry groups, such as Professional Convention Management Association (PCMA), Meeting Professionals International (MPI), International Special Events Society (ISES), and the American Society of Association Executives (ASAE), can be a valuable source. Also, the destination's **CVB** or DMO will have listings of DMCs that operate in and around its destination.

Association of Destination Management Executives

An important resource in finding a DMC is the Association of Destination Management Executives International (ADMEI). Founded in 1995, **ADMEI** is committed to the initiative that professional destination management is a critical and necessary component to every successful meeting or event. As a primary goal, ADMEI continuously seeks to identify and promote the value of destination management as a necessary resource for planners of meetings, events, and incentive travel programs. ADMEI's goals also include becoming the definitive source of information, education, and issues-based discussion of destination management for the meetings, events, incentive, and hospitality industries.

Professionals holding positions in the destination marketing field have the ability to gain an important professional designation. The designation of Destination Management Certified Professional (DMCP) was introduced by ADMEI in January 2000. This professional certification is only available to individuals who have qualified for an extensive examination administered by ADMEI. Applicants are screened through a detailed questionnaire, which chronicles the applicant's experience and industry education. ADMEI has also developed the Destination Management Company Accreditation® (ADMC) program designed to promote professional standards and recognize those firms that demonstrate excellence in the practice of destination management, and who adhere to the standards set forth by ADMEI. The ADMC designation assists the meeting planning community by identifying those DMCs that adhere to ADMC standards of practice, ethics, and industry knowledge.

Once a list of potential DMCs has been identified through references or research of the various industry associations, it is time to identify the best of the group. Factors that may be important before soliciting the RFP selection include:

- How long the company has been in business?
- What are the experience levels of the management and staff?
- What are the perceptions of the planner with the personalities of the management team?
- Is the DMC an affiliated member of any meeting and events professional organizations?

DMCs may make special arrangements for models, this one in costume. *George G. Fenich*

- Is the DMC adequately bonded, relative to the size and complexity of the program?
- What is the quality of the references provided by the DMC both in size of previous programs and ranking of professional providing the references?

The next step in the process is selecting a DMC that best meets the needs and budgetary guidelines. At this point, meeting and event professionals should formally notify potential DMCs by a RFP. Once the final selection has been made, it is important to begin working with the selected DMC to ensure that they have historical information related to the organization's participants that may impact the execution of the program.

FUTURE TRENDS

The destination management industry's varied representatives are not immune to the need for change. The following is a list of eight areas that DMC operators should take seriously in order to enhance their leadership and stature in meeting and event management circles and beyond.

1. *Take the Lead in Green Practices.* Be proactive in initiating sustainable practices by implementing leading edge methods for leaving a smaller carbon footprint, educating other parts of the hospitality industry through professional organizational training activities and the development and distribution of training materials. In addition, DMCs should develop new partnerships to share these activities and materials with other businesses in both the private and public sector.
2. *Work Together in Consortiums.* The DMC industry will continue to see a consolidation of service organizations. It will be important for smaller, niche DMCs to bond together in consortiums to ensure that business remains in the local community, and that the overall experience for meeting and event professionals is seamless from planning, execution, and payment.
3. *Identify and Develop New Business from Drive-To Markets.* Given the uncertainty of the economy and the unfriendly skies, businesses will begin to look for more local and regional sites for holding their meetings and events. This should lead DMCs to focus on developing new clients from locations that are closer to their destinations.

4. *Develop Crisis Networks.* Issues surrounding the safety and security of meeting attendees will continue to be a concern for corporations and associations. Successful DMCs will develop, implement, and execute crisis plans and business continuity networks in partnerships with other organizations within their communities.

5. *Emphasize Standards of Conduct and Operations.* DMCs will continue to receive scrutiny about the behavior of staff used to provide client services. It will become increasingly important that DMCs implement high standards of conduct for their employees and operations. The standards and operational policies should be defined, recognized, and understood by every employee, client, and the public in general as part of an established image and reputation.

6. *Relationship Management Strategy.* Corporations and associations that conduct business and meeting travel are quickly consolidating their travel, meeting, and event expenses into a more economically efficient model. Local and niche DMCs will need to build strong, lasting relationships with meetings and event professionals to ensure that they are on the list of approved vendors.

7. *Attentive to Competitive Forces.* Given the ubiquity of the Internet, and its convenience, successful large DMCs no longer need a continuous presence in a local market. Local, niche DMCs will need to increase the quality of customer contacts and services to meetings and events professionals and their attendees, to remain relevant in a competitive marketplace.

8. *Ethical Business Protocols.* DMCs rely heavily upon their confidential intellectual property, creative ideas, and research conducted for a specific client program. The industry's (DMCs, planners, as well as suppliers) adherence to the ADMEI Code of Ethics is vital for the continued growth and professionalism of the industry.

Summary

The niche that DMCs provide in the MEEC industry is important for meeting and event professionals. These organizations provide a crucial service because the customer companies and organizations that sponsor meetings and events will always need access to local expertise. The depth of local destination knowledge, the local contacts and connections, the community standing, buying power, and hands-on experience with the implementation of programs and events are not readily available to organizations outside of the destination. DMCs have evolved in some interesting ways. Many of the earlier DMCs evolved from the ranks of wholesale tour operators and ground operators. These early DMCs began by specializing in tours and transportation services for visiting travel groups. In the late 1950s, the specialization in association and higher-end corporate programs demanded a wider range of services, including dining programs, expanded activities, and special events.

Today, the competitive landscape of DMCs is filled multi-destination, national DMC companies that operate networks around the world. However, just as individual one-of-a-kind hotels still prosper along with the giant hotel chains, so do unique and specialized one-destination DMCs. The services requested of DMCs by meeting and event professionals are still evolving, and destination management services have been secured as a key component for success in meetings and events industry.

Today's network of professionals that work in the destination management segment of the MEEC industry have a wide range of industry associations for support and trade shows and conventions for marketing of their services. Chief among them is ADMEI and its DMC accreditation and executive certification programs.

The long-term outlook for DMCs is bright. The meeting and event industry that DMCs support is robust, and many existing firms are financially sound and poised to gain market share and increase their brand recognition despite temporary threats and business slowdowns. The industry is full of opportunities for long-term successful career options for new meeting and event professionals.

Key Words and Terms

For definitions, see GLOSSARY, or http://glossary.conventionindustry.org

ADMEI	destination management	field staff	program
client project	company (DMC)	incentive travel programs	request for proposal (RFP)
corporate meetings	destination marketing	meet and greet	site inspection
CVB	organization (DMO)	operations and production	special events

Review and Discussion Questions

1. What is a destination management company?
2. What services are offered by DMCs?
3. Compare and contrast the difference between a DMC and a DMO.
4. Create an organizational chart for a DMC.
5. How do DMCs generate their business leads?
6. What are the resources DMCs provide to a meeting and event professionals?
7. Describe the differences between the types of accounts that secure the services of DMCs.
8. What professional organizations support the professionals that work destination management industry?
9. List the services provided by DMAI.
10. Describe key factors that are considered when meeting and event professionals are selecting a DMC.

About the Chapter Contributor

William R. Host, CMP, is Associate Professor of hospitality and tourism management, focusing on meeting and event management at the Manfred Steinfeld School of Hospitality & Tourism Management at Roosevelt University in Chicago, Illinois. Prior to his teaching, Bill spent over 20 years in the industry as a meeting professional for a student religious organization, and international automotive trade association before forming HOST Meetings & Events Management.

Bill was installed in the MPI Chicago Area Chapter Hall of Fame in 2006 and was named by the PCMA Education Foundation as their 2010 Education Honoree for Lifetime Achievement.

Previous Edition Chapter Contributor

Brian Miller, Associate Professor at the University of Delaware.
Terry Epton, Executive Vice President, Host Global Alliance.

Special Events Management

Chapter Outline

Fireworks make an event even more special.   *Elen_studio/Fotolia*

Chapter Objectives

This chapter provides the reader with an understanding of the following:

- A working definition of a special event
- Understanding the importance of relationships in special event management
- The importance of a workable plan for staging a special event
- The planning tools used in special event management
- The importance of city and community infrastructures when hosting a special event
- The merchandising and promoting of a special event
- Sponsorships for special events
- Target markets for procuring attendance at a special event
- The basic operations for preparing for a special event
- The components of a special event budget
- The breakdown components of a special event
- Future trends in the industry

A WORKING DEFINITION OF A SPECIAL EVENT

A *special event* is an umbrella term that encompasses all functions that bring people together for a unique purpose. Most events require some sort of planning on the part of the organizer. A special event, such as a city festival or fair, can mean working with **community infrastructure**, merchandising, promoting, and in some cases dealing with the media. The event can be as small as the local community Kiwanis picnic or as large as the Olympics. Special events are imbedded in **meetings, expositions, events, and conventions (MEEC)**, and at amusement parks, parades, **fairs, festivals, and public events**.

The Convention Industry Council (CIC) glossary includes the following definition related to special events:

> *Special Event* One-time event staged for the purpose of celebration; unique activity.
>
> *Special Events Company* This type of company may contract to put on an entire event or only parts of one. A special events *Production* Company may present special effects and theatrical acts. They sometimes hire speakers as part of their contract.
>
> Source: http://www.conventionindustry.org/StandardsPractices/APEX/glossary.aspx. The APEX glossary is a product of the Convention Industry Council, copyright 2011, Used with Permission. www.conventionindustry.org

A special event can bring organizations together for the purpose of fund-raising, establishing a city or community as a local, regional, or national destination, and to stimulate the local economy. The event can also be an opportunity for an association or a corporation to favorably position itself with a community or with the mass consumer. Sponsoring a specific type of event can provide a marketing edge and another avenue for reaching customers. For example, Mercedes-Benz automobiles sponsor numerous PGA golf tournaments, in part because the demographics of the audience match its target clientele. It also does the same thing with the U.S. Open tennis tournament. Coors Light sponsors NASCAR races, Allstate sponsors the Sugar Bowl football game, and Macy's sponsors the Thanksgiving Day parade, and the list goes on and on.

Orchestrating a special event takes more than an idea. It takes planning, understanding your target market, having basic operational knowledge, using effective communications, working with volunteers or volunteer organizations, working within a budget, promoting the event, and even creating the logistics for breaking down an event. Simply stated, the event professional needs to understand the "who, what, where, and why" of the special event.

It All Begins with a Relationship

What do these special events have in common: a wedding reception, a 5K charity run, the Macy's Thanksgiving Day parade, and a company picnic? All are very special events, though very different. And, all are planned by someone who must understand the goals, the needs, and the desires of the client they are serving. The event professional has a responsibility to the client to do everything in his/her power to reach their goals, while working within the parameters of the given location, city, or facility.

How does the event professional begin to truly understand the vision of his/her client? And how does the client begin to trust the efforts of the event professional? Special events management begins and evolves by developing a very important relationship between the client and the event professional. The event professional must listen to the clients, hear their words, and see their vision. The event professional should have the capability to put that vision into a reality for the clients, given the expertise and the professionalism of the event professional.

An event professional and a client must have clear lines of communication between them. And as they talk and listen to each other, a viable plan can unfold. The event professional must always understand that the success of any event must begin with a relationship. Listen to the client, do what you say you will do, tend to the little things, and communicate without fail.

No matter what the profile of the event, each and every special event is, indeed, very special to someone, or to many. It becomes a great challenge to meet (and exceed) the expectations of your client, and this is one of the key roles of the event professional.

One very successful event that draws more than 100,000 visitors to Central Pennsylvania is the summer Central Pennsylvania Festival of the Arts™. This festival brings people to downtown State College and the University Park campus of PennState to celebrate the arts with its nationally recognized Sidewalk Sale and Exhibition, a gallery exhibition, and music, dance, and theatrical performances in a variety of traditional and nontraditional venues. The festival was founded in 1967 and was recently ranked first on the list of 100 Best Fine Arts and Design Shows in America by Sunshine Artist magazine.

The Presidential Inauguration Day Parade

While the tradition of the Inaugural parade dates back to the Inauguration of George Washington, the first organized parade unfolded at the Inauguration of James Madison in 1809. Here, Madison was escorted to the Capitol by a troop of cavalry. After taking his oath of office, Madison then watched the parade of militia. In William Henry Harrison's time, in 1841, floats were introduced to the parade. In addition, military bands, political groups, and college groups became parade participants.

As history progressed, African Americans joined Abraham Lincoln's Inaugural parade for the first time, increasing even further the number of participating groups in the parade. In 1873, President Grant reordered the events of the Inaugural Day to make the parade *after* the Inaugural Ceremony, rather than *before*. This tradition continues today.

Reviewing stands were built in 1881 for the Inauguration of President James Garfield. To combat the cold and sometimes harsh weather conditions, the grandstands became enclosed. Reviewing stands were also built for visitors.

Women became participants of the parade in 1917, and then, in 1921, President Warren Harding became the first president to ride in an automobile. This set a precedent until 1977, when President Jimmy Carter chose to walk in the parade with his wife and daughter, from the Capitol to the White House. The first televised Inaugural Parade was held in 1949 for President Harry S. Truman.

The largest parade occurred in 1953 at the Inaugural Parade of President Dwight D. Eisenhower. The parade included seventy-three bands, fifty-nine floats, horse, elephants, military troops, and civilian and military vehicles. The parade lasted for over four-and-a-half hours.

The size and sophistication of the parade has developed tremendously over the last 200 years, and the Inaugural Parade has evolved into a nationally lauded special event. At the 2009 Inauguration Parade, President Barack Obama hosted 15,000 participants, including 2000 military personnel. Forty-six bands were chosen to participate of the 1,000 that applied. Today, millions of Americans can view the parade, whether via television viewing, Internet access, or in person. This parade has truly become a tradition of celebration for all Americans.

Today, the Armed Forces Inaugural Committee is responsible for the organization of the parade, and the Presidential Inaugural Committee is responsible for selecting all participants of the parade.

A film festival can be a dream come true for moviegoers as they seek out famous actors who might be walking right next to them, as on the streets of Park City, Utah, during the Sundance Film Festival. Founded in 1981, the festival has grown to international recognition, attracting tens of thousands of visitors each year to this quaint little town to view over 3,000 film submissions.

These special events came from an historical tradition that ultimately grew to attract thousands of visitors to some very remote areas. Continuing to attract visitors requires planning and planning tools, such as an understanding of the community infrastructure, merchandising and promoting the event, developing sponsorships, and working with the media. This is the art and science of special events management.

HISTORY AND BACKGROUND

Festivals and special events have been part of human history since time immemorial. Humankind has celebrated births, weddings, and deaths throughout history and held special gatherings like the Olympics and gladiatorial combat. However, most historians credit the use of the term "special event" in modern history to a Disney "imagineer" named Robert Janni. The problem Disney faced was that the families who frequented the theme park were worn out after a day of adventure and most left by 5 PM each day, even though the park stayed open hours

Using Festivals in the Off-Season: "Rockin' Mountains"

The typical image of the Rocky Mountains and Colorado is one of snow-covered peaks in winter dotted with skiers. But what happens when summer rolls around and people cannot ski? What do the ski resorts do, shut down? The answer is a resounding "No!" They put on music festivals using the same facilities occupied by skiers in the winter. The setting is idyllic, with music carrying through the clean air with the awesome backdrop of mountain peaks.

This use of Colorado mountain ski facilities to host off-season musical events started in 1949, when concerts were held in the town of Aspen. At the time, it was called the Goethe Bicentennial celebration. Some of the events included the Minneapolis Symphony Orchestra playing in a tent that held 2,000 people. This special event has continued and grown into the Aspen Music Festival and School. Recently the event included more than 800 international musicians performing in over 300 events during the eight-week session. There are four major **venues**. The largest one is a tent that holds more than 2,000 people and is made from the same fabric as the Denver airport terminal.

Another ski resort that has turned to musical events to attract visitors in the off-season is Telluride, Colorado. Nearly every summer weekend, the town hosts a musical event. The biggest special event is the Telluride Bluegrass Festival, which has been held for over 40 years. It runs for four days in June and is capped at 11,000 people per day. Telluride also hosts a Jazz Festival, a Chamber Music Festival, and a Blues and Brews Festival.

In Winter Park just west of Denver, numerous weekends are occupied with music festivals. Concertgoers sit on the slopes and watch bands perform against the backdrop of the Continental Divide. The Winter Park Music Festival boasts a lineup of "old-school" music acts like Molly Hatchet and Cheap Trick. In July, they host the Winter Park Jazz festival for two days with artists covering a variety of genres. Also in July and covering two weekends is the Winter Park 30 Solshine Music Festival. This event features local artists and is presented free to the audiences.

Breckenridge also hosts a summer concert series that runs from late June until the middle of August. The event features everything from classical to rock music. They finance the event through a unique structure, raising one-fourth of its money through the Bon Appetit Series, which includes more intimate gatherings that range from country music concerts and wildflower hikes to scavenger hunts on Peak 7, tours of SouthPark, cabaret evenings, and Texas Hold'em tournaments.

longer. In order to keep attendees at the park, he proposed producing a nightly parade called the "Main Street Electric Parade" with numerous floats decked out with lights. It was a success in keeping people in the park in the evening. When asked by a reporter what he called this parade, he replied "A Special Event." The use of special events to attract or maintain crowds is still used to this day.

A special event is a celebration of something—that is what makes it special. Special Events can include:

- Civic Events
  - Centennials
  - Founders' Day
- Mega-Events
  - Olympics
  - America's Cup
  - United Nations Assembly's
  - WorldExpo's
- Festivals and Fairs
  - Marketplace of ancient days
  - Community Event
  - Fair = not for profit
  - Festival = for profit
- Expositions
  - Where suppliers meet buyers

- Education
- Entertainment
- Sporting Events
  - Super Bowl
  - World Series
  - Masters Golf Tournament
  - FIFA World Cup
- Social life-cycle events
  - Wedding
  - Anniversary
  - Birthday
  - Reunion
  - Bar Mitzvah (Bat Mitzvah)
- Meetings & Conventions
  - Political National Convention
  - National Restaurant Association convention in Chicago
  - PCMA annual conference
- Retail Events
  - Long-range promotional event
  - Store opening
  - New product launches
    - X-box
    - Apple
- Religious Events
  - Papal Inauguration
  - The Hajj (Mecca)
  - Easter
  - Kwanzaa
- Corporate Events
  - Holiday parties
  - Annual dinner
  - Company picnics
  - Conferences/meetings

PLANNING TOOLS FOR A SPECIAL EVENT

Special events management, like any other form of managing, requires planning tools. The first of these tools is a vision statement of your event. This vision statement should clearly identify the "who, what, when, where, and why" of the event. As the event begins to unfold, it is important to keep those involved focused on the vision. This can be accomplished by continually monitoring, evaluating, and, where possible, measuring the progress toward the outlined goals of the event (see chapter on "Planning and Producing MEEC Events").

The "who" of planning an event are those people or organizations that would like to host and organize it. In the case of the St. Patrick's Day Parade in Chicago, Illinois, it is the city that hosts and coordinates the marchers, the floats, and the bands. The "what" was a parade demonstrating Irish pride and local tradition. The "where" of the Parade is downtown Chicago, with the floats and bands marching down Michigan Avenue. The big question of "why" is one of tradition, pride, fun, and tourism. This, in turn, promotes the city and brings revenues to the local businesses. When the city decided to serve as the host of this event, it needed to incorporate the tools of special event management.

Some of the management tools that are used in staging events are as follows:

a. Flow charts and graphs for scheduling. Look at any program for a meeting/event; there are start and end times, times for coffee breaks, a time for lunch, and a time that the meeting resumes and ends. The flow chart can be as "romantic" as a wedding ceremony **agenda**. The chart can be the order or sequence of floats for a parade, the program for a talent show, or the agenda for a weeklong international conference. A flowchart scheduling an event's activities helps guide attendees and guests and makes the execution of the event flow smoothly. **Gantt Charts** are often used for many of these tasks.

b. Clearly defined setup and breakdown **schedules**. These provide the event manager with an opportunity to determine tasks that may have been overlooked in the initial planning process.

c. Policy statements developed to guide in the decision-making process. Policy statements provide a clear understanding of commitments and what is expected to fulfill them. Some of the commitments to be considered are human resources, sponsors, security, ticketing, volunteers, and paid personnel.

Understanding Community Infrastructure

Another key ingredient for planning a successful event is an understanding of the infrastructure in the community where the event is to take place. This infrastructure might include the CEO of the company, politicians, prominent business leaders of the community, civic and community groups, the media, and other community leaders. Without a "buy-in" from the city leadership, a community is less inclined to be supportive. The role of business leaders in the infrastructure could be to provide sponsorships, donations, staff, or a possible workplace for the coordination of the event. Many times, community groups serve as volunteer workers for the event and are also an extension of the advertising for it.

Early on, it must be recognized whether or not a community or a company is truly committed to hosting any type of special event that will call on its support. This support not only includes the financial commitment, but also in the physical and emotional commitment it will take to manage an event from start to finish. For a promoter or special events management company to maintain a positive reputation, there needs to be a solid infrastructure in place.

Merchandising and Promoting the Special Event

Merchandising and promoting a special event is another planning tool for attracting attendance and increasing the overall profitability for the event. Just because a community decides to host a craft fair or street festival does not mean that there will be the attendance necessary to meet vendors' and visitors' needs. Profit for the vendor and a memorable experience for the attendee are two main objectives for a special event. The special event requires all the promotional venues that an event management company or civic group is able to afford.

Understanding and utilizing the **promotional mix model** (see Figure 8-1) is pivotal in order to meet the goals of the event marketing plan. The role of promotion in special events management is the coordination of all the seller's efforts to set up channels of information and persuasion to sell or promote the event. Traditionally, the promotional mix has included four elements: advertising, sales promotion, publicity and/or public relations, and personal selling. However, this author views direct marketing and interactive media as additional elements of the promotional mix. Modern-day event marketers use many means to communicate with their target markets. Each element of the promotional mix is viewed as an integrated marketing communications tool. Each of these elements of the model has a distinctive role in attracting an attendee to the special event. Each takes on a variety of forms, and each has certain advantages.

Distinctive Roles of the Promotional Mix Model

Advertising is defined as any paid form of nonpersonal communication about the event. The nonpersonal component means advertising that involves mass media (e.g., TV, radio, magazines,

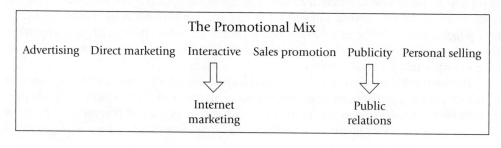

FIGURE 8-1 Elements of the Promotional Mix for Success Special Event Management

mobile phones, Web sites, and newspapers). Advertising is the best known and most widely discussed form of promotion because it is the most persuasive, especially if the event (e.g., a home and garden show) is targeted toward mass consumers. It can be used to create brand images or symbolic appeals for the brand, and generate immediate responses from prospective attendees.

Direct marketing is a form of advertising that communicates directly with the target customer with the intent of generating a response. It is much more than direct mail or catalogs. It involves a variety of activities, including database management, direct selling, telemarketing, direct-response ads, the Internet, and various broadcast and print media. The Internet has also fueled the growth of direct marketing. One of the large advantages of e-mail marketing is the ability to measure response rates. Interactive or Internet marketing also allows for a back-and-forth flow of information; users can participate in and modify the form and content of the information they receive in real time. Unlike traditional forms of marketing, such as advertising, which are one-way forms of communication, this type of media allows users to perform a variety of functions. It enables users to receive and alter information and images, make inquiries, respond to questions, and make purchases. Many event attendees will go to a Web site to garner information about a special event such as a concert and purchase their tickets directly online. For a special event such as the Aspen Music Festival, attendees can go to the festival's official Web site, view the schedule, learn about the event and the surrounding area, purchase tickets, and request additional information—all forms of direct marketing. In addition to the Internet, other forms of interactive media include CD-ROMs, kiosks, and interactive television.

Sales promotion is generally defined as those marketing activities that use incentives or discounts to increase sales or attendance. A popular form of sales promotion is the coupon. Many events will use a two-for-one attendance coupon to stimulate attendance on slower days. In addition, merchandise is often offered when purchasing several tickets at once.

Publicity and public relations is divided into two components. Publicity is the component that is not directly paid for, nor has an identified sponsor. When an event planner gets the media to cover or run a favorable story on a special event, it affects an attendee's awareness, knowledge, and opinions. Publicity is considered a credible form of promotion, but it is not always under the control of the organization or host of the event. In the case of South by Southwest (SXSW), prior to the event the organizers release press releases highlighting the performers or acts that are participating in the event. During the event reporters and camera crews cover the action on a daily basis. If those reporting the event have a positive experience, it will favorably affect the public's perception of the event. Unfortunately, the reverse is also true; the event professionals have little control.

Social Media has exploded as a preferred strategy for promotional initiatives. Social Media reaches the masses with minimal expense and relative ease of effort. This is also known as viral marketing. While there are many vehicles of social media, some of the more commonly used mediums include Facebook, Blogging, LinkedIn, Pinterest, Google+, and Twitter. Each of these mediums allows a message to be sent simultaneously to many people, projecting a controlled and positive message to the reader. In addition, the message that is sent is delivered immediately to the reader. (For more information, see Chapter 12, Technology.)

There are a variety of special events that take place to promote a destination or an occasion. One example is the SXSW event held in March each year in Austin, Texas. This nine-day event is the premier gathering of Music, Film, and Interactive professionals.

PUBLIC RELATIONS The purpose of public relations is to systematically plan and distribute information to attempt to control or manage the image and/or publicity of an event by building beneficial relationships with stakeholders and consumers. It has a broader objective than publicity because its purpose is to establish a positive image of the special event. Public relations and publicity are favored by festival and event directors because they reach the audience they are attempting to attract. Public relations can be the reason for hosting the special event altogether. Tobacco companies have used special events like a NASCAR race or tennis tournament to create a more positive image with consumers.

Personal selling is the final element of the promotional mix model, and it is a form of person-to-person communication in which a seller attempts to assist and/or persuade prospective event attendees. Typically, group tour sales are one of the best prospects for personal selling of a special event. There are several touring companies that purchase large groups of

Branding A Destination
South by Southwest

South by Southwest (**SXSW**) is a group of festivals and conferences that take place every spring in Austin, Texas, and covers music, film, and interactive technologies. It began small in 1987 but has grown each and every year since its inception. Currently, it is the largest music festival of its kind in the world boasting over 2,200 bands on 113 stages. The film festival is focused on attracting new directors while the interactive portion is focused on emerging technology. SXSW has launched a number of new products during the event but two of the more notable are Twitter and Foursquare. John Mayer launched his career by performing at SXSW. The film festival has launched numerous films over the years including in *The Hurt Locker*, which went on to win the Academy Award for Best Picture in 2010.

While the focus of the event has been to promote the three industries, it has also become a primary source of bringing tourism to Austin, Texas. It continues to be the single most profitable event for the City of Austin's hospitality industry. Recently the event created the following impact to the local economy:

- 41,700 registrations
- 13,000 individual hotel registrations totaling 56,000 room nights
- 155,000 conference and festival participants
- Employ a full-time staff of 120 employees
- A direct economic impact of $145.8 million (directly related to the local economy)
- An indirect impact of $37.5 million (increases in sales, income, and jobs associated with companies that benefit from SXSW expenditures
- Induced impacts of $34.9 million (spending by individuals as a result of increased earnings as a result of the conference).

tickets for special events. Unlike advertising, personal selling involves direct contact between the buyer and seller of the event, usually through face-to-face sales. Personal selling is by far the most expensive form of promotional activity when considered in terms of the number of consumers reached. Some examples of events that group tours attend may include: the Indianapolis 500, the Kentucky Derby, or the Jazz Fest in New Orleans. Group tour organizers will meet face-to-face with event professionals or talk via the telephone to purchase tickets for an event.

Sponsorships for Special Events

Sponsorships help to ensure profitable success for an event. They are an innovative way for event organizers to help underwrite and defray costs. Sponsorships should be considered more than just a charitable endeavor for a company—they can be a strong marketing tool.

Event sponsors provide funds or "in-kind" contributions and receive consideration in the form of logo usage and identity with the event. Recent trends of sponsorships show rapid growth. Sponsorship can take many forms. A large corporation, for instance, may have the means to provide financial sponsorship for an event. The mid-size and smaller organizations, however, may need to be more creative in their sponsorship methods. A smaller organization may, for example, provide product, rather than the financial contribution. Therefore, you may not see their banner hanging at the event, but you will have their product in your hand.

Many types of special events require sponsorship to be successful. Sporting events have long been the leader in securing sponsorships for teams and athletes. However, their market share has dropped as companies begin to distribute sponsorship dollars to other events, such as city festivals and the arts. This shift in sponsorships from sports events to that of festivals and the arts over the past decade has emerged because companies are cognizant of the effective tool that a sponsorship can be for overall company marketing plans. Sponsors are beginning to recognize that festivals are now as attractive as sports at generating a return on investment (ROI).

The Great Garlic Cook-Off
Gilroy, California

The Annual Gilroy Garlic Festival is held in the "Garlic Capital of the World," Gilroy, California, at Christmas Hill Park during the last full weekend of July.

This festival's origin lies in the pride of one man, Rudy Melone. Melone felt that Gilroy should celebrate its superior production of the "stinking rose," otherwise known as garlic. He then began what is referred to as "the preeminent food festival in America."

In December of each year, the Gilroy Garlic Festival begins its request for original garlic recipes. Citizens of Canada and the United States are asked to participate. Recipes are then submitted by amateur chefs, and eight are chosen to participate in the festival cook-off. Winners are awarded monetary prizes for their work well done.

Another tradition practiced by the Garlic Festival is the nomination of a "Miss Gilroy Garlic Festival Queen." Contestants are judged on a personal interview, talent, a garlic speech, and evening gown competition. The queen represents Gilroy at various festivities before and during the festival.

Over the last thirty-five years, the Garlic Festival has attracted over four million attendees and raised over $10,000,000 for local nonprofit organizations. Over 4,000 volunteers are recruited to work the event and participate in activities like picking up trash, parking cars, and serving lemonade. The Gilroy Garlic Festival is not only known for its garlic pride and knowledge but for its ability to bring the community of Gilroy together. Its Web site states, "Where else can one feast on food laced with over two tons of fresh garlic, enjoy three stages of musical entertainment, shop in arts and crafts, view the great garlic cook-off and other celebrity cooking demonstrations, spend time in the children's area, visit interactive displays set up by many of our sponsors, soak up some glorious sunshine, and mingle with a fun bunch of garlic-loving people?"

There are five compelling reasons why company sponsorships are an important option to consider:

1. Economic changes (both upturns and downturns)
2. Ability to target market segments
3. Ability to measure results
4. Fragmentation of the media
5. Growth of diverse population segments

Changes in the economic climate of the country will affect the goals, spending, and expectations of the sponsoring organization. In times of economic health, companies (both large and small) may be willing and able to more freely spend their promotional dollars on sponsorship. In economic downturns, however, organizations are likely to feel the necessity to account for the return they are receiving on their promotional spending. In other words, the sponsorship is seen as an investment, and the organization would like to know if, in fact, they are receiving a return on their investment. In either economic climate, sponsorships promote the intangible benefits of company visibility and overall goodwill.

When looking for sponsorships for a special event, organizers must determine if the event fits the company. Event professionals must always examine the company's goal, and be sure to research the competition. Special event organizers should aid the sponsors with promotional ideas that will help them meet their goals. Promoters of an event need to ensure that sponsors get their money's worth. Remember that sponsors have internal and external audiences to whom they are appealing.

"Cross-promotional opportunities" allow the sponsor to achieve the greatest visibility possible by capitalizing on more than one promotional opportunity within one event. For example, if PepsiCo sponsored an event, then that company would likely gain notable visibility through banners, logos, and so on. However, to further capitalize on this sponsorship, PepsiCo might further request that only Pepsi products be sold at the event. They are gaining visibility through the product that is being served at the event, and they may likely be earning revenue on the product that they are serving. This sponsorship would, therefore, serve as a triple benefit to the corporation. The internal audience of a corporation is its employees, and they must also be sold on the sponsorship of the event. A company needs to provide opportunities for employee involvement. If the special event is a charitable marathon, employees may be asked to actually participate in the marathon or raise funds for the charitable cause. Those employees who participate may be featured in promotional material or press releases.

New York City Marathon

Sponsorship

The New York City Marathon boasts 30,000 runners with more than 2 million spectators and is one of the largest live sporting events in the world, being broadcast to over 330 million viewers in more than 154 territories. Television coverage includes a live five-hour telecast on WNBC in New York, a one-hour national telecast on NBC, and various live and highlight shows internationally.

New York Road Runners and the New York City Marathon are fortunate to have the support and commitment of sponsors and strategic partners. Their continued support makes the New York City Marathon a world-class event year after year.

Sponsors

Title Sponsor:	Additional	Timex
ING U.S. (2013)	Sponsors	PowerBar
Tata Consultancy	Asics America	Dunkin' Donuts
Services (TCS)	Foot Locker	Gatorade
(beginning in	United Airlines	Poland Springs
2014)	Nissan	Phillips
	The Rudin Family	NY Times

Selling to the external audience of the corporation (the consumer) is done in a variety of ways. First, the company might feature its logo on the event's products. The company can promote its affiliation with the special event by providing its logo for outdoor banners and specialty advertising items, such as T-shirts, caps, or sunglasses. The types of specialty products are limitless and excellent venues for advertising. The sponsoring company may wish to appoint an employee spokesperson to handle radio or television interviews.

Working with the Media for an Event

Generating media coverage for a special event is one of the most effective methods for attracting attendance. Ideally, an event organizer wants to garner free television, radio, and print coverage. In order to attract the media, a promoter must understand what makes for good coverage and what does not.

When a camera crew is sent to film an event by assignment editors at a TV station, they will look for a story that can be easily illustrated with visuals captured by a camera. They also look for a vignette that can entertain viewers in thirty seconds or less. If an event organizer wants television or radio stations to cover the event, he or she needs to call it to their attention with a press release or press conference. There are no guarantees that the station or the newspaper will air the footage or print the story; however, the chances are better if a camera crew shoots footage or a reporter does an interview. Remember, special events provide ideal fodder for the evening news. This can be an interview with a celebrity who will be attending the event or an advance look at an art exhibit.

Event organizers try to present the unusual to the media. In 2007, Kentucky Fried Chicken decided to unveil a redesign of the company logo for the first time in over 10 years. The logo revision included bolder colors and changing the founder Col. Harland Sanders from his customary white suit and black bow tie into a red apron against a matching red background.

In order to unveil the logo redesign the company decided to create an 87,000-square-foot version that could be seen from space. The logo for this event was created out of 65,000 one-foot tiles that were set up in the Las Vegas desert. The new logo was then filmed by the Google satellite and uploaded to YouTube and Google Maps, resulting in over 600,000 views.

This also resulted in the story being carried on national news broadcasts and resulted in a multitude of media coverage over the next several weeks. Promoters of special events have long recognized what TV and radio coverage can do for an event. Here are some helpful hints for attracting television and radio coverage:

1. Early in the day is considered the best time to attract cameras and reporters. Remember, a crew must come out, film, get back to the studio, edit the film, and have the segment ready for the 5:00 or 6:00 PM newscast that night.
2. The best day of the week to attract news crews is Friday. That is because it is usually a quiet news day. Saturday and Sunday have even fewer distractions, but most stations do not have enough news crews working the weekend who can cover an event.
3. Giving advance notice for a special event is very helpful to assignment editors. Usually about three days' notice, with an explanation of the event via a press release and telephone follow-up, is very helpful in securing media coverage. If an interview is involved, a seven-day notice is a good time allotment for coverage.

UNDERSTANDING THE TARGET MARKET FOR YOUR SPECIAL EVENT

Bringing special events to a community has not changed much over the years; however, consumers have changed. They are much more selective and sophisticated about the events they will attend. Since the cost of attending events has risen, consumers are much more discerning about how they spend their entertainment dollars. This creates a demand for quality for any special event.

A Very Special Wedding

A couple from Texas wanted to be sure that their wedding was special, so they decided to have it in New Orleans. They were enamored with the charm of the city: moss-draped oak trees, antebellum homes, and horse-drawn carriages. They decided to invite 100 people and contacted a local destination management company (DMC) to make the arrangements. Their specification was that the DMC arrange a rehearsal dinner for 12 people and a reception for 100. Such costs as transportation to New Orleans, hotel accommodations, and the church were not part of the bid. Their stated budget for this wedding reception and dinner was $250,000. That's right—a quarter of a million dollars or $2,500 per guest! When the event professional heard this, her reaction was twofold: (1) how could she possibly put together this event and spend that much money, and (2) if that was their proposed budget, she would try to upsell them.

The rehearsal dinner was held in a private dining room at the famous Arnaud's restaurant in the French Quarter. The real money was spent on the reception. They rented the art deco Saenger Theater for the evening, but there was a problem. Like most theaters, the floor sloped toward the stage. So, they removed all the seats and built a new floor that was level, not sloped. The interior of the theater was so beautiful that it needed little decoration. The New Orleans Police Department was contracted to close the street between the church and theater to cars so that the period ambiance would not be disturbed for the couple and their guests while being transported in their horse-drawn carriages. When the couple and their guests entered for the evening, they were greeted by models in period costume and served mint juleps while a gospel group sang. A blues band followed, and the night was topped off by not one but two sets by Gladys Knight and the Pips. The affair was catered by Emeril Lagasse and only included heavy hors d'oeuvres, not even a sit-down dinner. The ultimate cost for this event was almost $300,000, and the couple was delighted.

The planner was Nanci Easterling of Food Art, Inc.

Understanding your target market is one of the most important components in the overall success of the event. It is critical for the event marketer and event professional to know the participant audience. Age, gender, religion, ethnicity—all must be understood. Depending on the type of event, the event professional must have an understanding of participant restrictions (i.e., religious, dietary) and participant needs. The event must be based on the overall needs and desires of the target market.

The most valuable outcome a special event can generate for a community is positive word of mouth. In order to create this positive awareness, an organizer recognizes that the event cannot appeal to all markets. A promoter will determine the target market for the community's event.

Target marketing is defined as clearly identifying who wants to attend a certain type of event. For example, a Justin Bieber concert has been determined to appeal to a young female audience between the ages of twelve and sixteen. To stage a profitable concert, promoters will direct their advertising dollars to that particular targeted audience. Subsequently, all promotional items will also be geared toward that age group.

Most communities know that a special event will have a positive economic impact on the community and the region. This has created competition to attract events. A city will commonly use inducements to lure the special event to the community. These inducements may include free entertainment space, security, parking, and even the "key to the city" to the celebrity providing the entertainment. A "city wide" is a commonly used term for those large events or conventions that impact the entire city. City wides are key to urban economics. When a large event or convention is hosted in a particular city, the economic effects are positive. Hotel rooms may completely sell out across the city, eateries are busy, and retail and cultural attractions may flourish due to the "city wide."

A successful event has two vital components. One is that the community is supportive of bringing the event to the city, and second is that the event meets the consumers' need. For example, every year on Labor Day weekend, New Orleans is host to a special event called "Southern Decadence." This three-day event, attended by over 125,000 gay and lesbian people, generates over $125 million for the city. New Orleans is probably one of the few communities in the United States that would be supportive of bringing such an event to its city.

PREPARING FOR THE SPECIAL EVENT

Basic operations for staging an event need to be established and include the following:

1. Secure a venue.
2. Obtain **permits**.
   a. Parade permits
   b. Liquor permits
   c. Sanitation permits
   d. Sales permits or licenses
   e. Fire safety permits
3. Involve **government agencies** where necessary (i.e., if using city recreation facilities, work with the department of parks and recreation).
4. Involve the health department if there will be food and beverage at the event.
5. Meet all relevant parties in person so that any misconceptions are cleared up early.
6. Secure all vendors and suppliers for the event.
7. Recognize the complexities of dealing with the public sector. Sometimes public agencies have a difficult time making decisions.
8. Recognize the logistics that a community must contend with for certain types of special events, such as street closures for a marathon.
9. Set up a security plan, which may include the security supplied by the venue and professional law enforcement. (Pay attention as to which security organization takes precedence.)
10. Secure liability insurance (the most vulnerable area are those liabilities attached to liquor and liquor laws).
11. Determine ticket prices if the special event involves ticketing.
12. Determine ticket sale distribution if the special event involves ticketing.

The type of special event being held will determine the degree of preparedness needed. The larger the event, the more involved the checklist. Preparedness should produce a profitable and well-managed event.

THE SPECIAL EVENT BUDGET

For any event to be considered a success, it must also be considered profitable. Profitability requires understanding the six key elements involved in the cost of an event. The basic items that make up the costs for a special event include the categories that follow.

Getting a Permit

San Diego, California's, event permitting process is fairly typical for most moderate-sized
cities. The city publishes a guide to indicate to
the event organizers what permits are necessary for their event. The city's Web site has a
planning guide and access to all of the forms
that might be required for any event.

Events or organized activities for 75 or
more people that involve street closures or
include event components requiring the coordination of a number of city departments or
other agencies such as the use of alcohol, on-
site cooking, food sales, or large-scale temporary structures typically are reviewed through
the Citywide Special Event Permit Process. Examples include festivals, parades, runs/walks,
farmer's markets, and other planned group
activities.

For an application to be considered complete, applicants must submit the following
minimum information required in sections of
the Citywide Special Event Permit Application
in sufficient detail that the material can be understood and assessed:

Host Organization Section (Complete)

Event Summary Section (Complete)

Event Infrastructure Section (All aspects that
relate to the specific event)

Operational Plan Section (All aspects that
relate to the specific event)

Site Plan/Route Map Section (Complete)

Community Outreach Section (Complete)

Insurance Section (Complete including all
required certificates of insurance and en-
dorsements)

Signature Section (Complete)

Any required documentation relevant to the
permit application processes and requirements set forth in the Special Events Planning Guide and Citywide Special

Event Permit Application (Complete)

Applicants are responsible for obtaining
all permits, authorization, and/or exemptions
required by other agencies with jurisdiction for
any element of the event (e.g., Alcohol Beverage Control Permits, Health Permits, California
Coast Guard, California Coastal Commission
approval, etc.).
http://www.sandiego.gov/specialevents/pdf/
planningguide.pdf

Rental Costs

Depending on the type of event, renting a facility such as a convention center or ground space to
put up a tent requires payment of a daily rental charge. Convention centers usually sell the space
based on a certain dollar amount per square footage used. Most facilities charge for space even on
the move-in and move-out days. Multiday events can usually negotiate a discount.

There are, of course, variations to the rental cost of event space. If, for example, an association is holding a conference in a hotel, the event space may be free of charge or offered at a
reduced rate if a certain number of hotel rooms are booked by the participating group. Furthermore, if the group requires food and beverage, then often the rental space is provided at a reduced
rate or complimentary with the establishment of a **food and beverage minimum**.

Security Costs

Most convention centers, rental halls, and hotels provide limited security. This could mean that
a guard is stationed at the front and rear entrances of the venue. Depending on the type of event,
such as a rock concert performed by a band that has raucous fans, more security may be required.
European Soccer (Football) matches require even more security. Actual costs will depend on the
city and the amount of security needed.

Production Costs

These are the costs associated with staging an event. The costs vary depending on the type
of special event. For example, if the special event is a large home and garden show, there are
costs associated with the setup of the trade show booths. As with many home and garden
shows, exhibitors bring in elaborate garden landscapes that are very time consuming and

labor intensive to set up and break down. Labor costs for decorators need to be calculated to estimate the production costs based on the type and size of trade show booth. There are also electrical and water fees needed for a home and garden show, and these costs must be included in the production costs. Other production costs include signage or banners for each booth and pipe and drape fees.

Labor Costs

The city where the special event is being held will affect the labor costs involved in the setup and breakdown of the event. Some cities are unionized, and this can add higher costs to an event because of the higher wages. Holding an event in very strict union cities means that the organizer of the event must leave more of the handling to the union crew. In some cities, the union allows the exhibitor to wheel his or her own cart with brochures and merchandise. In other cities, exhibitors cannot carry anything other than their own briefcases.

When selecting a city for an event, the role of unions has been an important influence. Most special event organizers will pass the higher costs on to the exhibitor or will increase ticket prices.

Marketing Costs

The costs associated with attracting attendees can make up a large portion of the budget. Here, the event organizer examines the best means of reaching the target market. Trying to reach a mass audience may mean running a series of television commercials, which can be very expensive. Most event organizers use a combination of promotions to attract the attendee. There will be elements of advertising, direct marketing, publicity and public relations, sales promotion, interactive or Internet marketing, and personal selling. All of these need to be budgeted.

Talent Costs

Virtually all special events use some type of talent or performers. They may include keynote speakers, band or orchestra, sports teams, vocalists, animals, and so on. While the organizer may have grandiose thoughts about the quality of the talent used, price has to be considered and matched to the special event budget. The high school class reunion probably cannot afford to have Jennifer Lopez or Taylor Swift perform.

Before an event, it is essential that an event professional do a projection of all costs and revenue. These projections are essential to whether a community will host another event. Repeat events are much easier to promote, especially when the organizers have made a profit. Before and during the event, it is critical that billing updates are completed and presented to the client on a regular (sometimes daily) basis. Any discrepancies or new costs should be handled at the point they occur. There should be no cost surprises at the end of an event.

BREAKDOWN OF THE SPECIAL EVENT

Special events have one thing in common: They all come to an end! Breaking down the event usually involves a number of steps. Once the attendees have gone, there are a variety of closing tasks that an organizer must complete.

First, the parking staff should expedite the flow of traffic away from the event. In some cases, community police are able to assist in traffic control.

A debriefing of staff should take place to determine what did or did not happen at the event. There may be issues pending that will need documentation. It is always best to have written reports to refer to for next year's event. Consider having the following sources add information to the report:

1. *Participants:* Interview some of the participants from the event. A customer's perception and expectation is an invaluable insight.
2. *Media and the Press:* Ask why it was or was not a press-worthy gathering.
3. *Staff and Management:* Get a variety of staff and other management involved in the event to give feedback.

4. *Vendors:* They also have a very unique perspective on how the event could be improved. Exhibitors and vendors MUST complete a survey. Because of their great perspective, exhibitors can provide some outstanding and constructive feedback for planning the next event.

The following should also be included in a final report on the event:

1. Finalize the income and expense statement. Did the event break even, make a profit, or experience a loss?
2. Finalize all contracts from the event. Fortunately, almost everything involved with putting together the event will have written documentation. Compare final billing with actual agreements for any discrepancies.
3. Send the media a final press release on the overall success of the event. Interviews with the press could be arranged. This could be especially newsworthy if the event generated significant revenues for the community.
4. Provide a written thank you for those volunteers who were involved with the event in any way. A celebration of some sort with the volunteers may be in order, especially if the event was financially and socially successful.

Once the elements of breakdown have taken place, the organizers can examine the important lessons of staging the event. What would they do or not do next year?

FUTURE TRENDS

The twenty-first century brings some evolving ideas into special events. The following are some noteworthy thoughts from special event planners, designers, and coordinators:

- Less is the new more. Clients are seeking the simple with a "flare."
- Clients want to appear to be responsible in their spending. Excessive overspending is no longer the desirable trend.
- "Stylish minimalism" refers to the idea that clients still want style, flare, and innovation in the overall event but choose to uphold a conservative budgetary perception.
- Quality is paramount, at a cost that the client sees as a "value."
- Frivolous events are seen as wasteful; events should have a purpose.
- Many events are now targeted toward service or charitable causes. This provides purpose to an event. Events may be targeted toward medical concerns (i.e., cancer research, heart disease, autism awareness, etc.) or toward relief on a national or international level (Haiti Relief, Hurricane Katrina Relief, etc.).
- Clients are looking for an entire "package"—an experience. The event planner is truly planning an experience—often referred to as "experience management." Some event planners believe that a good event should captivate the audience and offer "change" every half hour.
- Going green—environmentally, event professionals are urged to consider green solutions. Earthy, environmentally friendly efforts are becoming the expectation. Interestingly, because of the perceived lack of sophistication, "eco-friendly" efforts are more likely to be incorporated into an event, rather than a primary means of service. For example, recycled coffee cups may be offered at a coffee station, along with china cups and saucers.
- Technology is key in promotional efforts. More Internet promotions are desired, as event managers are able to quantify the number of "hits" that they receive on their promotional initiative.
- Technology will also impact the meeting space. Google Glass has the opportunity to create a more personal, staged, and shared attendee experience.
- Gamification—adding games to the meeting/event mix can create a healthy competition and measurable ROI for your events.
- Every client has his/her own unique set of needs and wants. Every client wants the undivided attention of the event professional; his/her needs must be recognized throughout the entire planning and execution of the event.
- Quality, cost, and relationship are three components that must be in balance for every special event.
- Face-to-face events are here to stay.

Summary

Creating a memorable event requires that an organizer meet and exceed an attendee's expectations. Recognizing that the special event could be for a meeting or convention, a parade, a festival, a fair, or an exhibit requires understanding the objectives of the event. Having the planning tools in place is the keystone for success in managing the gathering. Special events management works with and understands the community infrastructures to help support the event.

It can be costly if in advance an event professional does not decide which part of the promotional mix model of the event is used. The promotional mix model includes advertising, direct marketing, interactive or Internet marketing, sales promotion, publicity and public relations, and personal selling. Helping to defray costs by seeking sponsorships for a special event is another way to successfully market an event, and it is also an important marketing tool for the corporation sponsor.

Generating and working with the local and or national media is the most effective way for attracting attendance. An organizer also needs to understand what makes for good media coverage, and whether it is for print or broadcast. The target market for the special event must always be considered in the objectives, the promotions, and the continuation of the event.

The basic operations and/or logistics for the event follow the planning and promoting. A checklist of the items that need to be handled or looked into is a must for any event professional. Event professionals should also create checklists that will help develop the overall special event budget. This budget requires regular reviews of the statement of revenues and expenditures. The breakdown is the final step and includes another checklist for the closure of the event. Always remember your volunteers—without them, the event would not take place!

Key Words and Terms

For definitions, see GLOSSARY, or http://glossary.conventionindustry.org

agenda	food and beverage minimums	meetings, expositions, events and conventions (MEEC)	promotional mix model
community infrastructure	Gantt Chart		schedule
fairs, festivals, and public events	government agencies	permit	venue

Review and Discussion Questions

1. Discuss the types of events that a city might host.
2. What does the vision statement of an event provide for an organizer?
3. Discuss the importance of the event professionals' client relationship in event planning.
4. Discuss the types of planning tools that aid in successful event management.
5. What are the distinctive roles of the promotional mix model?
6. What are the benefits for sponsorships at a special event?
7. What are some tips for working with broadcast media?
8. What are some basic operations for staging an event?
9. Discuss costs associated with the event budget.
10. Outline the elements of breakdown for a special event.
11. Consider special event opportunities for your community. How would you offer advice as an event professional to encourage attendance?

About the Chapter Contributor

David Smiley received his M.S. degree in Hospitality & Tourism Management from the University of Central Florida and holds a Bachelor of Science degree from the Pennsylvania State University in Recreation and Park Management. He is a Lecturer in the School of Public Health at Indiana University Bloomington after serving 22 years in the industry, including 10 years with Rosen Hotels & Resorts. He also serves as the advisor to the school's student chapter of the Event Planning Association and is the advisor to the Tourism and Event Management Club.

Previous Edition Chapter Contributor

Joy Dickerson, WidenerUniversity.
Cynthia Vannucci, Metropolitan State College in Denver.

Planning and Producing MEEC Gatherings

Planning and organizing an international convention is a function of the MEEC Industry. *Designer_Andrea/Fotolia*

Chapter Objectives

This chapter provides the reader with an understanding of the following:

- The differences in association and corporate meeting planning
- The motivations that influence meeting objectives
- Writing clear and concise meeting objectives using the *SMART* technique
- The purpose of a needs analysis
- The process of site selection
- The information needed on an RFP
- Establishing budgetary goals
- The importance of evaluation
- The process of registration for a meeting or event
- The process of arranging housing for a meeting or event
- The elements of a meeting and event specification guide
- The importance of a pre- and post-convention meeting

INTRODUCTION

A meeting/event professional or organizer may be familiar with all of the elements of the MEEC industry. However, it takes good planning, organizing, directing, and control to put these diverse elements together and "make it work." In order to accomplish this, the organizer needs to understand the group, its wants, and its needs: Who are they? Why are they here? Then objectives can be set that will guide the program delivery to meet these wants and needs while staying within budget constraints. It should be noted that this chapter on planning and producing MEEC gatherings only touches upon the major issues involved. There are two new textbooks available that go into more detail. They are meant to be read in sequence: The first is *Planning and Management of Meetings, Expositions, Events and Conventions*, while the second is *Production and Logistics in Meetings, Expositions, Events and Conventions*. Both are by the author of this text, George G. Fenich, PhD. This chapter will focus more on the planning of meetings and somewhat less on producing meetings/events: The reader is reminded that the "process" and steps of planning are the same for any event, whether business or leisure oriented.

SETTING OBJECTIVES

Creating Meeting and Event Objectives

The first thing a meeting/event professional needs to determine is (1) Who is the group? and (2) What is the objective of this event? These simple questions are the basis of much of the planning process. An *objective* is defined as something strived for or accomplished and also as being the goal or aim. All meetings and events should begin with clear, concise, and measurable objectives. Objectives are the basis for virtually all components of the planning process, whether it is for corporate meetings, association meetings, special events, exhibitions (formerly referred to as trade shows), or virtual meetings held via the Internet. The objective of the meeting will impact site selection, food and beverage (F&B) requirements, transportation issues, communication channels, and especially program content.

Most people attend meetings for three reasons: education, networking, and to conduct business. Some people participate in association **annual meetings** for the networking and educational offerings. Others may attend primarily to develop business relationships and to generate leads or make sales. If the meeting/event professional does not design the program content and scheduling to accommodate these objectives, then the attendees may become dissatisfied.

Another key point is that program planning, especially for association meetings, begins months or years before the actual event. The average meeting attendee does not understand how much effort goes into planning even simple events, let alone something as complex as an association's annual meeting and trade show/exhibition. As with much of the hospitality industry, the real work goes on behind the scenes, and unless something goes wrong, the attendees are blissfully unaware of the planning process and the coordination and cooperation necessary to produce an event. The meeting/event professional and the support staff should be invisible to the attendee.

Good meeting objectives should focus on the attendees. What will make the attendees want to attend the meeting? What will be their **return on investment (ROI)**? What makes the event more desirable than that of a competitor? The following are some of the key meeting planning components that are directly affected by the meeting objectives.

IMPORTANCE OF EDUCATION

A key component of MEEC is to provide an environment conducive to education. Sponsors of meetings are increasingly cost-conscious with the planning and implementation of their events and have high expectations for the ROI achieved by employees or association members. Poor planning in logistics or in program content can spell disaster for the meeting/event professional. Gone are the days when conventions were viewed as primarily recreational events and expense accounts were plentiful. If the actual benefits of attending the meeting cannot be justified, then funding to attend or membership fees for an association may be withheld. In cases where the attendee is paying out of his or her own pocket to attend, good program content becomes a much more critical issue. People are usually much more careful with their own money than with someone else's. It is a fact that attendee expectations are seldom lowered. If child care and all meals are provided in one year, then the same (or better) services are expected the subsequent year. It is a constant challenge for the meeting/event professional to continuously improve the content and execution of meetings and conventions while keeping the price of attendance affordable.

Professional Certifications

Increasingly, people within a particular industry seek to differentiate themselves by becoming "certified" or "licensed" in a specific skill or to recognize that they have achieved a certain level of competence in a career field. Most people cannot afford the luxury of quitting their job to go back to school for academic instruction. Instead, they rely on their professional associations to provide current information and continuing education in their particular field. Programs may be offered at the annual convention, at regional seminars, or through distance education over the Internet, such as online classes and webinars. Individuals receive **continuing education units (CEUs)** for each workshop they attend, and these CEUs will be a part of the qualifications to become certified or licensed or renew a certificate or license. Physicians are a good example. To retain their medical license, doctors are required to take a certain amount of **continuing medical education (CME)** courses to keep current with innovations in health care. The MEEC industry also has numerous professional certifications (see Chapter 1).

NEEDS ANALYSIS

As part of setting objectives for a meeting, a needs analysis must be undertaken. A **needs analysis** is a method of determining the expectations for a particular meeting. A needs analysis can be as simple as asking senior management what they want to accomplish at a meeting and then designing the event around those expectations. It should be remembered that the needs of corporate and association meeting attendees are very different (see Chapter 2). The first step is to know the attendees by asking the question "Who are they?" A meeting/event professional must collect demographic information of both past and prospective attendees. This is much easier for an annual event, such as an association meeting or corporate management meeting. The meeting/event professional keeps a detailed **group history** of who attended the meeting, their likes and dislikes, and all pertinent information that can be used to improve future meetings. Questions to consider include the following:

- What is the age and gender of past attendees?
- What is their level of expertise—beginner, intermediate, advanced?
- What is their position within the organization's hierarchy—new employee, junior management, or senior management?
- What hotel amenities are preferred—indoor pools, spas, tennis courts, exercise rooms, wireless Internet access?
- Are there specific dietary restrictions for attendees (i.e., Kosher, Muslim, vegetarian, diabetic, gluten-free, food allergies, etc., or other medical dietary needs)?
- Who is paying the expenses? Most people are more cost-conscious if they are paying out of their own pocket rather than a company expense account.
- Will meeting attendees bring guests or children to the event?
- Are networking opportunities important?
- How far are attendees willing to travel to attend the meeting?
- Will international guests who require interpreters attend?
- Are special accommodations needed for people with disabilities?
- What are the educational outcomes expected at the meeting?

Some of this information can be answered by questions on the event registration form. Other information can be obtained through association membership or company records. Most meeting/event professionals do some type of evaluation after an event to provide feedback that can be used to improve the next meeting. This is covered later in this chapter.

DEVELOPING *SMART* OBJECTIVES

Once the meeting/event professional has determined the needs of the attendees and the sponsoring organization, objectives must be written in a clear and concise format so that all parties involved in the planning process understand and are focused on common goals. A common method of writing effective meeting objectives is to use the **SMART** approach. Each letter of the SMART approach reminds the meeting/event professional of critical components of a well-written objective.

Specific: Only one major concept is covered per objective.

Measurable: Must be able to quantify or measure that objectives have or have not been achieved.

Achievable: Is it possible to accomplish the objective?

Relevant: Is the objective important to the overall goals of the organization?

Time-related: The objective should include when the objective must be completed.

It is also good to begin meeting objectives with an action verb (e.g., *achieve, promote, understand, design*) and include cost factors if applicable. List by name of the person or department responsible for achieving the objectives.

Examples of Meeting Objectives

- The Meetings Department of the International Association of Real Estate Agents will "generate attendance of 7,500 people at the 2018 annual meeting to be held in Orlando, FL."
- The Education Committee of the National Association for Catering Executives (NACE) will "create a NACE professional certification program by the 2018 annual meeting."
- The Brettco Pharmaceutical Corporation will "hold a two-day conference, October 2 and 3 in Chicago, Illinois, for the 12 regional sales managers to launch five new product introductions for 2018. Total meeting costs are not to exceed $15,000."
- Jill Miller will "complete the graphic design for the convention program by May 3, 2018."

Designing well-written meeting objectives can be a very positive activity for the meeting/event professional. Objectives serve as signals to keep the planning process focused and on track. At the end of the meeting, the meeting/event professional can communicate to management what goals were achieved or exceeded, or what was not achieved and why. If objectives are met, it helps demonstrate the ROI that the meeting/event professional provides to the organization. If objectives are not met, then management can focus resources on finding out the causes of failure and correcting them for the next meeting.

SITE SELECTION

The site selection process can begin after meeting objectives are developed. The objectives will guide the meeting/event professional in deciding the physical location for the event, type of facility to use, transportation options, and many other meeting components. Depending on the type of meeting, site selection may take place days, weeks, months, or years before the actual event. For major conventions, a city is usually selected three to ten years in advance. Some large associations, such as the American Library Association, have determined meeting sites (cities) decades into the future. However, small corporate meetings usually have a much shorter lead time of a few weeks or months.

Contrary to popular belief, the association meeting professional is usually not the final decision maker when it comes to which city will be selected to host a convention. Typically, determining the actual site selection is a group decision made by a volunteer committee, with much input from the board of directors and the association staff. The meeting professional will review numerous reference materials, talk with other meeting/event professionals, and may make recommendations but usually does not personally make the final decision. The corporate meeting/event professional may have more influence over site selection, especially for smaller meetings. But for larger corporate meetings, the CEO or chairman of the board may make the decision. Sometimes, locations are chosen because of the availability of recreational activities like golf, shopping, or spa, not because the meeting facilities are outstanding. It differs with each organization.

Meeting/event professionals are regularly bombarded with site selection information. There are several trade publications like *Successful Meetings, Meetings and Conventions, Convene,* and *Corporate Meetings and Incentive Travel* that meeting/event professionals may subscribe to for low or no cost. Most are available online in addition to traditional print versions. There is an extensive *Trade Show Venue Directory* available online at the Trade Show News Network (TSNN). The magazines are either independently owned or are affiliated with one of the major meetings-related professional associations, such as the Professional Convention Management Association (PCMA) and Meeting Professional International (MPI). The magazines are funded through advertising sales from hotel chains, transportation companies, convention facilities, and many other service providers to the meetings/events industry. Other key advertisers are the actual locations competing for the convention dollar. The destination marketing organizations (DMOs), which represent locations around the world, may create multiple print or online marketing tools to promote regions ("Meetings on the Gulf Coast"), individual cities ("San Antonio Meeting/Event Professionals Guide"), states ("Conventions in California"), and countries ("The Korean Connection: Asia's Convention Destination"). These special advertising media can showcase local culture, attractions, and facilities; provide testimonials of past events; utilize streaming video for visual appeal; and serve to entice the meeting/event professional to consider their location. Other special supplements are designed to showcase other characteristics, such as "Second-Tier Cities," "Unique Venues," "Meetings on College Campuses," "Cruise Ship Conventions," "Affordable Meetings," or "Golf Destinations."

Large travel expos such as IMEX in Frankfurt, Germany, or IMEX America held in Las Vegas, Nevada, are also great opportunities for meeting/event professionals to gather information about possible locations for their meetings and events. They employ a "hosted buyer" strategy where the exhibitors pay for the travel expenses of the meeting/event professionals (buyers) in return for guaranteed appointments (see Chapter 5, "Exhibitions," for more information on IMEX and the hosted buyer concept).

Other factors to consider in site selection are the rotation of locations and the location of the majority of the attendees. In the United States, the meeting/event professional may want to "rotate" their conventions and hold a major convention in the East (Boston) one year, the South (New Orleans) the next, the West (San Francisco) the third year, and the Midwest (Chicago) the fourth year. This allows attendees to enjoy a wide variety of meeting locations, and attendees who live on one side of the country are not always traveling many hours and through several time zones to attend the meeting. But if most of the attendees live on the East Coast, it may be preferable to hold the meeting in a city conveniently located there. However, some conventions, such as the National Association of Broadcasters, MAGIC Marketplace, International Builder's Show, or the Consumer Electronics Show, are so large that they are extremely limited to their choice of cities due to the amount of sleeping rooms, meeting, and exhibition space required.

Cost is another consideration. In addition to the costs incurred by the meeting/event professional for meeting space and other essentials, the cost to the attendee should be considered. Some cities, mostly first-tier cities, are notoriously expensive for people to visit (the average daily

The Links at Spanish Bay, part of the famous Pebble Beach Golf Resort, is often chosen as a site for small meetings and incentive trips. *George G. Fenich*

rate [ADR] in New York City is over $500 per night). It all depends on what is important to the attendees—cost or location. Another option is to hold a meeting in a first-tier city at a first-class property in the off-season or during slow periods, such as around major holidays. Most hotels discount prices when business is slow. As witnessed by the global economic downturn that began in 2008, most hotels had to reduce their rates to attract a shrinking volume of MEEC gatherings. As economies and the willingness to spend money on travel continue to improve, it can be expected that rates for many services will rise.

The mode of travel is another factor in site selection. How will the attendees get to the location? Air? Road? Rail? In recent years, most major airline carriers have been struggling to survive, resulting in a number of mergers and acquisitions in the industry. Many people are still cautious about flying due to terrorism threats, the ordeal of getting through security at airports, packed airplanes, additional baggage fees, food charges, and a host of other challenges that make air travel distasteful. The availability of flights (**air lift**) can also be an important consideration in site selection. Those cities with the greatest number of flights include Chicago, Atlanta, Dallas, and Washington, DC. There are some cities that are convention destinations (have a convention center) and have no air lift, including Anchorage, Alaska; Huntington, West Virginia; Davenport, Iowa; and Wheeling, West Virginia.

The type of hotel or meeting facility is another major consideration. There are a variety of choices, including metropolitan hotels, suburban hotels, airport hotels, resort hotels, and casino hotels. In addition, there are facilities especially designed to hold meetings called "conference centers." The **International Association of Conference Centers** is an association in which the member facilities must meet a list of over thirty criteria to be considered an approved conference center. Visit their Web site for more information. Other options are full-service convention centers, cruise ships, and university campuses. These facilities are discussed at length in Chapter 4, "Meeting and Convention Venues."

Meeting space requirements are also critical in the site selection process. How many meeting or banquet rooms will be needed? How much space will staff offices, registration, and prefunction areas require? Floor plans with room dimensions are readily available in the facilities' sales brochures or on their Web sites. Good diagrams will also provide ceiling heights, seating capacities, entrances and exits, and location of columns and other obstructions. Most major hotel chain Web sites will provide direct links to their hotels and their specification information.

REQUEST FOR PROPOSAL

Once the meeting objectives are clearly defined and the basic location and logistics are drafted, the meeting professional creates a **Request for Proposal (RFP)**. The RFP is a written description of all the major needs for the meeting. The **Convention Industry Council (CIC)**, a federation of over thirty MEEC industry associations, has created a standardized format that may be used. It is copyright free.

Once the RFP is completed, it is disseminated to hotel properties and convention facilities that may be interested in submitting a bid for that meeting. Typically, the meeting/event professional can submit the RFP via the Internet directly to preferred hotels and the DMO or **Convention and Visitor Bureaus (CVBs)** of desirable cities for distribution to all properties, or can submit it to the DMAI Web site. Some hotel chains, such as Hyatt, guarantee a response to an RFP within twenty-four hours of receipt. The RFP also serves to allow hotels to examine the potential economic impact of the meeting and decide whether or not to create a bid for it. DMAI offers members an economic impact calculator. If the group has limited resources and can only afford an $89 room rate, then major luxury hotels may not be interested in the business. However, smaller properties or hotels in second-tier cities may be very interested in hosting the event. If a meeting facility decides to submit a proposal, then the sales department will review the meeting specifications and create a response.

Fam trips (familiarization trips) are another method of promoting a destination or particular facility to a meeting/event professional. Fam trips are a no- or low-cost trip for the meeting/event professional to personally review sites for their suitability for a meeting or event. These trips may be arranged by the local DMO or CVB or by the hotel directly. During the fam trip, the hotel or convention facility tries to impress the meeting/event professional by showcasing its property, amenities, services, and overall quality. Throughout the visit, the meeting/event professional should visit all F&B outlets, visit recreational areas, see a variety of sleeping rooms, check all meeting space, monitor the efficiency of the front desk and other personnel, note the cleanliness and overall appearance of the facility, and if possible meet with key hotel personnel. A seasoned meeting/event professional always has a long list of questions to ask. A lot depends on the selection of hotel. Make a mistake, and the whole meeting could be in jeopardy.

Once the meeting/event professional has reviewed the RFPs and conducted any necessary site visits, then the negotiations between the meeting/event professional and the sales department at a facility can begin. This process can be quite complex, and careful records of all communications, concessions, and financial expectations should be well documented.

BUDGETARY CONCERNS

Following the objectives, budgetary issues are usually the next major consideration in planning a meeting or event. How much will it cost to produce the event? Who will pay? How much will attendees be charged for registration, if anything? What types of F&B events are planned, and what will be served? Will meals be provided free or at an additional cost to the attendee? What additional revenue streams are available to produce and promote the meeting? Are sponsorships possible? If the event is being held for the first time, the meeting/event professional will have to do a lot of estimation of expenses and potential revenues. An event that is repeated benefits by having some historical data to compare and project costs. The basis for a meeting budget can be developed by establishing financial goals, identifying expenses, and identifying revenue sources.

Step 1: Establish Financial Goals

Financial goals are important and should incorporate SMART. They may be set by the meeting/event professional, association management, or by corporate mandate. Basically, what are the financial expectations of the event? Not every meeting or event is planned for profit. For example, an awards ceremony held by a company to honor top achievers represents a cost to the company. No profit is expected. Similarly, a corporate sales meeting may not have a profit motive. The ultimate goal of the meeting may be to determine how to increase business and thus "profit," but the meeting itself is not a profit generator; it is an expense for the company. Most association meetings, on the other hand, rely heavily on conventions to produce operating revenue for the association (see Chapter 2 for more details). For most associations, the annual meeting (and often accompanying trade show) is the second highest revenue producer after membership dues. The financial goal for an annual meeting may be based on increases or decreases in membership, general economic trends, political climate, competing events, location of the event, and many other influences. For any event, there are three possible financial goals:

- *Break-even:* revenue collected from all activities cover the expenses. No profit is expected.
- *Make profit:* revenues collected exceed expenses.
- *Deficit:* expenses exceed revenues.

Step 2: Identify Expenses

It is suggested that expenses be categorized by their different functions:

- **Indirect costs** should be listed as overhead or administrative line items in a program budget. These are expenses of the organization not directly related to the meeting, such as staff salaries, overhead, or equipment repair.
- **Fixed costs** are expenses incurred regardless of the number of attendees, such as meeting room rental or audiovisual equipment. The event professional could even set a specific dollar amount for profit as a fixed cost.
- **Variable costs** are those expenses that can vary based on the number of attendees (e.g., F&B).

Expenses will vary according to the overall objectives of the meeting and will be impacted by location, season, type of facility, services selected, and other factors. For example, a gallon of Starbucks coffee in San Francisco at a luxury hotel may cost $80 or more. A gallon of coffee at a moderate-priced hotel in Oklahoma City may only cost $25 or less.

Step 3: Identify Revenue Sources

There are many ways to fund meetings and events. Corporations include meeting costs in their operating budgets. The corporate meeting/event professional must work within the constraints of what is budgeted. Associations usually have to be a bit more creative in finding capital to plan and implement an event. Associations have to justify the cost of the meeting with the expected ROI of the attendee. It can be quite expensive to attend some association meetings. Consider a hypothetical example of one person attending an association annual meeting: transportation ($400), accommodations for three nights ($600), F&B ($300), registration fee ($500), and miscellaneous ($100), for a total of $1,900. Depending on the city and association, this amount could easily double. It is a complex process to create an exceptional and affordable event. If the registration fee is too high, people will not attend. If it is too low, the organization may not achieve revenue expectations. But there are more possible sources of funding available other than registration fees. These include the following:

- Corporate or association funding
- Private funding from individuals
- Exhibitor fees (if incorporating a trade show/exhibition)
- Sponsorships
- Selling logo merchandise
- Advertising fees, such as banners or ads in the convention program
- Local, state, or national government assistance
- Selling banner ads or links on the official Web site or on social media platforms
- Renting membership contact lists for marketing purposes
- Establishing "official partnerships" with other companies to promote their products for a fee or percentage of their revenues
- Contributions in cash or in-kind (services or products)

Estimating expenses and revenues can be accomplished by first calculating a break-even analysis—in other words, how much revenue must be collected to cover expenses.

COST CONTROL

To stay within budget and reach the financial objectives, it is important to exercise cost control measures. Cost control measures are tools for monitoring the budget. A large event for thousands of people may be managed by only a few meeting planning staff. The opportunities for costly mistakes are rampant. The most important factor is to make sure that the facility understands which person from the sponsoring organization has the authority to make additions or changes to what has been ordered. Typically, the CEO and the meeting planning staff are the only ones who have this "**signing authority**." For example, an association board member may have an expensive dinner in the hotel restaurant and say "put it on the association's bill." The restaurant cannot do so without the approval of a person who has signing authority. This helps keep unexpected expenses to a minimum.

Another cost control measure is to accurately estimate the number of meals that will be served. The **guarantee** is the amount of food that the meeting/event professional has instructed the facility to prepare and will be paid for. If the meeting/event professional estimates 500 people will attend a dinner and only 300 show up, the meeting/event professional is responsible for the 200 uneaten dinners—an expensive waste of money. This is covered in depth in Chapter 10, "Food and Beverage."

CONTROL IN MEEC

Creating and implementing most meetings is a team effort. Many meeting/event professionals will conduct an evaluation after each meeting to obtain feedback from the attendees, exhibitors, facility staff, outsourced contractors, and anyone else involved in the event. Individual sessions may be evaluated to determine whether speakers did a good job and whether the education was appropriate. Overall, evaluations may collect data on such things as the comfort of the hotel, ease of transportation to the location, desirability of location, quality of F&B, special events and networking opportunities, and number and quality of exhibitors at a trade show convention. This information may be collected by a written questionnaire after the event as well as by telephone, association or corporate Web site, or Web-based collection methods. One of the fastest and least expensive is to broadcast an e-mail with a link to the questionnaire. Many software packages are available that will design, distribute, collect data, and tabulate results for you. No special knowledge of statistics is required. Programs range from no cost such as SurveyMonkey to several hundred dollars such as SurveyPro. The data concerning speakers and logistics will assist the meeting/event professional and program planning committee to improve the programming for subsequent years.

The use of electronic **audience response systems** (ARS) has gained in popularity as costs for renting the equipment or purchasing software has dropped significantly. ARS allow meeting/event professionals to survey a variety of stakeholders via handheld devices or a "smartphone app" that transmits information to the meeting/event professional in real time. This allows the meeting/event professional to make adjustments to the meeting while it is still going on and can provide valuable data for future events.

Just as in setting good objectives, the meeting/event professional must first determine what is to be evaluated. For example: What information is needed, who will utilize it, and how will the results be communicated to those who participate in the evaluation? Evaluations can be time-consuming and expensive to design and implement. Unfortunately, some of the data collected by meeting/event professionals are often filed away and not used appropriately—especially if the results are negative toward the event. No board of directors or CEO wants to hear that the site they selected to hold a meeting did not meet attendees' expectations. However, negative comments may ultimately turn into a favorable marketing tool. If the attendees indicate they did not like the location of the meeting (Chicago in February), then by selecting a warmer climate (Palm Springs) for the next meeting, the meeting/event professional can promote how much the attendees' opinions matter and that the organization will follow the directives of the attendees.

Designing the Evaluation

A good evaluation form is simple, concise, and can be completed in a minimal amount of time. An evaluation for a meeting can be a single sentence: "Was this meeting a good use of your time?" Response options can be "Yes" or "No." This would be good for short departmental meetings or training sessions. For larger events with multiple sessions and activities, a more in-depth evaluation is called for. A good source for questions can be to review your event goals and objectives. If the meeting is an annual event, it is important to ask similar questions each year so that data may be collected and analyzed over time.

Timing is also an issue with administering evaluations. If data is collected on-site during or immediately after an event, it may increase the response rate. The meeting/event professional can remind attendees to complete and return evaluations before moving on to the next session. Other meeting/event professionals prefer to wait a few days to ask for feedback. This gives the attendee time to digest what actually occurred at the meeting and form an objective opinion when not clouded by the excitement of the event.

The process of evaluating a meeting should begin in the early stages of meeting planning and tie in with the meeting objectives. Costs for development, dissemination, analysis, and reporting should be included in the meeting budget. The evaluation serves as a valuable component of a meeting's history by recording what worked or did not work for a particular event. It is a cyclical process whereby the evaluation results feed directly into next year's meeting objectives. Committees plan most large meetings. Evaluation results are the means by which information is passed from one committee to the next.

PROGRAM IMPLEMENTATION

Once the basic objectives of the meeting have been identified, the site selected, and the budget set, the meeting program can be developed in detail. Some major concerns involved in this process are: Is the programming to be designed in a way that facilitates communication between departments within a corporation? Is the programming geared toward training new employees in the use of a particular computer system? Is the programming geared to educate the members of a professional association and lead toward a certification? To address these concerns, the meeting/ event professional must consider several factors, including the following:

- Program type
- Content, including track and level
- Session scheduling
- Speaker arrangements
- Refreshment breaks and meal functions
- Ancillary events
- Evaluation procedures

Program Types

Each type of program or session is designed for a specific purpose, which may range from providing information to all attendees, discussion of current events in small groups, hands-on training, and panel discussions. The following are typical descriptions of the major program types and formats.

GENERAL OR PLENARY SESSION A general or plenary session is primarily used as a venue to communicate with all conference attendees at one time in one location. Typically, the general session is what kicks off the meeting and includes welcoming remarks from management or association leadership; outlines the purpose or objectives of the meeting; introduces prominent officials; and recognizes major sponsors or others who helped plan the event, ceremonial duties, and other important matters of general interest. General sessions can last between 1 and 1.5 hours. Often, an important industry leader or a recognizable personality will give a **keynote address** that will help set the tone for the rest of the meeting. For a corporate meeting, this may be the CEO or the chairman of the board. An association may elect to hire a professional speaker in a particular subject area, such as business forecasting, political analysis, leadership and change, technology, or a topic that would be motivational to the audience. Many meeting/event professionals use highly recognizable political, sports, and entertainment personalities. These individuals are hired not because of their personal knowledge of the association and the various professions it represents but as a "hook" to attract people to come to the meeting. As a note, it is not uncommon to spend $75,000 to $100,000 or more (plus travel expenses) to hire a well-known sports or entertainment figure to speak at a general session. General sessions may also be held at the end of a convention to provide closure and summarize what was accomplished during the meeting or as a venue for presenting awards and recognizing sponsors. Attendance at closing general sessions is typically smaller than with opening sessions as people make travel plans to return home early.

CONCURRENT SESSION A concurrent session is a professional development or career enhancement session presented by a credentialed speaker who provides education on a specific topic in a conference-style format. Alternately, several speakers may form a panel to provide viewpoints on the topic at hand. Group discussions at individual tables may also be incorporated. Concurrent sessions typically serve groups of 150+ attendees, and several sessions may be offered simultaneously at a specific time. They typically last between 1 and 1.5 hours.

WORKSHOP OR BREAKOUT SESSIONS Workshops or breakouts are more intimate sessions that offer a more interactive learning experience in smaller groups. Participants may learn about the latest trends, challenges, and technologies of a specific field. These sessions are often presented by experienced members or peers of the association and may involve lectures, role-playing, simulation, problem solving, or group work. Workshop sessions usually serve groups of 150 or fewer attendees. These are the mainstay of any convention, and dozens or even hundreds of workshops may be offered throughout the course of the event, depending on the size of the meeting. A large association, such as the American Library Association, has more than 1,000 workshop sessions at its annual convention. Workshops typically last from fifty minutes to an hour.

ROUNDTABLE DISCUSSION GROUPS Roundtables are small, interactive sessions designed to cover specific topics of interest. Basically, eight to twelve attendees convene around a large round table, and a facilitator guides discussion about the topic at hand. Typically, several roundtable discussions will take place in one location, such as a large meeting room or ballroom. Attendees are free to join or leave a particular discussion group as desired. Roundtables can also be useful for continued and more intimate conversation with workshop speakers. The role of the facilitator is to keep the discussion on track and not allow any one attendee to monopolize the conversation. Roundtable discussion groups may also employ a **subject matter expert** to inform and moderate the group.

POSTER SESSIONS Poster sessions are another more intimate presentation method often used with academic or medical conferences. Rather than utilizing a variety of meeting rooms to accommodate speakers, panels or display boards are provided for presenters to display charts, photographs, a synopsis of their research, and so on for viewing. The presenter is scheduled to be at his or her display board at an appointed time so that interested attendees may visit informally and discuss the presentation.

Program Content

The average attendee will only be able to sit through three to six sessions on any given day. It is critical that the attendee be as well informed as possible about what each session will offer and the appropriateness of the session to his or her objectives for attending the meeting. For association meetings, programming objectives are developed months in advance and used extensively in marketing the convention to potential attendees. Program content is not a "one-size-fits-all" proposition. The content must be specifically designed to match the needs of the audience. A presentation on Basic Accounting 101 might be good for a junior manager but totally inappropriate for the chief financial officer. A good way to communicate to attendees how to select which programs to attend is to create tracks and levels. **Track** refers to separating programming into specific genres, such as computer skills, professional development, marketing, personal growth, legal issues, certification courses, or financial issues. A variety of workshops can be developed that concentrate on these specific areas. **Levels** refer to the skill level the program is designed for, whether it is beginning, intermediate, or advanced. Thus, the speaker who is assigned a session can develop content specifically tailored for a particular audience. Attendees can also determine if a session meets their level of expertise.

The following is an example of typical description of a session.

Session Description

Workshop 14: Effective Marketing through Social Media and E-Mail
Marketing:
Frank Wise, PhD
3:30 PM to 4:45 PM (1530–1645)
Room 314

With over 132 billion e-mail messages sent daily and billions of users on thousands of social media platforms, how can your company develop an effective marketing strategy to capitalize on these technologies? What are the most effective options to do so?

Attend this session to:

- Discover the top ten steps in developing effective electronic media marketing messages.
- Understand a variety of delivery platforms.
- Enhance your own effectiveness with social media.

Track: Marketing
Level: Intermediate

SESSION SCHEDULING

Timing is critical in program development. The meeting/event professional has to orchestrate every minute of every day to ensure that the meeting runs smoothly and punctually. Each day's agenda should be an exciting variety of activities that will stimulate attendees and make them want to attend the next meeting. One of the biggest mistakes meeting/event professionals make is double-booking events over the same time period. If a meeting/event professional schedules workshops from 8:00 AM to 1:00 PM and the tee time for the celebrity golf match is at 12:30 PM, then he or she stands to lose any of the attendees who want to attend the golfing event. Trade shows/exhibitions are another challenge. If workshops are scheduled at the same time that the trade show floor is open, attendees must choose between the two options. If attendees choose to attend the education sessions, the exhibitors will not get the traffic they expect. Conversely, if attendees go to the trade show rather than attend sessions, there may be empty meeting rooms and frustrated speakers.

Another major issue is allowing enough time for people to do what comes naturally. Do not expect to move 5,000 people from a general session into breakout sessions on the other side of the convention center in ten minutes. Plan thoughtfully. Allow sufficient time for people to use the restroom, check their e-mail, text messages, or voicemail, say "hello" to an old friend, and comfortably walk to their next workshop. If these delays are not planned for in advance, then there may be attendees disrupting workshop sessions by coming in late—or worse, by skipping sessions.

The following is a description of the schedule for an association meeting.

Typical Association Meeting Schedule

While no two conventions are the same, the following time line provides a good idea of a typical meetings flow.

Day One

8:00 AM. Staff office and pressroom area setup

Exhibition setup begins

Pre-convention meeting with facility staff

Registration set up

Day Two

8:00 AM. Association board meeting

Registration opens

Staff office opens

Exhibition setup continues

Set up for pre-convention workshops

1:00–4:00 PM. Pre-convention workshops (with break)

Various committee meetings

Program planning committee finalizes duties for meeting

5:00 PM. Private reception for board members and VIPs

7:00–9:30 PM. Opening reception

Day Three

6:30 AM. Staff meeting

8:00 AM. Registration opens

Coffee service begins

9:00 AM. General session

10:30 AM. Break

10:45 AM. Concurrent workshops

12:00–1:30 PM. Lunch

1:30–5:00 PM. Exhibition open

5:00 PM. Registration closes

Day Four

6:30 AM. Staff meeting

8:00 AM. Registration opens

Coffee service begins

9:00 AM–4:00 PM. Exhibition open

12:00–1:30 PM. Lunch provided on show floor

1:30–2:30 PM. Workshops

2:45–3:45 PM. Workshops

4:00–5:00 PM. Workshops

Teardown of trade show begins

5:00 PM. Registration closes

7:00 PM. Cocktail reception

8:00–10:00 PM. Banquet and awards ceremony

Day Five

7:00 AM. Staff meeting

8:00 AM. Registration opens

Trade show teardown continues

9:00–10:30 AM. Closing session

Pack up staff office

Pressroom closed

10:45 AM–12:00 PM. Program planning committee meets

12:00 PM. Registration closed

3:00 PM. Post-convention held with facility staff

REFRESHMENT BREAKS AND MEAL FUNCTIONS

As with scheduling workshops, it is important to provide time for attendees to eat and refresh themselves throughout the day. F&B functions can be quite expensive. But, depending on the objectives of the event, it may be more productive to feed attendees than have them wandering around a convention center or leaving the property to find something to eat. Refreshment breaks provide the opportunity to catch up with old friends, make business contacts, network, and grab a quick bite or reenergize with a cup of coffee or tea. Breaks and meals are excellent sponsorship opportunities. Companies gain attendee recognition by providing F&B. Attendees get fed and the host organization does not have to pay for it. Everybody wins!

Cocktail receptions and dinners provide their own set of challenges. Overindulgence in alcohol can not only be detrimental to the health of attendees but also has the potential to cause liability issues for the meeting/event professional. If alcoholic beverages are provided, facility staff should be trained as to when to stop serving individuals who have consumed too much. Provide lots of healthy snacks, and limit salty foods. There are a variety of ways the meeting/event professional can limit alcohol consumption. Drink tickets or a cash bar will greatly reduce consumption. Remember, hung-over attendees are not very focused!

SPEAKER ARRANGEMENTS

For large conventions, it is almost impossible for the meeting/event professional to independently arrange for all the different sessions and speakers. The meeting department often works together with the education department to develop the educational content of the meeting. In addition, a program committee comprised of industry leaders and those with special interests in education will volunteer to assist the meeting/event professional. These volunteers will work diligently to arrange what topics are appropriate for sessions and who the likely speakers might be. It is the job of the committee to be the gatekeeper of educational content. Subcommittees may be created to focus on finding a general session speaker, workshops, concurrent sessions, student member events, and so on.

VOLUNTEER SPEAKERS   Most associations cannot afford to pay all of the speakers at a large convention. A moderate-sized convention of 2,500 people may have 100 or more sessions offered at a three-day event. Remuneration for speakers may range from providing no assistance at all to paying a speaker fee and all expenses, such as the case with a paid general session speaker.

Benefits of Using Volunteer Speakers

- Reduces expenses (the person may already have budgeted to attend the meeting, so no housing or transportation costs are required)
- They are knowledgeable about important industry topics
- Popular industry leaders may increase attendance at sessions
- Builds relationships between speaker and event sponsor

Challenges of Using Volunteer Speakers

- May not adequately prepare for presentation
- May not be a good presenter, even if knowledgeable about topic
- May have a personal agenda; uses session to promote self or company

PAID SPEAKERS   A more expensive but often more reliable source of speakers is to contact one of the many speaker bureaus who represent thousands of potential speakers for your event. A **speaker bureau** is a professional talent broker who can help find the perfect speaker to match your event objectives and your budget. Typically, a speaker bureau has a stable of qualified professionals who can talk on whatever topic you desire. Fees and other amenities range from the affordable to the outrageous. If you are a small Midwestern association of county clerks, you are not going to be able to afford a world-famous athlete as your keynote speaker at your annual meeting. However, you might be able to afford a gold medal Olympian from the 1990s who can talk about teamwork and determination for a bargain price of $4,000.

Providing high-priced, popular, paid speakers will most likely increase attendance at your meeting. The smart way to provide such talent is to have the costs of the speaker sponsored by a key exhibitor or leader in the industry. The general session is a high-profile event, and it may be cost-effective for a company to fund the keynote speaker to promote itself to a

Sports stars are often used as keynote speakers in an effort to draw more attendees to a convention.
Cello Armstrong/Fotolia

maximum number of attendees. For example, a $30,000 speaker for a group of 5,000 attendees is only $6 per attendee. That may be less expensive than designing and distributing a traditional mailing!

Another source for speakers is local dignitaries, industry leaders, and university professors. As they are local, you will not incur transportation and lodging costs. In addition, their services are often free or very affordable. The local CVB or university can assist you in finding people who are willing to assist you. A small gift or honorarium is customary to thank these individuals for their time and effort.

Online Speaker Bureaus

Sources for well-known or affordable speakers can be found at a variety of Web sites. Speakers are separated into several categories based on subject matter and price. Streaming video is often available for you to view actual presentations online. Otherwise, the speaker bureau should be able to supply you with a recording of any person it represents. The best way to determine if a speaker is right for your audience is to attend an actual session and decide for yourself if he or she is worth the expense. The International Association of Speakers Bureaus or the National Speaker Bureau Association are good resources in locating a bureau to serve the needs of the organization.

SPEAKER GUIDELINES Speaker guidelines should be developed to inform the speakers (paid and nonpaid) of the logistics required to speak at an event as well as to clearly define the expectations of the organization. Speaker guidelines vary from one group to the next, but most should include the following:

- Background information about the association
- Date and location of meeting
- Special events or activities the speaker may attend
- Date, time, and location of speaker's room for presentation
- Presentation topic and duration
- Demographics and estimated number of attendees for the session
- Room set and audiovisual equipment requests and availability
- Request for short biography
- Names of other speakers, if applicable

- Remuneration policy
- Dress code
- Location of **speaker ready room**, where he or she can practice or relax prior to speaking
- Instructions for preparing abstracts or submitting final papers (typically for academic conferences)
- Instructions for having handouts available
- Transportation and lodging information
- Maps and diagrams of hotel or facility
- Deadlines for all materials that must be returned
- Hints for speaking to the group (i.e., attendees are very informal; attendees like time for questions and answers at the end of session)

It is not uncommon to include a variety of contractual agreements that must be signed by the speaker. These include:

Presenter Contract   This is a written agreement between the presenter and the sponsor to provide a presentation on a specific topic at a specific time. A contract should be used regardless of whether the speaker will be paid or not. The contract will verify in writing expenses that will be covered, the relationship between the two parties, promotional material needed to advertise the session, deadlines for audiovisual and handout materials, disclosure statements pertaining to any potential conflict of interest, selling or promoting products or services, penalties for failure to perform the presentation, and allowable conditions for termination of the contract.

Recording, Internet Authorization, and Waiver   If the session will be recorded in any digital format and made available on a Web site or online video platform, the speaker must be informed and must agree. Some speakers do not want their presentation materials to be accessed on the Internet, where they may be easily copied and used by others. Selling digital recordings of programs is an additional revenue stream for associations. Since attendees are limited in the number of sessions they can attend each day, by purchasing recordings of missed sessions, they can have the information from the sessions they missed. Additional information on the use of speakers, entertainers, and performers can be found in Chapter 9 of *Production and Logistics in Meetings, Expositions, Events and Conventions* by Fenich.

AUDIOVISUAL EQUIPMENT

Most hotels and meeting facilities do not allow meeting/event professionals to provide their own audiovisual equipment, such as LCD projectors, television monitors, and DVD players. The rental and servicing of this equipment is a huge revenue stream for facilities. Audiovisual equipment is extremely expensive to rent. In many instances, it costs as much to rent the equipment as it does to buy it. A 32-inch television, which may be purchased at a discount store for $350, may cost the meeting/event professional that amount in rental fees *each day*!

Thus, controlling audiovisual costs is very important. The event professional may wish to inform speakers that only an LCD projector and laptop computer are available. Thus, the speaker can craft his or her presentation to the media available. Another good idea is to provide speakers with a template to use in preparing overheads and handouts. You can request that all slides and handouts be developed with a certain font, such as Arial or Times New Roman, and dictate the text and background colors that should be used. Also provide a crisp logo for the organization or event. This will provide some uniformity in the "look" of your meeting.

Some attendees still expect traditional paper handouts at educational sessions. In an effort to reduce expenses and conserve resources, some groups have opted to put all handouts on a CD-ROM or flash drive and make it available free or for a nominal charge. Likewise, some groups will post all the handouts on their company Web site rather than distribute it at the meeting. Others will provide "print on demand" stations for those attendees who desire hard copy. If handouts will be used, remember to request a master copy well in advance of the meeting. You can e-mail the masters to a convenient copy shop at your destination and have everything printed and delivered to your meeting facility. Unfortunately, the fate of most handouts is to be thrown away at the hotel (too heavy to pack) or never referred to again.

MANAGING SPEAKERS ON SITE

For a large meeting with multiple speakers, keeping track of who is where and what is going on is a monumental task. Recruiting volunteers or hiring temporary staff to assist you will make a big difference. The worst thing that can happen is to have a speaker fail to show up for your meeting and the event professional does not realize it. Likewise, most speakers expect some sort of recognition for their time and effort. They want to feel "special."

A new trend is to develop "pre-convention" session activities so that attendees come better prepared to the education session. Social media such as Facebook, Twitter, LinkedIn, Pinterest, Google+, Tumblr, and blogs can be utilized months in advance for people to begin discussions on a topic. The speaker may facilitate discussion and will design the actual presentation based on what has transpired online. Similarly, some speakers will preassess the attendees to determine the level of knowledge of the group. After the session, attendees can be reassessed, and the amount of learning that occurred may be measured.

Ancillary Activities

There are a variety of activities that may be incorporated before, during, and after the actual scheduled program. In today's hectic business environment, many people try to squeeze a short vacation into their meeting schedule. More and more we are seeing husbands, wives, significant others, and children attending meetings as guests. Some meeting attendees tack on a few extra days at the beginning or end of the scheduled meeting to spend some quality time with their family and friends. Likewise, while the meeting attendee is attending workshops and trade shows, the guests want something to keep them occupied. Tours, shopping excursions, cultural events, sport events, dinners, museums, festivals, and theatrical shows are all popular diversions. Every city, no matter how small, has something of interest to explore. The key is not to let these ancillary activities interfere with your overall program objectives. Ancillary activities should not be more attractive than the program. Ancillary activities must be provided, and it is important that they are appropriate to the age, gender, and interests of the guests.

If possible, limit participation in planning ancillary activities for two reasons: additional effort and liability issues. As a meeting/event professional, you need to concentrate on what is going on in the meeting facility. You do not want to worry about whether the bus to the mall is on time. If possible, outsource the management of ancillary activities to a local **Destination Management Company (DMC)**. A DMC is a company that specializes in arranging activities and is an expert on the local area (see Chapter 3 on DMCs, for more information). Likewise, if something should happen and people are injured at an event that you arranged, you do not want to worry about liability issues. A prime example is if child care is offered by the sponsoring organization, additional insurance may be needed to protect the organization from any liability issues. Child care is definitely a service that must be outsourced to a professional child care service. Special licensing is needed to ensure the safety and security of children.

The safest route is to provide a list of local activities and the Web site address of the CVB. Let the attendees plan their own activities. Be warned: When holding meetings in popular resort locations like Orlando, Florida, or Las Vegas, Nevada, the "attractions" available can quickly become "distractions" for the attendees. It is not uncommon to lose a few attendees in Las Vegas when the call of the slot machines is louder than an hour-long workshop on a dry topic.

REGISTRATION

Registration

To attend most conventions or exhibitions, some type of registration is typically required. Registration is the process of gathering all pertinent information and fees necessary for an individual to attend the meeting. It is much more than merely collecting money. Registration data are a valuable asset to any association or organization that is sponsoring an event. Registration begins several weeks prior to the event and usually lasts right up to the final day. Discounts are often provided to attendees who register in advance. They are offered an **early bird rate** incentive to pay fees early. The association can then use that money to pay deposits or bills coming due. By registering early, the meeting/event professional can determine if registration numbers are at anticipated levels. If not, it can increase marketing or negotiate with the hotel or meeting facilities about lowering expectations and financial commitments that may have been promised.

Data collected on the registration form may include name, title, occupation, address, e-mail, phone, fax, membership category, desired workshop sessions, social functions, optional events, method of payment, special medical or dietary needs, and a liability waiver. A recent addition has been to ask attendees where they are staying while at the convention and their length of stay so that the impact of the meeting can be determined. Some organizations inquire about the size of the company, number of employees, or financial responsibility of the attendee (such as does he or she make or recommend purchase decisions). This registration data can be used before, during, and after the meeting. Registration does not typically occur at special or sports events.

Prior to the meeting, the data can be given or sold to exhibitors or advertisers so that they can promote their company, products, and services before the actual meeting. It may also be used to market to potential attendees who have not committed to attending. Advertising "we have 7,500 qualified buyers attending this year's convention" may entice more companies to register or exhibit. Preregistration data can also help the meeting/event professional monitor interest in special events or particular workshops that may be popular. If a particular workshop is getting a lot of interest, then the meeting/event professional can move it to a larger room or increase seating.

During the meeting, registration data can be used as a promotional tool for the press to gain media attention for the organization, sponsors, and exhibitors. It can also help the local DMO in justifying the costs of marketing and soliciting groups to come to their city. Hard facts, such as using 3,000 rooms and 200,000 square feet of meeting space, are music to the ears of hospitality companies. For the attendees, technology now allows them to automatically access via smartphone or computer on who is at a particular meeting and save the list for future use.

After the meeting, registration data can be used to update association membership records, solicit new members, or sold to interested parties. Most important, it can be used to help the meeting/event professional with logistics and to promote the next meeting. By examining registration data over time, it gives the organization a better view of who is attending its meeting and if there are any trends apparent, such as changes in gender, age, education, or title of attendees.

Registration Fees

There may be several different pricing structures for a single meeting. For association meetings, members typically receive a discount on the cost of registration. This helps encourage people to become members of the association. But not all members will pay the same price. For example, in 2014, the Professional Convention Management Association (PCMA) charged professional members (meeting/event professionals), $725; suppliers (hotel sales people, CVBs), $895; university faculty, $435; and student members, $250. These are the early bird preregistration prices available until about six weeks prior to the convention. After the **cutoff date** for preregistration, all prices increased by $50 to $100. Additional fees were added if the registrant did not stay in the room block at a host hotel. All attendees, regardless of how much they pay, receive the same opportunities for education and networking, and are invited to the scheduled meals, breaks, and receptions. However, additional activities, such as golf, tours, or special entertainment functions, may incur a separate cost.

For some events like the Exhibitor Show, an annual trade show for people in the exhibition industry, registration fees are priced based on what the attendee wants to attend. Entrance to the trade show is free, but education sessions may cost $295 or more per workshop. Additional events, such as dinners and receptions, may be purchased separately. All-inclusive registrations at the Exhibitor Show are also an option with full registration and attendance to all education programs costing well over $1,595.

Associations usually offer substantial registration discounts to their members. The "nonmember" rate to attend may well exceed the difference between the cost of membership and the member rate, making it desirable to join the association. This is a clever way for associations to increase their membership base and provides an opportunity to promote other products and services to the new members. Registration fees are often waived for VIPs, members of the press, speakers, and local dignitaries. Complimentary registrations must be monitored closely because there may be costs involved if the meeting has F&B or if other events are available.

Preregistration

Preregistration is the process of registering attendees weeks or months in advance of an event. This benefits the meeting/event professional in several ways. It provides information about who will be attending a meeting or event. It can help the meeting/event professional determine room capacities for educational sessions and can help the session speaker to estimate the number of people who may attend a session. Typically, advanced payment is also required to preregister. By receiving payment weeks or months ahead of the event, the meeting/event professional can use that money to pay bills or make necessary deposits for services. The early bird discount is a major incentive to preregister. Logistically, as people are arriving for the event, preregistration can reduce congestion in the registration area as well as reduce long lines and waiting time. A quick check-in to collect a name badge and other meeting materials and to confirm the person's arrival is all that is necessary.

Whether it is paper-based or electronic, the prospective attendee must complete a registration form, the more simple and easy to complete, the better.

ON-SITE REGISTRATION Like the front desk of a hotel, the registration area is the first experience an attendee has with a meeting, convention, or exhibition. A slow or inefficient registration process can set the tone for the entire meeting. The registration area should be heavily staffed the first day and should remain open throughout the event. If international guests are expected, registration materials may need to be translated, and interpreters may be necessary to facilitate a smooth check-in. If an exhibition is involved, having a separate area for exhibitor registration is a good idea.

Registration is one of the areas often outsourced by the meeting/event professional, especially for large events. It is a complex process that requires much training on the part of the registration attendants. Some hotels or convention centers have arrangements with temporary agencies that provide staff that do registration on a regular basis. Some registration management companies handle housing as well.

HOUSING

Not all meetings require housing (i.e., hotel) arrangements. But if housing is needed, there are basically four methods of handling housing for attendees:

1. Attendees arrange for their own room. Lists of hotels may be provided, but the meeting sponsor makes no prior arrangements regarding price negotiations or availability.
2. A group rate is negotiated by the meeting/event professional at one or more properties, and attendees respond directly to the reservations department of their choice.

Registration desk at a conference. The sign indicates where registrants should queue up based on the first initial of their last name. *Jetta Productions/Getty Images*

3. The meeting sponsor handles all housing, and attendees book rooms through them. Then the sponsor provides the hotel with a rooming list of confirmed guests.
4. A third-party **housing bureau** (outsourced company) handles all arrangements either for a fee or is paid by the DMO.

Having attendees make their own hotel reservations is the easiest method. It totally removes that responsibility from the meeting/event professional. But remember, the facility is going to base its pricing to host the event on the total revenues it anticipates from the group. Sleeping rooms represent the largest amount of potential revenue for the hotel. If rooms are not blocked (set aside for the group), it is most likely that a premium will be charged to the organization for renting meeting space and other services. The room block is a key negotiation tool for the meeting/event professional.

The last three options require that the meeting/event professional establish a rate for the attendees. The room rate will reflect prior negotiations with the sales department in which the total value of the meeting to the facility is considered. A certain number of rooms will be reserved, called a "block," and rooms are subtracted from this inventory as attendees request them. This can be a gamble for the meeting/event professional. As with F&B events, the meeting/event professional must estimate how many people will be attending. If the meeting/event professional blocks 100 rooms and only 75 rooms are used by the group, he or she may be held responsible for part, or all, of the cost of those unused rooms. The difference between rooms blocked and rooms "picked up" (actually used) is called **attrition** (for more information on attrition, see Chapter 11, "Legal Issues in the MEEC Industry"). A serious challenge to meeting/event professionals these days is attendees booking rooms outside the block. That is, they bypass the hotels for which the meeting/event professional negotiated special pricing and find other accommodations or even less expensive accommodations within the host hotels. If the host hotel charges $199 per day and a smaller and less luxurious hotel down the street is charging $99, a certain percentage of the attendees will opt for the lower price. Sometimes, by calling the hotel directly or by using a discount hotel broker on the Internet, attendees can get better prices in the same hotel for less than what the meeting/event professional negotiated. If large numbers of attendees do this, then the meeting/event professional is going to get stuck paying for a lot of unused rooms. One method of reducing this potentially expensive problem is to establish review dates in the hotel contract, whereby the meeting/event professional can reduce (or increase) the **room block** by a certain percentage at a certain time. The closer to the actual meeting dates, the less likely the hotel will allow a reduction in room block. The hotel must have time to try and sell any unused rooms and recoup any losses. A hotel room is a perishable commodity if it is not sold each day; the potential revenue is lost forever.

Having attendees call or reserve rooms online directly with the hotel is a good option. The attendees should benefit by the negotiated room rate, and the hotel handles the reservation processing directly. The meeting/event professional will need minimal involvement. For larger meetings where multiple properties are used, it is advisable to provide a range of hotel prices to accommodate the budgets of all the attendees.

Registration and Housing Companies

Several companies have evolved over the last few years that specialize in handling both conference registration and housing. Examples include companies such as Cvent, Conference-Direct, Experient, and Passkey.

Outsourcing the housing process to a third-party vendor or DMO is most prevalent with medium and large meetings. Some groups, such as the National Association of Broadcasters or Consumer Electronics Show, are so large that they require most of the hotel rooms in the host city. Housing for a so-called citywide meeting is best left to professionals who have the most current technology and are well equipped to handle thousands of housing requests. Making reservations through a housing service can be done by mail, phone, fax, Internet, and other mobile devices. The housing bureau may charge a fee per transaction. This cost may be paid by the sponsoring organization, or in some cases the local DMO will absorb some or all of the cost. Indeed, many CVBs and even hotels operate their own housing bureaus as a service to meeting/event professionals.

Handling attendee reservations in-house is possible but is easiest with small groups. If the event is a small, high-profile event, the meeting/event professional can have attendees reserve rooms with the organization, and a **rooming list** will be created to give to the hotel. The rooming list should include type of room, ADA requests, smoking or nonsmoking, arrival and departure dates, names of additional guests in the room, and special requests. Handling reservations in-house can be quite time-consuming and may require additional staffing. Alternatively, a housing bureau can be of great assistance.

MEETING AND EVENT SPECIFICATION GUIDE

One of the challenges in the meeting and events profession is that, historically, there were few standardized policies, procedures, and terminology. To begin a codification of definitions and standardized practices, an industry-wide task force called the **APEX Initiative** was created. As mentioned in Chapter 1, *APEX* stands for Accepted Practices Exchange, and one of its first accomplishments was the development of accepted practices regarding terminology. The committee found that many terms were used interchangeably to describe the document used by a meeting/event professional to communicate specific requirements for a function. Some of these terms included "catering event order," "meeting résumé," "event specifications guide," "staging guide operations manual," "production schedule," "room specs," "schedule of services," "working agenda," "specifications sheet," and "group résumé." After a considerable amount of effort and input from all types of meeting/event professionals, hotel convention service managers, DMCs, exhibit managers, and DMOs, the panel created a format that will greatly facilitate the communication between meeting/event professionals and the entities that service their meetings.

The panel developed the term **Event Specification Guide** that is defined as:

Event Specifications Guide (ESG). A comprehensive document that outlines the complete requirements and instructions for an event. This document is typically authored by the event meeting/event professional and is shared with all appropriate vendors as a vehicle to communicate the expectations of services for a project. The industry-accepted practice is to use the APEX ESG, which can be found at the Convention Industry Council Web site.

The ESG is a three-part document that includes the following:

1. *The Narrative:* general overview of the meeting or event
2. *Function Schedules:* timetable outlining all functions that compose the overall meeting or event
3. *Function Set Up Orders:* specifications for each separate function that is part of the overall meeting or event. This is used by the facility to inform setup crews, technicians, catering and banquet staff, and all other staff regarding what is required for each event.

There is also a standardized timetable for communication between the meeting/event professional and the facility and service providers. Recognizing that these guidelines may differ depending on the size, timing, and complexity of the individual event, they do provide a useful general format.

The ESG contains quite a bit of detailed information. Both the meeting/event professional along with catering and convention services staff will need access to a copy. If any changes are made, they should be recorded in all copies. Fortunately, as technology and connectivity improves, this document will be easier to maintain and update. What was once a five-pound,

Size of Event	Submit ESG in Advance	Receive Return from Facility and Vendors
1–500	4 weeks	2 weeks
501–1000	6 weeks	4 weeks
1000+	8 weeks	6 weeks

three-ring binder full of paper forms has been reduced to an app on a mobile device. Changes to the ESG can be made easily and accessed by the appropriate people.

PRE- AND POST-CON MEETINGS

What is certain for all meetings is that changes to the ESG are unavoidable. In fact, one of the chief responsibilities of a good meeting/event professional is to react and manage change—often unexpected change.

Pre-Convention Meetings

A day or two prior to the actual beginning of a meeting, the meeting/event professional should partake in a pre-convention (**pre-con**) meeting. This is a gathering of all critical people representing all departments within the facility who will impact the group. In addition to the convention service manager (CSM), who is the primary contact for the meeting/event professional, the following representatives may be requested to attend the meeting: catering or banquet manager or F&B director; audiovisual representative; sales manager; accounting manager; front desk manager; bell staff or concierge; housekeeping manager; security manager; engineering manager; switchboard manager; recreation manager; and all outside service providers, such as transportation, special events, and decorators. Often the general manager of the facility will stop by, be introduced, and welcome the meeting/event professional. The pre-con meeting allows the meeting/event professional to meet and visually connect with all the various people servicing the event. In most cases, this will be the first time the meeting/event professional meets many of these people. Each representative is introduced, and any changes or additions of duties in their respective departments are reviewed. After the individual departments have been discussed, the meeting/event professional should release the person to return to his or her duties. The ESG is reviewed page by page with the CSM. All changes are made, guarantees are confirmed, and last-minute instructions are conveyed. The pre-con is basically the last time the meeting/event professional has the opportunity to make any major changes without disrupting the facility. Once an event is in progress, it is very difficult and potentially costly to make major changes. If the meeting/event professional decides one hour before a session that the room should be set with only chairs rather than with tables and chairs as listed on the Function Sheet or BEO, it can cause havoc. Additional staff may be needed to remove the tables, and the meeting/event professional may be charged for the labor. Sometimes, the last-minute request of a meeting/event professional cannot be fulfilled. If fifty tables are requested just prior to an event, the hotel may not have them available or may not have scheduled staff for set up.

Post-Convention Review

At the conclusion of a major meeting, the meeting/event professional will create a written document to record all key events of the meeting. This is used for planning the next meeting. It also serves as a "report card" for the facility and the meeting manager. It will include what went right as well as what went wrong. Then, a post-convention (post-con) meeting is held. It is smaller than the pre-con and may include the planning staff, the CSM, the F&B director, the audiovisual manager, and a representative from the accounting department. This is the time to address any discrepancies in billing, service failures, and problems, or to praise facility staff for a job well done. Most major meetings will have a post-con; smaller meetings may not. In some cases, the meeting/event professional is just too mentally and physically exhausted to conduct a post-con meeting immediately following the event. A good night's rest and peace and quiet may be needed first.

FUTURE TRENDS

- Conference event apps will be critical for the success of events in the future. As people get accustomed to downloading apps to their smartphone or other portable devices they can more fully experience the event. Audience response systems will help event professionals to collect data in real time, which can be used to immediately impact their events. The ability to poll attendees will assist speakers in adjusting their presentations and insuring they are providing ROI to attendees.

- Social media is here to stay. Even older generations of event attendees are adapting to this platform for communicating with their colleagues. New social media are being developed at a blinding speed. As with most new technologies, some will be successful while others will fail. Ease of use and functionality will be key. Social media can be a great way to connect with old friends and network with business colleagues. For more information on technology in MEEC, see Chapter 12.

- Smartphones and tablets will be the dominant forms of portable media. Astute event professionals will make use of these devices and provide streaming video to enhance interest in their events. Static images in a Website gallery are just not going to be enough to satisfy attendee desires to be engulfed in the event experience. As the saying goes, "a picture is worth a thousand words." Now a dynamic video is worth a thousand pictures. Companies across all industry categories will be creating their own Internet channels and posting archived webinars to attract more attendees to their events and to preserve them for posterity.

- Twenty-five years ago some technologists forecast the end of the MEEC industry as we knew it. Why travel to a distant location when you have the ability to video chat or teleconference with customers and co-workers? The need for face-to-face meetings has never been stronger. While technology can improve our professional and personal lives in so many ways, the ability to shake hands, share a meal, and look someone straight in the eye has never been greater. Technology is a tool to help us communicate, network, streamline business practices, and adapt to our ever-changing environment, but it will never replace human contact. Ask yourself if you would like your wedding to be "virtual."

- Meeting/event professionals must continue to recognize and adapt to the multiple generations who are attending their events. One size does not fit all. The myriad of duties today's event professional is charged with accomplishing must take into consideration that not all attendees are the same. Educational content must be provided through multiple delivery mechanisms. Older attendees may not be comfortable with texting and balk at the notion of carrying around a complicated smartphone or tablet. Younger attendees may have less patience with a speaker who is not actively engaging them during their presentation. It will be a complicated road ahead for most meeting/event professionals.

- For many organizations, the days of lavish receptions and expensive junkets to exotic places for meetings are over. The "Great Recession" has forever changed the face of the MEEC industry. Cost control and accountability will be cornerstones for future events. Likewise, finding ways to create memorable experiences for attendees will be crucial. Boring chicken dinners in a ballroom just won't be acceptable.

- Lead time for planning MEEC events continue to bifurcate. Small event lead times will get shorter while large events will get longer.

Summary

Planning a meeting or event is a long process that often requires input from a lot of people or committees. Setting clearly defined objectives is the first essential step in creating effective program content and managing logistics. The meeting/event professional must begin with a clear understanding of the purpose and expectations of the meeting/event. The objectives will impact site or city selection, type of facility used, and the services required. The meeting/event professional must also understand the motivations of the attendees: Why should they attend? Is attendance voluntary or mandated by management? Planning a corporate event compared to an association event can be very different processes. Education has replaced recreation as the driving force for most meetings. However, people like to be entertained as well as educated, so the meeting/event professional must attend to all the needs of the attendees and provide both. The format of the education sessions as well as the setup of the meeting space should be appropriate to the objectives of the meeting.

Once the objectives are clear, a needs analysis should be conducted to further guide the meeting/event professional in selecting appropriate meeting space, speakers, and amenities that are expected from the attendees. The demographics of attendees must also be considered. Meetings and conventions represent enormous economic potential for cities. In the site selection process, the RFP is the announcement of what is required by the meeting/event professional. CVBs and individual hotels must evaluate the potential of the meeting and respond accordingly. Interested properties may invite the meeting/event professional for a fam trip to visit the property.

Evaluations of individual sessions, the overall conference, exhibitors, and other key items should be conducted to provide information for subsequent events. Creating a user-friendly format will ensure a good response.

Education has replaced recreation as the driving force for most meetings. However, people like to be entertained as well as educated, so the meeting/event professional must attend to all the needs of the attendees and provide both. The format of the education sessions as well as the setup of the meeting space should be appropriate to the objectives of the meeting. Program content should be designed with both a track and level that will target the majority of the attendees. Housing and registration are important components in implementing the plan for a meeting or event. Both paid and voluntary speakers can be utilized—each has positives and negatives. Care must be taken to ensure that speakers are adequately prepared to address the group and are contractually obligated to perform. Finally, ancillary activities like shopping trips, tours, child care, and other services that enhance an attendees' meeting experience should be planned thoughtfully so as not to interfere with the scheduled programming.

Because of the complexity of the meeting planning process, this chapter can only highlight some of the planning and producing activities involved. There two new books that provide more detail on the planning and production aspects of MEEC. They are *Planning and Management of Meetings, Expositions, Events and Conventions* and *Production and Logistics in Meetings, Expositions, Events and Conventions*, both by Fenich.

Key Words and Terms

For definitions, see GLOSSARY or http://glossary.conventionindustry.org

air lift	continuing medical education (CME)	guarantee	return on investment (ROI)
annual meeting	Convention and Visitor Bureaus (CVBs)	housing bureau	room block
APEX Initiative		International Association of Conference Centers	rooming list
attrition	cutoff date	keynote address	signing authority
audience response system	Destination Management Company (DMC)	level	SMART
citywide		needs analysis	speaker bureau
continuing education unit (CEU)	early bird rate	poster session	speaker ready room
Convention Industry Council (CIC)	fam trip	pre-con	subject matter expert
	group history	Request for Proposal (RFP)	track

Review and Discussion Questions

1. Why would a meeting/event professional hire a high-paid nationally known speaker for the keynote address?
2. What is the purpose of using program formats, levels, and tracks in designing effective meeting programming?
3. What is the purpose of using speaker contracts?
4. What are the benefits and challenges of using volunteer speakers compared to paid speakers?
5. Why are speaker guidelines used, and what should be included?
6. What are the benefits and challenges of providing ancillary activities?
7. What are the benefits and limitations of outsourcing components of a meeting, such as housing or registration?
8. How can meeting/event professionals use registration data before, during, and after a convention?
9. How does preregistration assist the meeting/event professional in planning a meeting?
10. Describe the four different methods of housing.
11. What is the purpose of an ESG? What information should it contain?
12. Explain the benefit of having a pre-con and post-con meeting.

About the Chapter Contributor

Curtis Love, PhD, is an Associate Professor in the William F. Harrah Hotel College at the University of Nevada Las Vegas (UNLV). His teaching and research concentrations are in the area of meetings, conventions, and exhibitions. Prior to joining UNLV, he was the Vice President of education for the Professional Convention Management Association.

CHAPTER 10

Food and Beverage

Meals are not always prepared in a kitchen.   *BestPhotoStudio/Fotolia*

Chapter Objectives

This chapter provides the reader with an understanding of the following:

- Types of catering operations and types of caterers
- Purpose of the meal function
- Types of meal functions, menu planning, menu design, and pricing
- Types of beverage functions, beverage menu planning, and pricing
- Liquor laws and third-party liability
- Space requirements and room setup

INTRODUCTION

Food and beverage is an area that many event professionals shy away from by out-sourcing planning and negotiation to third-party planners. It is often a mystery to many event professionals as to what is negotiable, how caterers price their services, and where caterers will make concessions.

161

The Convention Industry Council (CIC) Glossary provides the following definition:

Caterer (1) a food service vendor, often used to describe a vendor who specializes in banquets and theme parties. (2) An exclusive food & beverage contractor within a facility.

The quality of the food and beverage functions can impact the overall impressions of a meeting/event. While many simply see food as fuel, for others it is an important component of the overall experience. From planning menus to negotiating prices, catering is one area not to leave to chance. It is one of the major expenses of a meeting/event and an area where Murphy's Law prevails. Furthermore, the importance of cuisine must be emphasized. The choices and preparation of food have changed dramatically over the past few years—whether to go organic, ethnic, or vegetarian, for example. It is posited that food revenue is increasing steadily due to the increased choices of cuisine. However, beverage revenue may be in decline because sponsors of events do not want to assume liability for alcohol consumption.

Here are some questions to ask when planning for food and beverage:

1. Who will I work with planning the event?
2. Who will be on-site during the event?
3. When can I expect your written proposal?
4. What is your policy regarding deposits and cancellations?
5. When is the final payment due?
6. Are there other charges for setup, delivery, overtime, and so on?
7. Do you take credit cards? PayPal? Online payment?
8. When must I give you my final guarantee?
9. What percentage is overset above the guarantee?
10. What is the sales tax, and what are your gratuity and/or service charge policies?
11. What are the chef's best menu items?
12. What are your portion sizes?
13. Will wine be poured by the staff or placed on the tables?
14. How many staff will be working at the event?
15. What are your substitution policies for vegetarian plates and special meals?
16. Could you pass wine or champagne as guests arrive?
17. How many bartenders will be used during the cocktail hour?
18. Do you provide table numbers?
19. What size tables do you have?
20. What are the options for linen, chair covers, china, stemware, flatware, and charger plates?
21. What decorations do you provide for tables, buffets, and food stations?
22. Are you ADA compliant?
23. Can you provide a podium, mike, and overhead projector?
24. What are your "green" initiatives?

CATERED EVENTS

Catered events generally have one host and one bill, and most attendees eat the same meal. (Exceptions would be if an attendee arranged vegetarian, low-fat, or other special meals.) A mandatory gratuity is added to the check that can range from 18% to 24% of the total bill, and taxes can add another 5% to 9%. The distribution of this gratuity varies widely among venues and companies. In some companies, the gratuity goes exclusively to the servers and bartenders. In others, a portion goes to management, including the catering manager or the Convention Service Manager (CSM). A gratuity differs from a tip, as a tip is voluntary and is given at the discretion of the client for service over and above expectations. Service charges are a murky area, but they generally do not go to the service personnel. The lesson here is: when in doubt, ask. In many countries and cultures, service charges and tips do not exist.

Catered events can be held in just about any location. **Off-premise catering** requires transportation of food—either prepared or to be prepared on-site—to a location such as a tented area, museum, park, or attraction. Sometimes food is prepared in a kitchen and is transported fully cooked to the event site. At other times food is partially prepared in a kitchen and is finished at the site, or everything can be prepared from scratch at the site. Mobile kitchens can be set up just

A "wow" plate presentation.
George G. Fenich

about anywhere, using generators and/or propane and butane as fuel to heat cooking equipment. Off-premise caterers also generally must rent equipment, including tables, chairs, chafing dishes, plates, flatware, and glassware.

On-premise catering is defined as being held in a facility that has its own permanent kitchens and function rooms, such as a hotel, restaurant, or convention center. This allows the facility to keep permanent furniture, such as banquet style tables and chairs in their inventory. Event professionals are almost always required to use the catering department of the venue at the site of the meeting. In a citywide convention, one hotel is usually named the host hotel and holds most of the food functions, although some events often move attendees to a variety of venues. However, many meetings/events have at least one off-premise event, often the opening reception or closing gala or a themed event. Attendees want to experience some of the flavor of the destination, and they often get "cabin fever" if they never leave the hotel. Events can be held at an aquarium, a museum, a winery, or an historic mansion. For example, in St. Louis, many events are held at Busch stadium, home of the world champion Cardinals baseball team.

Off-premise Catering

In Orlando, it is much easier logistically to transport a 20-person board of directors' dinner to a local restaurant than to transport 1000+ attendees to Disney World. As an event professional, you may be responsible for simultaneously coordinating both off-premise catering events. In this case, a shuttle bus system must be set up to transport attendees back and forth, which can be expensive.

Many excellent restaurants have banquet rooms, and bigger restaurants have banquet sales coordinators. Arnaud's in New Orleans has a six-person sales staff, so banquets are big business. In Las Vegas, a trend in recent years has celebrity chefs create their own signature restaurants within the hotel, separate from the hotel's own food service operations. These restaurants, such as Spago in the Forum Shops at Caesars Palace or Delmonico's at the Venetian, also have their own banquet sales staff. The Web has made it easy to research what local restaurants have to offer. The MIM List, a free e-mail list server for event professionals sponsored by *Meeting News* magazine, is a great place to ask for suggestions and advice.

For an off-premise event, the first step for an event professional would be to create an RFP and send it to event managers or caterers in the area. The RFP would include basic information, such as the objective of the event, information on the company, workable dates, number of attendees, and approximate budget, as well as any special requests, such as the need for a parade area. Many catering companies have online RFPs. Once the event professional has had the opportunity to review the proposals, an interview and, if possible, a site inspection would follow.

During the site inspection, look at the ambiance of the space, the level of cleanliness and maintenance, and other amenities that may be required, such as parking and restrooms.

In many cases, off-premise events will be outsourced through a destination management company (DMC). DMCs are familiar with the location and have relationships established with unique venues in the area. For example, in Las Vegas the Liberace Mansion is available for parties. In New Orleans, Mardi Gras World, where the parade floats are made, is an outstanding setting for a party. Just about every destination has some distinctive spaces for parties: Southfork in Dallas, the Rock and Roll Hall of Fame in Cleveland, the Getty Museum in Los Angeles, and so on.

DMCs also know the best caterers, decorators, shuttle companies, entertainment, and any other supplier of products or services you may require. While DMCs charge for their services, they often can get quantity discounts because of the volume they purchase throughout the year. And if there is a problem with the product or service, the DMC can usually resolve it faster because of the amount of future business that would be jeopardized.

Two of the challenges with off-premise events are transportation and weather. Shuttle buses are an additional expense for the meeting. Weather can spoil the best-laid plans, so contingency measures must be arranged. Back-up shelter should be available, whether it is a tent or an inside function room. For example, outdoor luaus in Hawaii are frequently moved inside at the last minute because of the frequent tropical storms that pop up there.

During the initial site inspection, obtain a copy of the facility's banquet menus and policies. Do they offer the type of menu items that would be appropriate for your group? Ask if they are prepared to handle custom menus if you decide not to use their standard offerings. When planning custom menus, always check the skill level of the culinary team in the kitchen and the availability of special products that may be required.

Other important considerations include the demographics of the group. Menu choices would be different for the American Truck Drivers Association and the International Association of Retired Persons. The typical truck driver would probably prefer a big steak, while a retired person would likely prefer a smaller portion of chicken without heavy spices. You need to consider gender, age, ethnic background, profession, and so on.

On-premise Catering

Most meals are catered on-premise during a meeting. Serving attendees all at once prevents strain on the restaurant outlets, keeps attendees from leaving the property, and ensures that everyone will be back on time for the following sessions.

Conference centers offer a complete meeting package, which includes meals. Breakfast, lunch, and dinner are generally available in a cafeteria-type setup at any time the group decides to break. This keeps the group from having to break just because it is noon if they are in the middle of a productive session. If more than one group is in the facility, they will each be assigned different areas of the dining room. Refreshments are usually available at any time as well, allowing breaks at appropriate times. Conference centers can also provide banquets and receptions on request.

Convention centers and stadiums usually have concession stands open. More and more, exhibitions are holding their own opening reception or providing lunch on the show floor to attract attendees into the exhibits. Most convention centers are public entities, and the food service is contracted out to companies like ARAMARK or Sodexo. These contract food service companies often have exclusive contracts, and other vendors or caterers are not allowed to work in the facility.

The venues mentioned earlier generally also have full-service restaurants on the property. If the group will use the restaurant, check the capacity and hours relative to the needs of the group. For example, the association ICHRIE held one of its annual conventions at a major hotel in Palm Springs, California, during late July. They attracted about 700 attendees and were virtually the only people in the 1,500-room hotel. ICHRIE felt that the five freestanding restaurants would be more than adequate to meet the dining needs of the group (dining off-site was not a practical option). This would normally be true. However, since it was low season for the hotel, they closed all but two of the restaurants, with the result that ICHRIE convention attendees were faced with waits of over two hours to be seated for dinner.

Event professionals also need to stay abreast of current food trends. They do so by reading trade journals, such as *Meeting News, Successful Meetings, Convene,* or *Meetings & Conventions.* Many of the event and food trade publications, such as *Event Solutions, Special Events, Hotel F&B Director,* and *Catering* are wonderful resources as well and can be accessed online.

STYLE OF SERVICE

There are many ways to serve a meal, from self-service to VIP white-glove service (see Table 10-1). While there is some disagreement on a few of the following definitions, the following are based on the CIC glossary. The White House protocol is also being followed in this book. The White House publishes the *Green Book,* which explains how everything is to be done for

Table 10-1 Types of Functions	
Continental breakfast	Typically includes an assortment of breads and pastries, juice and coffee, although it can be upgraded with the addition of sliced fruit, yogurt, and/or cold cereals. Most are self-service with limited seating, unless an additional fee for "seated continental service" is assessed.
Full, served breakfast	The entrees are plated in the kitchen and would normally include some type of egg like Eggs Benedict, a meat like bacon or sausage, a potato item like hash browns, fruit, and coffee.
Breakfast buffet	Includes a wide assortment of foods including fruits and fruit juices, egg dishes, meats, potatoes, and breads.
Refreshment breaks	These are often beverages only but may include snacks, such as cookies, bagels, or fruit.
Brunch	This is a late-morning meal and includes both breakfast and lunch items. A brunch can be a buffet or a plated, served meal.
Buffet lunch	This can be a cold or hot buffet, with a variety of salads, vegetables, meats, and so on. A deli buffet may include a make-your-own sandwich area.
Box lunch	Normally only available for carrying away from the hotel to an off-premise location. They can be eaten on a bus if there is a long ride to a destination (such as a ride from San Francisco to the Napa Valley for a day's activities) or eaten at the destination (such as a picnic area to hear the Boston Pops Orchestra). Box lunches can also be provided to attendees at a trade show.
Full, served lunch	This is a plated lunch, usually a three-course hot meal, and often includes a salad, a main course, and a dessert. A one-course cold meal is sometimes provided, such as a Grilled Chicken Caesar Salad.
Receptions	These are networking events with limited seating, which allow for conversation and interaction during the event. Food is usually placed on stations around the room and may also include butler style service. Beverage service is always offered at these events. Light receptions may only include dry snacks and beverages and often precede a dinner. Heavy receptions would include hot and cold appetizers, perhaps an action station, and are often planned to replace a dinner.
Dinner buffet	This would include a variety of salads, vegetables, entrees, desserts, and beverages. Often meats are carved and served by attendants.
Full, served dinner	This could be a three- to five-course meal, including an appetizer, soup, salad, main course, and a dessert. Food is preplated in the kitchen and served to each guest seated at round tables in the dining room. This style of service is often referred to as American Style Service.
Off-site event	This is any event held away from the host hotel. It could be a reception at a famous landmark, such as the Queen Mary in Long Beach, or a picnic at a local beach or park.
Theme party	This is a gala event with flair. It can be a reception, buffet, or served meal. Themes can run the gamut. An example would be an international theme, where different stations are set up with food from Italy, China, Japan, Mexico, Germany, and so on.

Dessert Buffet Table. *George G. Fenich*

presidential protocol. However, because of confusion in the area, it is important to be sure that the event professional and the catering representative agree on what the service styles mean for the event. (Unfortunately, the *Green Book* is not available to the public, as it also includes information on presidential security, among others.)

- *Buffet:* Food is attractively arranged on tables. Guests serve themselves and then take their plates to a table to sit and eat. Beverages are usually served at the tables. Buffets are generally more expensive than plated served meals because there is no portion control, and surpluses must be built in to assure adequate supplies of each food item. Be sure to allow adequate space around the table for lines to form, and to allow efficient replenishment by the service staff. Consider the flow, and do not make guests backtrack to get an item. For example, place the salad dressings after the salad so that guests do not have to step back on the next guest to dress their salad. Provide one buffet line per 100 guests, with 120 being the break point.
- *Attended Buffet/Cafeteria:* Guests are served by chefs or attendants. This is more elegant and provides better portion control.
- *Combination Buffet:* Inexpensive items, such as salads, are presented buffet style, where guests help themselves. Expensive items, such as meats, are served by an attendant for portion control.
- *Action Stations:* Sometimes referred to as "performance stations" or "exhibition cooking." **Action stations** are similar to an attended buffet, except food is freshly prepared as guests wait and watch. Some common action stations include pastas, grilled meats or shrimp, omelets, crepes, sushi, flaming desserts, Caesar salad, Belgian waffles, and carved meats.
- *Reception:* Light foods are served buffet style or are passed on trays by servers (**butler service**). Guests usually stand and serve themselves and do not usually sit down to eat. Receptions are often referred to as "Walk and Talks." Small plates should always be included for these events, since some cost control can be managed by selecting the appropriate service pieces. Some receptions serve only finger food (food eaten with the fingers), while others offer fork food (food that requires a fork to eat).
- *Family Style/English Service:* Guests are seated, and large serving platters and bowls of food are placed on the dining table by the servers. Guests pass the food around the table. A host often will carve the meat. This is an expensive style of service. Surpluses must be built into the price to account for potentially high food cost and additional service equipment.

- **Plated/American Style Service:** Guests are seated and served food that has been preportioned and plated in the kitchen. *Food is served from the left of the guest.* The meat or entree is placed directly in front of the guest at the six o'clock position. *Beverages are served from the right of the guest. When the guest has finished, both plates and glassware are removed from the right.* **American Service** is the most functional, most common, most economical, most controllable, and most efficient type of service. This type of service usually has a server/guest ratio of 1:20 or 1:30, depending on the level of the hotel.
- **Preset:** Some foods are already on the table when guests arrive. The most common items to preset are water, butter, bread, and appetizer and/or salad. At luncheons, where time is of the essence, the dessert is often preset as well. These are all cold items that hold up well.
- **Butler Service:** At receptions, *butler service* refers to having hors d'oeuvres passed on trays, where the guests help themselves.
- **Russian Service:** (1) Banquet Russian: The food is fully prepared in the kitchen. All courses are served either from platters or an Escoffier dish. Tureens are used for soup and special bowls for salad. The server places the proper plate in front of the guest, who is seated. After the plates are placed, the server returns with a tray of food and, moving counterclockwise around the table, serves the food from the guest's left with the right hand. With this style of service, the server controls the amount served to each guest. (2) Restaurant Russian: Guests are seated. Foods are cooked tableside on a *réchaud* (portable cooking stove) that is on a *gueridon* (tableside cart with wheels). Servers place the food on platters (usually silver), and then guests serve themselves. Service is *from the left*.
- **Banquet French:** Guests are seated. Platters of food are assembled in the kitchen. Servers take the platters to the tables and serve from the left, placing the food on the guest's plate using two large silver forks or one fork and one spoon. Servers must be highly trained for this type of service. The use of the forks and spoons together in one hand is a skill that must be practiced. Many hotels are now permitting the use of silver salad tongs.
- **Cart French:** Less commonly used for banquets, except for small VIP functions, this style is used in fine restaurants. Guests are seated, and foods are prepared tableside using a réchaud on a gueridon. Cold foods, such as salads, are prepared on the gueridon, sans réchaud. Servers plate the finished foods directly on the guest plate, which is then placed in front of the guest *from the right*. Bread, butter, and salad are served from the left, while beverages are served from the right. All are removed from the right.
- **Hand Service:** Guests are seated. There is one server for every two guests. Servers wear white gloves. Foods are preplated. Each server carries two plates from the kitchen and stands behind the two guests assigned to him or her. At a signal from the room captain, all

servings are set in front of all guests at the same time, synchronized. This procedure can be used for all courses, just the main course, or just the dessert. This is a very elegant and impressive style of service used mainly for VIP events because there is significant additional labor required.

- *A La Carte:* Guests are given a choice of 2–3 entrees, with a minimum of 2 predetermined courses served before the entrée choice.
- *Waiter Parade:* An elegant touch where white-gloved servers march into the room and parade around the perimeter carrying food on trays, often to dramatic music and lighting. This is especially effective with a Flaming Baked Alaska Dessert Parade. The room lighting is dimmed, and a row of flaming trays carried by the waiters slowly encircles the room. When the entire room is encircled, the music stops and service starts. (Flaming dishes should never be brought close to a guest. After the parade, the dessert is brought to a side area, where it is sliced and served.)
- *Mixing Service Styles:* You can change service styles within the meal. The whole meal does not have to conform to one type of service. For example, you can have your appetizer pre-set, have the salads "Frenched" (dressing added after salads are placed on table), the main course served American, with a dessert buffet.

MENUS

In times past, menus rarely changed. Today, change is necessary to keep pace with the changing tastes of the public. Most food trades journals run features on "What's Hot and What's Not." Table 10-2 lists some items that are generally always "hot," while Table 10-3 lists consumption guidelines.

Table 10-2 "Hot" Menu Items	
Seasonal food	The use of locally grown produce, in season, was first popularized some years ago by Chef Alice Waters. These foods are served when they are at the peak of flavor, enhancing the quality of the event.
Ethnic foods	With the influx of peoples from other cultures into the United States has come the unique cuisine of many areas of the world. The American palate has grown beyond the ethnic foods of the past, such as Italian, Chinese, and Mexican, to include the foods of many Asian countries, the Middle East, and South America.
High-quality ingredients	People may pinch pennies at the grocery store, but when they eat out at a banquet, they want the best. No longer satisfied with frozen, sweetened strawberries, they want fresh Driscoll strawberries on their shortcake. They want giant Idaho baked potatoes and Angus beef.
Fresh ingredients	Frozen, canned, and dried foods, once seen as the newest, greatest technology, have worn out their novelty. The loss of these food's flavors during preservation has made fresh food highly prized.
New and unusual ingredients	With improvements in production, technology and transportation, new foodstuffs have appeared in marketplaces that were previously unknown to most Americans. These include artisanal breads and cheeses, heirloom tomatoes, lemon grass, Yukon Gold potatoes, purple potatoes, and blood oranges.
Safe foods	Organic foods and foods free from pollution and pesticides.
Highly creative presentations	Plate presentations are increasingly important. We eat with our eyes before anything hits our taste buds. Contemporary presentations should focus on the primary menu components, and garnishes should be minimal (based on the time food might be on display or stored in a hot box).
Excellent service	Food served promptly (while still hot) and friendly, courteous services are important considerations in the enjoyment of a meal.

Table 10-3 Food Consumption Guidelines		
Type of Reception	**Type of Eaters**	**Number of Hors D'Oeuvres per Person**
2 hours or less (dinner following)	Light	3–4 pieces
	Moderate	5–7 pieces
	Heavy	8+ pieces
2 hours or less (no dinner)	Light	6–8 pieces
	Moderate	10–12 pieces
	Heavy	12+ pieces
2–3 hours (no dinner)	Light	8–10 pieces
	Moderate	10–12 pieces
	Heavy	16+ pieces

FOOD CONSUMPTION PATTERNS

The most important information in deciding how much food to order is the history of the group: Who are they? Why are they here? A pretty good determination can be made based on previous years. If this is a new group, or the history is not available, then consider the demographics of the attendees.

Some General Guidelines

Guests generally eat more during the first hour of a reception and may eat an average of 7 hors d'oeuvres per person during this hour. These general guidelines will vary based on the demographics of the group.

The amount of food consumed may also depend on how many square feet of space is available for guests to move around in (smaller equals less consumption).

MENU RESTRICTIONS

Banquet servers should know the ingredients and preparation method of every item on the menu. Many attendees have allergies or are restricted from eating certain items like sugar or salt due to health concerns. Others do not eat certain foods due to their religious restrictions, and others are vegetarians who do not eat meat. There are three basic types of vegetarians:

- Type one: vegetarians who will not eat red meat but will eat chicken and fish.
- Type two: "lacto-ovo" vegetarians who will not eat anything that has to be killed but will eat animal by-products (cheese, eggs, milk, etc.).
- Type three: "vegans" who will not eat anything from any animal source, including animal by-products such as honey, butter, and dairy.

When in doubt, assume attendees who identify themselves as vegetarian are vegans. To serve a vegan a plate of vegetables with butter and/or cheese would not be appropriate.

Other dietary restrictions include people who are lactose intolerant, which means they have difficulty digesting anything containing milk or milk products. Today, people have imposed dietary restrictions upon themselves in an effort to eat in a more healthy fashion, including those on low carbohydrate diets, high fiber diets, and so on. Religious restrictions may also impact food and diet. For example, people who maintain a Kosher diet will not eat anything that does not follow Kosher guidelines, will not mix dairy products with meat products, and will keep separate kitchens for dairy and for meat.

It is a good idea to have attendees fill out a form indicating if they have menu restrictions. This information can then be communicated to the catering manager, who will ensure that the proper number and type of alternative menu items are available. At meetings of the National Association of Catering Executives, attendees are provided with complete menus of every event, along with a form where they can indicate which meals they need to have changed.

FOOD AND BEVERAGE ATTRITION

Most event professionals do not like **attrition** clauses, although they benefit both event professionals and venues because they set down legal obligations for both sides and establish liability limits. When a contract is signed, both parties want the food and beverage guarantee to be met. But caterers want to be certain and up-front, while event professionals want to wait until the last minute to give the final guarantee. If the guarantee is too high, the event professional might have to pay for it in the form of attrition.

Attrition hits the event professional in the pocketbook if the **guarantee** is not met. The event professional agrees in the contract to buy a specific number of meals or to spend a specific amount of money on group food and beverage; the caterer's obligation is to provide the service and the food. If the guarantee is not met, the event professional must pay the difference between the guarantee and the actual amount or an agreed-on percentage of the actual amount (see Chapter 11 on legal issues for more information on attrition).

The event professional may also lose concessions that he or she has negotiated. Function space often is provided free of charge because of the revenue the group brings into a hotel through sleeping rooms and catered events. If the revenue does not come in, the hotel can charge for services that normally would have been complimentary, such as labor. The hotel could also reassign or reduce space being held for the event professional if minimums are not met.

Catering sales managers must strive to maximize revenue per available hotel room. They need a way to guarantee that money when booking a group. Event professionals should know how much revenue their meeting produces before negotiating an attrition clause. Caterers should pin down how much money the group will be spending on catering instead of getting a head count, since food prices fluctuate.

When using a dollar amount guarantee, provide some flexibility as to how the money may be spent. The contract can indicate that food and beverage fees could be reduced if the catered event is replaced with other business.

BEVERAGE EVENTS

Reasons for a Beverage Event

Beverage events are popular and include refreshment breaks and receptions. Beverage breaks not only provide liquid repasts and possibly a snack but also allow the attendee to get up, stretch, visit the restroom, call the office, and possibly move into another room for the next breakout session.

Receptions are slightly different because most include alcoholic beverages and probably more variety and quantity of food options. Reasons for receptions include:

Socializing: To provide a relaxed atmosphere that encourages interaction among guests.

Networking: To provide an opportunity to discuss business and develop new contacts.

Categories of Liquor

The categories of alcoholic beverage offered to a customer for a catered event are liquor (distilled spirits), wine, and beer. The caterer typically offers tiers of these options, representing different price and quality levels: **Well**, **Call**, and **Premium** brands. The event professional will choose the tier most appropriate for their guests and the event budget.

Well Brands: These are sometimes called "house liquors." It is less expensive liquor, such as Kentucky Gentleman Bourbon. Well brands are served when someone does not "call" a specific brand.

Call Brands: These are priced in the midrange and are generally asked for by name, such as Jim Beam Bourbon or Beefeater's Gin.

Premium Brands: These are high-quality, expensive liquors, such as Crown Royal, Chivas Regal, or Tanqueray Gin.

Spirits

All premium brands are available in 750-ml and 1-liter bottles. One 750-ml bottle equals 20 (1¼-ounce) servings; a 1-liter bottle equals 27 (1¼-ounce) servings (see Table 10-4). Consumption will average three drinks per person during a normal reception period.

Table 10-4	Number of Drinks per Bottle			
		1 Ounce	**1¼ Ounce**	**1½ Ounce**
1 Liter	33.8 ounces	33	27	22
750 ml	25.3 ounces	25	20	16

Wine/Champagne

All premium brands are available in 750-ml bottles and/or 1.5 liters (magnums):

> One 750-ml bottle = five 5-ounce servings
>
> One 1.5-liter bottle = ten 5-ounce servings

Consumption will average three glasses per person during a normal reception period, assuming that 50% of the people will order wine; you should order thirty 750-ml bottles for every 100 guests.

Champagne should be served in a flute glass instead of the classic "coupe" because there is less surface exposed to the air, so the bubbles do not escape as fast, causing the champagne to go flat (see Figure 10-1).

Beer

The caterer should always offer a variety of domestic and imported choices, as well as a contemporary list of "craft" beers from small, independent, and traditional brewers (Dogfish Head 60 Minute IPA, Bell's Two Hearted Ale).

How Beverages Are Sold

BY THE BOTTLE   *Common for open bars and poured wine at meal functions.*

The event professional pays for all of the liquor bottles that are opened. A physical inventory is taken at the beginning and end of the function to determine liquor usage. Most venues charge for each opened bottle, even if only one drink was poured from it. This method saves money but is inconvenient to monitor and calculate. The event professional will not know the final cost until the event is over. Usually, the group history will give some indication of how much consumption to expect. Open bottles may not be removed from the property. Unopened bottles may not be removed unless the venue has an off-sale liquor license. You can, however, have them delivered to a hospitality suite or to the room of a VIP to use during the meeting.

BY THE DRINK   *Also called "Consumption Bar."*

The host is charged for each individual beverage consumed during the event. Normally, the price per drink is high enough to cover all relevant expenses (limes, stirrers, napkins, etc.). Individual drink prices are set to yield a standard beverage cost percentage set by the hotel. This is the amount of profit the hotel expects to make from the sale of the liquor. Cost percentages

Flute   Coupe

FIGURE 10-1 Flute and Coupe
Pearson Education, Inc.

range from 12% to 18% for spirits and usually around 25% for wine. The event professional will not know the final cost until the event is over.

PER PERSON   This method is more expensive for the event professional but involves less work and aggravation. The event professional chooses a plan, such as premium liquors for one hour, and then tells the caterer how many people are coming ($25 per person × 500 guests = $12,500). Costs are known ahead of time—no surprises. Tickets are collected from attendees at the door, and the guarantee is monitored.

CHARGE PER HOUR   *This is similar to per person.*

This method often includes a sliding scale, with a higher cost for the first hour. This is because guests usually eat and drink more during the first hour, then level off. You must provide a firm guarantee before negotiating a per-hour charge. Or, you can combine *per person, per hour*: $25 per person for the first hour, and $20 per person for the second hour, so hosting 100 guests for a two-hour reception would cost $4,500 [$25 × 100 = $2,500 (+) $20 × 100 = $2,000 (=) $4,500]. No consideration is given for those who arrive late or leave early; the fee is $45 per person, regardless.

FLAT-RATE CHARGE   The host pays a flat rate for the function based on the assumption that each guest will drink about two drinks per hour for the first hour and one drink per hour thereafter (Check history and demographics of your group.) Costs will vary based on the number of attendees; whether well, call, or premium brands are poured; and the type of food served.

OPEN BAR   *Also called "Host Bar."*

Guests do not pay for their drinks; a host or sponsor pays for them. Guests usually drink as much as they want of what they want. Liquor consumption is higher because someone else is paying. The sponsor can be the meeting itself, an exhibitor, a similar organization, and so on. For example, at the Super Show, which features sporting goods, Nike may sponsor a bar.

CASH BAR   *Also called "No-Host Bar."*

Guests buy their own drinks, usually purchasing tickets from a cashier to exchange with a bartender for a drink. At small functions, the bartender may collect and serve, eliminating the cost of a cashier. Cashiers are usually charged as extra labor. Cashiers provide better control and speed up service. Bartenders do not have to handle dirty money and then handle glassware.

Calculate Total Cost to Determine the Best Option

If the hotel charges $80 for a bottle of bourbon that yields twenty-seven 1¼ ounce drinks, each drink costs the client $2.96. If guests are expected to drink two drinks per hour, for a one-hour reception for 1,000 people, purchasing by the bottle would cost $6,000.

If purchased by the drink, at $4.00 per drink, the same group would cost $8,000.

If purchased at $10 per person, it would cost $10,000.
So, you can see, the hotel makes more money selling per person.

COMBINATION BAR   A host purchases tickets and gives each attendee a certain number (usually two). If the guest wants a third drink, he or she must purchase it himself or herself. Or, the host can pay for the first hour, and the bar reverts to a cash bar for the second hour. This method provides free drinks to guests but retains control over costs and potential liability for providing unlimited drinks.

LIMITED CONSUMPTION BAR   Pricing by the drink. Cash register used. The host establishes a dollar amount. When the cash register reaches that amount, the bar is closed. The host may decide to reopen as a cash bar.

Labor Charges

Extra charges are usually levied for bartenders and/or **barbacks**, cocktail servers, cashiers, security, and **corkage**. These items are negotiable, depending on the value of the business. For example, if a bar sells over $500 in liquor, the bartender charge may be waived.

A "barback" is the bartender's helper—restocking liquor, keeping fresh ice, clean glasses, and so on—at the bar so that the bartender will not have to do it himself during service.

"Corkage" is the fee added to liquor brought into the hotel but not purchased from the hotel. The hotel charges this fee to cover the cost of labor, use of the glasses (which must be delivered to the room, washed, and placed back in storage), mixers, olives, lemon peels, and so forth.

One bar or bartender per every 100 guests is standard. If all guests are arriving at once, or if there is concern about guests standing in long lines, one bar or bartender for every 50 or 75 guests can be used. Unless yours is a very lucrative group, the hotel passes on the labor charges to you.

HOSPITALITY SUITES

Hospitality suites are places for attendees to gather outside of the meeting events. They are normally open late in the evening, after 10:00 PM, but occasionally around the clock. Three types of hospitality suites are:

Morning: Continental breakfast

Afternoon: Snacks and sodas

Evening: Liquor and snacks

Some suites offer a full bar, and some beer and wine only. Some have lots of food, others have only dry snacks. Some offer desserts and specialty coffees. Consider ordering more food if the attendees have had an open evening.

Hospitality suites are usually held in a client's suite on a sleeping room floor, usually handled by room service, and usually sold by catering. Sometimes they are held in a public function room and are both sold and serviced by catering.

Hospitality suites can be hosted by the sponsoring organization, a chapter of the organization, an exhibitor, a non-exhibiting corporation, an allied association, or a person running for an office in the organization.

Watch for "underground hospitality suites" where unofficial parties pop up. In these types of hospitality suites, you only gain liability and lose revenue. The court case resulting from the Tailhook Scandal, in which a female was groped in a hallway at a military meeting at the Las Vegas Hilton, set a precedent that a hotel can no longer claim that it does not know what is going on within the property.

Another factor to keep in mind is that liquor laws vary from state to state and county to county. You should always check the laws in your specific location.

Examples

In Las Vegas and New Orleans, liquor can be sold 24/7.

In California, liquor cannot be sold between 2 AM and 6 AM.

In Atlanta, liquor may not be served until noon on Sundays.

In some states, liquor may not be sold at all on Sundays.

There are generally four types of illegal liquor sales, wherever you are located:

- Sales to minors
- Sales to intoxicated persons
- Sales outside legal hours
- Sales with an improper liquor license

There are on-sale licenses, off-sale licenses, and beer and wine licenses. Licenses also stay with the property. For example, if your hotel has a liquor license, it is not valid in the public park across the street. The caterer would need to obtain a special temporary permit.

Event professionals who wish to bring their own liquor into an establishment must check local laws and be prepared to pay the establishment a per-bottle corkage fee.

Grand Hall

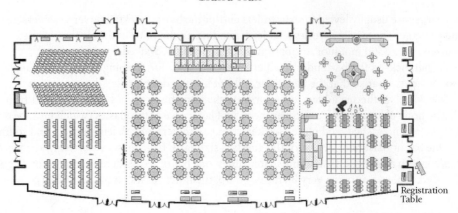

Registration
Table

FIGURE 10-2 Sample Room
Layout *Pearson Education, Inc.*

ROOMS

Room Setups

The way the room is set up is critically important to the success of any event. The room set can affect the flow of service, the amount of food and beverage consumed, and even the mood of the guests. The ambiance can make or break a meal function—be it a continental breakfast or a formal dinner. (See Figure 10-2)

Room setup includes tables, chairs, decor, and other equipment, such as portable bars, stages, and audiovisual equipment. It is essential that you communicate *exactly* how you want the room to be set to the banquet setup manager. This is accomplished on the **Banquet Event Order (BEO)** form and by using room layout software. These types of programs allow you to place tables, chairs, and other equipment into a meeting room plan. Room software demos may be viewed on a number of Web sites, including Meeting Matrix, Optimum Settings, and Room Viewer.

Room Rental Charges

Can they be waived? It varies depending on the venue. If the event is part of an event that also requires the use of sleeping rooms, it is easier to negotiate the room rental charge from the hotel. When undertaking catering events at hotels that are handled by the catering department rather than the sales department because there are no room nights involved, an event professional rarely encounters a rental fee for the space. Rather, there will be a minimum revenue requirement based on the amount of space needed for the event. The group may have to spend $50,000 to secure a ballroom for an event, which frequently means that guests eat *very* well. However, in event venues, otherwise known as off-premise venues, it depends on how the venue has set up its charge/ profit schedule. Most off-site venues charge a rental fee. Some charge a rental fee, some an admission fee per guest, and a few charge both and then add on catering, rentals, and service costs. The types of charges are almost always dependent on the size or projected profitability of the event. Everything is negotiable. At several venues, it may be possible to negotiate removing the rental charge when bringing a large or highly profitable event to the property; it varies depending on the venue.

AISLE SPACE Aisles allow people to move easily around the room without squeezing through chairs and disturbing seated guests. They also provide a buffer between the seating areas and the food and beverage areas. Aisles between tables and around food and beverage stations should be a bare minimum of 36-inch wide (3 feet), but it would be preferable to have 48 inches. Also, leave a three-foot minimum aisle around the perimeter of the room. Cross aisles should be six-foot wide. Check with the local fire marshal for local rules and regulations.

TABLES Allow 10 square feet per person at rectangular banquet tables. Allow 12.5 square feet per person at rounds. This assumes the facility is using standard 20- by 20-inch chairs.

Remember to deduct space taken up for furniture before calculating the number of people. Include large sofas found in many hospitality suites, buffet tables, portable bars, plants, decor and props, check-in tables, and so forth. Also, allow three square feet per person for dance floors. And always remember to check local fire codes.

Service

REQUIREMENTS   One bartender per every 100 guests is standard. If guests will arrive all at once, or you do not want long lines, you could have one bartender for every 50 or 75 guests, but there may be an additional labor charge. See Table 10-5.

Service is critical. Many excellent meals are ruined by poor service. Meal service levels can run from one server per eight guests to one server per forty guests. Most hotel staffing guides allow for a ratio of 1/32, but most event professionals want 1/20 or 1/16 with either poured wine or French Service.

Savvy event professionals negotiate for the following:

General

Rounds of 10:1 server for every two tables

Rounds of 8:1 server for every five tables

With poured wine or French Service

Round of 10:2 servers for every three tables

Round of 8:1 server for every two tables

Buffets 1/30–40

One server per thirty to forty guests

1 runner per 100 to 125 guests

French or Russian Service

Rounds of eight or ten

One server per table

One busser per three tables

Supervision   One room captain. One section captain for every 250 guests (25 rounds of 10).

Table 10-5 Space Requirements		

Space Requirements for Tables

Rounds	60-inch round =	5-foot diameter =	Round of 8
	72-inch round =	6-foot diameter =	Round of 10
	66-inch round =	Compromise size	Seats 8–10
Rectangle	6-foot long	30-inch wide	Banquet 6
	8-foot long	30-inch wide	Banquet 8
Schoolroom or classroom	6- or 8-foot long	18- or 24-inch wide	
Half-moon table	Half of a round Table		
Serpentine	¼ hollowed-out	round table	

Space Requirements for Receptions

Minimum (tight)	5½ – 6 square feet per person
Comfortably crowded	7½ square feet per person
Ample room	10+ square feet per person

Set Over Guarantee.   This is negotiable. It is the percentage of guests that the hotel will prepare for beyond the guarantee, in case additional, unexpected people show up.

Average overset is 5%, but you must look at the numbers, not just the percentages.

100 guests = 10% overset

100–1,000 guests = 5% overset

Over 1,000 guests = 3% overset

COCKTAIL SERVERS   Cocktail servers can only carry from twelve to sixteen drinks per trip. Counting the time to take the order, the time to wait for the drinks at the service bar, and the time it takes to find the guest and deliver the drink, it takes at least fifteen minutes per trip to the bar. This only makes it possible to serve from forty-eight to sixty-four drinks per hour. Cocktail servers are usually only used at small or VIP functions.

SERVICE TIMING   Fifteen minutes before you want to start serving, dim the lights, ring chimes, start music, open doors, and so on to get the guests to start moving to their tables.

The salad course should take from twenty to thirty minutes, depending on dressing or style of service. The main course should take from thirty to fifty minutes from serving to plate removal. Dessert should take from twenty to thirty minutes.

A typical luncheon: One hour and fifteen minutes

A typical dinner: Two hours

Tablescapes

The tabletop is the stage—it sets expectations and should reflect the theme of the event. Once seated, the focus is mainly on the table, so it is imperative that it not be overlooked.

The centerpiece should not block sight lines for people sitting across the table from each other. Centerpieces should be low or high with a Lucite or slender pole in the middle portion.

The *cover* is the place setting and includes placement of flatware, china, and glassware.

"Napery" is the term to include all table linens, including tablecloths, overlays, napkins, and table skirting.

Other décor may include ribbons, greenery, or other items relating to the theme of the meal.

Examples

Trailing flower garlands or ribbons between place settings

Different colored napkins at each cover

This "wow" dessert included a chocolate hand. *George G. Fenich*

Creative napkin folds at each cover

Creative centerpieces

Major props for **tablescapes** can be rented from prop houses, service contractors, party stores, or be provided by the hotel or club. Other props are small, decorative pieces that can be found in many places, such as:

Auto supply stores

Toy or crafts stores

Garden centers

Ethnic food stores or import shops

Travel agencies (destination posters)

Sports clubs or stores

Medical supply stores

Military surplus stores

FUTURE TRENDS

- There will likely be gradual and sustained efforts to embrace and integrate "green" products and practices.
- The trend is toward clean/slick/simple presentations and efficient service.
- There will continue to be a focus on big/bold flavor profiles.
- There is a trend toward fresh, locally/regionally sourced foods and products from outstanding specialty producers (Cowgirl Creamery, Niman Ranch).
- There is a growing trend to include a signature portfolio of "house made"' items (potato chips, jams, yogurt, jerky, olives, spice rubs).
- Strategic use of well-known branded products (Boars Head, Starbucks, Evian, Pellegrino).
- Tapas style small plates as reception choices.
- The food truck! Popular even now in Paris! An interesting addition to receptions as a themed station.
- Continued focus on providing additional craft beer options and bolder options for varietal wines.
- Investment in improved display and action station equipment (hinged chafing dishes, small convection burners, steamers, deep-fryers, self-draining cold beverage containers, stainless steel buffet table tops, rolling/folding buffet tables, display racks, lighted back-bar units).

Other Food Trends

- ***Classic Dishes Are New Again:*** Fads are on hold. People are looking for sophisticated interpretations of familiar food.
- ***Chicken Is Back in Style:*** There is a movement toward "anti-luxury," so chicken is preferred over beef for a closing dinner.
- ***Small Surprises:*** Even if budgets for meals are reduced, a "wow" item can be included to build some "buzz."
- ***Breakfast Can Be Tweaked:*** Some venues are allowing multiple groups to share the same breakfast buffet, thus saving cost. Another trend is to consolidate breakfast and lunch into brunch, thereby making it one meal instead of two, which results in cost savings.
- ***Easier Prep:*** Event professionals will choose foods that don't require extra labor such as making special sauces or preparing individual servings.

- ***Meal Mingling:*** More meals are focusing on networking opportunities in lieu of a large, long, sit-down meal. Lunches are going to a more "grab and go" style or on small, tapas style items. Dinners are often replaced by receptions.
- ***Organic Décor:*** Using cotton tablecloths instead of linen, low-cost candlescapes instead of laurels. "Compostable" plates and utensils are now more common.
- ***Locally Grown:*** The green movement has created more interest in products that are locally grown. The "story" of where food came from is being included on printed menus.
- ***Waste Reduction:*** There is continued focus on reducing the "waste" produced by meetings, conventions, and events.

Summary

Food and beverage is an integral part of most meetings. Astute planning can save a tremendous amount of money. Knowing what is negotiable and how to negotiate is critical. Food and beverage events create memories and provide a necessary service beyond being a refueling stop. While most attendees do not specify food and beverage events as a reason for attending a meeting, when asked later about a meeting, they will often rave (or complain) about these events. Catered events can set the tone of the meeting and create great memories that can result in future business, not only from the event professional but also from every guest in attendance.

Key Words and Terms

For definitions, see GLOSSARY, or http://glossary.conventionindustry.org

action station	barbacks	guarantee	set over guarantee
American Service	butler service	on-premise catering	tablescapes
attrition	catered event	off-premise catering	
Banquet Event Order (BEO)	corkage	room setup	

Review and Discussion Questions

1. What is the first step for an event professional when planning for an off-premise event? List five types of functions and give a brief description of each.
2. Describe how Family Style/English Service and Plated/American Style service differ.
3. What is the most important information to consider when deciding how much food to order for a group?
4. What is the average number of hors d'oeuvres a guest will eat during the first hour of an event?
5. What are the three categories of liquor?
6. What is the function of a hospitality suite, and what are the three types?
7. What are the important aspects of an event that are affected by how the room is set up?
8. When catering an event at a hotel, and no room nights are involved, which department handles the booking of the event?
9. Why is it imperative that the tabletop not be overlooked?

About the Chapter Contributor

Perry Lynch joined the faculty of the Rosen College of Hospitality Management at the University of Central Florida in 2006, after a 23-year career in catering and convention service with Marriott Hotels.

Previous Edition Chapter Contributor

Patti J. Shock, emeritus professor and chair in the Harrah College of Hotel Administration at the University of Nevada–Las Vegas.

CHAPTER 11

Legal Issues in the MEEC Industry

Knowledge of legal issues will save MEEC professionals money and keep them out of court. *Brian Jackson/Fotolia*

Chapter Objectives

This chapter provides the reader with an understanding of the following:

- The fine points of negotiation between the organizer and suppliers
- The concept of risk management and ways to deal with risk
- Taxation
- Employment laws
- The concept of intellectual property and how it relates to MEEC
- Ethics and unique applications in MEEC

INTRODUCTION

Whether we like it or not, we live in a very litigious society. Thus, legal issues are becoming increasingly important, especially in the MEEC industry. There are legal aspects or issues in almost everything we do as meeting planners and organizers. Contracts are a part of virtually every event and have become increasingly complex. One reason that contracts can be so long and complex is that the parties to the contract try to eliminate as much ambiguity as possible. Ideally, contracts will be as clear as possible upon reading by the average person. We enter into negotiations regardless of whether we are the buyer (meeting organizers) or suppliers (hotels, DMCs, caterers, etc.). We have to be concerned about risks such as force majeure (emergencies, crises, or disasters), people getting injured, and failures to perform. We also have to be concerned with national, state, and local laws that impact how we put on an event, who we employ, and the entertainment we use. In this chapter, we delve into many of these issues and provide some insight into legal issues. Remember that this chapter does not take the place of consulting with an attorney who is knowledgeable about MEEC and licensed to practice in your jurisdiction. Further, legal and ethical issues vary by country. This chapter uses a U.S. framework but has broad applicability around the globe.

NEGOTIATION

Negotiation is the process by which a meeting planner and a hotel representative (or other supplier) reach an agreement on the terms and conditions that will govern their relationship before, during, and after a meeting, convention, exposition, or event.

While many believe that the goal of a negotiation is to create a "win–win" situation, some say there can be no "win–win" because generally one or both parties have to compromise on some things. The real "winner" may be the party who is better prepared entering the negotiation and has the best bargaining leverage. In this regard, hotel representatives generally have an advantage over planners, since the hotels usually know more about the planner's organization than the planner knows about the lodging industry or the specific hotel under consideration. There are almost as many approaches to negotiating strategy as there are negotiators. One negotiator has offered these tips:

- *Do your homework.* Develop a "game plan" of the outcomes sought, and prioritize your needs and wants. Learn as much about the other side's position as you can.
- *Keep your eyes on the prize.* Do not forget the outcome sought.
- *Leave something on the table.* It may provide an opportunity to come back later and renew the negotiations.
- *Do not be the first one to make an offer.* Letting the other person make the first move sets the outside parameters for the negotiation.
- *Bluff, but do not lie.*
- *When there is a roadblock, find a more creative path.* Thinking "outside the box" often leads to a solution.
- *Timing is everything.* Remember that time always works against the person who does not have it and that 90% of negotiation usually occurs in the last 10% of the time allocated.
- *Listen, listen, listen … and do not get emotional.* Letting emotions rule a negotiation will cause one to lose sight of what result is important.

When negotiating meeting contracts—or any contracts—it is wise to keep some general rules in mind. The following general rules will help with the negotiation of a meeting contract:

- *Go into the negotiations with a plan.* A skilled negotiator knows his or her "bottom line," that is, what is really needed, what is just wanted, and what can be given up to reach a compromise result.
- *Always go into a contract negotiation with an alternative location or service provider in mind.* Bargaining leverage is better if the other party knows you can go somewhere else with your business.
- *Be thorough.* Put everything negotiated in the contract. Develop your own contract if necessary.
- *Do not assume anything.* Meeting industry personnel change frequently, and oral agreements or assumptions can be easily forgotten or misunderstood. Put it in writing.
- *Be specific.* For example, do not state "food and beverage prices will be guaranteed *12 to 18* months out." Instead, specify that "food and beverage prices will be guaranteed 12 months prior to the meeting" and make sure there is a cap on the amount they can increase from the time of signing the contract to that date.
- *Beware of language that sounds acceptable but is not specific.* For example, what does a "tentative first option" mean? Words like "reasonable," "anticipated," and "projected" should be avoided, since they mean different things to different people.
- *Do not accept something just because it is preprinted on the contract or the proposal is given to you by the other party.* Everything is negotiable.
- *Read the small print.* For example, the "boilerplate" language about indemnification of parties in the event of negligence can make a major difference in the resolution of liability after an accident or injury.
- *Look for mutuality in the contract's provisions.* For example, do not sign a contract in which the "hold harmless" clause only protects one of the parties. Such provisions should

be applicable to both parties. And never give one party the unilateral right to do anything, such as change the location of meeting rooms without consent of the meeting organizer.

In addition to the general "rules" applicable to all contract negotiations, there are some special rules about hotel contracts that should also be kept in mind:

- Remember that a meeting contract provides a "package" of funds to a hotel. Think in terms of overall financial benefit to the hotel (i.e., its total income from room rates, food and beverage, and so on), and allocate this to the organization's benefit.
- Never sign a contract in which major items like room rates are left to future negotiation. Future rates can always be set as a percentage of then-current "rack" or maximum increase over then-current "group" rates. This applies to rooms, catered food and beverage, audiovisual, and other expense items.
- Specify special room rates—such as for staff and speakers—and indicate any upgrades for them. Indicate whether these are included in the complimentary room formula, and specify what that formula is.
- While it is preferable to have specific meeting and function rooms designated in the contract, a secondary negotiation position is that they should be assigned at least 12 months prior to the meeting/event, depending on the time of the first promotional mailing. Do not permit a change in assigned meeting rooms without approval of the meeting organizer, but be prepared to agree to alternate space or pay for original space if the group numbers decrease significantly.
- Do not agree to any changes that are not spelled out either in the contract or in a later addendum. If an addendum is used, make sure that it references the underlying agreement and supercedes the language in it; and if it is signed at the time of the agreement, make sure that the agreement references the addendum. Be sure that all documents are signed by individuals who are authorized to bind the parties.

One of the most frequently overlooked yet most important parts of a hotel contract includes the names of the contracting parties. While the meeting's organizer is listed (an independent planner should always sign as an agent for the organizer or have an authorized representative of the organizer sign), the name of the hotel is, in almost all cases, simply listed as the name on the hotel marquee, like "Sheraton Boston."

But the hotel's name is merely a trade name—that is, the name under which the property's owner or management company does business. In today's hotel environment, it may actually be a franchise of a national "chain" operated by a company that the planner has never heard of. For example, one of the country's largest hotel management companies is Interstate Hotels & Resorts, Inc. Included in the more than 300 hotels that it manages are properties operating under the following "chain" names: Marriott, Holiday Inn, Hilton, Sheraton, and Radisson. Thus, if a contract with one of Interstate's properties simply states that it is with the "Gaithersburg (MD) Marriott," the planner might never know that the actual contracting party is Interstate Hotels & Resorts.

Every meeting contract should contain the following provision, usually as the introductory paragraph:

> "This Agreement dated _____ is between (official legal name of entity), a (name of state) (corporation) (partnership) doing business as (name of hotel) and having its principal place of business at (address of contracting party, not hotel) and (name of meeting organizer), a (name of state) (corporation) (partnership) having its principal place of business at (address of meeting organizer)."

Sleeping rooms generate the major share of hotel revenue, so this is often the biggest concern to hotels.

Catered food and beverage is also important but only if it is the "right" kind of food and beverage function, since not all functions are equal in value. For example, a seated dinner for 100 people is worth more to a hotel—in revenue and profit—than a coffee break or continental breakfast for the same number of people.

The type of entity organizing the meeting. Hotels know from experience that certain types of meeting attendees are likely to spend more at hotel food outlets (restaurants, room service, etc.) than other types of attendees who may venture outside the property for meals at more expensive restaurants. From experience, a hotel is also able to estimate the number of attendees who will not show up or who will check out early. Early departures and no-shows deprive the hotel of expected revenue.

If a meeting planner is going to successfully negotiate with a hotel, the planner should:

- Understand the relative strengths and weaknesses of the meeting as a "piece of business" that the hotel may be interested in: "how much is the piece of business worth?"
- Understand how a hotel evaluates business.
- Understand the competitive marketplace in which the hotel operates—for instance, its strengths, weaknesses, and occupancy patterns.
- Position the meeting in its best light, using detailed information and history of prior meetings to support this approach. The hotel may base its evaluation of a meeting, especially one it has never hosted before, on its perception of the industry or profession represented by the meeting organizer. Thus, the meeting organizer can counter any negative impressions, or play up positive ones by providing the hotel with as much information as possible on the organizer's meeting history. Especially helpful is information pertaining to previous meeting room blocks and subsequent room utilization, total spending on sleeping rooms, food and beverage, equipment rental, and ancillary services like recreational activities or in-room movies.
- Many hoteliers, particularly those who have been in the industry for many years, sum up meeting negotiations with this simple maxim: **Dates, Rates, and Space**—*You Can Only Have Two.*" By this maxim, for example, the planner can get the dates and meeting space he or she wants for a meeting, but may have to give a little on the rate. In reality, much more than space, room rates, and meeting dates are negotiable. Consider contract issues such as earning complimentary rooms for a certain number of reserved rooms, cutoff dates, rates after cutoff, attrition and cancellation clauses, meeting or exhibit space rental, comp suites, staff rates, limo service, audiovisual rates, VIP amenities, parking fees, and food and beverage provisions. In short, *everything* about a hotel (supplier) contract is negotiable. Likewise, in any other vendor or supplier contract, there are many negotiable items.
- Determine where the meeting organizer can be flexible. A negotiation often requires both parties to make concessions in order to reach an equitable, acceptable agreement. For example, if a planner understands that the meeting's space-to-rooms ratio is greater than customary, the planner can help his or her position by altering program format, eliminating 24-hour "holds" on meeting or function space that allows the hotel to sell the space in unused hours. The planner who refuses to be flexible is not likely to get the best deal. Changing arrival and departure dates to more closely fit the hotel's occupancy pattern can also lead to a successful negotiation. Moving the meeting forward or backward one or more weeks can also result in savings, especially if the preferred time coincides with a period of high sleeping room demand.

To understand how a hotel approaches a meeting negotiation, the planner must first know about the hotel. Some of the necessary information is obvious:

- The hotel's location—is it near an airport, downtown, or close to a convention center?
- The hotel's type—is it a resort with a golf course, tennis court, and other amenities; a "convention" hotel with a great deal of meeting space; or a small venue with limited meeting facilities?

However, some of the information that is important to know is not so obvious, and may in fact change depending on the time of the year. For example, it is important to know the mix between the hotel's transient business (that derived from individual business guests or tourists) and groups. Within the group sector, it is valuable to know how much business is derived from corporate, government, and association sources. It is also important to know what the hotel regards as "high" season, when room demand is highest, and "low" season, when demand is at its annual low. This information is important because it helps the planner understand the hotel's position in the negotiation process, and it may provide some helpful hints in structuring a planner's proposal to meet the hotel's needs.

Seasonal fluctuations may be driven by outside factors, such as events in the city where the hotel is located. For example, an informed planner will know that it is difficult to book rooms

Jazz Fest draws upward of 100,000 attendees per day to New Orleans in late April.   *Anton Gvozdikov/ Fotolia*

in New Orleans during Mardi Gras or during that city's annual Jazz Fest (in late April and early May) because hotels can sell their rooms to individual tourists at higher rates than to groups. Many hotels in Palm Springs, California, are heavily booked during spring break; therefore, favorable meeting rates may be difficult to obtain then.

The arrival and departure patterns of the majority of a hotel's guests are also important for a planner to know. For example, a hotel in Las Vegas is generally difficult to book for weekend meetings, since that city attracts large numbers of individual visitors who come to spend the weekend. A hotel that caters to many individual business guests may have greater availability on Friday and Saturday nights, when business travelers are not there. A national survey indicates that, for typical hotels, occupancy is lowest on Sunday evenings and highest on Wednesdays.

While hotels generate revenue from a variety of sources—and recently have become more sophisticated in analyzing these "profit centers"—the primary source of hotel income is sleeping room revenue; one industry research report estimates that, on the whole, more than 67% of all hotel revenue is generated from sleeping rooms.

Sleeping room revenue is profitable, with more than 73% of the income going to the "bottom line" as gross profit. This profit figure does not take into account expenses for marketing, engineering, general and administrative overhead, or any items related to debt service, such as mortgage payments and insurance. While food and beverage operations is the second largest source of revenue, this source is far less profitable, with about 25% being recorded as profit.

Hotels set their sleeping room rates—at least the published or so-called **rack rates**—in a number of ways. First, the hotel wants to achieve a total return on its investment. However, since nearly 50% of all rooms in all hotels are sold at less than rack rate, hotels vary their actual rates depending on a number of supply and demand factors, including time of year (which is a function of demand).

Most hotels have adopted the concept of **yield management**, also called revenue management, pioneered by the airline industry. In this approach, hotels are able to vary their rates almost daily, depending on the actual and anticipated demand for rooms at a particular time. The "yield management" concept may have some negative impact on meeting planners. For example, a planner who books a meeting fifteen to eighteen months in advance may find that, as the meeting nears, total hotel room utilization is lower than the hotel anticipated, so the hotel, hoping to generate additional revenue, will promote special pricing that may turn out to be less than what was offered to the meeting organizer. A contractual provision prohibiting this practice—which many hotels will not agree to—or at least giving the meeting organizer credit toward its room block for rooms booked at these lower prices can help take the sting out of yield management practices.

CONTRACTS

In far too many instances, **contracts** for meetings, conventions, and trade shows, and the ancillary services provided in connection with these events, contain self-serving statements, lack specificity, and fail to reflect the total negotiation between the parties. This is understandable since neither meeting planners nor hotel sales representatives generally receive training in the law governing these agreements.

By definition, a contract is an agreement two parties that details the intention of the parties to do (or not do) specific things. For example, at its most basic, a meetings contract says the meeting's organizer agrees to use a certain number of rooms and services and the hotel agrees to provide the rooms and services outlined.

A contract need not be called a contract but can be referred to as an "agreement," a "letter of agreement," a "memorandum of understanding," and sometimes a "letter of intent" or "proposal." The title of the document or understanding is not important—its contents are. For example, if a document called a "proposal" sets forth details of a meeting and contains the legal elements of a contract, it becomes a binding contract when signed by both parties. So, don't let the name at the top of the document mislead you.

The essential elements of a contract are:

- An offer by one party.
- Acceptance of the offer as presented by another party. This is typically done by signing the contract.
- Consideration (i.e., the price negotiated and paid for the agreement). Although consideration is usually expressed in monetary terms, it need not be—for example, mutual promises are often treated as consideration in a valid contract.

Offers can be terminated prior to acceptance in one of several ways:

- At the expiration of a specified time (e.g., "This offer is only good for twenty-four hours." After twenty-four hours, the other party cannot accept it because it expired.).
- At the expiration of a reasonable time period.
- On specific revocation by the offeror. In this case, however, the revocation must be communicated to the offeree to be effective.

A rejection of the offer by the offeree or the proposal of a counteroffer terminates the original offer, but a request for additional information about the offer is not construed as a rejection of the offer. For example, if an individual responds to an offer by saying, "I accept, with the following addition," that is not really an acceptance but the proposal of a counteroffer, which the original offeror must then consider and either accept or reject.

Often, a meeting contract proposal from a hotel will contain a specified termination period for the offer. These "offers" are usually couched in the phrase "tentative first option" or in a similar wording. Because the meeting organizer pays or promises nothing for this "option," it is, in reality, nothing more than a contract offer, which must be specifically accepted by the meeting planner. There is no legal obligation on the part of the hotel to keep the option or offer open for the time period stated.

In a meeting context, the hotel, venue, or vendor is usually the offeror—that is, the written agreement is generally proposed, after some preliminary negotiation, by them to the planner. The meeting organizer becomes the offeree, but a counteroffer is often made.

In order for an offer to be accepted, the acceptance must be unequivocal and in the same terms as the offer. Any deviation from the offer's terms is not acceptance; it is a counteroffer, which must then be accepted by the original offeror in order for a valid contract to exist.

Acceptance must be communicated to the offeror using the same means as the offeror used. In other words, if the offer is made in writing, the acceptance must be in writing. Mere silence on the part of the offeree is never construed as acceptance, and an offeror cannot impose an agreement on the other party by stating that the contract will be assumed if no response is given by a specified date.

As indicated, consideration is the price negotiated and paid for the agreement. While consideration generally involves money paid for the other party's promise to perform certain functions—for example, money paid to a hotel for the provision of sleeping rooms, meeting space, and food and beverage functions—it could also be an exchange of mutual promises, as in a barter situation.

Consideration must be what the law regards as "sufficient," not from a monetary standpoint, but from the standpoint of whether the act or return promises results in either a benefit to the promisor or a detriment to the promisee. The fairness of the agreed exchange is legally irrelevant; thus, the law is not concerned about whether one party "overpaid" for what he or she received. One need not make an affirmative promise or payment of money; for instance, forbearance, not doing something that someone is legally entitled to do, can also be a consideration in a contract.

It is important that both promises must be legally enforceable to constitute valid *consideration*. For example, a promise to commit an illegal act is not *consideration* because the law will not require one to commit that act.

Although a contract does not have to be in writing to be enforceable, every law student learns that it is better to have a written document since there can be less chance for a misunderstanding about the terms of the agreement. However, under what is called the "Statute of Frauds," some contracts must be in writing to be enforceable. This statute was first passed in England in 1677, and in one form or another has become a part of the law of virtually every state in the United States. The exception is Louisiana, where law is based on French Napoleonic code.

Among the agreements that must be in writing are contracts for the sale or lease of real estate and contracts that are not to be performed within one year of agreement. The latter includes contracts for meetings and other events that are to be held more than one year in the future. The former could also include a meeting contract, since the agreement might be construed as an organizer's "lease" of hotel space. The law requires these contracts to be in writing because they are viewed as more important documents than "ordinary" agreements. However, as indicated, planners are strongly encouraged to put all contracts in writing to avoid the possibility of misunderstandings.

A valid written contract must contain the identity of the parties, an identification or recitation of the subject matter and terms of agreement, and a statement of consideration. Often, where the consideration may not be obvious, a contract will state that it is entered into for "good and valuable consideration, the receipt and sufficiency of which are acknowledged by the parties."

When a contract is in writing, it is generally subject to the so-called "parol" evidence or "four-corners" rule of interpretation. Thus, where the written contract is intended to be the complete and final expression of the rights and duties of the parties, evidence of prior oral or written negotiations or agreements or contemporaneous oral agreements cannot be considered by a court charged with interpreting the contract. Many contracts contain what is often called an "entire agreement" clause, which specifies that the written document contains the entire agreement between the parties and supersedes all previous oral or written negotiations or agreements.

Parol Evidence

Parol evidence (or evidence of oral agreement) can be used in limited instances, especially where the plain meaning of words in the written document may be in doubt. A court will generally construe a contract most strongly against the party that prepared the written document; and if there is a conflict between printed and handwritten words or phrases, the latter will prevail.

Many contracts, especially meeting contracts, contain addenda prepared at the same time or sometimes subsequent to the signing of the contract. In cases where the terms of an addendum differ from those of the contract, the addendum generally prevails, although it is a good idea when using an addendum to specifically provide that in the event of differences, the addendum will prevail.

Planning and executing a meeting may involve the negotiation of several contracts. Obviously, the major—and perhaps most important—agreement is the one with the hotel and/or trade show facility. However, there can also be agreements covering a myriad of ancillary services, such as temporary employees, security, audiovisual equipment, destination management (e.g., tours and local transportation), entertainment, outside food and beverage, exhibitor services or decorating, and housing bureaus. Moreover, agreements may be negotiated with "official" transportation providers like travel agencies, airlines, and rental car companies.

Attrition, cancellation, and termination provisions in a hotel are frequently confusing. If not carefully drafted, they can lead to many problems (and much expense) if a meeting organizer does not fill the room block or wishes to change his or her mind for some reason.

Attrition

Attrition clauses (sometimes also referred to as *performance* or *"slippage clauses"*) provide for the payment of damages to the hotel when a meeting organizer fails to fully utilize the room block specified in the contract. Most hotels regard the contracted room block as a commitment by the meeting organizer to fill the number of room nights specified. However, in at least one case, a court determined that the room block did not represent a commitment by the meeting organizer; that decision was predicated, in part, on contract language that indicated that room reservations would be made by individuals and not by the meeting organizer.

A well-written attrition provision should provide the organizing entity with the ability to reduce the room block by a specified amount (e.g., 10% to 20%) up to a specified time prior to the meeting (e.g., six to twelve months) without incurring damages. Thereafter, damages should only accrue if the organizer fails to occupy a specified percentage (e.g., 85% to 90%) of its adjusted (not the original) room block. Occupancy should be measured on a cumulative room night basis, not on a night-by-night basis.

Because hotels sometimes offer rates to the general public as part of special promotional packages that are lower than those available to the meeting attendees, it is important that the meeting room **pickup** be measured by all attendance, regardless of the rate paid. This may involve some extra work on the part of the hotel and the meeting organizer, but the result could save the organization money, especially if the meeting attendance is not as expected. For example, the meeting contract could include language similar to the following:

> Group shall receive credit for all rooms used by attendees, regardless of the rate paid or the method of booking. Hotel shall cooperate with Group in identifying these attendees and shall charge no fee for assisting Group.

Using this language, an organization would submit its meeting registration list to the hotel and ask that the hotel match the list against those guests who are in-house at the time. An alternate approach, which many hotels reject, is to have the hotel give the group its in-house guest list and have the group do the matching.

Damages triggered by the failure to meet a room block commitment should be specified in dollars, not measured by a percentage of some vague figure such as "anticipated room revenue." The latter may provide the hotel with an opportunity to include estimated spending on such things as telephone calls, in-room movies, and the like. The specified damages should be based on the hotel's lost profit, not its lost revenue. With sleeping rooms, for example, the average industry profit margin is 75% to 80%, so the per-room attrition fee should not exceed 80% of the group's single room rate. The industry standard for food and beverage profit is 25% to 30%. In any event, damages for failure to meet a room block commitment should never be payable if the hotel is able to resell the rooms; the contract should impose a specific requirement on the hotel to try and resell the rooms and, if possible, require the hotel to resell the rooms in the organization's room block first.

Attrition clauses often appear in the portion of a contract that discusses meeting room rental fees, with the contract providing that meeting room rental fees will be imposed, typically on a sliding scale basis, if the room block is not filled. If the clause appears in conjunction with meeting room rental, it should not also appear somewhere else, resulting in a double charge, and language should be inserted making it clear that the meeting room rental fee is the only charge to be imposed in the event that the room block is not completely utilized.

Some meeting organizers have attempted to insert a provision that is, in essence, the reciprocal of an attrition clause. Such a provision would state that if the group exceeds its room block by a specified percentage (usually the same as the attrition percentage), the hotel would provide a monetary payment of a specified amount to the organizer's master account, recognizing the additional revenue generated by the larger-than-anticipated attendance. Hotels, however, have been generally reluctant to agree to such a provision, even though it can be argued that it is merely the reciprocal for damages for failure to fill a room block.

Cancellation

This is the provision that provides for damages should the meeting be canceled for reasons other than those specified, either in the same clause or in the termination provision. More often than not, this provision in a hotel-provided agreement is one-sided. It provides damages to the hotel in the event the meeting organizer cancels. A properly drafted agreement should provide for damages in the event either party (including the hotel) cancels without a valid reason. However, as indicated previously, some contract drafters believe that damages should not be specified in the event of a hotel cancellation because it only provides the hotel with an amount that it can use to buy out of an agreement.

If a cancellation clause will trigger a monetary payment to the hotel, the payment should be specified in dollars (not percentages of something) and should be based on the hotel's lost profit rather than lost revenue. When lost room revenue is involved, make sure to measure lost sales against the normal occupancy for the particular time of the year, not against the hotel's capacity. Damages should not be payable if the hotel resells the space. While many contract drafters strive for mutuality in provisions, there is a difference of opinion regarding specified damages in a contract for cancellation by the hotel. Some believe that this is important; others point out that it only provides the hotel with a predetermined figure that it can use to "buy out" of a deal and that may not actually reflect the true damages to the meeting organizer of hotel cancellation.

The meeting organizer should not have the right to cancel solely to book the meeting in another hotel or another city, or for the hotel to book another, more lucrative meeting in place of the one contracted for. However, a meeting organizer should be able to cancel, without payment of damages, if the hotel ownership, management, or brand affiliation changes; if the meeting size outgrows the hotel; if the hotel's quality rating (e.g., as measured by the American Automobile Association) changes; or for reasons that make it inappropriate or impractical to hold the meeting there. The latter language should be broad enough to cover so-called boycott situations, where a group decides not to hold a meeting in a particular location because of action taken by government. As an example, the organizer of a major shooting sports trade show—SHOT—canceled the event after the sponsoring city sued gun manufacturers who were the show's major exhibitors.

In some cases, cancellation is provided without damages as long as it is done within a specified time (e.g., two to three years) prior to the meeting. This gives the hotel ample opportunity to resell the space.

The damages triggered by a cancellation are sometimes stated on a sliding scale basis, with greater damages being paid the closer to the meeting date the cancellation occurs. Damages should be expressed as "liquidated damages" or a cancellation fee, not as a penalty, since the law generally does not recognize penalty provisions. As with damages in an attrition clause, damages should be expressed in dollar amounts, not room revenue (so that sales tax can be avoided) and should only be payable if the hotel cannot resell the space.

Termination

Sometimes called a **force majeure** or **Act of God** clause, this provision permits either party to terminate the contract without damages if fulfillment of the obligations imposed in the agreement is rendered impossible by occurrences outside of the control of either party. This usually includes such things as labor strikes, severe weather, and transportation difficulties. This provision sometimes contains the "inappropriate or impractical" situation referred to in the discussion of cancellation provisions. However, many hotels seek to limit termination to situations where performance becomes illegal or impossible, so some negotiation is usually required.

Example Terminology

Provide the ability to cancel a meeting without penalty or damages if:

a. Hotel ownership, management, or brand affiliation (often called the "flag") is changed.
b. The meeting outgrows hotel space or substantially shrinks in size.
c. The hotel does not perform satisfactorily at an earlier meeting (e.g., in the event of a multiyear contract with the same company).
d. An adverse change in the hotel's quality rating, as measured by the American Automobile Association or the Mobil Travel Guide.

Contracts provided to planners by hotels generally vary significantly from property to property, even within the same chain. Some of the variance can be attributed to the fact that some "chain" properties are managed by outside parties, making standardization difficult. Often, however, it has been the result of a lack of attention to the meeting contracting process by the chains themselves. Some hotels have resisted development of "standard" contracts, saying that all meetings are different and thus one contract cannot "fit all." More recently, though, most major hotel chains have adopted or are considering "standard" agreements, even though some of the provisions contain multiple options for use by sales representatives.

Because of the differences in contracts supplied by hotels, and because it is often so easy for planners, even experienced ones, to overlook key elements of a contract, many meeting organizers are developing their own "standard" contract. While many meeting organizers may be unsure of the costs involved in having a competent attorney prepare this type of document, such costs are minimal when compared with the time (and therefore expense) involved in reviewing each and every contract proposed by a hotel, whether the review is conducted by counsel or by a meeting planner or other staff member.

An organizer's development of its own contract will ensure that its particular needs are met and will minimize the chances of subsequent legal problems caused by a misunderstanding of the terms of the agreement.

Dispute Resolution

No matter how carefully a contract is written, disputes may occur either because the parties might disagree as to their individual rights and obligations or because one of the parties may perform less than had been promised. These controversies seldom involve precedent-setting legal issues; rather, they concern an evaluation of facts and interpretation of contract terms. When these differences arise, parties often prefer to settle them privately and informally in the kind of businesslike way that encourages continued business relationships.

Sometimes, however, such resolution is not possible. This leaves the "aggrieved" party with three options: Forget the possibility of reaching a solution and walk away from the problem, go to court and sue, or resolve the dispute through other means.

Going to court can be an expensive and time-consuming proposition, with crowded court dockets delaying a decision for several months, or in some cases several years. Attorney fees can mount up quickly, especially if extensive pretrial proceedings are involved. Depending on the court's location, one of the parties may have to expend additional fees for travel expenses. Since court cases are matters of public record, potentially adverse publicity may result.

For this reason, arbitration is gaining favor as a means of settling disputes. "Arbitration" is one form of alternative dispute resolution. In arbitration, one or more arbiters are chosen to hear the each party's side of the dispute and make a decision about the outcome. Under rules administered by the American Arbitration Association, arbitration is designed for quick, practical, and inexpensive settlements. It is, at the same time, an orderly proceeding, governed by rules of procedure and standards of conduct prescribed by law. Either party can utilize lawyers, but there is a minimum of pretrial procedures. If arbitration is chosen as the dispute-mechanism procedure in the contract, the parties also generally agree that the results are binding; that is, they cannot be appealed to a court of law. The contract should also specify the location of the arbitration. Arbitration is not generally a matter of public record, so all of the proceedings can remain private.

While the filing fee required to commence an arbitration proceeding is generally higher—often considerably so—than that required to begin litigation in the courts, the overall cost of arbitration is frequently significantly lower. This is because of the absence of extensive pretrial maneuvering and because attorneys are often discouraged or even prohibited from participating as representatives of the parties. The "downside" to arbitration is that some believe arbitrators may often "split the difference" in a dispute, seeking an equitable solution rather than following the letter of the law.

If the parties choose arbitration as a means of settling disputes, the choice should be made before disagreements arise, and language governing the arbitration option should be included in the meeting contract. If arbitration is not selected, the contract should spell out which state's law (e.g., where the meeting took place or where the meeting organizer is located) will be utilized to resolve a court dispute.

Under the American system of justice, each party to a court suit or arbitration proceeding is required to bear the costs of its own attorneys unless the agreement provides that the winning party is entitled to have the loser pay its attorneys' fees and costs.

Finally, a well-drafted contract should specify the damages to be awarded in the event of a breach by either party. Such an approach takes the decision out of the hands of a judge or an arbitrator and leaves the dispute resolver only to determine whether a breach of the agreement occurred. Damages are typically stated as "liquidated damages"; that is, damages that the parties agree in advance will be the result of a breach. Courts will generally not honor a contract provision that imposes a "penalty" on the one breaching the agreement, so that term should be avoided. As an example, a conference was held in a Las Vegas hotel, but the meeting organizer failed to pay the $57,000 master bill presented by the hotel for the meeting expenses. After multiple unsuccessful efforts to get the meeting organizer to pay the bill, the hotel decided to bill the individual attendees for a pro rata share of the master bill. After many upset attendees and much negative media, the hotel reversed its position and went back to pursuing the meeting organizer for the payment.

RISK MANAGEMENT

What Is Risk? What Is Risk Management?

All meetings involve an element of **risk**. *Risk* is the possibility of suffering loss or harm. *Risk management* is the process of assessing, analyzing, mitigating, and controlling risk. Risk is the "what" and risk management is the "how." Risk is used here as an umbrella term to include loss or harm caused by everyday occurrences as well as emergencies, disasters, crises, and catastrophes, all of which are defined differently based on the scope and impact.

Imagine that an exhibition is to be held outdoors and during setup, torrential rains come, making it impossible to complete setup or to hold the exhibition. This is an example of a risk. Now imagine that the wise exhibition planner has rented tents under which the exhibits can be placed so that the show can go on. That's risk management.

The stages of risk management are:

1. Preparedness
2. Mitigation
3. Response
4. Recovery

The outdoor exhibition example earlier can be used to simply and quickly walk through the steps of risk management.

How do you plan for natural risks like fires and tornadoes?

1. *Preparedness:* The exhibition organizer would have *assessed and analyzed* the possible risks during the planning stage. Risks identified during the assessment might have included not only rain (and other inclement weather) but accidental injuries, violence, airline stoppages (preventing exhibitors or attendees from getting to the destination), and so on. In analyzing these risks, the exhibition planner looks at the *probability* that each risk would occur and the *consequences* if it did. The planner probably decided that an airline stoppage was less likely to occur than rain, and so might focus more on planning for rain.

2. *Mitigation:* In the *mitigation* stage, the planner would try to determine what he or she could do to decrease the probability that rain would occur (and quickly realize it's hard to control the weather!) and to decrease the consequences if it did rain. Realizing that the latter was more manageable, the planner would have had a tent rental company on standby (or rented them just in case if the budget allowed), contracted with a backup indoor venue, purchased event cancellation insurance in case the exhibition was rained out, and carefully monitored the weather reports on the days leading up to the exhibition. Part of the mitigation phase is creating and implementing contingency plans.

3. *Response:* The tricky thing about risk response is figuring out both *when* to respond and *how.* If two days prior to the event dates, the weather forecast is calling for 60% chance of rain on the exhibition date, should the planner implement the rain plan? Does that mean getting the tents or just alerting exhibitors to the possible change in plans? If the planner waits until the morning of the exhibition, does that give him or her enough time to implement the rain plan? The answers to these questions really depend on the size and scope of the event as well as the nature of the plan.

4. *Recovery:* A risk that results in loss or harm can cause damage to property, people, or to more intangible aspects—like the organizer or planner's reputation. In the case of the outdoor exhibition, recovery might just include refunding exhibitor's or attendee's fees who didn't attend, or filing a claim with the insurance company. In the case of a full-blown disaster or crisis, however, the recovery stage can be much more serious and take a much longer time.

Despite the obvious importance, some of the reasons meeting planners may not have a plan are that they don't have enough time or staff, their organization doesn't require it, they don't have a risk management budget, or they simply don't know what to do!

How Risk Management Affects Your Meeting or Event

Risk management isn't just another thing that planners have to do; it is just part of the meeting planning process. It should inform decisions on a myriad of meeting and event logistics. For example, the meeting organizer may decide not to choose a coastal destination for an event during hurricane season. The planner may decide to choose one facility over another because security is better, and so on.

PREPAREDNESS AND MITIGATION   Conducting a risk assessment and analysis will also help the planner determine which mitigation measures should be implemented. Examples of some common mitigation measures include:

- Contracts—signed prior to the meeting or event, contracts mitigate risk by narrowing or shifting liability to the responsible party or they specify exactly what the monetary damage fees (e.g., attrition or cancellation) might be for underperformance of the contract.
- Insurance—the mitigation effect of insurance is that it shifts some of the liability for financial loss to the insurance company. In exchange for paying a premium, the meeting/event organizer knows that the insurance company will pay a claim for loss or damage if it falls within the boundaries of the insurance policy.
- Security—hiring security guards to provide physical security and/or monitor a property is a way of mitigating the risk of injury or loss.

RESPONSE   Meeting and event planners focus primarily on the preparedness and mitigation stages of risk management. That is, planners are responsible for determining what the risks might be, how they might affect the meeting or event, and implementing measures to reduce the likelihood that the risk will occur and the impact if it does occur. However, not everything is within the control of the planner.

Should a realized risk adversely affect a meeting or event in spite of the best planning, the meeting/event professional needs to have a risk team ready to respond. Depending on the nature of the realized risk, the response may be as simple as sending an announcement to participants about a change in the program. Or, it may be as complex as having to help coordinate an emergency evacuation and provide first aid to the injured. A simple response will be up to the planner's risk team. A complex response will likely require emergency professionals: firefighters to put out a fire, police to regain control of a crowd, and emergency medical professionals to administer first aid. The response must fit the realized risk.

RECOVERY   Recovery also depends on the nature of the realized risk. If the rain in our ongoing example is so bad that the outdoor exhibition has to be cancelled, recovery would include insurance paying claims for the losses suffered by the exhibition organizer as well as the actions by the organizer to overcome any bad press, upset members or exhibitors so that the organization can survive both from a financial and a public relations standpoint.

- *Workers' compensation* insurance is mandatory in all U.S. states. It provides coverage for employees who are injured on the job. While most states permit employers to either self-insure or purchase coverage from private companies, a few states (such as Nevada) require employers to purchase this insurance only through a state fund. This could cause a problem if an organization holds a meeting in Nevada and hires temporary employees to perform services at the meeting. To avoid this problem, organizations should utilize individuals provided by a temporary agency located in that state.

- *Comprehensive general liability* (CGL) policies are the business equivalent of a homeowner's policy. They protect the organization against personal injury claims and loss (including theft) or damage to the insured's property as well as the property of others. Although these policies are designed to cover "all risks," they frequently have exclusions, and it is important to carefully review what is not covered as well as what is included within the policy's scope.

It is not clear from many of these policies whether they insure against events that occur outside of the organization's premises, such as at meetings, conventions, and trade shows. If they do not cover these types of events, they should be amended to cover them or additional insurance should be secured. Furthermore, many general liability policies may not cover liability resulting from alcoholic beverage service without a specific amendment. Athletic events, such as obstacle courses or races, may also be excluded from coverage without a specific endorsement. In addition, it is important to be sure that the policy specifically refers to and covers contractual liabilities, like those that would be incurred under a meeting contract.

Another coverage that should be checked as part of any CGL policy is alcohol server liability. Serving alcoholic beverages at an event, especially if the guests are going to drive home afterward, can subject the organizing entity to the risk of litigation if an attendee becomes intoxicated at the event and then is involved in an automobile accident. Such an occurrence led to a lawsuit in Washington, DC, against a company holding a holiday party for its employees at an off-site location.

Planners should review the definition of who is the "insured" under the policy, since it may be important to extend coverage to the organization's employees and volunteers as well as the organization itself. Frequently, a hotel or convention center will require that it be designated as an "additional named insured"; this is easily done through the insurance broker who procured the policy.

How much insurance to carry is also a concern for planners. While multimillion dollar awards are all too common in liability cases, the typical general liability policy has coverage limits of 2 to 4 million dollars. If additional coverage is desired, it is relatively easy to obtain an "umbrella" policy that provides coverage in the 5 to 10 million dollar range.

- *Association professional liability* (APL) policies protect the organization and its officers, directors, staff, and volunteers against personal liability arising from their official actions. This type of policy is broader than a traditional directors and officers (D&O) liability policy in that it covers the organization as an entity as well as individuals.

Unlike many other forms of insurance, APL policies issued by different companies vary greatly, and organizations may find that certain coverages, such as antitrust or libel protection, may not be available from a particular company. Therefore, it is important to obtain several sample policies and premium quotations in order to properly evaluate options. The lowest-cost policy may not always be the best.

- The APL policy generally does not protect the organization against the kind of liability that is covered by the CGL policy. APL premiums are generally considerably higher than those for general business liability, although some carriers are attempting to cut premiums by writing APL policies in conjunction with comprehensive general liability coverage.

- *Event cancellation* policies are a specialized form of protection, insuring against unforeseen circumstances, such as labor disputes, inclement weather, or damage to the convention or meeting facility. The failure of a featured speaker or entertainer to appear may or may not be included in the coverage. These policies often cover the organization's personal property (such as computers and other equipment) utilized at the convention or meeting and the loss or theft of on-site convention receipts. However, this coverage is generally in excess of any other existing personal property or loss of money coverage that an organization may carry. It is not intended to be used as "first dollar" coverage against loss to personal property and/or money and receipts.

- Planners should seek to include coverage for reduced attendance as well as total cancellation at an event, although most policies will not protect against the lack of attendance for reasons other than unforeseen circumstances. Many policies will include so-called remedial action taken by a meeting organizer, such as purchasing fans to deal with a failed air-conditioning system. In addition, some policies will provide automatic coverage for smaller meetings (e.g., under $50,000 budgeted gross revenue) when an organization's major meetings are covered. This coverage only applies to the period of time the coverage is in force for major meetings. These policies also do not protect against liability to third parties.

- *Exhibitors liability* policies provide protection to the organization for damage caused by exhibitors. In addition, these policies generally protect the organization for loss or damage that it causes as part of its convention or meeting management. Many policies also provide host liquor liability coverage. One company quotes a premium on the basis of $50 per exhibitor, with a $500 minimum. This type of coverage may not be necessary if all exhibitors are major companies and the exhibitor contract includes a provision requiring indemnification of the organization for damage caused by the exhibitor's negligence.

AMERICANS WITH DISABILITIES ACT

Federal legislation makes it illegal to discriminate against or fail to provide a "reasonable accommodation" for people with disabilities. The legislation resulted in passage of the Americans with Disabilities Act (**ADA**) of 1990, which places responsibility on the owners and operators of public facilities to make reasonable accommodations for people with many types of disabilities. A **disability** is "a physical or mental impairment that substantially limits a major life activity of an individual." This may include people in wheelchairs, those with visual impairments, hearing impairments, and food intake restrictions as well as "invisible disabilities" like those having cancer, epilepsy, or other conditions that may not be immediately visible. The ADA Amendment Act of 2008 became effective January 1, 2009; so criteria for identifying a person with a disability and the appropriate "reasonable accommodation" have been more broadly construed in recent years.

The following is the stated purpose of ADA:

1. to provide a clear and comprehensive national mandate for the elimination of discrimination against individuals with disabilities;
2. to provide clear, strong, consistent, enforceable standards addressing discrimination against individuals with disabilities;
3. to ensure that the federal government plays a central role in enforcing the standards on behalf of individuals with disabilities; and
4. to invoke the sweep of congressional authority, including the power to enforce the Fourteenth Amendment and to regulate commerce, in order to address the major areas of discrimination faced day-to-day by people with disabilities.

For more information on the Americans with Disabilities Act, see the U.S. government's ADA Web site, www.ada.gov.

This act applies to meeting planners and organizers as well as facilities and vendors. Meeting organizers must (1) determine the extent to which attendees have disabilities and (2) make reasonable efforts to accommodate the special needs of those attendees at no cost to the attendee. As a result, we now see sections on registration forms asking if the attendee has any special needs. One of the most common relates to dietary needs, such as the individual who is lactose intolerant (cannot drink milk or consume milk products). The planner would not have to provide milk substitutes for that attendee because the situation does not impair a major life function. Another example is the attendee who is hearing impaired. The planner would have to provide a "sign language" interpreter. Readers may have seen these interpreters in class or during important speeches. For those with vision impairment, the planner may have to provide documents with extra large type or produced in Braille. Failure to accommodate attendees with disabilities can result in legal action and fines. Furthermore, the accommodations requirement is not limited to attendees. It applies to employees as well.

The planner must be aware of the ramifications of the ADA and be sure that all facilities used meet the standards. The planner must also be sure that their activities and programs meet the guidelines set forth in the act. Be aware, however, that this act only applies to events and meetings in the United States. Canada does not have the equivalent of the ADA, and many of its facilities do not meet the standards put forth in the act. Accessibility and accommodation of those with disabilities varies significantly from county to county.

INTELLECTUAL PROPERTY

The right of the authors of "original works of authorship" includes literary, dramatic, musical, artistic, and certain other intellectual works. For more information on copyrights, see the U.S. government's copyright Web site www.copyright.gov.

Many meetings and trade shows feature events at which music is played, either by live musicians or through the use of prerecorded CDs. Music may be provided as a background (such as at a cocktail reception) or as a primary focus of attention (such as at a dinner dance or concert). At trade shows, individual exhibitors as well as the organizing entity can provide music.

Regardless of how music is provided, it is important to remember that under the federal **copyright** act, the music is being "performed," and according to many court decisions, the entity organizing the event is considered to be controlling the "performance," even if that "control" means only hiring an orchestra without telling them what to play. The only recognized exemption to the "performance" rule is for music played over a single receiver (radio or TV) of a type usually found in the home.

The American Society of Composers, Authors and Publishers (**ASCAP**) and Broadcast Music, Inc. (**BMI**) are membership organizations that represent individuals who hold the copyright to approximately 95% of the music written in the United States. ASCAP and BMI exist to obtain license fees from those who "perform" copyrighted music, including radio stations, retail stores, hotels, and organizations that organize meetings, conventions, and trade shows. A 1979 decision of the U.S. Supreme Court conferred on ASCAP and BMI a special, limited exemption from normal antitrust law principles. This decision has enabled them to develop "blanket" licensing agreements for the various industries that utilize live or recorded music.

Following negotiations with major meeting industry organizations (such as the International Association of Exhibits and Events and the American Society of Association Executives) in the late 1980s, both ASCAP and BMI developed special licensing agreements and fee structures for meetings, conventions, trade shows, and expositions. These special agreements were designed to replace earlier agreements under which hotels paid licensing fees for meetings held by others on the property. Although the negotiated agreements technically expired at the end of 1994, ASCAP and BMI have extended them on a year-to-year basis, with slight increases in licensing fees. Under court decrees, ASCAP and BMI are forbidden to grant special "deals" to individual meetings, so the agreements, which must be signed, are the same for all meetings and cannot be altered to meet the needs of a particular meeting. Failure to sign these agreements— and agreements with *both* organizations must be signed—could subject a meeting or trade show organizer to costly and embarrassing litigation for copyright infringement.

Under copyright law, an organization cannot meet its obligation by requiring the musicians performing the music or the booking agency or hotel that provided the musicians to obtain ASCAP and BMI licenses. The entity organizing the event must obtain the requisite licenses.

Jibbitz, Inc., the official maker of snap-on accessories for Crocs (shoes), attended the WSA trade show as an exhibitor. At the trade show, the Jibbitz exhibit staff noticed another exhibitor promoting the sale of snap-on accessories for Crocs. Because Jibbitz, Inc. (as a wholly owned subsidiary of Crocs, Inc.) was the only official maker of these accessories, it filed a trademark infringement lawsuit against the other exhibitor. Jibbitz, Inc. was awarded $56 million in damages.

Recording or Videotaping Speakers

An organization organizing a meeting will often want to make audio or video recordings of certain speakers or programs, either for the purpose of selling copies to meeting attendees to those who could not attend, or for archival purposes.

Speakers or program participants have a common law copyright interest in their presentations, and the law prohibits the organizing organization from selling audio or video copies of the presentation without obtaining the written permission of the presenter. Many professional speakers who also market books or recordings of their presentations frequently refuse to provide consent to be recorded by the meeting organizer.

Permission can be obtained by having each speaker whose session is to be recorded sign a copyright waiver, a simple document acknowledging that the speaker's session is going to be recorded and giving the organizing entity permission to sell the recordings made of the speaker's presentation. If the recording is to be done by a commercial audiovisual company, a sample waiver form can usually be obtained from that company, or the sample form following this summary can be used.

LABOR ISSUES

Preparation for on-site work at meetings and trade shows often involves long hours and the use of individuals on a temporary or part-time basis to provide administrative or other support. It is therefore important for organizations to understand how federal employment law requirements impact these situations.

The Federal Fair Labor Standards Act (FLSA), adopted in 1938, is more commonly known as the law that prescribes a minimum wage for a large segment of the working population. Another major provision of the FLSA, and one frequently misunderstood, requires that all workers subject to the law's minimum wage coverage *must* receive overtime pay at the rate of $1\frac{1}{2}$ times their "regular" rate of pay *unless* they are specifically exempted by the statute.

There are many common misconceptions that employers have about the FLSA's overtime provisions, including the following, all of which are not true:

- Only hourly employees (and not those paid on a regular salary basis) are eligible for overtime.
- Overtime pay can be avoided by giving employees compensatory time off instead.
- Overtime need only be paid to those who receive advance approval to work more than forty hours in a week.

Over the years, the Department of Labor regulations and court decisions have made it clear that overtime pay cannot be avoided by a promise to provide compensatory time off in another workweek, even if the employee agrees to the procedure. According to the U.S. Department of Labor, the only way so-called comp time is legal is if it is given in the same week that the extra hours are worked or in another week of the same pay period, and if the extra time off is sufficient to offset the amount of overtime worked (i.e., at the time-and-one-half rate).

The use of comp time is probably the most common violation of FLSA overtime pay requirements, and it occurs frequently. This is because many employees, particularly those who are paid by salary, would rather have an extra day off from work at a convenient time to deal with medical appointments, holiday shopping, or simply "attitude adjustment." Compensatory time is also frequently—but not legally—provided when a nonexempt employee works long hours in connection with a meeting or convention, then is given extra time off in some later pay period to make up for the extra work.

Overtime cannot be limited to situations where extra work is approved in advance. The law is also clear that premium pay must be paid whenever the employee works in excess of 40 hours per week—or is on call for extra work—even when the extra effort has not specifically been approved in advance. Thus, if a nonexempt employee works a few extra hours in the days prior to a meeting to complete all assignments for that meeting, the employee must be paid overtime.

Overtime pay is not limited to lower salaried employees or those paid on an hourly basis. The FLSA requires *all* employees to receive overtime unless they fall under one of the law's specific exemptions. The most generally available exemptions are the so-called white-collar exemptions for professional, executive, and administrative employees.

In order to determine whether an employee falls within one of these exemptions, one should review the FLSA and applicable regulations and interpretations carefully. What is explained here is simply a summary. It is also most important to remember that the exemptions only apply to those whose actual work activity falls within the definitions; job titles are meaningless in determining whether an employee is exempt.

- The professional exemption is available only to those whose job requires that they possess a skill obtainable only through an advanced degree. This is generally limited to lawyers, physicians, architects, and some engineers. An employee whose employer prefers, or even requires, an advanced degree cannot be exempt from overtime unless the actual job being performed—such as general counsel—requires such an education.
- The executive exemption is available only to those whose primary duty is management and who regularly supervise the work of two or more full-time employees (or their part-time equivalents). Thus, someone who has the title "Director" but who only supervises an administrative assistant or secretary is not exempt from overtime under this category.
- The administrative exemption is probably the most difficult to understand, although it may be available to those employees who cannot qualify under either of the other two white-collar exemptions. According to the Labor Department regulations, an administrative employee is one whose primary duty is the performance of nonmanual (i.e., office) work directly related to management policies and who, in the course of that work, generally exercises discretion and independent judgment. The regulations make clear that an administrative assistant is not exempt from overtime merely because he or she exercises discretion over such things as what office supplies to order or how to process meeting or convention registrations. These decisions are viewed as merely carrying out established management policy.

It is important for all employers to know which of their employees are exempt from overtime pay requirements and which are not. This is especially significant when employees are asked to work long hours at meetings or conventions, particularly those held out of town, or to "pitch in" and help complete a large project. When in doubt about overtime, an organization should review job descriptions with a competent human resources professional or experienced counsel.

ETHICS IN MEEC

The preceding part of this chapter deals with legal issues, and the event professional can look to legislation or legal advisors for assistance in dealing with them. There are many other issues, actions, or activities in MEEC that may be legal but may raise questions of ethics. Ethics guide our personal and professional lives. Furthermore, the issue of ethics has come to center stage with the unethical practices of businesses like Enron, Imclone, Martha Stewart, and others. Ethics is addressed on the evening news and on the front page of newspapers today. The MEEC industry, by its very nature, offers a multitude of opportunities for unethical behavior or practices.

How someone responds to an issue regarding ethics is personally and culturally based. What is ethical behavior in one community or society may be considered unethical in another. Loyalty to personal friends versus an employer is another ethical consideration faced in the MEEC industry. Ethical issues and personal conduct are an important aspect of any industry, including MEEC. The topic cannot possibly be covered in a few paragraphs. Thus, readers are encouraged to seek additional sources of information on this topic.

SUPPLIER RELATIONS

Some planners feel suppliers are out to make a buck and will do anything they can to get the contract for an event. Some believe that suppliers and vendors will promise anything but may not deliver on their promises. While promising more than can be delivered, or embellishing their abilities may be legal, it may not be ethical. On the other hand, many suppliers and vendors feel meeting/event professionals tend toward overstatement, for example, in estimating the number of rooms they will use in a hotel and the amount their group spends on food and beverage. This too is an ethical question. The solution to these issues is to put everything in writing, preferably in the contract.

Even with a contract, the buyer (planner or organizer) and the seller (vendor or supplier) should be as open, forthright, and honest as possible in dealing with each other. A relationship not built on trust is a fragile relationship, at best. Furthermore, given the increasing importance of relationship marketing, honest and ethical behavior can lead to future business.

Still another ethical issue deals with the ownership and use of intellectual material. Destination management companies (DMCs) in particular often complain that meeting planners submit requests for proposals (RFPs) to many suppliers and the DMCs spend quite a bit of time, energy, and money to develop creative ideas and programs to secure the planners business. However, there are many cases in which a planner will take the ideas developed by one DMC and have another implement them, or the planner may then do this on his or her own. Is this legal? Yes. Is it ethical? No.

Still another issue for suppliers concerns the offering of gifts. Should an event professional accept gifts and privileges from a supplier or vendor? If amenities are accepted, is there some obligation on the part of the salesperson to repay the supplier by steering business in the vendor's direction? When does one cross the line from ethical to unethical behavior? Is it proper to accept a Christmas gift, but not proper to accept football tickets when offered? Event professionals working for the U.S. government are prohibited from accepting any gift with a value of $50 or more.

Another ethical question regards so-called familiarization or "fam" trips. Fam trips bring potential clients on an all-expenses-paid trip to a destination with the hope that they will bring their business to the community. But what if a planner or organizer is invited on a fam trip to a destination but has no intention of ever holding a MEEC gathering in that location? Should the planner accept the trip? If accepted, is there some implicit expectation that the planner *will* bring business to the locale? Although it is perfectly legal to accept a trip with no intention of bringing business to the locale, is it ethical?

The planner or organizer of a large MEEC gathering has significant clout and power based on the economic and social impact of the gathering. He or she may ask for special consideration or favors based on this power. It may be ethical to exert this influence on behalf of the group such as when negotiating room rates, catering rates, and complimentary services. However, is it ethical for the planner or organizer to request personal favors that only benefit himself or herself? Is it ethical for the planner to accept personal favors from a supplier or community?

Examples of ethical issues and questions abound in the MEEC industry. An individual must adhere to a personal code of ethics, and many industry associations have developed their own code of ethics to which members must adhere. Colleges and universities have recognized the need to address ethics by implementing courses on the subject. The discussion of ethics in this chapter is meant to make readers aware that ethics is an important aspect of the study of the MEEC industry, but it is not meant as a comprehensive treatise.

FUTURE TRENDS

- Legal issues and precedents continue to vary by geographic region—even within the same country.
- Laws that are seemingly unrelated to the meetings industry will nonetheless affect the meetings industry.
- As developing countries mature, the complexity of legal issues will increase.
- Who has the upper hand in negotiation—the organizer or the vendor—will depend upon the economy. In a good economy where demand is strong, the supplier has the upper hand; in a weak economy, it is the organizer or buyer.

- Attendees, speakers, and other meeting participants will become more informed and savvy about legal issues that protect their rights such as ADA and intellectual property.
- The need for competent legal advice will remain: for organizers and vendors alike.

Summary

Legal issues are an increasingly important factor in the MEEC industry. This chapter is meant to provide insights into some of these issues, such as negotiation, contracts, labor, and intellectual property. There are other issues that were not discussed, and entire books are devoted to them. Readers are reminded to seek legal counsel whenever appropriate.

Now that you have completed this chapter you should be competent in the following Meeting and Business Event Competency Standards:

MBECS – Skill Measure Value of Meeting or Business Event

Sub skills	Skills (standards)
A 3.04	Evaluate effectiveness of risk management plan

MBECS – Skill 6: Manage Risk Management Plan

Sub skills	Skills (standards)
C 6.01	Identify risks
C 6.02	Analyze risks
C 6.03	Develop management and implementation plan
C 6.04	Develop and implement emergency response plan
C 6.05	Arrange security

MBECS – Skill 17: Engage Speakers and Performers

Sub skills	Skills (standards)
H 17.04	Secure contracts and communicate expectations

MBECS – Skill 32: Professionalism

Sub skills	Skills (standards)
K 32.03	Demonstrate ethical behavior

Key Words and Terms

For definitions, see GLOSSARY, or http://glossary.conventionindustry.org

Act of God	BMI	disability	rack rates
ADA	CGL	force majeure	risk
APL	contract	negotiation	yield management
ASCAP	copyright	parol evidence	
attrition	dates, rates, and space	pickup	

Review and Discussion Questions

1. Discuss the negotiation process. What are the important points for each party to be aware of?
2. Define a contract.
3. What laws are important to know with regard to contracts?
4. Discuss negotiating contracts.
5. Discuss attrition.
6. What is the difference between cancellation and termination with regard to events?
7. Discuss the different types of risks a planner may face and how to deal with them.
8. What is the ADA, and how does it impact events and gatherings?
9. What is intellectual property, and why should a planner or organizer be aware of it?
10. What are some of the labor issues unique to MEEC?

About the Chapter Contributor

Tyra W. Hilliard, PhD, JD, CMP, is a speaker, writer, and multipreneur focused mainly on the topics of law, risk management, and change. She has created and delivered many presentations on these and related topics throughout North America as well as in more than a dozen countries in Europe and Asia.

The meetings industry has been very good to Tyra during her 20+ years of involvement. She was named Professional Convention Management Association (PCMA) 2013 "Educator of the Year," chaired the Convention Industry Council's APEX Contracts Panel, and was honored for professional achievement as an Educator by the PCMA Education Foundation. She was also recognized with the MPI Chairwoman's Award for her work on the Meeting & Business Events Competencies & Standards Committee.

Tyra has worked in many aspects of the meetings industry—she has been an attorney, a meeting planner, a catering manager, a convention and visitors bureau sales manager, and an association executive.

Her industry experience gives her a unique perspective on the legal and business aspects of meeting and event management.

She is one of very few people to have a PhD in Hospitality, be a practicing attorney, and earn the Certified Meeting Professional (CMP).

Contact Information:

Tyra W. Hilliard, Ph.D., JD, CMP, Associate Professor
117 Rosemont Street
Saint Simons Island, GA 31522
Phone: (912)506-8708
Tyra.Hilliard@gmail.com
http://www.tyrahilliard.com

Previous Edition Chapter Contributor

James M. Goldberg is a principal in the Washington, DC, law firm of Goldberg & Associates, PLLC.

CHAPTER 12

Technology and the Meeting Professional

Satellite technology is used to beam MEEC programming to remote locations.
Tsuneomp/Fotolia

Chapter Objectives

After reading this chapter, the learner will be able to:

- Recognize how technology currently impacts meeting professionals
- Identify new technologies that support meeting/event marketing and communications
- Understand the critical technology terms that apply to the hospitality industry
- Recognize the best Web portals for researching industry information
- Understand how social media is impacting the meetings industry

INTRODUCTION

Advancements in technology over the past five years are creating seismic shifts in how meetings are marketed and produced. It's not that rates, dates, and space aren't still the key negotiation items, nor is it that technology has eliminated the need for face-to-face meetings. In fact, both of these components remain as true today as they did 30 years ago.

What has radically changed, and exponentially increased, are the tools at the disposal of the meeting/event professional. **Social media** and mobile devices have become an inextricable part of the event landscape. Event and guest bandwidth needs continue to grow in importance and in many cases become a tipping point in the site selection process.

Conference attendees, in large part due to the increase of generation Y attendees, are now demanding a less passive, more interactive experience at the event. Meetings that preach "turn your phones off" in the meeting space now find that attendees believe this is an antiquated model. Attendee engagement through social media and mobile devices are the lifeblood of most successful events.

From mature to late breaking technologies, this chapter will provide the information required to be knowledgeable about what technology is impacting the MEEC industry and how it will help ensure success.

BEFORE THE EVENT OR CONFERENCE

Technology-savvy meeting professionals have more tools than ever before to help research, promote, and organize their event. While this "pre-event" use of technology was once the primary use of technology in the MEEC, it still can be said that technology applications are of great support to the conference planner in this phase of the event's lifecycle. From desktop uses to virtual site selection support, not to mention the ubiquitous Web-based marketing tools, the planners certainly have plenty of choices in making the process work for them.

Virtual Site Selection and Research

ONLINE RFPS As the World Wide Web developed in the mid to late 1990s, one of the first tools available, both through convention and visitors bureau (CVB) Web sites and hotel and third-party planning sites, was the one that allowed the planner to create an efficient online **RFP** (Request for Proposal—the tool many planners use to distribute information to hotels about potential meetings). The model continues to shift from a fee-based RFP to a free approach, from the sites of hotels and CVBs to those of third-party organizations. The idea remains the same: Allow the planners to input their specifications (specs) easily, and allow the Web to be the conduit for distributing the information to potential cities and hotels.

Without standardization, each RFP has its own nuances, which could cost the planner time in completing each one. Planners still need to determine which vehicle (CVB-based, hotel-based, or third-party-based) is best to distribute their meeting specs.

Some planners eschew the RFP forms, and just use e-mail and the Internet to save time in their process by allowing an Office-based spec sheet to be distributed. No matter how one looks at it, the technology is saving significant time in helping planners distribute their meeting requirements.

VIRTUAL TOURS Industry stats have estimated that over one-half of all meetings are booked without a formal site inspection, a number that continues to grow. While there is no substitute for visiting a hotel or destination, the Web's visual capabilities have allowed planners to at least get a sense of a facility if time or budgetary restrictions prevent their physical inspection.

The concept of a virtual site inspection has morphed over the years, from its meager beginnings in using only pictures of meeting rooms. Videos and 360° panoramic tours of meeting spaces and sleeping rooms are now the norm, and at a significantly lower cost than ever.

Technology and Site Inspection

While **virtual tours** offer the planner a feel for a site, it can never fully replace the actual site visit. In addition to the visit confirming (or not) the virtues of a hotel or event facility, a new critical component is in the inspection of the property's technological capabilities. This is both in the meeting space as well as in the guest room.

The thread that applies to both meeting and guest room technologies is in the bandwidth requirements. Bandwidth will be extensively covered later in this chapter.

While bandwidth hogs much of the tech site inspection conversation, it is not the only part of the site analysis. How a property integrates technology into their on-site experience is another consideration. Hotels are using tablets and smartphones to enhance the guest experience. From a downloadable hotel app to an in-room iPad acting as a virtual concierge, this guest room enhancement is becoming more heavily used. Perhaps in a few years, we won't even need to discuss this, as it will be a standard part of the guest experience.

There are plenty other tech features that can enhance the value of the hotel to the planner, by creating a better on-site experience for the guest. Mobile hotel check-ins expedite the guests' arrival. Strategically placed device charging stations are always appreciated. A well thought out hotel app can make for a better on-site experience.

So, it is clear that while the event professional needs to continue to do their due diligence with the traditional site inspection elements, they should now add technology to that list.

Meeting Industry Information Portals

While less elegant, but still enormously useful, industry information **portals** continue to thrive. While search engines are incredibly useful for general research, the MEEC industry has a great deal of information at the fingertips of the savvy Web users who can find resources and tools at their disposal in a few clicks. There are many sites that have great information, but their discussion is focused only on where registration (or paid subscription) is not a requirement of entry.

Any discussion of information portals for the hospitality industry begins with the Web site of Corbin Ball. From his home page, linking onto his favorites page presents the viewer with nearly 3,000 industry-related Web sites, organized categorically. Ball keeps the site updated frequently and has plenty of additional information of value for the meeting professional.

A newer Web portal, also designed for planners, is the Meeting Pool. It is on a smaller scale than Corbin's site; this site includes the "Event Tech Decision Engine," designed to facilitate choosing of tech vendors for the event.

MARKETING AND COMMUNICATIONS

Are event Web sites obsolete? Perhaps not yet. However with the enormous growth of social media tools for event information and conversation, coupled with the mobile devices becoming the go-to tool to connect to the Web, an expensive, "old school" Web site, without a leaner mobile version, isn't going to serve the audience as well in the coming years.

Web Sites and Strategic Communications

It used to be all about one-way communication: Information sent from the event organizers to the (potential) attendees. In the past few years, as social network sites have become synonymous with real-time communication, the model of event communication has clearly become a two-way model.

Web sites are still an important part of the communication conversation. Not only do they need to integrate a two-way communication model, but they still must serve the purpose of efficiently providing critical information to the conference attendees. The best online event models have both successful social media and mobile strategies and are easy to find, navigate, and even make purchases from the event Web site.

Event Web Sites

Overshadowed in the social media revolution is that one-way tools still have some importance in MEEC. The event Web site is to today what the conference marketing brochure was a generation ago: a place to provide information, create interest, and, hopefully, offer people one way to register for the conference.

The best Web sites integrate a two-way strategy (such as including Facebook and Twitter feeds), but having that site that can allow people to find out everything they need to know about the event is of critical importance. The core rules of a successful conference Web site include:

The need for a clear, easy way to find information.

Focus on the 5 Ws about the conference or event (who, what, where, when, and why).

The ability to make the sale (in the MEEC industry, the payment process on the registration form).

A frequent issue with event organizers is not getting information on the Web site early enough. While there is no definitive time frame, it is clear that if you're running an annual event, information about next year's meeting should be ready to go live the day that this year's meeting concludes. It's just common sense. If people are pleased with the conference, why shouldn't you allow them to register for next year when their memories are still vivid from the past event?

Social Media
Odua Images/Fotolia

Social Media

While the conference Web site is still the fulcrum of the online marketing presence, the usage of social media tools to enhance the traditional Web presence is an essential element of today's online meeting, marketing, and communcations.

Do you want to know a sure-fire way to kill a conference? Make sure you don't use any social media. While the value of social media is difficult to accurately quantify (though there aren't a shortage of tools telling you how you should be doing that), the effect of social media in meetings and every form of communication today is undeniable. The quantity of social media options for the planners is staggering. The following are the ones making the greatest impact today.

TWITTER   For many event professionals **Twitter**, and not Facebook, is the essential conference social tool. Twitter has become the real-time conversation place. While the amount of content flowing on Twitter is overwhelming, it can be fine tuned, and made highly useful, for the event professional.

At the core of the Twitter value is the hashtag (#). Used before a keyword, such as the event's acronym (e.g., #MPIWEC14), the hashtag provides a way for posts to be threaded and aggregated. It has become standard for many planners to establish their event hashtag at the start of the event's promotion and marketing cycle, allowing the organic conversation to take place and keep the conference dialogue going.

Aside from events, hashtags also allow the event industry to share fantastic content with one another. Many industry professionals agree that both the quality and quantity of content on Twitter surpasses any traditional media designed for the MEEC industry. One such example is the #eventprofs tag, which all meeting professionals need to follow.

CURATION TOOLS   Due to the extreme amount of content coming at us (which can be referred to as the Social Tsunami), we need tools to help filter this flow. Social and mobile curation tools are designed for that purpose. Meeting professionals can (and should) be effective content publishers about their event. Two spectacular tools to help this include Paper.li and the mobile app Flipboard. Planners, as well as suppliers, can use the tools to create their own event magazine at no cost.

FACEBOOK   The 600-pound gorilla of social media is indeed Facebook. With over 1 billion users, its reach cannot be denied. Event specific Facebook pages are becoming more frequently used, though many say the value of those aren't as great as they had hoped.

Facebook does have excellent meeting communities for people to share and follow industry content. At the apex of this is the MeCo (Meetings Community) Group. This is the Facebook extension of MeCo's popular Google Group list (also an excellent meeting professional online destination). This group offers an excellent peer to peer industry conversation.

In early 2014, Facebook released its first curation app. Called Facebook Paper, it is designed to transform Facebook's news feed into a richer content, story telling, and sharing platform. Time will tell how valuable a tool this may become to event planners.

YOUTUBE   It is surprising, with the amount of video on the Web, that every conference and organization does not have its own YouTube channel. Stats continually show that video posts have better traction and response than text and/or photos. A conference YouTube channel can include event promotion, speaker and attendee interviews, and other snippets of valuable content for the attendees. In our industry, Collinson Media marketplaces (Connect, Collaborate, and Rejuvenate) have continued to use their YouTube channel and videos in a "best of class" approach.

LINKEDIN   LinkedIn may be more rolodex than true social media, but many planners, especially baby boomers, find it to be their go-to social tool. LinkedIn has a content curation service (called Pulse), though many users find their greatest value to be the groups and high level communities hosted on LinkedIn.

GOOGLE+   Google's social media offering is not the ghost town that critics claim. In fact, many people believe that the level of professional interaction is greater here than any other social media. Google+ also spawned one of the best tech tools of the past five years. Google Hangouts (now an independent app) allows anyone to host free video conferences for up to 10 people. It also has seamless publishing of these videos out to the user's YouTube channel.

Other Social Tools

Over the past few years, visually based social media has exploded onto the scene. Many planners (especially special event and wedding planners) use Pinterest as their essential social tool. With its focus solely on images, it has a very passionate following.

Mobile/social tool Instagram has seen great adoption in the MEEC industry, as planners can get attendees to be involved in the documenting of their meeting. Combining the power of the visual image with the content threading of the hashtag, it's becoming a frequently used meeting tool.

Another facet of social media usage in our industry is the meeting's customized social community. Frequently integrated within conference apps, these services allow a private social channel for conference goers. Companies such as Pathable and IntroNetworks can design and customize these experiences for events.

Regarding "legacy" social media, there still is a great value proposition for many groups. **Blogging** continues to be a great way to establish content expertise, as well as enhance search engine optimization. **Podcasting** still can offer great streamed educational content. **RSS** (Really Simple Syndication) feeds, somewhat supplanted by Twitter, Facebook, and other curation tools, still can provide the user the ability to aggregate and stream content to their followers.

What's next on the social media horizon for meeting professionals? The continued use of these tools is a given. The integration of social media with your mobile experience will also continue to grow. As for new tools, just wait a few days. We haven't seen the end of discovery and development in this area.

Room Design Software

Another level of more efficient communications is how the planners can share information with the facility to ensure that their wants and needs are translated into the actions of the facility. Conference resumes create a very effective flow chart of what has to happen, and at what time.

Certain aspects of the event (themed parties, banquets, or just unique setups) are not as efficiently communicated by the written work. In these cases, planners use CAD (computer-aided design) **room design software** to enhance the communications.

The MEEC industry has many versions of this type of software. They tend to be simple to use but can greatly range in price. Some work better for meetings; others focus on special events. Two products that provide this capability include Meeting Matrix and Vivien.

The latest in-room design enhancements is the 3-D room tour. Once you create your room setup, a click of a button transforms it into a virtual 3-D tour, with the room setup precisely as the event professional diagrammed. In some cases, the hotel can enhance that by providing the actual room images (carpeting, windows, lighting, sconces) as part of the 3-D walkthrough. In this case, you may not even be sure if the image is real or virtual.

Selling the Show Floor

Another way technology is enhancing the event communications and marketing is by assisting the trade show manager in selling the show floor. Traditional exhibit sales were focused on a document called the Exhibit Prospectus, along with a generic layout of the show floor.

By posting the show floor diagram on the Web, and using its interactivity, trade show managers can now offer potential buyers a better look at where they might want their booth. Advantages of this include updated layouts (as the show floor diagram is frequently modified when exhibitors buy space) as well as helping buyers locate a floor space that is either near or far from their competitors (depending on their approach). The use of colors to represent booths can help differentiate which ones are available, and the ones where premium costs apply.

Almost every trade show now uses some kind of virtual enhancement to the trade show floor selling process. These sites also include a downloadable version of the Exhibit Prospectus, as well as other information of use for the exhibitor. One of the better known vendors is Expocad.

Online Registration

A few years ago, when discussing event technology, the topic of online registration would dominate the conversation. One of the first critical benefits of the technology to the MEEC industry,

3-D view of exhibition booth
Vegel/Fotolia

the ability to register for the event online, truly enhanced the marketing and communication of the event organizers.

Currently, the industry needs to look at online registration as a relatively mature technology, which most planners who need to use it do. It is interesting to note that some meetings still do not use online registration. Many meetings, especially internal meetings where attendance is mandatory, do not wish to incur the expense of establishing a professional online registration presence, preferring to use more traditional, or even e-mail approaches to handling meeting registration.

With this said, there are still a number of issues that confront planners when establishing the online registration process. The largest one for many planners is the integration of data. If it is agreed conceptually that even in the best of circumstances, 100% of the attendees will not use an online service, then the planners' challenge is to make sure that when they integrate the data, there are no inaccuracies or duplication of records. Ensuring that the online service can properly export into whichever tool you are using to maintain the remaining records (such as Excel) is a critical question to ask when considering companies to use.

Another issue that is raised by organizations using online services is in the added, unexpected expenses. One particular area of concern is in the creation of additional reports. The planner has two approaches to offset this issue. One is understanding all of the reports they might require and having this discussion negotiated into the package when purchasing the service. The other, more technology-savvy approach is to learn how to use the report writing feature. Many online registration services use the product "Crystal Reports" to generate reports for the client. For others, they still download content into Excel to manage the data.

Regarding online resources that can perform the online registration service, there are too many to mention. Research using an industry portal, such as Corbin Ball and his industry favorites, will give the user a plethora of options from which to choose.

Desktop Applications

While there are dozens of industry specific software packages on the market, the clear leader in the MEEC industry is still the basic MS Office Suite. With Word, Excel, Access, and PowerPoint, the event professional has the tools on his/her desktop to manage all components of any event. However, it is important to note that the "desktop" of the planner is now less a traditional desktop or laptop PC as it may be the tablet or other mobile devices where planners and suppliers do the majority of their work.

MS office is beginning to shift to becoming more of a Web-based tool. Office 365 is the Web-based version of the standard MS tools. Continuing to compete with other online office-based tools, such as Google Drive, these tools continue to be standards for meeting professionals, with the only twist being the portability of the device on which they need to be utilized.

However, this general package does not fill every need. Many planners, especially in organizations with noncentralized meeting departments, need tools that allow information to be shared across the organization. The industry has a number of tools that foster better information centralization.

At the core of this need to centralize information is the ability for organizations to be aware on the amount of purchasing leverage they have. The individual planning a small meeting within a large organization is at a disadvantage in terms of negotiation, unless they can combine their hotel room contracting with others within the organization. This is where third-party software tools can have a significant advantage over the MS Suite. While more expensive, they frequently provide exceptional cross-organization value by allowing organizations to bundle their purchasing needs.

The Convention Industry Council, the organization that manages the Certified Meeting Professional (CMP) examination, has been at the forefront of establishing the **Accepted Practices Exchange (APEX)**—for the MEEC industry. The essential concept of APEX is to make the industry more efficient by creating a set of standards that all parties within the industry would accept. As was noted earlier, APEX is also involved in helping planners understand conference bandwidth needs better. (A great link to learn more about APEX is found at the Convention Industry Web site, http://www.conventionindustry.org/standardspractices/apex.aspx.)

DURING THE EVENT

You've created the ideal Web site. The social networks are in place and active. You efficiently communicated and marketed to your prospective attendees and exhibitors. You established an ongoing dialogue with your constituents using the various technologies. Is your technology usage finished? Of course not.

Even before you go on-site with the meeting/event, you need to be considering how you want technology to support your goals and objectives at the conference. From your setup work to awareness of the devices that can complement your (and your attendees') goals, technology is playing an enormous role in creating a successful conference/event experience for all of the event's shareholders—planners, exhibitors, and attendees.

Setting Up Your Infrastructure

The event professional understands the importance of negotiations with hotels. From rates, dates, and space to every other aspect of the event, the professionals, armed with knowledge and information about their event and the destination, can have a productive give and take with the hotel, to create a win–win event.

However, many event professionals are fearful about or unaware of the technologies. Thus, they leave out any discussion of the technology during this part of the planning process. And, this can be a very expensive omission. The technology-savvy planner, however, understands enough about the technologies that support their event so that they know the need to plan for (even negotiate) it during the initial stages of planning.

As was discussed earlier, planners need to think about issues of bandwidth. They also need to think about how they will use the Internet and other technologies to support their goals. In addition, the technology-savvy planners will think about how their attendees will want to use technology to enhance their meeting experience. While Jane Planner may not be able to implement all of these technologies, she can identify which ones are most critical (and useful) to successfully achieve everyone's goals, thereby allowing the technology to play a spectacular supporting role in the success of the conference or event.

Bandwidth

Simply defined, bandwidth is the maximum speed of the Internet coming into a facility or a space such as a meeting or guest room. Today's planner needs to be aware of the four major components to investigate and inquire about:

> Guest room
>
> Speaker/presentations
>
> HQ office needs
>
> Attendees meeting room needs

A critical question that the planner should ask about in these four areas is whether the hotel or venue can offer shared or dedicated bandwidth. As the names imply, shared bandwidth is where the internet pipeline is shared among the users. Hotel sleeping rooms are one example of this. Bandwidth in public spaces (like your neighborhood coffee bar) also is shared. Attendee bandwidth in the meeting space also falls under this category.

However, is shared bandwidth acceptable when your CEO is giving the big presentation, complete with streaming content from the Web? Since the speed of shared bandwidth is based on the number of users at any given time (as well as how they are using it), one cannot imagine any planner wanting to take that risk. Additionally, the organization's on-site management needs should also be a dedicated stream of bandwidth.

Today's planners have tools to test the bandwidth while they are on the site visit. The free app/Web tool "SpeedTest" allows the immediate testing of bandwidth into a space. Planners should understand that this is a snapshot at a given point of time and needs to be supplemented with conversations with the hotel or venue. The Convention Industry Council's APEX has created the industry's first Event Bandwidth Estimator, allowing planners to estimate their bandwidth needs based on projected attendees and fundamental categories of usage. For many meetings, bandwidth requirements are so critical for the success of the conference that they are part of the event contract.

Technology Is Great: When It Works

A MEEC Industry conference included a session that was meant to be at the cutting edge of technology. Attendees sitting at tables were each provided a tablet while others were invited to use their smart devices. All were provided log on information. The concept was to have content streamed to each attendee. Two-way communication was incorporated where attendees could send text to the presenters and participate in audience polling. The session began well. However as more and more attendees logged on, communication slowed and eventually the entire session crashed. This was due to insufficient bandwidth. Technology is great: when it works.

Conference Apps

Perhaps the biggest shift in the usage of meeting technology over the past few years is the development and standardization of the conference mobile app. Just a few years ago, when smartphones such as the iPhone and Android were in their infancy, there was no thought about how a mobile device could somehow become the attendee's essential tool to navigate the conference. Yet fast forward a few years, and more tech-savvy (and "greener") planners are reducing their carbon footprint by minimizing (or in some cases eliminating) the need for conference programs and printed handouts by replacing them with **conference apps**.

Today's planner should begin thinking about producing a conference app at least a few months prior to the event, if not at the beginning stages of the event's life cycle. At its most essential, the conference app provides all of the information that had previously been published in the conference program and more.

Two Essential Flavors

When thinking about creating an app for your conference or event, the first, and possibly most important consideration, is the style of app to choose. The two major approaches are "native apps" and "Web-based" apps. Both have pros and cons to them.

Native apps are the style of apps that we have become accustomed to using. These "programs" are downloaded and live inside of the mobile device. While connectivity is still important on-site for these devices, it is for either the downloading of the app, or the interactivity (primarily in social feeds) that is one of the apps' features. As the name implies, being a native app does mean that continual internet connectivity is not absolutely necessary for these to work. A major challenge and discussion point for the native app is in regard to the operating system for which it is written in order to be utilized. It has become trendy to build great apps for iOS (iPhone, iPad) devices, which has the negative impact of eliminating any user with an Android or other smart phone. The smart conference planner will make sure that whichever type of app is developed, that they maximize the number of attendees who can utilize it. Otherwise, why bother at all?

Web-based apps are more like mobile Web sites, optimized for the smaller screen. As such, for these to work at events, adequate bandwidth must be available to all conference attendees. Since many properties (and planners) still do not provide for this, this type of app won't work well in a limited bandwidth environment. However, on the plus side of this process is that an attendee with any smart device (one that has a browser) can use this service.

App pricing also runs the gamut. Freemium, ad-based models, such as Guidebook and Bloodhound, provide the planner the opportunity to create a low-cost/free version. This is especially useful when implementing the conference app for the first time. EventMobi, a Web-based app provider in the industry, couples their product with the ability for the planner to design it themselves. Other top players in the meeting app industry include QuickMobile, CrowdCompass, DoubleDutch, and E-proDirect. This is definitely a changing landscape.

One other app conversation that is part of the productivity tools of today's planners are the apps that they use to get their work done. The challenge in discussing this is how quickly new apps (and new needs) are being developed. For the current time, here's a list of a few apps, which many event professionals have found exceptionally helpful.

> Cloud Storage—Dropbox
>
> Notetaking—Evernote
>
> File Reading—Good Reader
>
> Translation Tool—Word Lens
>
> Airport Flight Info—Flight Board

Wired versus Wireless or Both?

When considering the bandwidth needs of an event, another consideration in MEEC venues is how the bandwidth is delivered to the attendee. Facilities have the capability of both wired and wireless connectivity. The tech-savvy planner will discuss both these options during their site visit. Wired connectivity tends to be a bit more stable but is clearly of little value to the attendee who wants and needs their connectivity wherever they are at the event.

If the planner is really thinking through the area of connectivity thoroughly, they will even find out how good the cellular signal is within the facility. Phones that have 4G LTE capabilities (which most major ones do) can provide high-speed bandwidth through their cellular signal, thereby reducing the reliance (and in some cases cost) of expensive dedicated wireless bandwidth. Like any technology, this should be tested throughout the venue to see which carriers work well and where the dead spots may be.

Digital Recording and Streaming Media

The General Session is a critical part of any annual meeting or conference. The marketing success of many conferences depends on the quality (and often name recognition) of the keynote speakers because they establish the tone of a conference.

However, there are many people who cannot attend and would like to watch/hear the talk, either in real time or on an archived basis. The organization can extend its keynotes (as well as other meeting components) to those who cannot attend by digitally recording the event and streaming it over the Internet (frequently referred to as Webcasting) or creating podcasting content to share or sell.

If you have never done this at a meeting, be aware that a lot of extra coordination and support is required, especially with video content. The event professional will need to have cameras (and video/audio engineers) in the session to ensure that the recorded material is of good quality. Also needed is a company to digitize the video into a format that can be electronically distributed. The event professional will need to determine whether the event should be streamed live (always a more risky proposition) or archived. Another issue to decide is whether people will have free access to it, or will the organization charge a fee for people to virtually attend?

While learning about the technical side, the event professional must also understand a great deal about their audience, and what they might want to view online. Age and demographics certainly play a role in whether an entire session should be digitized, or if a highlights approach is best for their group. The adage "Know Your Group" applies to all aspects of meeting planning, even the technological side.

NFC and RFID

These two acronyms are at the core of many of the interactive technologies available on-site at conferences. **NFC** stands for Near Field Communications, which is a short-range, high-frequency wireless technology, allowing for information exchange between certain devices. **RFID** stands for radio frequency identification and are the tags (readers) that can be used to access these signals. RFID tags are commonplace as anyone living in a city knows with tolls from bridges or tunnels using RFID tags (known by a variety of names, including EZPass, SmartPass, and others) to quickly pay these fees. They also can be used to inventory products in a company's warehouse, enabling workers to better track their products. RFIDs and NFC are finding a use in the MEEC industry as well, mainly in use in **interactive nametags**.

Interactive Nametags and Networking Devices

Although not as trendy as it was a few years ago, perhaps the most widely used RFID is occurring in nametags. Either attached to a slim piece of paper behind the badge, or as part of a slightly larger wearable nametag device, the RFID-based service offers better networking and interactivity between conference attendees, as well as between attendees and vendors.

RFID devices frequently contain program contents, surveys, instant messaging capabilities, and other interactive tools for the attendee to utilize while at the event. The badge is now their communication device and program (as well as nametag) for the duration of the event. However, with the development of the smartphone, it is unclear whether this technology will continue to be used for the long haul.

The interactive, RFID-driven nametag, has two well-defined meeting-specific uses:

CEU Tracking   Many organizations need to track attendance at each educational session in order to provide CEUs (continuing education units) for the attendee (in many industries, these units are critical to maintain certification required for employment). The RFID-based tag, coupled with readers in each room, can automatically track attendance, so that proper CEUs can be awarded. Medical and scientific meetings are conferences where a significant value of attending is to allow the individual to obtain the required CEUs.

Interactive Message Centers   In the older days, conference message centers consisted of a phone (and a hired attendant to take messages), along with a cork board and push pins. Today's RFID-based systems can provide an electronic board that, as you walk past the board, will display your name and indicate whether you have any messages waiting. This is a far cry from cork board and push pins.

When thinking about the networking advantages of RFID devices, don't forget about the pre-event attendee networking options discussed earlier in the chapter. Today's attendee, when supported by a technology-savvy meeting professional, can truly take advantage of the enormous benefits of conference networking by using these systems. Tomorrow, perhaps these services will be completely integrated into ones personal mobile device.

Lead Retrieval Systems

For many years, trade shows and exhibits have used **Lead Retrieval Systems** to help capture customer information. The process begins with the meeting organizer asking questions during the registration process that will help identify information of importance to the exhibitor. These questions often include the attendees purchasing responsibility, and nature of products and services in which they may have interest.

The information is coded into a badge, though it needn't be an RFID. From the 1990s through today, many groups still use a simple bar coding on the badge (or even a credit card–based system) that can contain this information.

When the attendee enters the trade show floor and interacts with an exhibitor, the exhibit staff members can ask to swipe the badge with their lead retrieval device (typically, these are rented to the exhibitor for the duration of the show by a vendor who is supporting the meeting). Once swiped, this information now resides in their handheld lead retrieval device. At day's end, the exhibitors can download this information to their spreadsheet or database, and have customized thank you notes e-mailed to the attendee before their work for the day is complete (not to mention excellent information about their prospective clients).

The job of the event professional in this process is to identify and select a system or service that can support the lead retrieval process. Since exhibitors require this level of information to determine whether exhibiting at a function will potentially help their business, lead retrieval systems are primarily used for exhibitions and trade shows. However, these systems have also been used to help facilitate attendee surveying using automated kiosks around the event.

Also available to the planner is what is known as a reverse lead retrieval system. Instead of the exhibitor scanning the badge of the attendee, the attendee uses a handheld device to scan information positioned in the booth of the exhibitor. When utilized, it is frequently found in the larger shows.

As for the future of lead retrieval systems, it is clear that the integration of this functionality into the smartphone (and frequently the conference app) is the new approach. With all of the devices that people carry around today, one more piece of hardware isn't high on the wish list.

The "Virtual" Trade Show Booth Model

RetailNext was looking for a way to stand out on the crowded floor at Retail's Big Show, hosted by the National Retail Federation at the Jacob K. Javits Convention Center. The company decided to try a new tactic to entice attendees to stop at its booth: a life-size, lifelike virtual presenter from **Prsonas**.

The company positioned the virtual presenter in a high-traffic spot in its booth. While in idle mode, the unit would look around and wave to attract attention from passersby. As attendees got near, motion sensors triggered it to speak a welcome message that invited them to select an option from an attached touch screen, such as watching a video about RetailNext or submitting contact information. As attendees stepped away from the unit, it would say good-bye and thank them for visiting the booth, and RetailNext staff members were nearby to answer any questions.

This was one of the first virtual presenters created with Prsonas's new computer-generated system, which creates the lifelike image entirely through computer animation rather than shooting video of a real actor. Live talent is used for the voice recordings, because it is warmer and more engaging than a computer-generated voice. Clients provide the scripting for the presenter's messages—which can be recorded in multiple languages—and they also customize its appearance, choosing hairstyle and color, eye color, and clothing.

The virtual presenter can be configured to swipe attendee badges for lead capture or process credit cards for exhibitors that are selling products in their booths. The system captures data such as how many people interacted with the presenter, the duration of the interactions, and which topics on the touch screen were most popular.

Audience Response Systems and Speaker Interaction

If you've ever watched certain audience participation game shows, you've seen the host poll the audience to determine their opinion about a question. The audience is outfitted with small keypads that allow them to answer questions quickly and have their data tallied immediately. This is the essence of the **Audience Response System** (ARS).

Historically, ARS systems have been expensive propositions for the planner to implement, but today's technologies have made it a more affordable, and in today's two-way communication lifestyle, a more necessary part of many meetings. One such service is Poll Everywhere, which uses SMS (texting), in addition to Web and Twitter voting that interfaces with a real-time Web-based poll. The audience members respond, and the data are instantaneously updated and posted for all to see.

Another product that has simplified the ARS process is Turning Point that allows for real-time poll integration into PowerPoint. In addition to using handsets, their latest product also supports certain mobile device-specific responding.

Twitter is also used to help facilitate interactivity during a session, whether it's for the purpose of providing an audience chat discussion or used as a way to send messages and questions directly to a speaker. SMS (through texting of questions to a session moderator) is another way that these technologies have created a better real-time connection between a speaker and his/her audience.

What may be the hottest technology for speaker interaction are the apps and services that allow the speaker's presentation to be delivered directly to the attendees mobile device. Services such as SlideKlowd, Nice Meeting, and Eventpad include features such as real-time polling integrated into the app, as well as the ability to download handouts directly onto mobile devices, among other bells and whistles. It is clearly early in the development cycle and usage of these tools. The next few years will determine how these will be used and developed further.

Attendee Blogging and the Social Conference

Event blogging, while not as popular as it was a few years ago, still provides the event professional a way to integrate better attendee interaction within the event. The meeting professionals' responsibility, if they wish to facilitate attendee blogging, is to provide wireless broadband connectivity in any/all of the meeting rooms and prefunction space. Although this can result in

Google Glass in use
Martin Matthews/Fotolia

a significant cost, the establishment of this wireless environment allows the attendees to enter sessions and utilize their computers.

Various social media tools can truly extend the conference outside of its four walls. While following attendee blogs is one way, Twitter, with the ubiquitous hashtag, could be the best tool out there to help extend the event. It has become easy for non-attendees to feel part of some of the activity. Tools such as Tagboard make it easy for the attendee to follow the conference Twitter stream in a newsmagazine-style layout.

Recently, the service Conferize has provided a tool for attendees to be able to aggregate the social feeds of an event, including Twitter, Instagram, YouTube, and others, so that they can keep up with the speakers, sessions, and activities.

Clearly, conference apps, with their significant social component, can also be used by attendees and non-attendees alike to follow the real-time conversation at the event.

Augmented Reality

For both pre- and on-site event functionality, what may be the next big thing are augmented reality tools. **Augmented Reality** (AR) is a tool that allows attendees to use their mobile device to see beyond what is visible to the naked eye. Layers of AR content can be created to supplement typical marketing and event content. The highest profile of these tools is the upcoming release of Google Glass; this small screen, sitting at your eye level and connected to the Web, provides a personal interactive tool for all attendees. Pricing and privacy issues may not make this the ultimate AR tool, but it will likely be the first of the major players in this space and possibly may define how these tools are used in the future.

Some groups are already using AR in their marketing. In 2013, Omni Hotels, in conjunction with AR app developer Aurasma, created what many believe is the first augmented reality print ad for the hospitality industry. By hovering a smart device over the ad (while in the app), the phone will deliver "second screen" content to the user, in the form of video, Web sites, or many other options. Another major player in the AR space is Layar. How these tools impact the MEEC industry will depend more on the creativity of the meeting professional than on the development of the devices.

POST-CONFERENCE TECHNOLOGY APPLICATIONS

Technology has clearly served a great purpose in the marketing and running of the meeting or event. However, it continues to be a useful tool once the meeting or event is completed. From the post-conference evaluation process to the digital highlights (which weave into the marketing for the next conference), there is more to review regarding technology applications in our industry.

Evaluations and Surveys

Many organizers have moved the meeting/event evaluation process from a paper-based process on-site (it can be digitized as well) to a post-conference/event, online approach. While there is much debate over whether post-conference/event evaluations provide the greatest number of responses and best accuracy of information (since the survey is not being completed at the time of the event), we are such a digital society that most meetings have moved in this direction.

Regardless of one's position, it is a system in use by many event professionals. In fact, Web-based tools such as SurveyMonkey have become increasingly popular for this process. The Web-based services not only distribute the evaluations, but also tally them and provide the planner with easy-to-read analysis of the questions they posed to the attendees. In fact, many integrated online solutions for meeting professionals include event survey functionality. For those looking for a free alternative, Google Drive has survey functionality built into its cloud-based set of tools.

This process should not be limited to conference evaluations. Any event professional who is involved in the programming process understands that learning about the needs of his or her audience is one of the best tools to identify program elements that create greater value for the attendee. The online survey, independent of the event evaluation, can be of significant support to that process.

Marketing the Media

The essence of post-event technology is to extend the conference past the traditional time borders. A conference is no longer bound to a Monday to Thursday time frame. It can begin with attendee networking months prior to the opening session, by using tools such as pre-event networking. After the conference, the event professional can provide content to those who didn't attend (or even those who wish to view it again).

Conference YouTube channels are at the core of this experience. Video is such a fundamental tool of today's online media; it should be a given for every event professional that they take video at the event and use it in their follow-up marketing. Professionals should also be aware of newer video tools, such as the app Vine, which allows for the creation of 6-second videos. You may not think this is the content approach for you, but the success of this tool for many may have you thinking otherwise.

As for delivery, especially in a live environment, the event professional needs to make certain that they have the servers and technology (including bandwidth) available so that whoever wishes to log on and view the event can do so without the signal degrading or breaking up.

The professionals best marketing tool is the success of their previous event. The digitization and distribution of this content is then an absolutely critical tool for not only generating revenue from this year's event, but continuing to attract attendees in future years.

VIRTUAL GATHERINGS

As event-based technology is discussed, the need to also focus on the purely virtual meeting must be included. Many smaller meetings, where stakeholders cannot afford (in terms of either time or money) to travel to attend, can be run virtually. The generic term "webinar" seems to have become the standard term used to describe the online services that allow audio, data, and sometimes streaming content to be delivered over the Internet.

Webinars

The creation of a successful **webinar** is very different than a live event. All day live events are rarely successful (who's going to sit at their desk all day to actively view a meeting?). Short burst training (sometimes as short as 15–20 minutes) can be as, if not more, effective than more standard session durations of sixty to ninety minutes. The speaker, who is getting no visual or audio cues from the audience, must be able to keep the audience engaged. Q&A tends to be relegated to a specified time frame following the session.

There are many webinar providers that a professional can use. One such service is Ready Talk. The event professional should make certain that the service that is used is priced properly for their needs. Additional questions include how the service handles the audio (**VoIP**

Case: The Pitfall of Virtual Meetings

Jessica, who is a meeting planner for a big corporation, has just been told by her manager that their company is going to start making budget cuts due to the economic downturn, and that the corporate meetings were going to be part of these budget cuts. Jessica began to worry about possibly losing her job and began doing some research on potential alternatives that cut costs for meetings.

Jessica came across virtual meetings. She thought that this would be the perfect alternative for face-to-face meetings because it would still give the corporation a way to network and communicate with their clients and customers, and also save money. The next day, Jessica went to her manager to present her idea about the virtual meetings. Her manager liked the idea and set up a meeting with the corporation managers to oversee the idea. Before the meeting with the corporate managers, Jessica wanted to do some more research on virtual meetings, so she contacted one of the virtual meeting companies to hear more about the software and also ask them questions. As Jessica was getting off the phone, she was sold on the idea. Jessica met with the corporate managers, and they also believed she had a great alternative for face-to-face meetings, so they began the process of starting up the virtual meetings.

Jessica was planning her first meeting through virtual events, and she was excited about it. She planned the first virtual meeting just like any other meeting except that she had to contact all the clients that are attending and send them software, with help from the virtual event company.

The first virtual meeting day was here and everything seemed to be ready to go. The virtual meeting began at 2:00 PM with a rough start. Jessica forgot that there are different time zones throughout the country. So, when her company logged on there were only a few attendees online. They started the meeting anyways, but the sound and video qualities began to go in and out. The corporate managers began to get flustered and even embarrassed because they were meeting with very important clients. Without the corporate managers being able to close the meeting, the screen cut off. The corporate managers were upset about the event that occurred because they did not want to lose possible business over technical difficulties. They were also a little upset with Jessica because they were putting a lot of faith in her, hoping the virtual meeting idea was going to be a success. The corporate managers then set up meeting with Jessica and the virtual event company the next day to talk about whether or not they should give the virtual events another try.

or teleconferencing), the maximum capacity of the virtual event, whether the service provides interactive tools such as chat and polling, and how easy it is for the event organizers and speaker to switch the view from the platform being used to their desktop, so they can showcase their applications and browser.

A more expensive, yet far more interactive, approach comes from Cisco, whose TelePresence videoconferencing provides face-to-face communications between the attendees. With HD and top-quality audio, events or meetings held using this service can seem to tear down the walls between real and virtual events.

Hybrid Meetings

A **hybrid meeting** is one that simultaneously takes place in a live and virtual environment. Hybrid meetings help event professionals extend their live events to those who cannot attend. However, successful hybrid meetings are more than just streaming the video of the speaker. Organizers need to put thought into creating compelling content and delivery that interact successfully with both the live and virtual audience. It is not as simple as just switching on a camera and streaming content.

Virtual Trade Shows

The promise of **virtual trade shows** from its inception of a few years ago has not been met. Perhaps it was too ahead of its time, but for whatever reason, tools such as Second Life (which is no longer a major player in the tech space) and other virtual trade show providers did not catch fire.

Case: Virtual Meeting Space at the Convention Center

Technology is becoming well known in every industry; soon it will take over the convention industry. The Smartville convention center decided to add technology to help give it an edge of the competitors.

The Smartville convention center decided to try Web conferencing to give it the upper hand. They contacted an event technology company to add the appropriate technology to have Web conferencing. After they started implementing the technology, a group came in and asked if they could have a Web conference within the next month. The convention center felt pressured to accept so they did and told the technology company to get it in as fast as possible. When deciding whether or not to implement a new technological upgrade, the convention center became concerned about what types of stipulations came with installing the system in less than month.

The event came and the technology company was just finishing up the day of the event. Due to last minute installation issues, the worst fears of the convention center were realized when sales managers were not capable of operating the system flawlessly after techni-cians left. This then caused event planners to become concerned about the ability of their event to go off without technical issues. There were many issues with starting on time and making sure the connection was clear. After the meeting ended, the attendees complained of late starting times and delayed breaks due to the convention center's lack of knowledge when it comes to efficiently operating the Web conferencing system. Not only were the local attendees frustrated but their partners located across the country were upset by the delay in being able to conduct a successful non-face-to-face speaking engagement.

The convention center tried to implement the technology too fast. They should have waited to have this event on a later date to ensure that the technology was running smoothly and the staff was prepared. If they had more time, they would have had a better first impression on the community with the Web conferencing. The question came up for the convention center as to what to do as far as keeping the technology. It will be hard to market the technology now that they had such an unsuccessful event.

At its most basic, a virtual trade show can be an online trade show floor plan, with hyper-text links to the sites of the exhibitors for the attendees to visit. However, a virtual trade show can also be a virtual experience in itself, with the attendee virtually walking through the event and clicking on information (or in some cases, actually chatting with sales reps). Digitell is still one of the major players in this area.

While some people fear that these virtual events will replace face-to-face ones, it is pretty clear that for the foreseeable future, these services work best as an adjunct to actual events, or used when a face-to-face event isn't possible to hold. Whichever format is used, the main benefit of a virtual trade show of this style is that it greatly extends the trade show from the two to three days of live exhibits to potentially a year round buying and selling marketplace.

FUTURE TRENDS

The only future trend we can confidently state is that change will continue to be thrown at us at an exponential rate. While futurists with crystal balls can only guess what the meeting or event of 2025 will look like, for the near future, what's clear is that the impact of social and mobile tools on the MEEC industry is still growing and maturing. Social media enables everything, including your events, to be shared in real time. Mobile apps and services will continue to develop and not only provide better real-time content, but hope to better alleviate some of the carbon footprint of MEEC events.

Clearly a trend to watch in the future of meetings is mobile commerce. "Mcommerce" will help redefine how payments are made at events by using mobile devices as the transaction model. Tools such as the Square app are already in use today, helping to reduce costs of credit card processing while expediting the experience for both the event professional and attendee. There is concern about mcommerce and security, and clearly this trend is something to watch in the upcoming months.

Summary

Today's technology-savvy meeting/event professional has an arsenal of tools at their disposal to enhance their organization's event, both from the focal point of the attendee and from the organization. Social media has become an enormous focal point for many event planners to integrate into their event marketing and management. Since time, money, and objectives don't require every technology to be integrated, the true role of the event professional today is to identify and determine those tools that add the greatest value to their meetings/events, while continuing to learn about other technologies that could also impact their organization. Technology is also used in the "green movement" (see Chapter 13 on green meetings).

Now that you have completed this chapter you should be competent in the following Meeting and Business Event Competency Standards:

MBECS – Skill 10: Perform Administrative Tasks

Sub skills	Skills (standards)
E 10:02	Manage information system

MBECS – Skill 32: Exhibit Professional Behavior

Sub skills	Skills (standards)
K 32.10	Keep up to date with changes in the meetings and event industry

MBECS – Skill 33: Communication

Sub skills	Skills (standards)
L 33.03	Use communication tools

Key Words and Terms

For definitions, see GLOSSARY, or http://glossary.conventionindustry.org

augmented reality
Accepted Practices Exchange (APEX)
audience response systems
blogging
conference apps
hybrid meetings
interactive nametags
lead retrieval systems
NFC
podcasting
portal
RFID
RFP
room design software
RSS
social media
Twitter
virtual tours
virtual trade shows
VoIP
webinars

Review and Discussion Questions

1. How can technology impact site selection?
2. List three new technologies that support meeting networking.
3. What are the seven types of Web-based gatherings?
4. How is third-party software used, and what is its advantage?
5. Why has the Web become so important to meeting planners and suppliers?
6. What are the five facets of the e-marketing strategy of the technology-savvy meeting professional?
7. In addition to enhancing live networking, RFID nametags frequently contain what other interactive tools?
8. What is the major benefit of attendee blogging during a session?
9. List four types of e-conferencing and discuss each.
10. What are some of the benefits of using online evaluations?
11. What is the main benefit of a virtual trade show?
12. What is green technology?

About the Chapter Contributors

James Spellos is the president of a company called Meeting U. He is a consultant and frequent speaker on technology issues in the MEEC industry.
Kathryn Hashimoto, PhD is a member of the faculty in the School of Hospitality Leadership at East Carolina University.

Previous Edition Chapter Contributor

Dennis Rudd, Ed.D. and Kathleen Taylor Brown of Robert Morris College

CHAPTER 13

Green Meetings and Social Responsibility

Chapter Outline

The Vancouver Convention Center is a green facility including grass on its roof.
liquid Studios/Fotolia

Chapter Objectives

After reading this chapter, the learner will be able to:

- Define "green meetings"
- Define "social responsibility"
- Describe best practices in green meetings
- Identify opportunities for meetings and events to be more environmentally sensitive
- Discuss the costs associated with "being green"
- Define "greenwashing" and identify key areas where greenwashing occurs

INTRODUCTION TO GREEN MEETINGS

The **Green Movement**, as it was initially referred to, was first started in the 1960s with environmentalists advocating the sustainable management of resources and the protection of the natural environment through changes in public policy and individual behavior. The year 1970 brought the First Earth Day, which by design created public awareness of environmental abuses and is ultimately credited with being the impetus for the Safe Drinking Water Act as well as the Endangered Species Act. In addition, the gas crisis of the 1970s helped create further public awareness of the finite supply of our natural resources. The economic prosperity of the 1980s and 1990s shifted public focus away from green and sustainability issues and towards a fast, disposable society. It wasn't until 2005 and the arrival of Hurricane Katrina that the world started truly paying attention to the potential catastrophic effects of global warming and the wastefulness that was taking place all over the world. And it was even more recently that meeting professionals began to fully consider the importance of environmentally friendly events. As more planners strive to minimize their events' environmental impacts, suppliers are also working to make their products and services more earth-friendly.

Tidbit		

Earth Overshoot Day—Date calculated to measure the point in time when our consumption for the year exceeds the planet's ability to replenish. It is important to note that as a planet we are exhausting our natural resources earlier and earlier each year.

1992	October 31
2002	October 3
2012	August 22

The movement toward green meetings within the MEEC industry is impacting all areas of meeting planning. Meeting professionals are actively learning the ins and outs of executing green meetings, and meeting suppliers are jumping on board accordingly. Meeting professionals, clients, customers, venues, exhibitors, contractors, and suppliers are actively taking part in the green movement. When meeting professionals begin planning more eco-friendly meetings, the ripple effect has an impact on all parties involved.

Definition of a **green meeting**: A common expression describing a meeting that incorporates environmental considerations to minimize its negative impact on the environment (CIC).

WHY GO GREEN—THE BOTTOM LINE

In an industry as hectic as the meetings and events industry where every detail is important, it is easy to understand why planners, suppliers, vendors, and facility managers want to streamline wherever possible. So why should industry professionals take on the extra challenge of going green?

The answer boils down to a few important points:

Economic

It makes good business sense to go green, and companies that choose to do so are reporting higher gross margins, higher return on sales, higher return on assets, and a stronger cash flow than their less sustainable competitors. Once a company has made the commitment to go green within its own organization, it is easier to follow the same guidelines for meetings and events that will ultimately lead to a better return on investment (ROI).

Taking small steps to go green can make an enormous difference in a company's bottom line, as well as in the environment. In addition to the monetary savings to these groups, the

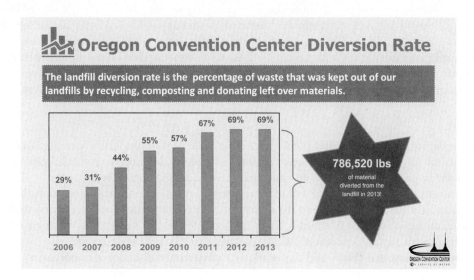

Provided with Permission of the Oregon Convention Center

amount of waste deposited into a landfill was dramatically reduced, just by making these small changes.

Simply switching from bottled water to pitchers of water for attendees saved $1.5 million at an event attended by 40,000 people over a five-day period. Reusing name badge holders saved another group over $1,500 in just one year. It is common to ask hotel guests to hang their towels if they wish to reuse them. This practice saves one large hotel chain 10–17% annually per hotel on hot water and sewage costs. Oracle's sustainability efforts during their annual OpenWorld event saved the company $1.7 million combined over the past five years. Among their many green efforts, they saved $420,000 by reevaluating their signage policies. Signage is now made from lighter, reusable materials and is sourced from local companies.

Another example of environmental responsibility is to reduce the amount of printed materials associated with a meeting or event. Many groups have eliminated the old practice of automatically printing a conference and meeting programs for each attendee. Instead, they take advantage of technology to encourage attendees to access important information via the Web. One group reduced paper usage at its annual meeting enough to save 26 trees and $6,000.

ECONOMICS OF BOTTLED WATER

- Bottled water costs 2,000 times as much as tap water
- Researchers discovered that one-third of all bottled water is actually tap water.
- Eighty percent of all water bottles end up in a landfill (where they do not break down) or are incinerated (where they emit harmful toxins into the air).
- Americans purchase one-half billion dollars' worth of bottled water each week, enough bottles to circle the globe five times.
- On an annual basis, the oil needed to produce the water bottles in the United States could fuel one million cars, in America alone.

Tidbit

The economics of sourcing locally is no more apparent than with the case of one popular west coast conference hotel. By switching from Atlantic Salmon to Pacific Salmon, costs went from $21 per pound to $6 per pound.

Increasingly, companies are looking at sustainability, both personal and company-wide, as a galvanizing force to get their employees to become more engaged in their work. Sustainability arguably provides one of the most engaging topics for a theme of an employee engagement program. People are curious about it, and many people can relate to it. Sustainability encompasses people's health (healthy food, clean drinking water, etc.), the health of the environment (clean air, clean water, healthy ecosystems providing ecological services like keeping disease at bay), societal issues (safe public parks, walkable communities, connecting with our neighbors, getting people together and away from the TV), and economic sustainability (people's paychecks, business success, etc.). Workplace programs dealing with sustainability issues lend themselves well to improving employee satisfaction, morale, productivity, and retention. And just as importantly for the entrepreneur or manager, it also has terrific potential for contributing to the bottom line of the company.

Social

Corporate Social Responsibility (CSR) refers to a widespread approach where organizations consider the long-term interest of the communities in which they operate and take responsibility for the impact of their actions on employees, customers/members, the community, and the environment. Although the concept of social responsibility is not necessarily a new one, the idea that businesses should contribute to the welfare of their communities both locally and globally is one of the trends of the millennium. Everyone wants to feel like he or she is making a difference. In a recent report, generation Y employees were asked what they are looking for in future employers. Almost two-thirds said that workplace environmental policy is important to them.

WORKING TOWARDS **0%WASTE**

GUIDE TO REDUCING WASTE AT YOUR EVENT

Dear Event Planner,

Built with sustainability in mind, the Oregon Convention Center (OCC) is a leader in green building and other environmentally responsible business practices.

What this means for you is that you're reducing the environmental impact of your event just by choosing to host your event at OCC. Since we are a LEED certified building, many green event components are built into our daily operations, such as event recycling and composting, water and energy efficient upgrades, and purchasing local food for our catering.

Our goal is to maintain our leadership as the preferred venue for green meetings. A large component in meeting this goal is to reduce waste generated by events in our facility. Please assist us in our efforts by reviewing this packet, resources you'll find are:

1) Materials Checklist
2) Recycling and Composting Guide
3) Recycling Stations for Exhibitors, Decorators and Attendees
4) 5 Ways to Reduce Waste at your event

We are thrilled that you have selected Portland and the Oregon Convention Center as your venue for your upcoming event. Together we can make a positive impact on the environment.

Greening your event,

Erin Rowland

Erin Rowland
Sustainability Coordinator

WHY GREEN EVENTS?

According to the Convention Industry Council, a green meeting or event incorporates environmental considerations to minimize its negative impact on the environment. In addition to the environmental benefits, green meetings have *many other benefits including:*

SAVE MONEY
by conserving resources

MEET EXPECTATIONS
of your stakeholders and attendees

SUPPORT COMMUNITIES
in need by donating excess materials

Create
COMPETITIVE ADVANTAGE
and reputation

Educate and
INFLUENCE LONG TERM SUSTAINABLE BEHAVIOR with exhibitors, decorators and attendees

Recyclable

- ☐ Aluminum Cans
- ☐ Glass Bottles and Jars
- ☐ Clean Paper *(Brochures, Programs, Fliers, Etc.)*
- ☐ Cardboard Boxes
- ☐ Cardboard Signage
- ☐ Plastic Shrink Wrap, Sheet Plastic, Bubble Wrap
- ☐ Plastic Bottles and Containers
- ☐ Plastic Plant Pots
- ☐ Block Styrofoam
- ☐ Styrofoam Peanuts *(must be bagged)*
- ☐ Vinyl Tablecloths

- ☐ Wood Pallets*
- ☐ Construction Debris*
- ☐ Lumber or Other Wood Scraps*
- ☐ Brick, Concrete, or Other Construction Debris*
- ☐ Scrap Metal
- ☐ Grease*

Compostable

- ☐ Yard Debris*
- ☐ Food Scraps
- ☐ Paper Products and Compostable Serviceware *(contact Sustainability Coordinator for approved list)*

Donations

- ☐ Donate-able Goods *(Books, T-Shirts, Office Supplies, Trinkets, Décor, Potted Plants, Bags, Craft Materials, Garden Supplies, Etc.)*
- ☐ Donate-able Food *(Dry Goods, Prepared Foods, Perishable Food, Frozen Food, Pet Food)*
- ☐ Donate-able Name Badges
- ☐ Donate-able Yard/Garden Items

> *** Additional charges may apply to handle this material**

Landfill

- ☐ Plastic Food Serviceware
- ☐ Plastic Beverage Cups
- ☐ Plastic Utensils
- ☐ Plastic Signage
- ☐ Food Packaging
- ☐ Vinyl Banners
- ☐ Foam Core Signage

Other

_____

_____

_____

RECYCLING AND COMPOSTING GUIDE Please consider only using products at this event that are recyclable or compostable at the OCC.

Cardboard Boxes and Signs

Metal Containers

Plastic Containers, Pots and Buckets

Glass Containers

Compostable Serviceware

Paper

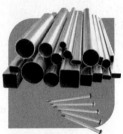

Scrap Metal

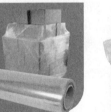

Plastic Film and Shrink Wrap

Block Styrofoam

Plants, Trees and Yard Debris

Wood

Construction Debris

Vinyl Tablecloths

Kitchen Grease

Food Scraps

At OCC we provide recycling stations for exhibitors, decorators, and attendees that include separate streams for recyclable, compostable and landfill materials.

COMPOST
FOOD SCRAPS AND SERVICEWARE *SERVED AT THE OCC*

RECYCLE
PLASTIC BOTTLES, CANS, PAPER

LANDFILL
WHEN IN DOUBT, THROW IT OUT

MOVE IN AND MOVE OUT BINS

We provide several containers to be used by exhibitors and decorators during show move in and move out.

Mixed Recycle and Glass Recycle

Food Scraps and Compostable Serviceware

Yard and Construction Debris, Scrap Metal, Brick, Wood

Cardboard, Plastic Film, Styrofoam, Vinyl

Landfill

Please ensure your vendors and exhibitors are using compostable serviceware to participate in our efforts in

WORKING TOWARDS 0% WASTE

FIVE
WAYS TO REDUCE WASTE

1 DESIGN YOUR SIGNAGE TO BE REUSABLE OR RECYCLABLE

Avoid printing signs on foam core – **it's not recyclable!** Choose a recyclable alternative like EcoBoard™ or better yet, design signage without date specific information so that it can be reused again.

2 KNOW WHAT'S RECYCLABLE AT THE OREGON CONVENTION CENTER

Recycling varies from city to city and business to business. Review what we can recycle at our facility and purchase products that we can recycle or compost and encourage your exhibitors to do the same.

3 SUBMIT MATERIALS CHECKLIST

Please check off all materials that might be generated from your event. This will allow us to provide you the best event recycling services possible!

4 DONATE LEFT OVER MATERIALS

We are often able to donate leftover goods and materials to local community organizations. This could include *decorations, giveaways, bags, office supplies, construction materials, unused food* and more. Let us know if you anticipate any left-over goods and we'll happily coordinate for you.

5 COMMUNICATE WITH EXHIBITORS AND DECORATORS

Exhibitors and decorators can be some of your biggest *allies in waste reduction.* Ask us for tips on how to communicate your efforts to staff, sponsors and attendees *– a great PR opportunity!*

WANT TO LEARN MORE?

Check out these great resources to read case studies and learn more about industry best practices for green events.

www.apexsolution.org   www.epa.gov   www.gmicglobal.org   www.usgbc.org

Oregon Convention Center

Further, more than half of those surveyed said that investment in community is important when deciding on future employers. Employers need to take note! Employees who are satisfied with their organization's commitment to social and environmental responsibility are likely to be more positive, happier, and more productive than those working for less socially responsible employers. Businesses that recognize the importance of social responsibility often have employees who tend to be more satisfied with their jobs.

How does this work? Employees who work in organizations that support green efforts could be healthier due to working in an office that is naturally lighted or better ventilated for energy savings. They may be encouraged to take the stairs or ride their bike to work, obviously contributing to their personal health. In addition to obvious health reasons, employees like to be a part of something that is good overall. According to a recent survey, 92% Americans are interested in an increased use of solar power. If you are working for a company that is using solar power, you are likely to feel that you are participating in making a positive contribution. Encouraging employees to become participants in green efforts often means encouraging them to live a healthier and more active lifestyle, thus leading to happier and more productive individuals in the workforce.

Meeting and event attendees are also positively impacted by sustainable efforts and enthusiastically participate in reduce, reuse, and recycle programs. One industry expert reminds us that most attendees participate in environmentally responsible efforts on a daily basis at home and consider it a non-issue to continue to act responsibly when attending events.

Social responsibility can take many formats. Some organizations encourage attendees to become actively involved in a project while attending an event. **Experiential CSR**, a socially responsible experience is a term recently coined. Some examples of experiential CSR include:

- **Stop Hunger Now**—a meal packaging program. Through this program a group of 40–50 volunteers can package 10,000 meals in two hours. Meals are then delivered to the local shelters.
- **American Red Cross**—groups large or small can volunteer to fill emergency preparedness kits.
- **Clean the World**—recycles soap and partially used toiletries. In less than 90 minutes, volunteers can sanitize 3,000 bars of soap and wrap another 140 pounds. Soap is then delivered around the world to places where simple hand cleansing reduces the number of childhood deaths from pneumonia and diarrheal disease by up to 60%.
- **The Community Footprints Program**—organized through Ritz Carlton Hotels. They make it easy for groups staying in their hotels to give back to the local community. With their "VolunTeaming" assistance, groups have worked with Habitat for Humanity, harvested local crops to donate to the local food bank, and helped clean up and preserve historic parks.

When asked to evaluate, attendees who have engaged in these and other meaningful Experiential CSR programs are significantly more satisfied with their overall MEEC experience.

CSR does not always have to include the experiential component. In many cases the group cannot engage in local volunteerism, yet the desire to be socially responsible still exists. Programs like American Forests' Meeting ReLeaf fill that gap. At a cost of $1 per attendee, ReLeaf will plant one tree per attendee. One tree provides 260 pounds of oxygen per year (which is enough for two people) and captures 760 gallons of water in its lifetime, thus reducing run off, erosion, and storm water damage.

Triple Bottom Line

Perhaps answering the question of "why go green?" includes more than a single bottom line could report. Some experts consider the "triple bottom line" as a more accurate measure of a company's accomplishments and a better answer to the question. Considering the triple bottom line of people, planet, and profit expands the concept of success to include ecological and social accomplishments in addition to financial accomplishments of an organization. Research suggests that many forward thinking organizations, associations, and companies are applying the triple bottom line concept as they measure success and answer to stakeholders.

OPPORTUNITIES TO GO GREEN

According to recent studies, more than half of all meeting professionals are considering environmental practices as they plan their conferences. No longer is it possible to limit considerations to sleeping rooms. At all major events held by Meeting Professionals International (MPI), the board of directors purposefully considers the eight areas of "green meetings" as defined by the Convention Industry Council (CIC). These include: destination selection, transportation, venues, accommodation, food and beverage, communications, on-site operations, and expositions.

Planning a green meeting used to be thought of as difficult and expensive, when in reality, it may be as simple as paying attention to the decisions that are made regarding company policies. Here are some simple steps professionals can follow to make their next meeting green:

- *Create Standards:* Establish environmental standards within the business. Get buy-in from the organization's management and clientele. Select suppliers that share those environmental standards. The 'Ask for It' program is an example of how event professionals can convey their expectations to their suppliers. As the name implies, event professionals are encouraged to request sustainable practices from their suppliers. This program goes one step further and reinforces the expectation by certifying suppliers against the standards. Standards should be shared with participants so that everyone involved understands the expectations as they relate to the standards.
- *Use Technology:* Take advantage of technology to reduce the need for paper. With easy-to-use Web site platforms, electronic registration vehicles, and e-mail, there is virtually no need to produce printed materials. To cut down on travel costs, utilize podcasting, webinars, and video streaming are great options. In doing so, planners may find an increase in attendance because they are making it easier for more people to attend. Select Web site platforms that will allow for personalized post-event thank you notes and feedback surveys.
- *Choose a Local Destination:* Ninety percent of an event's carbon footprint comes from air travel. Whenever possible, event professionals should choose a destination close to where participants live to reduce the distance that must be traveled to attend. If air travel is necessary, event professionals should choose a venue or hotel that is close to the airport or is within walking distance of off-site events. Research public transportation options in the host city.

This salad is served on a plate that is totally compostable.
George G. Fenich

Decorating with nature.
George G. Fenich

- *Reduce, Reuse, and Recycle:* Proper recycling bins should be added to the event supplies list, and the staff should be trained in the proper ways to recycle. Venues should be asked to provide visible and accessible recycling services for paper, metal, plastic, and glass. Banquet managers should be asked about composting options or giveaway programs and also the option of using real china for meals. If this is not possible, choose disposable plates made from renewable resources that will biodegrade in a landfill. Collect name badge holders and lanyards for use the next year.
- *Volume Up:* Encourage food and beverage providers to serve sugar, creamer, and other condiments in bulk dispensers rather than individual packets. Find hotels that use dispensers for shampoo and lotions. Request that water stations not offer bottled water, but pitchers of water or water coolers. Give attendees a water bottle for their personal use throughout the meeting.
- *Eat Local:* Speak with the banquet manager about using local fruits and vegetables that are in season. Include more vegetarian meals, as they require less carbon energy to prepare. Obtain an accurate headcount prior to finalizing the amount of food to order to avoid waste.
- *Decorate with Nature:* Use local flowers and plants to decorate your tables and leave them in pots so that you can use them as gifts or prizes. This ensures that they are not wasted once the meeting is over.
- *Use Paper Wisely:* If print materials are necessary, use chlorine-free, recycled paper and vegetable-based inks. Print on both sides of the paper and only print materials for a participant if requested. Use "print-on-demand" stations rather than printing copies for each attendee.
- *Save Energy:* Look for venues and hotels that have an energy efficient policy in place. Coordinate with the venue to ensure that lights, audiovisual equipment, and air-conditioning in meeting spaces will be turned off when not in use. Remind attendees to conserve energy in the guest rooms by turning off lights when they leave and not leaving electronics plugged in and powered on unnecessarily.
- *Inform Everyone:* Tell participants, speakers, suppliers, vendors, and the media about your sustainability efforts and your expectations from them as event partners. Communication is the key in encouraging and securing active participation from all involved parties. For example, in the speaker contract, green expectations should be made very clear so that speakers do not arrive with printed handouts when electronic versions of the handouts are expected.
- *Sources:* Companies will recycle items such as meeting banners into useful and creative things like messenger bags, wallets, tote bags, and laptop sleeves.

SAVOR . . . Chicago at McCormick Place

Contributed by Connie Chambers, General Manager

"A garden is a living reminder of our commitment to environmental and social responsibilities." SAVOR . . . Chicago, the food service operator at McCormick Place Convention Center in Chicago, incorporates sustainability into every aspect of the operation operating the Midwest's largest farm-to-fork rooftop garden. Producing over 6,000 pounds of organically grown vegetables and flowers takes a trained staff and a utilization plan. SAVOR partnered with Windy City Harvest to provide the expertise in urban agriculture, collaboration that benefits the communities, and produces the high-value, nutritious produce utilized in catering and restaurant operations at McCormick Place.

Windy City Harvest trains adults in a six-month certification program learning hands-on sustainable horticulture and urban agriculture skills. Participants earn a certification from the Richard J. Daley College that readies participants for permanent employment in new "green collar" jobs sector.

Crop determination for the 19,000 gross square foot garden is determined by the soil composition and SAVOR . . . Chicago's utilization plan. Crops are selected based on root depth requirements, heat and sun tolerance, and mature rates. Spring and fall plantings consist of pansies, calendula, sweet peas, English daisies, cilantro, grape tomatoes, lettuce, kale, Swiss chard, carrots, and other hearty crops. In the summer, nasturtium, parsley, chives, peppers, tomatoes, eggplant, kales and a variety of herbs are planted and harvested. Quantities are determined on by the utilization plan and to ensure ample amount to incorporate into menus and daily features.

Phasing for the vegetative rooftop began with trials of different soil composition and a control area containing only compost. The soil composition zones included five areas plus a control. Area 1 plantings were in existing media with amendments such as worm castings and compost. Area 2 plantings consisted of 75% existing media and 25% compost/worm castings; area 3 consisted of 50% existing media and 50% compost/worm castings; and area 4 consisted of 25% existing media and 75% compost/worm castings. Trial crops will include lettuce, kale, collard greens, tomatoes (bush varieties), beans (bush varieties), peppers, herbs (basil, thyme, chives, parsley, cilantro, lavender, rosemary and oregano), and cover crops.

Produce distribution is handled on a weekly basis. The Chef is provided an availability list of items ready to harvest to incorporate into menu planning and weekly purchasing plan. SAVOR staff determines what they want from the availability list, and the Windy City Harvest team harvest, process, and package produce for pickup and transport across campus to the main production kitchen less than a block away.

SAVOR . . . Chicago and McCormick Place Convention Center understands the importance of providing visitors and attendees with responsible choices. Reducing waste, composting, limiting chemical use and offering local, organic and antibiotic free options are woven into the operating culture fueling the community with jobs and its visitors with pride in aligning with like-minded partners.

Provided by Connie Chambers of Savor . . . Chicago, Chicago, Illinois

The McCormick Place Convention Center in Chicago has added a rooftop garden. *McCormick Place*

Chefs at McCormick Place use items grown on the rooftop for meals served to attendees.
McCormick Place

GREENWASHING

Definition

The term **greenwashing** refers to any misrepresentation by a company that leads the consumer to believe that its policies and products are environmentally responsible, when its claims are false, misleading, or cannot be verified. Greenwashing is also used to identify the practice of companies spending more money on the campaign to notify customers of their environmentally friendly efforts, than the efforts themselves. Another term, **green sheen**, has also been used in a similar way. This term refers to companies that are making a concerted effort to show that they are adopting green practices regardless of whether their claims are true.

The actual practice of greenwashing began in the mid 1960s when companies were eager to be seen as part of the environmental movement that was taking shape. As these practices continued to evolve, they eventually became known as "greenwashing," a term that was first used in an essay written by environmentalist Jay Westerveld in 1968. His essay reviewed the practice of placing a card on the pillow in each hotel room explaining that the hotel encourages reuse of guest towels for environmental responsibility. Upon closer examination of this practice, Westerveld surmised that, in most cases, the hotel's main reason for the practice was to increase profits.

Today, as consumers become more and more aware of environmentally sound practices, companies are responding by incorporating these green efforts into their business standards. As these companies compete for consumers, many become too eager to tout their green campaigns, achievement, or standards. As awareness grows, it is becoming more difficult for even the consumer to distinguish between those companies that are actually implementing green practices and those who are greenwashing.

Identifying

The meeting industry continues to respond to this challenge in many ways. One of the first steps was to identify greenwashing. In December of 2007, the TerraChoice Environmental Marketing Consulting Company became known for a study in which the "Six Sins of Greenwashing" were identified. Through a later study, an additional "sin" was added. Here is a list of the "sins" with an example to illustrate each point

- *Sin of the Hidden Trade-Off:* Providing an organic product that requires shipping instead of an equally beneficial local product.
- *Sin of No Proof:* Stating that eco-friendly cleaners are being used but not being able to produce evidence of these claims when asked.
- *Sin of Vagueness:* Using terms that are not particularly clear, such as a zero-waste conference.

- *Sin of Irrelevance:* Using or referencing environmental efforts or products that do not make sense (such as a water-conserving light bulb.)
- *Sin of Fibbing:* Stating that the property or product has a specific certification when it does not, or there is no such certification in existence.
- *Sin of the Lesser of Two Evils:* Claiming eco-friendly statements about products or services that are by nature, not eco-friendly. Using "environmentally friendly pesticides" or planning a "carbon neutral conference" where no emissions were actually reduced.
- *Sin of Worshipping False Labels:* Claiming a third-party endorsement through the use of words or images when no such endorsement exists. Using a label, for example, that by design implies that the product is eco-friendly, when it is not.

Prevention

Now that we have some idea of how to identify greenwashing, how do we prevent it within our conferences, meetings, and events?

First, meeting professionals must be aware, knowledgeable, and not afraid to ask questions. As this area of the industry continues to evolve, it is the responsibility of all event professionals to stay on top of current trends, regulations, and questions regarding this topic. Meeting professionals must take responsibility for understanding what is being said and ensuring that the terms being used are credible and make sense. Just because something is "natural" or "organic," for example, does not mean that it is healthy.

Understanding the criteria for certifications and labels is also important. A meeting professional now has to have a greater understanding of how the location became certified and what is included within the certification. Again, the responsibility falls upon the meeting professional to investigate.

A back-of-the-house tour should be part of the due-diligence process of the meeting professional and can be very helpful in validating (or not validating) the green claims being stated by any given company. Greenwashing can be spotted on these types of tours if one is aware and observant. If a claim was made by the participating venue, for example, that recycling opportunities were readily available, and will be made available for all attendees, evidence of this should be apparent during the back-of-the-house tour. The event professional should be able to observe where the recycled material is stored and the process that takes place once it is removed from the event space. If the venue has made claims that local produce is used for all meals, evidence of this could be apparent during this tour as well. Boxes from local companies may be observed, or the event professional may have an opportunity to speak with those working in the kitchen area. These tours provide opportunities for the venue contact to validate their claims and/or often prompt questions by the meeting professional that validates or contradicts the claim. Lastly, planners must practice being green within their departments and companies so that they can be an advocate and lead by example. While there are numerous checklists available that can be used to assist meeting professionals with planning a green meeting, the checklist included at the end of this chapter is a good place to start. Once a planner is aware of the obstacles greenwashing can present, it is easier to identify those areas of concern and proceed in a positive manner with the planning of a green meeting.

GREEN MEETING STANDARDS

The hospitality industry is moving quickly toward the very real possibility of green meetings becoming the norm of the future. Evidence that corroborates this theory lies in the number of green guidelines and certifications that are currently available. With new guidelines in place to set an industry standard in green practices, greenwashing will soon become much more difficult for companies to get away with and much easier for meeting professionals to identify. As greenwashing becomes less of an issue within the industry, meeting professionals will have the ability to ask the right questions with more confidence that the answers they receive will be within their expectations. Greenwashing may never disappear completely, but now that industry standards are in place, the threat is reduced.

These green meeting standards help identify, unify, and contain these efforts. While there are numerous certifications available, the CIC along with the ASTM (originally known as the American Society for Testing and Materials) has created standards that can be used throughout the MEEC industry.

ASTM/APEX Green Meeting Standards

The U.S. Environmental Protection Agency (EPA) and the Green Meeting Industry Council (GMIC) have developed nine standards for sustainable meetings and events. These were developed in a collaborative effort between APEX (the Convention Industry Council's Accepted Practices Exchange) and ASTM (An ANSI certified international standard development organization) and are the first and only standards of this kind in the MEEC industry. The standards are referred to as the APEX/ASTM Environmentally Sustainable Event Standards

The standards cover nine individual sectors of the MEEC industry as noted in Figure 13.1 below. They include:

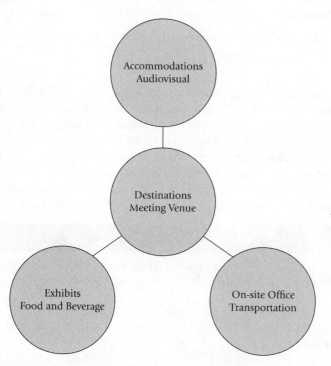

FIGURE 13.1   Nine Standards

Each of the above standards is broken down into nine separate subcategories as seen below. These address the environmental and social areas to be included in each sector. They are:

ASTM International is an American National Standards Institute (ANSI)-accredited standards developing organization. Although the APEX process has always followed the voluntary consensus model mandated by ASTM and ANSI, APEX elected to take the extra step in partnering with ASTM in order to create the standards above that were accepted by both the meetings industry and those outside the industry such as the federal government. The ASTM/APEX Green Meeting and Event Standards are designed

- to be measurable.
- in a tiered system to allow for different levels of interaction.
- for both the planners as well as the suppliers.
- to complement other recognized standards in the MEEC industry such as ISO 20121(see below).

For detailed information on these standards, go to the CIC Web site.

ISO 20121

ISO 20121 is an international management system standard designed to help MEEC organizations improve the sustainability of their events as they relate to products, services, and related activities. It is the international version of a British standard established in 2007, and specifically created to coincide with the 2012 London Olympics. ISO 20121 is designed to address all areas of the MEEC industry. Successful implementation of the standard will allow corresponding organizations to seek certification through an independent accrediting body. Although ISO 20121and ASTM/APEX represent two different approaches to defining a sustainable events standard, they are designed to work independently or in collaboration with one another.

Sands Expo, The Venetian and The Palazzo Reach Green Milestone for Meetings & Conventions

The meetings complex that includes Sands Expo and the Congress Center at The Venetian and The Palazzo Las Vegas has further solidified itself as a true industry leader by being named the first venue in the world to achieve the advanced "level two" industry certification for environmentally sustainable meetings, events, trade shows, and conferences. The certification—called Level Two Certification to the ASTM Standard—is a designation of the meeting industry's comprehensive standards for environmentally sustainable meetings, created through a partnership of the Convention Industry Council's APEX initiative and ASTM International. For more information, contact Keith Salwoski, the Venetian in Las Vegas.

Third-Party Industry Certifications

Third-party certifications are not a new concept. In the early 1900s the Pure Food and Drug Act (PFDA) was established to assure the public of safe food products. Over the years the PFDA's realm of responsibility expanded to all products marketed to consumers. Eventually the Consumer Product Safety Commission (CPSC) was established. CPSC requires the full disclosure of any health hazards linked to chemicals used in household products. In the 1970s and 1980s, the public became concerned about the effect of manufactured products on the environment. Ecolabels such as "environmentally friendly," "green," "organic," "compostable," and "post-consumerwaste" resulted from a consumer demand for products that are environmentally safe. Today, "green" products are commonplace.

Green Certifications and Ecolabels are all around us. Importantly, they confirm that a product or service meets a certain standard. They offer independent third-party proof of a product or service's green qualifications.

In addition to ASTM/APEX and ISO 20121, there is a plethora of, eco-friendly, third-party certifications that are recognized within the MEEC industry. The following is a list of the various certifications that apply to MEEC.

A. Accommodations
- The Hotel Association of Canada's (HAC) Green Key Eco-Rating Program
- Audubon GreenLeaf Eco-Rating Program

- Green Hotel Association
- Coalition for Environmentally Responsible Economies (CERES) Green Hotel Initiative
- Green Globe 21
- Ecotel Certification
- International Tourism Partnership
- Leadership in Energy & Environmental Design (LEED)
- Building Owners and Managers Association (BOMA) of Canada
- Energy Star Qualified Buildings

B. Catering/Food & Beverage
- Marine Stewardship Council (MSC)
- Fair Trade Certified
- USDA Certified Organic
- Conseil des Appellations Agroalimentaires du Québec

C. Décor/Trade Show Rentals
- The Sierra Eco Label
- VeriFlora™
- The Flower Label Program (FLP)
- Rainforest Alliance Certification

D. Event Logistics
- Audubon GreenLeaf™ Eco-Rating Program
- Green-e Program
- Gold Standard

E. Printing/Promotional/Gifts
- Forest Stewardship Council (FSC)
- The Programme for the Endorsement of Forest Certification Schemes (PEFC)
- The Sustainable Forestry Initiative(r) Program (SFI)
- American Tree Farm System (ATFS)
- Waterless Printing Association
- Rainforest Alliance
- Green Seal

F. Transportation/Tours
- Green Globe 21 (GG21) Sustainable Travel & Tourism Certification
- International Ecotourism Standard (IES)
- Blue Flag
- Green Seal
- World Wildlife Fund's (WWF) Membership Travel Program
- International Tourism Partnership

G. Venues
- The Hotel Association of Canada's (HAC) Green Key Eco-Rating Program
- Leadership in Energy & Environmental Design (LEED)
- Audubon Green Leaf™ Eco-Rating Program
- BS 8901:ISO20121
- Green Hotels Association
- Green Globe 21
- National Geographic GeoTourism Award
- Ecotel Certification

In addition to the certifications that suppliers, vendors, and venues can earn, meeting professionals can educate themselves and earn a certification in green meetings. The Certification in Green Meetings & Events (CGME) is designed to assist meeting professionals with all stages of the meeting planning process in a way that promotes social and environmental responsibility. This certification is not required in order to plan green meetings and events, but it does offer credibility to the planner and ensures the client that the planner is well-versed with regard to green practices. The Green Meetings Industry Council offers another opportunity for planners. They offer a six month distance education course leading to a Certificate in

Sustainable Event Planning. The industry is likely to see many more of these programs pop up in the near future.

While not all of the meeting industry certifications are noted here, the list of these certifications continues to change. New certifications are added, some are blended together, and some have simply outlived their usefulness and have been replaced by a more meaningful certification. From a meeting professional's perspective, it is important to gain a thorough understanding of what is required for each certification that is claimed. Planners have to do their homework and verify that the certification in question is of value. They all have individualized requirements, but the overall goal is to bring a level of quality to the ever-evolving practice of incorporating eco-friendly applications. Due diligence on the part of the meeting professional will ensure that there is no misrepresentation to the attendees of the meeting and will also help guarantee that the green goals for the meeting will be met.

Sustainability Report
FSA 2013

Food Services of America
2013 Trends Show

SUSTAINABILITY REPORT

Prepared by:
Lindsey Newkirk
Sustainability Program Assistant
Oregon Convention Center
Portland, Oregon
November 14, 2013

Foreword

This document serves as the means to provide a comprehensive overview of both the sustainability operations at the Oregon Convention Center that lower the impact of the FSA Trends Show, as well as to highlight additional sustainability efforts administered in collaboration with FSA in order to further increase sustainability efforts.

Content of this report may be used to generate information required in meeting internal goals or certification reporting.

OCC Landfill Diversion Overview

With an extensive recycling, composting, donation and waste avoidance program, OCC continues to increase the amount of waste diverted from the landfill each year; in fact, 69% for the entire facility in 2012/2013. As we continue to increase our own efforts, it was only natural to continue a collaboration to assist FSA with their Zero Waste efforts.

Event Overview

For the third year in a row, FSA has established a goal of being a zero waste event. As a food based event that generates several thousands of pounds of material in only one day, it is imperative to 1) plan in advance, 2) engage relevant stakeholders to establish roles and expectations and 3) measure results. All of which were continued components in this year's success.

Sustainability at a Glance

4970lbs of material generated; of which 4255lbs was diverted from the landfill through recycling, composting and post event food donations. 2080lbs of food was donated to the Oregon Food Bank which is equal to 1600 meals for hungry people.

OUTCOME: 86% LANDFILL DIVERSION RATE

Zero Waste Details

Zero Waste Defined: The only peer-reviewed internationally accepted definition of Zero Waste was developed by the Zero Waste International Alliance (ZWIA) to assist businesses and communities in defining their own goals for Zero Waste:

> "Zero Waste is a goal that is both pragmatic and visionary, to guide people to emulate sustainable natural cycles, where all discarded materials are resources for others to use. Zero Waste means designing and managing products and processes to reduce the volume and toxicity of waste and materials, conserve and recover all resources, and not burn or bury them. Implementing Zero Waste will eliminate all discharges to land, water or air that may be a threat to planetary, human, animal or plant health."

According to ZWIA, "Businesses and communities that achieve over 90% diversion of waste from landfills and incinerators are considered to be successful in achieving Zero Waste, or darn close."

Services Received

Standard Housekeeping Services Received:

- Well-marked recycling stations placed throughout exhibit halls during show days
- Labeled recycling cages and other recycling receptacles are placed to capture large volumes of recyclables during move in and out
- Recycle stations serviced by OCC staff during show hours
- Sorting guide provided to all exhibitors

Additional Services Received:

- "Working Towards Zero Waste" project management
- Sustainability Stations monitored by OCC staff during show hours and move out
- OCC housekeeping staff provided porter service to exhibitors
- Post event food donations coordination with the Oregon Food Bank
- All materials weighed in order to calculate event diversion rate
- Approximately five hours of staff time was spent time after the show sorting through the non-manned recycling station containers to increase diversion efforts
- Sustainability report

Results

The landfill diversion rate for the FSA 2013 Food Trends Show was 86%. Great improvements were made to this years' event, resulting in a 3% increase in the events diversion rate from the year prior.

Three new contributions assisted with this years' advancement including 1) eliminating the small trash bins at exhibitor booths, 2) using OCC staff to monitor sustainability stations including exhibitor move out, and 3) conducting an exhibitor training prior to show opening to review recycling goals, expectations, sorting and the post event food donation opportunities.

(continued)

A huge success of the show was that 2080 pounds of food was donated to the Oregon Food Bank. This made up over 40% of all of the material diverted from the landfill and is equal to providing 1600 meals for hungry people.

The continued success of this program is in large part due to the commitment of FSA staff to continually find ways to improve their efforts and the hard work of the organizers to obtain buy in from exhibitors.

Material Break Down

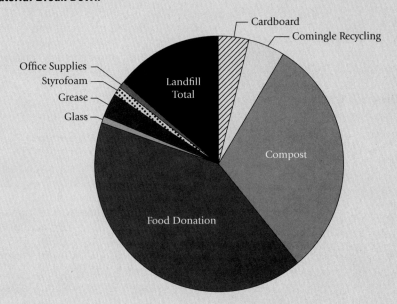

Notes on Materials:

- Co-Mingle Recycling includes paper, plastic and aluminum
- Compost included food scraps and compostable food service ware
- Excess food was donated to the Oregon Food Bank
- Landfill waste includes non-recyclable and non-compostable materials; a large part of which was food contaminated containers and non-recyclable packaging.

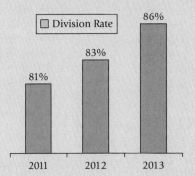

Year to Date

Keys to Success in 2013
FSA

- Made commitment to continue with zero waste efforts
- Educated exhibitors about zero waste goals, expectations and requirements
- Provided a commissary with compostable food serviceware for exhibitors that were initially non-compliant

*New for 2013

- Hired OCC staff instead of outside contractors to monitor sustainability station and us sed OCC staff to provide porter (previously OCC allowed the use of outside staff for porter service, even though that is outside OCC policy) service to exhibitors, thus employing staff that are well trained and passionate about recycling

- Coordinated an all exhibitor training to review goals, expectations and requirements
- Eliminated majority of exhibitor booth trash cans in replacement of increased number of recycle stations

OCC

- Provided recommendations for improvement
- Provided guides for exhibitors and vendors for sorting materials and donating food
- Provided well marked recycle stations
- Coordinated post event food donations
- Weighed all materials to calculate event diversion rate

*New for 2013

- Improved internal planning process and preparation for the show
- Provided training to exhibitors prior to show opening
- Coordinated sustainability station monitors to stay after event close to help direct exhibitors for proper waste and recycling disposal during move out
- Wrote press release; posted on OCC website and distributed to local media contacts

Challenges & Recommendations for Improvement

The majority of challenges identified in 2012 were mitigated with the improvements made in 2013. Remaining challenges and recommendations for improvement include:

1. **Non-Compliance:** Some exhibitors did not understanding the requirement to use compostable service ware and were using traditional plastics. While they were identified and asked to get compostable replacements from the FAS commissary, it was already a few hours into the show. It is recommended to continue finding ways to educate exhibitors and to walk the show floor prior to opening to catch non- compliance as soon as possible. Increased compliance could come from one to one phone calls, requirement of a signed pledge or incentives.
2. **Food Bank Volunteers:** Some lost opportunity with left over food being thrown away instead of donated. It is recommended that OFB volunteers are allowed on the show floor 15 minutes prior to close to start talking with exhibitors that are packing up.
3. **Monitored Sustainability Stations:** OCC provided non-staffed recycling bins on the show floor in addition to staffed Sustainability Stations. It was noticed there was a high level of contamination and missed opportunity for proper sorting of material at the non-staffed recycling stations. It is recommended for next year, to only use staffed Sustainability Station. OCC staff spent time after the show sorting material from the unstaffed recycling station to improve the diversion efforts.

Oregon Convention Center

EVALUATING EFFORTS

If you can measure it, you can manage it. This is a common mantra in many sectors of the business world. It applies equally well to green meetings and sustainable efforts. It is important for meeting professionals and companies to set clear goals in the beginning so that it is possible to measure the success or failure of an event. Fortunately, because of the growing interest in conducting green meetings, a few tools have been created to help in the measurement/evaluation process.

Carbon Footprint Calculator

A carbon footprint is a measure of the impact human activities have on the environment due to the release of greenhouse gases as measured in units of carbon dioxide ($CO2$). The **Carbon Footprint Calculator** allows planners to easily see which destination sites have the least amount of carbon emissions generated by air travel based on points of origin. A planner can calculate **event miles** by tracking the amount of miles traveled by participants, staff, and speakers to the location and the amount of carbon emissions associated with this travel. Once the site has been selected and the resulting carbon footprint calculated, planners can communicate this information to attendees so that they can make an informed decision about participating. Planners can also offer options for attendees to neutralize carbon emissions through various **carbon offset** programs. Planting trees is an example of a carbon offset program.

City Scorecard

The Scorecard ranks cities according to environmental programs that are administered by the local convention and visitors' bureau, convention center, and hotels offered in the city's conference package. With this instrument is it easy to quickly see the top "green cities" and know that their efforts have been verified by a third party, MeetGreen, and been found valid.

Grand Carolina Resort and Spa

The resort was chosen to host the 1,000 delegates over six days. While it was not particularly "green" at the outset, management responded to the client's greening requirements by altering standard operating procedures and implementing capital improvements, such as installing solar panels. Delegates joined in the effort by reducing their own consumption while on-site.

For the duration of the event, data were collected each day on utility usage and waste generation, and reported the following morning at general sessions. Total consumption was compared with the average of a similar convention held the previous year. The results were impressive: Total electricity consumption had been reduced by 21%, water use by 48%, and solid waste by 34%. The greening measures were estimated to save the resort over $1 million per year.

As the need for measurable outcomes continues to grow and companies look for ROI on green strategies, the ability to measure sustainability factors will become increasingly important. Look for new and more sophisticated tools that track carbon, energy, and water footprints, BS 8901, and overall conference achievements. Newer tools will work hand in hand with established tools such as paper savings calculators and the MeetGreen Calculator.

McCORMICK PLACE

For Immediate Release

Contact: Mary Kay Marquisos
McCormick Place/MPEA
312-791-6237

McCORMICK PLACE COMMITS TO UTILIZING 100 PERCENT WIND ENERGY

Announcement comes as WINDPOWER 2013 Conference and Exhibition
takes place at McCormick Place (May 5–8)

CHICAGO May 7, 2013, McCormick Place officials today announced that the nation's largest convention center has committed to offsetting 100 percent of its electricity usage with clean, affordable wind energy. This important announcement was made in conjunction with the WINDPOWER 2013 Conference and Exhibition taking place at McCormick Place from May 5–8.

McCormick Place has purchased Green-e Renewable Energy Certificates (RECs) generated from wind power to match 100 percent of the annual electricity demand. In total, McCormick Place will purchase an estimated 130 million kilowatt-hours of wind power each year over the course of a new three-year REC purchase program provided by Sterling Planet.

"McCormick Place is a perfect example of how even the largest facilities in the world can lead the way towards a sustainable future for all," Governor Pat Quinn said. "Green energy is good business, and I congratulate

McCormick Place for taking this important step that will improve our environment while creating jobs and driving our economy forward."

"I congratulate McCormick Place on to committing to clean, renewable wind energy as its sole source of electricity," said Mayor Rahm Emanuel. "McCormick Place continues to dominate as the best destination for any convention or trade show, bringing thousands of visitors to Chicago every year. Moving to 100 percent wind energy will increase job opportunities and economic development, while moving towards a sustainable future for the City of Chicago. It is also clear proof that sustainability can go hand in hand with the creating of a vibrant, thriving business environment."

The RECs will guarantee that an equal amount of renewable energy is delivered to the electric grid and will provide carbon avoidance of an estimated 730,931,248 pounds of carbon dioxide emissions.

McCormick Place

Besides evaluating efforts numerically, planners need to evaluate the bigger picture. They and the organizations they work with need to ask some hard questions. Is going green always the right thing to do, regardless of cost in resources and dollars? What about evaluating the efforts from the perspective of event itself as well as what occurs before and after the event. Consider the following:

Using bamboo plates is commonly considered a green alternative to disposable tableware because it is reusable and because bamboo regenerates quickly and is biodegradable. However, the manufacture of bamboo into plates is expensive. In addition, the chemicals used to make bamboo into plates and other tableware may be harmful to the environment.

Large water jugs are a great alternative to individual bottles of water. However, if the water has to be transported from far away, and empty water jugs have to be transported back, are we just trading landfill space for carbon emissions?

GOING GREEN VERSUS SUSTAINABILITY

While sometimes used interchangeably, the terms "Going Green" and "Sustainability" have different meanings.

Going Green is a phrase referring to individual action that a person (or company) can consciously take to curb harmful effects on the environment through consumer habits, behavior, and lifestyle. The term **Green** is usually product or service specific; and while taking the current state of the environment into consideration, it is not usually associated with the overall impact of future generations.

Sustainability is a more encompassing term that includes implementing and executing a plan to save resources while improving performance. This term suggests that the impact that a company has on the environment, society, and the economy has been taken into consideration.

Green Meetings Concierge at the Venetian Macao
by Gene Capuano, Vice President Convention and Exhibition Operations

The Venetian Macao Convention & Exhibition Operations team is committed to environmental responsibility by promoting sustainable development through our Green Meetings program, as part of the company's global Sands ECO360° sustainability strategy. Green Meetings has a number of components in which we explain, discuss and create sustainable objectives for our clients and their events. While we have high performance facilities and standard sustainable practices in place, we are focused on creating a customized sustainable event for each and every client that wishes to take part in the program. This is a great way for them to be able to see the impact their event has on the environment, track material usage, look at ways to create healthier food options for their guests and involve the local community as well. We are able to provide what we call a "Green Meetings Concierge," which provides them with dedicated staff to walk them through the process, assist with creating achievable objectives, and show them the finished product in an "Impact Statement" that they can hopefully use as a benchmark for future events.

There is no mistaking that we are a large facility, which uses a lot of energy and resources, so it is our social responsibility to make sure we are being as sustainable as possible with our operation. More important, it is how we educate our staff and work with them to make these initiatives fun and impactful, not only at work, but in their lives outside of work, and in the community. If we can achieve this with our staff, then they will be able to project this to our clients and their events.

The education doesn't stop with our staff. We are heavily involved in community activities, such as student visits from local schools with children of all ages. Our goal is to show them what we are doing here to preserve our environment, but just as important, hear their ideas for their own sustainable future. This type of community outreach always gives us new ideas that we can add to our Green Meetings program, which benefits our operation and our clients.

We are definitely proud of what we have achieved so far, but there is a long way to go, and as we continue to grow as a company here in Macau we will continue to challenge ourselves to find new ways to sustain our operation, environment and community.

Used with permission of Sands China LTD.

Sustainability is doing business in a way that meets current consumer demands, while not impacting the ability for future generations to meet their demands. *Green* can be considered as a part of, or a bi-product of, sustainability.

Fad or Here to Stay? The industry of green meetings is quickly growing and all indicators point to these practices eventually becoming the norm within the meeting industry. With large green meetings taking place and the ripple effect continuing to impact all involved, many companies are changing the way they do business with positive results. As more and more associations and corporations make demands for green efforts, suppliers will respond and those that can't will not compete.

In a 2009 TripAdvisor survey, over a third of respondents said they would visit an eco-friendly hotel or resort in 2009. Also, 32% of respondents said they would be more environmentally aware with their travel decisions than they have in the past. The data indicate that we will continue to see an increase in green efforts by clients and customers. Meeting professionals are being challenged by their clients, and they in turn are challenging their vendors as they plan and execute meetings. The end result is green meetings, a better environment, happier employees, happier attendees, and an overall contribution to the state of our world.

FUTURE TRENDS

The following are some of the trends we are likely to see in MEEC sustainability.

- Increasing numbers of planners will have green meeting policies that will extend to suppliers.
- Green meeting practices will continue to be incorporated into increasing numbers of events.
- Increasing numbers of groups will have policies associating social responsibility with their meetings and events.
- Many national governments are likely to demand that the meetings and events they organize and sponsor incorporate "green elements."
- There will be increasing "accountability" and requirements that planners "prove" their meetings and events are green.
- There will continue to be an increased focus on cost versus benefits of "going green." Being able to document and calculate the true cost of going green versus the true benefits will be crucial.
- Some green activities that are now voluntary will become legal requirements.
- The number of certifications will be reduced as the most relevant ones survive and the rest either blend together or disappear.
- Educational training and workshop programs for providers of sustainable events will become more abundant.

Summary

This chapter dealt with the most recent developments in the MEEC industry: green meetings and social responsibility. These are not "fads"; they are facts of life in the twenty-first century. The challenge is how to incorporate green elements along with social responsibility into meetings and events.

Now that you have completed this chapter you should be competent in the following Meeting and Business Event Competency Standards:

MBECS – Skill 2: Develop Sustainability Plan for Meeting or Event

Sub skills		Skills (standards)
A2.012	Implement sustainability management plan	
A2.02	Demonstrate environmental responsibility	

Key Words and Terms

For definitions, see GLOSSARY, or http://glossary.conventionindustry.org

carbon footprint calculator	event miles	green	green sheen
carbon offset	experiential CSR	green meeting	greenwashing
corporate social responsibility (CSR)	going green	green movement	sustainability

Review and Discussion Questions

1. Discuss the economic advantages and disadvantages of a meeting going green.
2. How does a meeting manager evaluate green efforts?
3. Explain the difference between the terms "going green" and "sustainability" and give examples for each that support your answer.
4. How can greenwashing be regulated within the industry and handled by a meeting professional?
5. What is corporate social responsibility (CSR)? What role does CSR play in the MEEC industry?

About the Chapter Contributors

Nancy Bailey is the president of Carolina Event Consultants, a South Carolina–based event and meeting planning firm. She has been working in the event planning industry for more than ten years offering professional planning advice and services to corporations, associations, and not-for-profit organizations. Nancy graduated with a BA in public relations and a minor in hotel, restaurant, and tourism management from the University of South Carolina.

Dr. Carole Sox currently teaches at the University of South Carolina within the School of Hotel, Restaurant and Tourism Management. She started her career at the National Gallery of Art in Washington, DC, and was employed there for approximately ten years. She then worked for a national company in the Marketing and Communications Departments where she managed the local, regional, and national meetings for the corporation. She earned her BS at St. Mary's College of Maryland and her MSM at Southern Wesleyan University.

Dr. Sandy Strick, a graduate of Purdue University, has been on the faculty of the School of Hotel, Restaurant and Tourism at the University of South Carolina for over twenty five years. She teaches Meeting Management, Wine and Spirits, and Multicultural Human Resources. Dr. Strick is the coauthor of *Meetings and Events and Introduction to the Industry*, one of the first textbooks in the discipline of meetings' management. She is a Certified Hospitality Educator and Director of Graduate Studies.

APPENDIX A

GREEN MEETING CHECKLIST

The following can be used as a practical guide in determining where and how your meeting or event is achieving a higher green standard.

Communications and Marketing

Paper Reduction

- Minimize paper usage by encouraging participants to register online
- Give preference to electronic documentation over paper or use double-sided copying and printing
- Provide materials via PDA download or online where possible
- When printing, use recycled stock or Forest Stewardship Council (FSC)-certified stock
- Format any distribution materials to minimize the amount of printed paper
- Use a digital registration bag when possible
- Collect name badge holders for recycling
- Inform staff, attendees, and stakeholders of event environmental practices
- Work with event staff to evaluate past events of a similar scope and size to forecast the amount of materials and handouts needed

Selecting Recyclable & Recycled Materials

- Use recycled, high (100%) post-consumer content paper where possible
- Use FSC-certified paper
- Print materials on an Energy Star certified printer and use vegetable-based inks
- Limit the use of paper that is difficult to recycle, such as glossy paper, goldenrod, and florescent paper

Promotional Materials

- Distribute registration materials electronically.
- Various forms of social media such as Facebook, Twitter, and Instagram should be utilized for advertising and promotion.
- Request that all banners and signs are reusable and made from recycled content
- Give preference to mailing labels that use water-based adhesives
- Send event confirmations electronically or mail only when requested
- Limit the number of event program books available on-hand, encouraging participants to access the event program online

On-Site Event Materials

- Print any event collateral locally rather than shipping it to the event
- Reuse plastic name badge holders/lanyards and make recycle bins easily accessible
- Use digital signage when possible
- Computerize registration process at the opening of the event
- Transmit handouts, brochures, and session notes electronically after the event via e-mail and post to Web site
- Encourage exchange of electronic event materials via USB drives
- Use dry erase boards instead of paper flip charts
- Provide pens and notepads only if requested by participants and use pens and notepads made with recycled content
- Ensure that event sponsors subscribe to the environmental guidelines for promotional materials

Sponsor and Guest Materials

- Encourage speakers/guests to provide electronic copies of handouts and post the materials to the event/organization Web site
- When unavoidable, request that speakers/guests subscribe to the environmental guidelines for any promotional materials that must be printed

(continued)

Food and Beverage

General
Confirm the guaranteed number of event participants in order to eliminate excessive food waste

Elimination of Disposable Service Ware
- Give preference to reusable glassware and dishware over disposable
- Encourage participants to use mugs in a coffee stations and water coolers instead of disposable cups
- Use biodegradable disposable if using disposables is unavoidable
- Replace plastic/wooden stir sticks with reusable spoons
- Use cloth napkins and tablecloths

Food Service
- Source locally grown organic ingredients and in-season vegetables from local farmers
- Use fairly traded products (particularly fair trade, shade grown, organic coffee, tea, chocolate, and cocoa)
- Avoid bottled water by requesting water be served from pitchers
- Consider giving attendees a reusable water bottle for use throughout the event. Have water coolers available for easy refill
- Avoid excess and throw-away packing by encouraging suppliers to use reusable containers
- Ensure food and beverage packaging is recyclable
- Give preference to condiments, ingredients, and beverages purchased in bulk
- Request that all food and beverage condiments are served in bulk containers rather than individual packets
- Use only edible garnishes
- Arrange the donation of leftover untouched prepared food to local shelters and/or food kitchens
- Offer vegetarian meal selections (vegetables require less energy input than meat selections)
- Serve only seafood that was harvested in a responsible manner (farmed versus fished, management of operation)

Alcoholic Beverages
- Feature locally sourced alcoholic beverages
- Give preference to reusable ceramic or wood-corked coasters over disposable coasters
- Replace disposable drink napkins with cloth napkin or compostable alternatives
- Request alcoholic beverages only from producers whose packaging and containers can be easily recycled
- Ensure that all bottles and cans are property recycled

Food Composting
- Verify that kitchen waste and prepared food that has been touched is composted
- Ensure that leftover untouched prepared food is not composted and instead consumed as staff meals or donated to local food banks, missions, or charities

Contracts and Suppliers
- Clearly outline and communicate the event's sustainability guidelines to all contractors and suppliers
- Include all the food and beverage sustainability guidelines in supplier contracts

Event Production

Recycling Initiatives
- Place recycling containers in various easy-to-access areas with adequate signage
- Arrange for recycling areas to be staffed with advisors that can guide recycling efforts and address any questions/concerns
- Provide small trash bins at reception areas only if requested and provide no trash bins if the event's objective is zero-waste
- Give participants advance notice of the general recycling programs at the event via e-mail or post the information on the event's Web site
- Communicate recycling waste prevention initiatives to event participants at the opening/general sessions and periodically remind participants of the initiatives at intermissions

Recycling Signage
- Display clear signage indicating the type of recyclable material each container accepts, differentiating from cans, bottles, paper, organics, and so on.
- Request digital signage if available or use paper with recycled content
- Signage without a logo can be reusable
- If paper signage is used, follow the same guidelines outlined in Communications & Marketing

Design and Decor
- Request that centerpieces and decorations such as flowers be organic. It is even better if they can be reused for future events
- If organic centerpieces such as potted plants are used, encourage participants to take the items with them, or donated to a local charity to be reused
- Request that any other design features or decor items use materials that are both recycled and recyclable

Food Service Suppliers
- Request that reusable containers that are used to transport any items/materials to and from the event
- Create a no waste policy that places the responsibility of disposing any garbage on the suppliers and/or vendors
- Consider charging a fee for excessive waste left at the event

Cleaning Services
- Ensure that housekeeping staff uses only nontoxic, eco-friendly cleaning solutions such as Certified Green Seal products
- Request that housekeeping staff replace paper cleaning towels with reusable cloth towels

Energy and Electricity
- Purchase green power (or offset power consumption) during the event and notify participants of the renewably-sourced electricity
- Request venue thermostat be set to comfortable temperatures that use minimal energy. Consider requesting further temperature adjustments during "off" hours to conserve as much energy as possible
- Take advantage of naturally lit meeting and exhibit space

Event Staff
- Get buy-in from the staff prior to the beginning of the event by communicating the event's sustainability guidelines

- Ensure that the staff is effectively trained on appropriate environmental behavior such as sorting recyclables, minimizing waste, and composting organic waste
- Create a green committee comprised of stakeholders from various parties to oversee the event and monitor the event's sustainability guidelines
- Develop a reward program that encourages responsible behavior from event participants, staff, and committee members

Exhibits and Exhibitors

Reducing Packaging for Giveaways

- Request that all exhibitors not over-package any giveaways. Hold exhibitors responsible for discarding/recycling the packaging
- Encourage exhibitors to select giveaways made of recyclable materials or reusable items
- Consider sourcing eco-SWAG (souvenirs, wearable, and gifts)

Exhibitor Promotional Materials

- Extend environmental guidelines for communications and marketing materials to the promotional materials and exhibitors
- Communicate the expected number of participants to exhibitors in order to minimize any additional waste
- Encourage exhibitors to bring smaller quantities of promotional materials and require that exhibitors offer access to electronic materials on their Web site as an alternative

Packaging Materials

- Encourage exhibitors to reuse any boxes or packing that was used on arrival at the event venue
- Enforce a pack-in/pack-out policy or zero-waste criteria to ensure exhibitors leave with everything that was brought to the event
- Discourage exhibitors from using any external chemical substances on-site

Event Closing Protocol

- Develop check-out procedures that require exhibitors to interact with event staff prior to departure, ensuring their area is clean and waste-free
- Enforce fines for exhibitors that leave discarded materials, trash, carpet, or anything that accompanied them to the event

Recycled-Content in Display Booths and Exhibits

- Encourage exhibitors to use recycled content in the fabrication and assembly of display booths/exhibits
- Encourage exhibitors to use booths/exhibits with minimal or no logo so that they can be reused for future events

Reward Green Exhibitors

- Reward exhibitors with a "Green Exhibitor Award" at the end of the event, recognizing the exhibitor in front of all participants

Accommodations

General

- Identify any accommodation providers that are certified by an eco-rating program, such as the Green Key
- Highlight any accommodation providers that subscribe to a specific industry environmental code of practice
- Request in-house environmental policies/guidelines of potential accommodation providers and consider eliminating any accommodation providers whose environmental policies/guidelines do not support the event's sustainability goals

- Schedule a site visit with accommodation providers to verify on-site environmental practices
- Request that the accommodation provider dedicate a channel at the hotel that contains specific information about the event as well as any important updates
- Request that hotels change linens and towels every other day unless specifically requested by the guest

Accommodation Location

- Give preference to hotels that can accommodate the entire event or are within walking distance of the event venue, thereby eliminating the need for transportation
- Encourage participants to walk whenever possible and provide online walking directions if needed
- If transportation is necessary, consider providing operating g a shuttle service from the hotel to the event venue and back

Cooperation from Event Participants

- Ask event participants to reuse the linen at their hotels rather than use the laundry service everyday
- Remind participants to turn off lights, television, and air conditioners or heaters when leaving their hotel room for an extended period of time

Transportation

General

- Allow Web-conferencing abilities for participants that cannot physically travel to the event
- Establish an idle-free zone around the event venue

Low-Impact Air Travel

- Notify event participants of the various airlines that allow passengers to offset their emissions

Emissions Offsets

- Partner with local offset companies and request them to setup a display booth/exhibit at the event and sell offsets directly to participant
- Work with offset companies to offer emissions offsets at a discount rate if purchased in bulk
- Ask a representative from a local offset company to deliver a brief presentation on the importance of offsetting emissions
- Offer reduced attendance fees to event participants that purchase emissions offsets

Shuttle to/from Hotel

- Encourage all participants to travel together to or from the event
- Work with accommodation providers to develop a convenient schedule of pickup and drop-off times and locations

Zero Emission Alternatives

- Partner with local bicycle vendors to arrange bicycle rentals that give participants the option to ride between the hotel and event and explore the city
- Establish appropriate bicycle storage areas with the facility manager

Mass-Transit Passes

- For hotels located across town or outside of walking distance, provide participants a bus or mass transit pass and directions on how to travel between the hotel and event

(continued)

- Include the cost of a transit pass in the overall fee of attending the event, for delegates who must use transportation to reach the event

Hybrid Vehicle Rentals

- For participants who require a private vehicle, partner with car rental companies that offer hybrid vehicles
- Request that hybrid models are on reservation and ready for pickup before the event
- Work with parking operators to allocate a certain amount of parking stalls for participants that arrive to the event in a hybrid vehicle

Hybrid Taxis

- Use taxi companies that have a large hybrid fleet and encourage participants to specifically request hybrid taxis
- Notify taxi companies of the event prior to the start date and communicate the event's sustainability guidelines

Car-Pooling

- Encourage car-pooling by dedicating a section of either the event's Web site or the organization's Web site that permits local participants and car rental users to make arrangements
- Work with parking operators to allocate a certain amount of parking stalls for participants that carpool to the event

Information Technology
Web site and Online Content

- Request that the event venue or client organization create a section of its Web site that contains event materials accessible only by participants
- Notify and periodically remind participants of the Web site and its content

Equipment

- Encourage laptop usage over desktop computers, as laptops typically use less energy than desktops
- Ensure sufficient outlet for recharging batteries
- Use liquid crystal display (LCD) monitors instead of cathode ray tube (CRT) monitors
- Activate sleep mode on any equipment used in the event's production, including projectors, computers in the registration area, and personal computers of participants
- If purchasing any equipment for the event, give preference to Energy Star products that use less energy

Recycled Components

- Request that recycled print cartridges are used when printing event-related materials
- Request that recycled print cartridges contain vegetable-based inks

- Recycle any electronic waste, such as print cartridges, that is left behind at the end of the event

APPENDIX B

TERMINOLOGY

FSC FSC is a nonprofit organization that sets certain high standards to make sure that forestry is practiced in an environmentally responsible and socially beneficial manner. If a product, often a piece of wood outdoor furniture, is labeled as "FSC Certified," it means that the wood used in the piece and the manufacturer that made it met the requirements of the FSC.

ENERGY Energy Star is a U.S. government program created in 1992 by the U.S.

STAR Environmental Protection Agency in an attempt to reduce energy consumption and greenhouse gas emission by power plants. What began originally as a voluntary labeling program has grown in to one of the largest efforts worldwide to promote energy efficient consumer products.

SWAG Souvenir, wearable, and gifts typically found at tradeshows or other promotional events

GREEN POWER Energy produced from renewable or nonpolluting and nonhazardous technologies such as air turbines (windmills), geothermal power plants, and solar cells.

FAIR TRADE PRODUCTS For a product to carry either the International Fair-trade Certification Mark or the Fair Trade Certified Mark, it must come from FLO-CERT (the inspection and certification body for labeled Fair-trade), inspected and certified producer organizations.

The crops must be grown and harvested in accordance with the international Fair-trade standards set by FLO International.

The supply chair must also have been monitored by FLO-CERT, to ensure the integrity of labeled products.

CERTIFIED GREEN SEAL A product is eligible for green seal certification when it has passed rigorous testing and evaluation using a life-cycle approach, which means they evaluate a product or service beginning with material extraction, continuing with manufacturing and use, and ending with recycling and disposal.

CHAPTER 14

International Aspects in MEEC

MEEC organizers must be prepared to work with diverse people and cuisines. *bikeriderlondon/Shutterstock*

Chapter Objectives

This chapter provides the reader with an understanding of the following:

- How trade fairs exhibitions and conferences vary around the world
- The status of the trade fair and conference industry in different regions
- The terminology and protocol differences among various countries
- Aspects to consider before committing to an international trade fair or conference

Chapter Outline

INTRODUCTION

The growth of international communications and travel has brought about impressive changes in how the world does business. Thirty years ago, only the largest companies were considered "international." Today, there are few large companies that do not have an international presence.

Consequently, the meetings, expositions, events, and conventions (MEEC) industries have expanded internationally. In this chapter, we look at how the international scope of MEEC has evolved and how it differs in various parts of the world.

The Union of International Fairs (UFI) publishes regular, and impressive, statistics about the international **trade fair** industry. UFI estimated that 30,700 exhibitions are held annually, occupying 1.3 billion square feet of total net exhibition space. These events feature 2.8 million exhibitors and welcome 260 million visitors.

International meetings also contribute very greatly to the economy, for example, in the creation of jobs: 214,000 in Australia and up to 1 million in the United Kingdom.[1] Regardless of the location, the purposes of international meetings and exhibitions remain the same—communication, learning, networking, and marketing.

HOW MEEC VARIES AROUND THE GLOBE

Despite similarities of purpose, cultural and business influences have created different models for meetings and exhibitions in various parts of the world. In this section, the types of meetings and exhibitions held in different regions of the world are surveyed, with a discussion of how they differ in scope and operation, and what areas of the world are embracing trade fairs as a primary method of marketing. Included at the end of this chapter is a compilation of international trade fair and meetings organizations.

The World's Largest Fairs

The Canton Fair

China Import and Export Fair, also known as the Canton Fair, has been held in Guangzhou every spring and autumn since 1957. The exhibition occupies over 10 million square feet and features almost 60,000 booths. It attracts 24,500 exhibitors and over 189,000 buyers.

Hannover Messe (Fair)

In 2013, over 217,000 visitors from 93 countries came to Hannover Messe. Five million business contacts were made in five days, and in 2014, the fair focuses on core industrial technology in:

- Industrial Automation
- Energy
- Digital Factory
- Industrial Supply
- Research & Technology

One of many buildings where the Canton Fair is held in Guangzhou, china   *George G. Fenich*

---

[1] MPI Foundation (2013), *The Economic Impact of the UK Meeting & Event Industry*, Appendix 1

Europe

The trade fair industry's roots are in Europe. During the Middle Ages, the concept began with farmers and craftsmen bringing their products and wares to the town center to link with their customers. Although the wars of last century devastated European industry, today Europe is the focal point of international trade fairs and exhibitions.

There are three primary reasons for this. First is location—Europe has always been the crossroads of the world. International hub airports in Frankfurt, London, Amsterdam, Paris, and Madrid enable visitors and cargo to arrive easily from all parts of the world. In addition, a superlative network of rail transportation within Europe enables many cities to be within speedy reach from one another. For example, the Eurostar links London to Paris and Brussels within 2 hours. The second reason for the growth of trade fairs is Europe's industrial base. With reconstruction help from the United States, Europe was able to recover its manufacturing and distribution base within a few decades of World War II. With the help of their governments, European industrial centers develop excellent trade fair facilities. The third reason is the adoption of the euro as the currency of trade rather than francs, marks, lira, and so on. This facilitates trade throughout the European Union.

The Largest Exhibition Venue

Hannover Fairgrounds is the world's largest exhibition site. It features almost 11 million square feet of exhibit space in 27 exhibit halls and open air display area. The site includes a Convention Center with 35 conference rooms, 42 restaurants seating 14,000 parking facilities for 50,000 banks, laundry, pharmacy, and Münchner Halle—the world's largest trade fair beer hall. Hannover Fairgrounds offers separate units that provide partitioned areas with their own infrastructure and several events can run concurrently. More importantly, the regional government and the management company have worked together to establish excellent transportation and lodging facilities.

Report from CeBIT 2013

CeBIT, the world's biggest high tech fair, attracted around 285,000 visitors. Over 4,000 companies from 70 countries participated in CeBIT 2013. Germany's chancellor, Poland's prime minister, and Germany's federal minister of economics and technology were among the prominent delegates, as were more international industry and government delegations than ever before, for example, from Asia, the United States, Australia, and Europe. The show introduced a networking service, the Match and Meet delegation service, which was used by more than 350 international participants.

The show's dedicated recruiting arena allowed businesses to get in touch with promising candidates, often resulting in employment contracts being signed right on-site.

A total of over 7 million business meetings took place over the five days of the event. Online exposure was very much on the rise, especially via social media channels.

Germany is usually thought of as the center of industry and trade fairs in Europe. Spending by international visitors to Germany on business travel reached over $18 billion per year, and three of the world's five largest exhibition centers can be found in Hannover, Frankfurt, and Cologne.[2]

Italy is another focus of international trade fair activity. Milan is the fashion trade fair center of the world. Other important centers can be found in Bologna and Verona, while in Spain trade fair activity is concentrated around Barcelona, Valencia, and Madrid.

---

[2]German Convention Bureau(2013), *Business travel is a key economic factor for Destination Germany and AUMA (2012), German Trade Fair Industry Review 2012*

The Grassmarket has been a focal point in the Old Town for 500 years and a trading place since the beginning of the City of Edinburgh, Scotland   *The StockCube/Fotolia*

In 2012, the nations of the United Kingdom hosted over 1,600 trade exhibitions with more than 13 million buyers and suppliers and generating $18 billion of economic benefit for the United Kingdom.[3] Top exhibitions included:

- Farnborough International Air Show
- International Spring Fair (Birmingham)
- World Travel Market (London)

The Benelux nations also have a strong trade fair program. Excellent facilities exist in Amsterdam, Rotterdam, Brussels, and at Schiphol Airport. Paris, too, hosts numerous international events throughout the year.

Perhaps, the greatest growth of trade fairs in Europe is occurring in the countries of Eastern Europe. New facilities have opened in Zagreb, Belgrade, Warsaw, Moscow, and most recently in St. Petersburg, where the first stage of the new ExpoForum center launched in 2014.

It is probably true to say that the growth of the European Union, its common currency of the Euro, and the removal of trade barriers and tariffs has helped the European trade fair and exhibition industry to grow.

Large International Trade Fairs and Congresses

MITT MITT Russia (Moscow International Travel & Tourism Exhibition) is held annually. MITT is the largest travel and tourism exhibition in Russia for international companies to promote themselves to the Russian outbound travel and tourism market. For the past 20 years, MITT has become a well-established event in the industry and is one of the top five travel exhibitions in the world. Newcomers to MITT included national groups from the Philippines, Uruguay, Paraguay, Guatemala, and Ecuador.

MITT Russia occupies an exhibition space of almost 600,000 square feet over eight exhibition halls. With over 3,000 companies from 198 countries and Russian regions, it attracts some 74,000 visitors over four days. The first three days of MITT are trade only; the fourth day is open to the general public.

MITT is more than an exhibition. A comprehensive and educational business program takes place alongside the show, for visitors and exhibitors to attend. The recent program included:

- The 5th Moscow International Tourism Business Summit
- Seminars, consultations, and company presentations
- The 3rd Moscow Medical & Health Tourism Congress
- MITT Awards

---

[3]Business Visits and Events Partnership (2012), *The 2012 Things You Should Know about Events in Britain*

MITT Russia also featured the MITT Inaugural Summit of Ministers. The first summit brought together national tourism ministers and senior government representatives from Azerbaijan, Catalonia, Cuba, Dubai, Ethiopia, Greece, Hong Kong, Italy, Latvia, Montenegro, Morocco, Romania, Serbia, South Africa, Tanzania, Tunisia, Ukraine, the United States, and Vietnam.

Topics discussed included:

- Increasing tourist flow—the removal of barriers, simplifying procedures, and creating the right conditions
- Tourist safety—protecting the rights of tourists
- Region and event marketing—generating interest in cultural and national attractions
- Using technology effectively in the tourism industry

Adapted from: www.mitt.ru, *MITT 2013 Post Show Report*

The European Society of Cardiology (ESC) Congress

Europe also holds many international association meetings. The ESC Congress is the world's largest cardiovascular event and has been held annually since 1962. It takes place over five days in Amsterdam in early September. Figures are staggering: almost 30,000 health professionals and stakeholders (clinicians, scientists, epidemiologists, nurses, technicians, health care industry, opinion leaders, and policy makers) from 145 countries attended. They discussed topics arranged in themed scientific villages at the RAI exhibition and conference center. The Congress also features an exhibition where 204 companies display their goods and services.

The figures below show that international meetings now make increasing use of technological tools to communicate even more widely. The audience was not limited to on-site participants as it had a virtual reach of:

- 847, 000+ views/year (103 000+ unique visitors) on ESC Congress 365 (the ESC Congress scientific content platform).
- 42, 000 views of the live streaming video (published on the home page during the congress).
- 24, 000 viewers on ESC TV (the ESC Congress video channel).

The Congress changes venue every year: One year it is held at the Fira Gran Via 2 in Barcelona and the next at the ExCeL center in London.[4]

Asia

The growth of trade fairs and exhibitions in Asia has been phenomenal over the past fifteen years. New facilities and government promotions have taken the industry from its infancy to world class in little more than a decade. Primarily, Asian trade fairs focus on high technology, consumer electronics, and food. However, all types of manufacturing and service industries are well represented. Asian trade fairs and exhibitions are either sponsored by trade organizations, such as the world trade centers, or individual governments.

Taiwan and Singapore have been the backbone of Asian trade fairs and exhibitions. Taiwan has excellent facilities and routinely sponsors trade fairs in the semiconductor, consumer electronics, and food industries. Taiwan is also an important exhibitor at trade fairs and exhibitions in North America and Europe.

Singapore is a major "destination" city and consequently attracts many visitors to its textile, fashion, food, and electronics trade fairs. It has multiple facilities all linked to world-class shopping and entertainment complexes. Singapore is also attractive because it provides excellent transportation facilities with a world-class airport. The government of Singapore is very active in promoting exhibitions. International Enterprise Singapore, formerly known as the Singapore Trade Development Board, encourages Singapore's export and the Singapore Exhibition and Convention Bureau (SECB) is the lead agency for marketing Singapore as an international exhibition city. It provides financial and marketing support for trade fairs organized by both Singaporean and international organizers.

---

[4]Adapted from: http://www.escardio.org/ESC2013

China

The section that follows on China is largely based on a contribution by Dr. Wang Chunlei, Associate Professor in the Department of Event Management, School of Tourism and Event Management, Shanghai University of International Business and Economics, Shanghai.

The phrase "Convention & Exhibition" in Chinese was put forward in the late 1980s in China. If we input the Chinese characters of "Convention & Exhibition" in Google, we can get various words such as "meeting industry," "exhibition industry," "Convention & Exhibition industry," or "Convention & Exhibition tourism industry." In other words, the professionals and the scholars in China have different opinions on the range of convention and exhibition industries. As in other parts of Asia, the acronym MICE (Meetings, Incentives, Conferences, and Events or Exhibitions) is also very popular in China.

But just like many other countries, "event" is becoming a more and more popular term in China. Accordingly, event management has gradually got the common recognition and acceptance by industrial practitioners as an independent science.

With annual gross domestic product (GDP) growth rates of nearly 8% in recent years and continued economic reform, China has become one of the world's largest markets for the sale of raw materials and products. China's economy is now second in the world, after that of the United States. Economic prosperity, coupled with the liberalization of the regulatory regime as part of China's World Trade Organization (WTO), and entry commitments have been the greatest stimuli to the rapid and sustainable development of the Chinese convention and exhibition industries. At the same time, incentive travel, festivals, and special events are becoming more and more popular with local governments.

CONVENTION AND EXHIBITION INDUSTRIES IN CHINA   In 1978, only six international conventions and exhibitions were held in China, and it held and took part in twenty-one exhibitions abroad. The first exhibition company, Shanghai International Exhibition Company (SIEC), was established in 1985. Today, the quantities and scales of exhibitions in China have been increased by hundred folds and penetrated into all fields of the national economy; as a consequence, each industry had its own international professional exhibitions. There is over 51 million square feet of national indoor exhibition space in China's main venues, about 15% of the world's total. In this respect, China is second in the world after the United States.[5]

The Convention and Exhibition Services industry in China is calculated to be worth almost $3.5 billion in, up over 8% from the previous year and is growing at 9% annually. It is estimated that about 5,200 conventions and exhibitions are held in China annuals.[6]

Trade events have developed rapidly in recent years due to the growth of China's business, manufacturing, and services sectors. Revenue from industrial product conventions and exhibitions is estimated to account for about almost a third of the total industry revenue.

The Chinese government takes services increasingly seriously. The 2nd China Beijing International Fair for Trade in Services (CIFTIS) held at the China National Convention Centre in 2013 took as its theme "Trade in Services: the New Engine for Value Enhancement." A United Nations Conference on Trade & Development ran concurrently. Over 1,900 exhibitors attracted 138,000 trade and public visitors and the show extended over 750,000 square feet; 119 domestic and foreign dignitaries, government ministers, heads of international organizations, and foreign ambassadors participated in more than 150 activities.[7] This is a significant show that clearly demonstrates the government emphasis and desire to push and encourage the 12 new UN service sectors.

Five convention and exhibition economic belts, the Yangtze River Delta, Zhujiang Delta, Bohai Bay Area, and Northeast and Central China, have been formed in the mainland, and many trade shows have reached as far west as Chengdu, Sichuan Province; Chongqing city; and Xi'an, Shaanxi Province. As far as the scales and impacts of exhibition projects go, Beijing, Shanghai, and Guangzhou have been the most important three cities of Chinese convention and exhibition industries. As one form of economic concentration, some cities have grown into regional centers, such as Dalian, Shenzhen, Chengdu, Hangzhou, Nanjing, Ningbo, Suzhou, Qingdao, Xiamen, Xi'an, Wuhan, Nanning, Kunming, and Chongqing.

---

[5]UFI (2012), *Global Exhibition Statistics*

[6]ACMR-IbisWorld (2013), *Convention &Exhibition Services in China: Market Research Report*

[7]http://www.iccaworld.com

In addition, both Hong Kong and Macau, which are Special Administrative Regions of China, have an important place in international MEEC. As a free port with a major international airport hub, Hong Kong was nominated "Best Business City in the World" by *Business Traveler Asia-Pacific* in 2012 and "Best City for Business Events" in 2013 by the MICE publication *CEI Asia* magazine. Hong Kong's main venues are the Hong Kong Convention and Exhibition Center, the Asia WorldExpo, and the Hong Kong International Trade and Exhibition Center. Recently Hong Kong hosted three of the world's largest travel exhibitions and ten of Asia's largest trade exhibitions.[8] Macau, on the other hand, is a favorite incentive destination and its many casinos attract numerous international travelers to the "Vegas of the East."

It is probably true to say that, even though Chinese exhibition and meetings industry is developing very rapidly, there are some areas for improvement: The industry is still poorly positioned in many cities, government gets involved in industry management, domestic exhibition companies are relatively weak in comparison to their international competitors, and professional education and training is still not developed sufficiently. Organizing an event in China is also administratively and legally complex: Different government departments are designated to oversee an exhibition that corresponds with its industry and level. That is to say, if a trade show organizer plans to launch an exhibition in Shanghai, it must receive approval from the relevant municipal government departments mainly according to the exhibition's theme, the scope of exhibitors or attendees (international or domestic), and the qualification of the organizer.

The UFI Special Interest Group on China recently identified some key points to consider for international organizers wanting to hold an event in China[9]. These are:

- Need to understand local regulations and licensing requirements
- Importance of a local partner
- Rise of e-commerce and online competitors
- Increasing labor costs
- Challenge to find skilled and professional managers

However, Chinese companies and the government are becoming increasingly aware of the need for greater internationalization. For example, the China Convention and Exhibition Society (CCES) and China Association for Exhibition Centers (CAEC) have partnered up with international organizations to train and promote their members.

In addition, many Chinese cities began to realize the importance of meetings, which could contribute to the balanced development of the convention industry and the exhibition industry.

FESTIVALS AND SPECIAL EVENTS (FSE) IN CHINA With the rapid development of the national economy and the improvement of living standards in China, festivals and special events with various themes are welcomed by more and more local governments, and especially the tourism industry. Generally speaking, the Chinese FSE industry shows different attributes: The content of events is colorful, including entertainment, sports, and trade shows; the industries of culture, tourism, sports, and manufacturing have been integrated together; there are public service and private products in most festivals and special events. The most important fact is that culture and arts are becoming much more important when developing festivals or special events in China.

But even here, government intervention is prominent, and not just in infrastructure development, policy formulation, and marketing to visitors for local hallmark festivals (especially international events). It is a common practice that a lot of festivals and special events are hosted or subcontracted by different levels of Chinese government.

In addition, in a broad sense, many Chinese city governments still manage FSE in a classification-and level-oriented manner. It means that the government dismisses its macro-administration and delegates authority to individual departments such as commerce, domestic trade, science and technology, culture, and trade promotion committees. This kind of administration system could easily lead to political issues. And under the pattern of cross administration, the government is far from bringing out its strength in adjusting and controlling that should be segmented into statistics, planning, making policy, or regulations.

INCENTIVE TRAVEL IN CHINA Incentive travel is a new kind of business in the Chinese tourism industry but with a huge potential market. With more and more Chinese organizations and

[8]Hong Kong Trade Development Council (2013), *Convention and Exhibition Industry in Hong Kong*
[9]UFI China special interest group, *UFI Info, December 13/January 14*

companies making use of incentive travel, a lot of traditional travel agencies in China began to change their business model or offer new services. Economic success has generated an increase in incentive travel—Chinese companies hold incentives more frequently and travel to more destinations and with a higher number of employees. This trend is expected to increase in the next few years, with small corporate meetings also on the rise, mainly commissioned by pharmaceutical/medical, education, IT, and financial companies.

Some professional trade shows address this sector. The largest and most international are the China Incentive Business Travel & Meetings Exhibition (CIBTM) and the Incentive Travel & Convention, Meeting IT & CM China. The first international exhibition in China dedicated to the business travel, incentives, and conferences, CIBTM, was launched in 2005. Both shows offer exhibitors the opportunity to meet qualified buyers with an interest in different business travel products and services.

Furthermore, with plenty of tourism resources, competitive prices, and a good tourism image, China is expected to become one of the most popular incentive travel destinations in the world. On the other hand, with its rapid economic prosperity, China is also becoming one of the key incentive travel markets. And many countries such as Australia, the Netherlands, and Egypt are enhancing marketing to trade customers and residents in China.

Thailand

Thailand is a major center for clothing and textile trade shows as well as for food and agribusiness along with automotive and engineering fairs. Excellent transportation facilities in Bangkok make it easy for visitors to arrive from around the world. The IMPACT Exhibition and Convention Centre is Thailand's largest, with a total indoor space of over 1.5 million square feet. In 2013 the largest event held at IMPACT was THAIFEX—World of Food Asia 2013 with 50,000 delegates and visitors.

Korea

COEX, Kintex, and Songdo Convensia can be called Korea's three main exhibition centers. All three are situated in or very near the capital Seoul and host a variety of events (exhibitions and meetings). COEX is not just an events venue with almost 5 million square feet of floor space but it also hosts Asia's largest underground mall, three five star hotels, office blocks, a department, and a subway station. Kintex (or Korea International Exhibition Center) is in Goyang City. Its exhibition and meeting space was expanded in 2011 to almost 1.2 million square feet of floor space. It is a run as a partnership between the Korean national government investment agency and regional and municipal administrations. Songdo Convensia, situated next to Korea's main international airport, Incheon, offers the largest column-free space in Asia and is operated by the local tourism organization.

Other Asian Countries

Other countries nurturing trade fair programs with government promotion include Vietnam, Malaysia, and India. In these countries, the facilities are usually owned and operated by the government, and promotional activities are sponsored by various government agencies. Vietnam has taken a strong position in clothing and food trade fairs, while India is at the forefront of Asian information technology and software shows.

Australia

Australia has a long track record of hosting high-profile international events, especially association congresses and incentives. In a recent year, delegate expenditure was calculated to be worth almost AUD$13 billion (US$ 11.4 billion) to the Australian economy, and trend studies forecast the potential for this to increase to AUD$16 billion (US$ 14 billion) by 2020. Australia's major cities such as Sydney, Brisbane, Perth, and Adelaide all have internationally renowned conference and exhibition centers, while the capital, Canberra, is currently studying the feasibility of a new multipurpose center with over 130,000 square feet of exhibition and a plenary hall for 3,000 delegates. In 2013, Melbourne was voted Australasia's leading meetings and conference destination in the World Travel Market Awards.

Africa

The section that follows on Africa is largely based on the contribution by Uwe P. Hermann, a faculty member and researcher in the Department of Tourism Management, Tshwane University of Technology, Pretoria, South Africa.

The MEEC industry in Africa has seen significant growth over the past few decades, particularly in South Africa. Since the early 1990s, South Africa has become an increasingly important player not only on the continent but also worldwide, culminating in the highly successful hosting of the FIFA World Cup in 2010. The International Congress and Convention Association recently ranked South Africa in 37th position worldwide as a meeting destination. In the African context, however the country is far ahead: The closest African rivals, Morocco and Egypt, occupy 63rd and 69th position, respectively, and South Africa provides 29% of Africa's indoor exhibition space.[10] Cape Town is the most popular urban meeting destination in Africa. The city hosted the first Africa Travel Week in April 2014, when three large travel and meeting related fairs were held at the Cape Town International Convention Centre (CTICC): The World Tourism Market Africa, IBTM Africa, and the International Luxury Travel Show Africa are expected to attract almost 4,500 leisure, luxury travel, and meeting planning professionals.

Traditionally, the MEEC industry in South Africa is concentrated around hotel venues and game lodges, but considerable development has taken place in the creation of large multipurpose conference and exhibition facilities. In South Africa, three cities dominate the MEEC industry, namely, Cape Town, Durban, and Johannesburg. To support the development of MEEC in South Africa, the Tourism Grading Council of South Africa launched a star grading system for meetings and exhibition venues; this initiative is considered a world first. The FIFA World Cup also left behind a nationwide legacy of improvements in telecommunications and broadcast technology and public transport as well as a highly positive reputation for the country as a successful destination for major events.

Large numbers of domestic trade fairs and conventions dominate the South African industry, predominantly around Johannesburg, although South Africa as a destination for trade fairs is growing rapidly. Major venues in South Africa include:

- Cape Town International Convention Centre
- Durban International Convention Centre
- East London International Convention Centre
- Johannesburg Expo Centre
- Sandton International Convention Centre (Johannesburg)
- Tshwane Events Centre (Pretoria Showgrounds)

The Johannesburg Expo Centre currently is the largest exhibition venue on the continent, offering over 1 million square feet of space. The Cape Town International Convention Centre held 537 events, generated over 1.3 million visitor days, and almost R3 billion (US$ 276 million) for the South African economy in a recent year.[11] Upcoming cities in the MEEC industry in South Africa include Bloemfontein, Port Elizabeth, and Pretoria.

Egypt will soon see the opening of the Cairo Expo City with over 1.42 million square feet of exhibition space with additional conference center facilities. The project impresses through its modernistic design, which is meant to represent the patterns of the Nile delta. Other venues with significance may also be found in Botswana, Nigeria, Senegal, Uganda, and Zimbabwe.

The South African Tourism INDABA is an annual event that has been held in Durban since 1997, one of the largest tourism marketing events on the African continent. In 2013 this exhibition attracted 10,000 attendees, including almost 1,800 international visitors from 78 countries, and hosted 1,467 exhibitors from the Southern African region.[12]

The major problems facing the development and hosting of MEEC in Africa include the low per capita income of the population, low levels of professionalism, the general poor standing of the continent compared to other parts of the world, and the relative high costs of travel, especially to South Africa.

---

[10]http://www.ibtmevents.com

[11]http://www.cticc.co.za/

[12]http://www.indaba-southafrica.co.za/

Middle East

Trade fairs and exhibitions in the Middle East are most prominent in Dubai and Abu Dhabi in the United Arab Emirates, due to excellent government promotion, new facilities, and ease of travel access. Both Dubai and Abu Dhabi have international airports with service to every continent. This "crossroads" concept, as well as the fact that exhibition facilities are located at or near the international airports, is emphasized heavily in promotional materials. For example, both Dubai and Abu Dhabi strongly promote the duty-free zones near their airports and the extensive duty-free shopping available at their facilities. In addition, the regional market for consumer goods is very strong and puts the focus of trade fairs on items like furniture, automobiles, and consumer electronics.

In 2020, Dubai will hold the World Expo, the first Middle Eastern nation to do so. It is expected that the expo will attract more than 25 million visitors and positively impact UAE's GDP by $23 billion between 2015 and 2021 and create 277,000 new jobs.[13]

It is also fair to say that Qatar has been working very hard to attract both exhibition and meeting planners. The Qatar National Convention Centre, which opened in 2011, was built according to U.S. Green Building Council's Leadership in Energy and Environment Design (LEED) gold-certification standards.

Latin America

The huge population base of Latin America makes it well suited for trade fairs and exhibitions. Until recently, most of the Latin American trade fairs and exhibitions have been regional. However, new facilities and promotional efforts have set the stage for a growth in international exhibitions. New facilities in Sao Paulo, Brazil, and Mexico City are hubs for this activity. The Las Americas Exhibition Center in Mexico City provides the latest in technology to support exhibitors and attendees. In addition, the center is built within an entertainment complex that includes a horse racing track, restaurants, hotels, and a shopping center.

Brazil in particular is in the limelight, hosting both the soccer World Cup in 2014 and the Olympic summer games in 2016. A report by Ernst & Young Terco estimates that the 2014 World Cup[14] contributed over US$60 billion to the country, creating 3.63 million jobs. The event also no doubt helped change Brazil's reputation from just soccer and samba to that of an innovative country with plenty of research and development, a robust economy, and modern cities.

OWNERSHIP, SPONSORSHIP, AND MANAGEMENT MODELS

In the United States, many trade shows are adjuncts to association meetings and are owned by the association. Others are sponsored by private, entrepreneurial companies and operated on a for-profit basis. Ownership and management are usually accomplished by two companies working toward the success of the show. Other service companies support the industry by helping both the trade show management company and exhibitors.

This model is not always followed for international trade fairs and exhibitions. While there are very important commercial trade show organizing companies (especially in the United Kingdom), in some countries, such as Germany and Italy, it is the venues that do not just rent the space but also organize the fairs. Often governments, in collaboration with organizing companies, plan and operate the trade fairs. For example, the government of China plays a major role in the sponsorship of most trade fairs held in Beijing, Hong Kong, and Shanghai.

Professional Congress Organizer

In the United States, organizers and sponsors of large congresses will typically work with a DMO (CVB) and/or a DMC or third-party planning consultant. Outside the United States, there is an alternative, the Professional Congress Organizer (PCO). The PCO represents the client in dealing with the DMO, DMC, hotel, restaurant, transportation company, and other suppliers. The PCO will negotiate with vendors on behalf of the client. PCOs also tend to be more familiar with international issues like customs, taxation, and government regulations. The PCO

---

[13]http://www.ibtmevents.com

[14]Ernst & Young Terco (2011), *Sustainable Brazil, Social and Economic Impacts of the 2014 World Cup*

may even handle financial transactions, letters of credit, and foreign bank accounts. PCOs are often involved in the content of shows and SEPs. PCOs have their own association called the International Association of Professional Congress Organizers (IAPCO).

Global Commercial Exhibition Organizing Companies

There is a leaderboard of five truly global trade fair organizing companies, which operate across the world in all main markets. Here is the list:

1. Reed Exhibitions
2. Messe Frankfurt
3. UBM
4. GL Events
5. Messe Dusseldorf

IMPORTANT INTERNATIONAL MEETING AND TRADE FAIR ASSOCIATIONS

World Trade Centers Association

The World Trade Centers Association stimulates trade and investment opportunities for international businesses, commercial property developers, and economic development agencies looking to connect globally and prosper locally. The association serves as an "international ecosystem" of global connections, integrated trade services, and iconic properties under the umbrella of a prestigious brand.

The exclusive "World Trade Center" and "WTC" branded properties and trade service organizations are located in more than 90 countries and supported by 15,000 WTC professionals that deliver integrated, reciprocal resources to solve their members' and clients' business needs.

World Trade Centers are an ideal resource for hosting and leveraging large international events. Many WTCs house world-class exhibition halls, meeting rooms, and conference facilities, which are complimented by a worldwide network of international business professionals, and government and economic development agency partners to enhance their international event promotion, management, and recruitment. An excellent example is Taipei World Trade Center (TWTC), which operates the Exhibition Hall 1, Nangang Exhibition Hall, and the Taipei International Convention Center (TICC) and holds more then 80 trade shows annually. In addition, TWTC organizes over 30 international trade exhibitions each year, including some of Asia's largest—the Taipei International Cycle Show and Computex Taipei.

The International Congress and Convention Association

The International Congress and Convention Association (ICCA) is the global community for the world's meetings industry. It is the only association that comprises a membership representing the main specialists in handling, transporting, and accommodating international events.

ICCA's network of over 950 suppliers to the international meetings industry spans the globe, with members in over 90 countries, regrouping companies and organizations, which have a strategic commitment to provide top quality products and services for international meetings. ICCA tracks over 17,900 regularly occurring association meetings, which rotate between at least three countries. Access to this data and association clients is the primary reason why companies and organizations belong to ICCA.

International meeting planners can rely on the ICCA network to find solutions for all their event objectives, as ICCA members represent the top destinations worldwide, and the most experienced specialist suppliers.

Speaking on the occasion of ICCA's 50th anniversary, Martin Sirk, CEO, said: "What the long-term data tell us is a story that is dramatic: What is shown is an incredible picture of growth and dynamism, and a trend that justifies even more investment by destinations and suppliers into the international association market, in anticipation of what the future holds."

ICCA has offices in the Netherlands, Malaysia, the United States, and Uruguay.

Adapted from http://www.iccaworld.com/abouticca.cfm (used with permission of ICCA CEO Martin Sirk).

INTERNATIONAL MEEC CONSIDERATIONS

Lessons to Be Learned

It is important for trade fair, event, and exhibition managers to learn the reasons for success in different aspects of the international marketplace. For example, North American trade show managers can learn from their European colleagues in three areas:

- *Excellence of Infrastructure:* Public transportation systems in Europe provide excellent support of trade fairs and exhibitions.
- *Logistics:* International trade fair organizers are, by necessity, experts in logistics. Because the lifeblood of many international shows is the international exhibitor, many have specialized departments devoted to helping exhibitors overcome obstacles for exhibiting in their countries. Shipping and storage procedures are simplified and expedited by these agencies to help make exhibiting in their countries as easy as possible.
- *Support Organizations:* In America, many trade shows are sponsored and organized by associations. In other parts of the world, trade fairs and exhibitions are sponsored and organized by trade promotion organizations, such as the world trade centers or government agencies.

Methods of Exhibiting

There are a number of differences between exhibiting at an American trade show and at an international trade fair or exhibition. These differences need to be a part of the basic research before initiating an international trade fair program.

Typically, companies have choices in how they will exhibit at an international trade fair or exhibition. The U.S. government sponsors U.S. pavilions at many trade fairs, and a U.S. company can work through the government to be part of the U.S. exhibit. If a company does decide to be a part of the exhibit, the U.S. Department of Commerce can provide significant help.

Another option is to exhibit under the auspices of another company that is organizing a pavilion. Similar to U.S. government sponsorship, a private company may be the main interface, and contractual arrangements are made with it. Companies should fully investigate this type of situation to ensure that the organizing company is reputable and has experience in the host country and with the desired trade fair.

Joint ventures can also be formed between companies, particularly when one has experience exhibiting at a certain trade fair. In this case, it is important that companies be sure that their products or services do not compete with each other. This type of arrangement works best when the two companies' products complement each other and it is an excellent way for a company to enter the international trade fair marketplace and gain valuable experience.

"Going it alone" is another option for companies entering the international trade fair arena. Many large companies choose this route because they have the budget and staff to support the complexities of international exhibiting. Smaller companies must ensure that they have a clear understanding of all the requirements, costs, and scheduling before committing to this route. For example, smaller companies must factor in all the personnel time and costs involved in verifying that all tasks are completed. Assuming that the preparation time for an international trade show is the same as that for a domestic trade show can be a very costly mistake.

Terminology

In many parts of the world, an exhibit is not called an exhibit—or even a booth. Rather, it is called a **stand**. And this is only the beginning of the differences in terminology. Depending on where the trade fair is being held and who is managing it, participating companies must be familiar with those differences.

For example, in Germany the following terms must be understood:

- **Ausstellung:** Consumer show
- **Kongress:** Meeting or convention
- **Gesellschaft:** Company or society
- **GmBH:** Limited liability company
- **Messe:** Trade fair
- **Messegelande:** Fair site

And in the United Kingdom:

- **PLC:** Public limited company
- **Trade Exhibition:** Trade show

Contractual and Procedural Issues

In addition to terminology differences, contractual and procedural differences abound. Labor rules in the United States are very different from those in Europe or Asia. In Asia, there are few unions and no jurisdictional issues. Exhibitors have much more freedom in what they can do within their exhibit. In Europe, although there are unions, they are much more flexible than many in the United States.

Companies should not assume that setup or logistical contracts read the same as those in their home country. Substantial differences exist from country to country and from trade fair to trade fair. Companies should read each contract closely and adhere to all the requirements. If something is not understood, it should be brought to the attention of show management immediately.

Customs Clearance

Exhibition organizers at international shows provide access to experienced international freight forwarders, who also act as custom brokers, to ensure that everything is in order and arrives on time. The freight forwarders are knowledgeable about the custom regulations for the host country and take action to ensure that exhibitors know of every requirement and deadline.

Typically, goods can be temporarily imported to an international show site without having to pay duties or taxes, using either a **carnet** or a **trade fair bond**. A carnet can be very complicated to obtain, and a hefty bond must often be established. However, most trade fair venues offer trade fair bonds, which are simple to arrange. Again, the international freight forwarders are the point of contact for trade fair bonds. Be sure to inquire about host country rules on giveaways and promotional materials. In some countries, a duty is charged when the value is above a certain limit; in others, a duty is not charged for materials used for this purpose.

First International Trade Show

At one point before joining the academe, Dr. George G. Fenich had the job of running all the marketing and trade shows for a company. On one occasion, one of his technical representatives arrived at an international trade show the day before it was to open only to find that the written materials and brochures had been lost. He called the home office of the company and asked that a new set of brochures be sent "overnight express" to be there in time for the opening of the show. The problem was that, while the shipment could get there overnight, it would take three or four days to clear customs, and the trade show would have ended.

Freight forwarders are also cognizant of the estimated time for materials to clear customs, and they factor these times into the schedules that they provide to exhibitors. Companies fully adhere to these schedules to ensure that their materials arrive on time. Countries vary widely in the amount of time to clear customs, so be very aware of the differences if you are exhibiting in more than one country. Do not assume that because it takes only one day to clear customs in Paris or Frankfurt that it will be the same in Dubai or Taipei.

Protocol

It is the responsibility of the company trade fair manager to research the business customs of the host country and the individual trade fair. Staff should then be thoroughly trained on these differences before departing for the trade fair. Always remember that what is acceptable in one country or at one trade fair may very well be offensive in the next country or at another trade fair. Although English is normally the "official" language of international trade fairs, it is not safe to assume that all attendees or other exhibitors speak English. The wise company will ensure that at least some of the staff is bilingual, particularly in the host country's language.

Exhibit staff members will be greeting people from many countries to their international exhibit. It is imperative that they be familiar with the appropriate greetings for different cultures and forms of address. Although most visitors will not be offended if protocol is not strictly followed, it does give visitors a positive impression if their cultural standards are observed. It is also important for visitors to be aware of negative gestures for various cultures. What is a normal gesture in one culture may be extremely offensive in another. Gift giving and invitations are other areas that require research and training before embarking on an international trade fair program. Staff should also be aware of other cultural factors concerning dining and traveling in the host country. If spouses are traveling to the host country, they should be given briefings on the host country and its cultural expectations as well.

Examples

- In Indonesia, greetings are stately and formal. Do not rush. Hurried introductions (which commonly occur in trade fair settings) show a lack of respect.
- In the Netherlands, always avoid giving an impression of superiority. Egalitarianism is a central tenet of Dutch society. Everyone in a Dutch company, from the boss to menial laborers, is considered valuable and worthy of respect.
- When interacting with French visitors to an exhibit, never use first names until you are told to do so.
- In China, discussion of politics is taboo and is actually not understood.
- Germans generally take a long time to establish a close business relationship and may appear cold in the beginning. This will change with time.
- Be very careful regarding what your exhibit staff wears. What is the customary business dress for the host country? For example, Japan is still very formal when it comes to dressing for business, so you should avoid flashy jewelry or colors that are too bright.
- At a business meeting in Saudi Arabia, coffee is often served toward the end of the meeting as an indication that the meeting is about to end.
- Also, in most Arabic countries, the left hand is considered dirty, so you should never eat or accept anything with this hand. Be sure when giving gifts or promotional materials that you do so with the right hand.
- When giving away gifts in Switzerland, avoid giving away knives—it is considered bad luck.
- If a Japanese person gives you a gift, do not throw away the wrapping or tear it up. It is considered part of the gift.
- Aside from handshakes, there is no public contact between the sexes in many countries. Do not kiss or hug a person of the opposite sex in public—even if it is your spouse. On the other hand, in some countries contact is permitted between people of the same sex. Men may hold hands with men and even walk with arms around each other; this is interpreted as nothing but friendship.
- Westerners frequently find Arabic names confusing. The best solution is to request the names of anyone you meet, speak to, or correspond with. Find out their full names (for correspondence) as well as how they are to be addressed in person.
- Understand the hierarchies of doing business within a foreign country. For example, the managing director in England equates to the CEO in an American firm.
- Keep in mind that many English do not consider themselves European. This is vital when discussing issues regarding the European Union.
- In many European countries, employees get four or five weeks of summer vacation. Some countries virtually shut down for the month of August.
- When negotiating in China, always give many alternatives so that the Chinese negotiators have room to negate several options with dignity. Also, always keep the same negotiating team throughout the process.
- The traditional Chinese greeting is a bow. When bowing to a superior, you should bow more deeply and allow him or her to rise first.
- In many Asian countries, it is not appreciated to pat people on the shoulder or initiate any physical contact.
- In Japan, the host will always treat when you are taken out. Allow your host to order for you. Be enthusiastic while eating and show great thanks afterward.

The exchange of business cards with Asians is very formal.
Sunabesyou/Fotolia

- In Japan, business cards are presented after a bow or handshake. Present your card, using both hands, with the Japanese side facing your colleague, in such a manner that it can be read immediately. Handle cards very carefully, and do not put them in your pocket or wallet. Never write on a person's business card in his or her presence.
- Age and rank are very important in Korea, so it is usually easiest to establish a relationship with a businessperson of your own age.
- Hospitality is very important in Taiwan. Expect to be invited out every night after hours. This will entail visiting local nightspots and clubs, and may go until the wee hours of the morning.
- Avoid pouring wine at a social occasion in Argentina. There are several complex taboos associated with wine pouring that a foreigner can unknowingly violate. For example, pouring with the left hand, a common practice in the United States, is a major insult in Argentina.
- In the United States, the hand gesture where the thumb and forefinger are forming a circle with the other three fingers raised is considered the "OK" sign.
  - In Brazil, it is considered a vulgar or obscene gesture.
  - In Greece and Russia, it is considered impolite.
  - In Japan, it signifies money.
  - In southern France, it means zero or worthless.
- In the United States, waving the hand back and forth is a means of saying hello.
  - In Greece, it is called the *moutza* and is a serious insult: The closer the hand is to the face of the other, the more threatening it is.
  - In Peru, waving the whole hand back and forth can signal "no."
  - In most of the world, making a fist with the thumb raised means "OK."
  - In Australia, it is a rude gesture.

These are simply a few of the cultural issues that foreign businesspeople must face. Before traveling to any country, it is wise to consult as many sources as possible to learn the appropriate business and social behaviors for the culture. Take the time to learn the appropriate behavior in the host country and the greeting expectations for potential visitors to the trade fair.

The following are aspects of international trade fairs that are different from U.S. exhibitions. Keep in mind that these are generalizations and do not apply to all situations.

- Hospitality events are generally held on the exhibit floor, with many companies providing food and beverages as a matter of course in their exhibit.

- Height restrictions may be nonexistent. Many large exhibits may be two or three levels.
- Rules on smoking in the exhibit hall may not exist, and many exhibitors and attendees may smoke in the exhibits.
- Some trade fair organizing companies may not offer "lead retrieval" systems that U.S. companies are accustomed to. It is always wise for a company to bring its own method of capturing leads.
- International trade fairs are often longer in duration than U.S. trade shows and often are open on weekends as well. Although in Europe the show may run from 9 AM to 6 PM, in Brazil or other Latin American countries it is common for trade fairs to open at 2 PM and run until 10 or 11 PM at night.
- Be aware that most of the world outside the United States is metric. Voltages may differ, and exhibitors may need plug-in adaptors or transformers.

Determining Whether to Participate

Because exhibiting at an international trade fair or exhibition is a significant investment, it is important that companies seriously consider if this move makes good business sense. First, consider the following top-level questions:

- Would international trade fair exhibiting support our business objectives?
- Who is our international audience that can be reached through a trade fair program?
- What trade fairs or exhibitions are available in our industry?
- What is the audience profile for each potential trade fair or exhibition?
- Do we have a system in place to determine our return on investment?

If these questions support a company's decision to initiate an international trade fair program, the following questions help analyze the situation before making a final decision:

- What are the costs associated with exhibiting at each potential trade fair or exhibition? Companies must be sure to calculate the costs for travel, shipping, translated materials, and other items that are not a normal part of domestic exhibiting.
- What are the cultural consequences of exhibiting at each potential trade fair or exhibition? Investigate how the fair operates, what cultural rules may apply, and provide training for all staff who will participate.
- Does the company have the personnel resources to support adding international trade fairs to its marketing mix? International trade fairs are often longer than domestic trade shows and therefore may require more staff.
- What type of participation is best for the company? Explore the options that are available— U.S. Pavilion, joint venture, or going it alone.
- Have all the requirements for each trade fair been identified and analyzed? Every trade fair is different, and an exhibiting company must be clear on all requirements before committing funds and resources.
- Does senior management support an international trade fair program? An international trade fair or exhibition is a serious investment—one that should require commitment from the highest levels of company management.
- Are the logistic requirements fully understood? Although trade fair management companies generally provide detailed instructions to exhibitors, it is imperative that key people in the company understand all the requirements, especially deadlines, for shipping materials.

Other Considerations

- Visas may be required for entry and exit.
- Items that Americans take for granted may have to be declared upon entry to a country. For example, brochures and written materials must be declared and taxes paid on them.
- Many international destinations require payment of departure taxes.
- Most countries require that payment be made to ensure that goods exhibited at a trade show are exported and not sold within the country. A freight handling company can arrange a bond as security.
- AND many more! When in doubt, ask.

TRADE FAIR CERTIFICATION

The **U.S. Department of Commerce** has developed a program to promote exports of U.S. products and services abroad. The **Trade Fair Certification Program** endorses independent and association show organizers who manage and organize overseas events. The certification helps trade fairs attract more exhibitors, provides additional support and value-added services for exhibitors, and promotes the event through a variety of publications and sources. Requirements for Department of Commerce Trade Fair Certification include the following:

- Must have either a U.S. Pavilion or commitment to attract at least ten U.S. exhibiting companies.
- Must have a U.S. office or agent.
- Must have exhibited before.[15]

FUTURE TRENDS

- Rapid expansion of the MEEC industry will occur in developing countries such as those in Africa, the Middle East, and Latin America. Mega events such as the FIFA World Cup (football or soccer depending upon your location) and the Olympics create goodwill toward the organizing destinations.
- Rapid expansion of the MEEC industry is also occurring in China. Facilities continue to be built or expanded. Some, such as the "birds nest" stadium built for the 2008 Beijing Olympics, have unique architectural features.
- As MEEC planners reach out to increasingly international audiences, technology will be used more and more to promote events and to hold so-called "hybrid" events, a mixture between face-to-face and virtual elements.
- Environmental factors such as the economy or natural disasters will cause ripple effects well beyond local boundaries.
- As proud as many nationalities are of their "native" language, English is increasingly the common language of the MEEC industry.

---

[15]http://export.gov/tradeevents/eg_main_018558.asp

Summary

The growth of international trade fairs and exhibitions and international meetings has been phenomenal over the past fifteen years. Europe, the historical home of trade fairs, continues to strengthen its hold on the world's largest trade fairs and those with the most significant economic impact. Asia has made great strides by building state-of-the-art facilities and promoting its efforts throughout the world. The Middle East, Africa, and Latin America all have strong efforts under way to capture a larger piece of the international trade fair and exhibition and convention market.

Worldwide communications, easy travel access, and open markets have been a boon to the international event industry.

Few large companies can afford not to be in the international marketplace today. What was once the playground of only the world's largest companies is now a necessity for most companies of any size. Trade fairs and exhibitions are the easiest method for these companies to enter the marketplace and meet their potential customers.

Exhibiting at international trade fairs is not easy. Cultural and business differences present a new set of challenges for the exhibitor, along with more complex logistics and travel procedures. Companies must seriously analyze all factors before committing to an international trade fair program.

Key Words and Terms

For definitions, see GLOSSARY, or http://glossary.conventionindustry.org

ausstellung	International Congress and	messegelande	trade fair bond
carnet	Convention Association	PLC	stand
gesellschaft	kongress	trade exhibition	U.S. Department of Commerce
gmBH	messe	trade fair	trade fair certification program

Review and Discussion Questions

1. List some ways that international trade fairs may differ from U.S. trade shows.
2. What are two reasons for Europe's strength in the international trade fair industry?
3. What is the purpose of the World Trade Centers Association or of ICCA?
4. What are some of the complexities that a company must consider before exhibiting at an international trade fair or exhibition?
5. What options does a company have for participating in an international trade fair or exhibition?
6. Before proceeding with your exhibition or conference outside of North America, list at least five pieces of knowledge you will require before moving ahead. Where will you get the information from?

About the Chapter Contributor

Mady Keup is Course Director for the Master of Science program in Strategic Event Management and Tourism Management at SKEMA Business School in France. Mady was Head of the London Convention Bureau (now London & Partners) for five years, and she is an MPI (Meeting Professionals International) accredited trainer and an instructor for Destination Sales Training in Europe & the Middle East on behalf of Destination Marketing Association International (DMAI). Mady travels extensively for consultancy and training in Europe, Middle East, and North America.

Previous Edition Chapter Contributor
Sandy Biback, CMP, CMM, lecturer of Meetings and Conventions.

CHAPTER 15

Putting It All Together

MEEC events are like puzzles—eventually they must be put together. *Maksim Kabakou/Fotolia*

Chapter Objectives

This chapter provides the reader with an understanding of the following:

- Key tasks in creating a citywide meeting/event
- Method to create a statement of conference objectives
- Ways to identify budget expenses and income sources
- Timetable for implementation of different meeting planning tasks
- Process of conducting a site inspection
- Assessment of success of the meeting

INTRODUCTION

Many books contain a concluding chapter that repeats and summarizes the elements of the earlier chapters. In this textbook, a fictitious case study of a citywide convention serves the same purpose. The goal of this case study is to bring together all the previous chapters. Throughout this text, you have read about the tasks associated with meeting/event planning. Through this case study, you will learn more about topics from the previous chapters, and how they apply to a citywide annual conference for 3,000 attendees. The objective of this case study is to help you understand the various tasks a planner or event professional (these terms will be used interchangeably through the chapter) must complete in order for a meeting, exposition, event, or convention MEEC to be successful. In addition, this case study will help the reader

More Shampoo Please

The Hilton New Orleans Riverside is a large convention hotel. The hotel contains over 1,600 guest rooms and suites, 130,000 square feet of meeting space, and a 90,000-square-foot health and fitness center. Needless to say it hosts countless meetings and conventions. Whenever a convention attended predominantly by females is booked into the hotel the housekeeping staff is instructed to double the amount of shampoo and towels in each guest room: women use more of each. The hotel also increases the strength of their linen laundry department: Makeup is more difficult to remove from linens.

understand the complexities of the budget and timetable, as well as the many people with whom an event professional must communicate.

This case study uses a three-year planning timetable for one citywide conference. The meeting planning cycle is continuous, and it is important to understand that two of the key skills an event professional must possess are the abilities to organize and to multitask. Event professionals typically work on three to five meetings or events simultaneously, each in different stages of development.

As you review the budget portion of the case study, it is important to understand that many variables, including the time of year the meeting is held, the planner's ability to negotiate, the value of the business to the facility, and the trade-offs, will affect the budget. This budget is broad and was created to highlight the many details the planner must consider.

THE ASSOCIATION

As a meeting or event planner, it is important to understand your audience—the attendees of the event. For association meeting planners, this is critical as they market the conference to association members and to potential members. The meeting planner must also communicate information about his or her association members to suppliers for the convention. The better a supplier understands the audience of the meeting planner, the better the supplier can serve them. For example, if a hotel knows that the majority of the people attending a meeting are women, the hotel might add products that women use, such as hand cream or shower caps, to the room amenities.

The American Small Animal Association (ASAA) is an example of a typical association in the United States. The ASAA is an 8,000-member nonprofit association whose members are veterinarians from throughout the United States who specialize in care for small animals. The ASAA was founded ten years ago by a group of veterinarians who saw the need to update research and to network with other veterinarians specializing in small animal care. Over 60% of the organization's membership operates independently owned veterinary clinics; the remainder of the association members are suppliers to the veterinary industry. The suppliers include pharmaceutical companies, prescription food companies, and product suppliers. Although the number of women members is increasing, 60% of the members are male; 55% Caucasian; 30% African American; and 15% a mix of Latino, Asian, and Native American. It is important to know the makeup of the organization so that the event can meet its wants and needs. The planner or organizer must ask two questions: Who is the group? Why are its members here?

An executive committee and a board of directors operate the ASAA, while the executive director and seven committee members oversee the day-to-day operations of the association. Members of the board of directors are elected from seven established regions and serve two-year terms. All board elections take place during the annual meeting and are announced during the final night.

Sue Rodriguez is the director of meetings for the ASAA and is a full-time employee. Sue is one of the five full-time employees and is responsible for coordinating the seven regional meetings and the annual conference; she reports directly to the executive director. Planning for the annual conference begins three years in advance of the meeting date. For the past five years, attendance at the annual conference has increased 5% per year; and last year, 37% of the membership attended the meeting. This increase is attributed to the success of the trade show portion of the conference that was added five years ago.

AMERICAN SMALL

ANIMAL ASSOCIATION

Logo for the (fictitious) American Small Animal Association.
George G. Fenich

Goals

To begin preparation for the annual conference, Sue reviews past annual conference evaluations from attendees and members of the board of directors. The board of directors wanted to save money by cutting down on the cost related to networking activities, but the members indicated how important it is to have time to meet other professionals from around the country. The board also would like to see the money collected from this conference increased by 10% because other than membership dues, the annual conference is the largest revenue source for the association. Last year, the ASAA created the Small Animal Preventive Disease Certificate (SAPDC). During the annual convention, veterinarians earn five continuing education units (CEUs) and learn about the preventive medicines that can be used to save the lives of small animals. Additionally the board of directors request that a **Corporate Social Responsibility (CSR)** segment be included in the annual conference. Once a destination is selected for the annual meeting, Sue will work with the local community to identify not-for-profit organizations that need help.

To help focus her thoughts, Sue reads the ASAA mission statement: The mission of ASAA is to provide an educational forum for members to exchange ideas and develop ways to ensure the health of small animals. This mission is accomplished by providing quality education for its members, offering assistance to new veterinarian clinics, and providing a forum for members to meet and to assist each other with emerging technologies.

To help Sue measure **return on investment (ROI)**, she creates operational and educational objectives. The operational objective for this conference is to increase meeting profits by 5% over last year's conference. Sue works with the program committee to create the educational objective for this meeting, which is to increase the number of attendees enrolled in SAPDC classes by 10% and to provide additional networking opportunities. Sue hopes to meet these objectives by offering a four-day conference focused on education and networking that will result in an increase of conference profits by 5%.

Budget

To create the budget (see Tables 15-1 and 15-2), Sue reviews the past meeting budgets. For her expenses, she includes the cost of marketing materials, the convention center, host hotel, decorator, audiovisual equipment, speakers, entertainment, and staff. In addition, Sue must consider operational objectives for the meeting. To locate income sources, Sue looks at past meeting **sponsors** and exhibitors.

Table 15-1 Budget Income		
Budget	**Income**	**Registration**
		3,000 attendees
Members		1,680 attendees
early (at 60% = 1,008 people)	$600 p/p	$604,800
late (at 40% = 672 people)	$800 p/p	$537,600
Nonmembers		600 attendees
early (at 50% = 300 people)	$700 p/p	$210,000
late (at 50% = 300 people)	$900 p/p	$270,000
Student (at 5% = 120 people)	$100 p/p	$12,000
Speakers (100 people)	$300 p/p	$30,000
Exhibitors	Included in exhibit fee	
Registration Total		**$1,664,400**
SAPDC (500 people)	$100 p/p	$50,000
Exhibitors	$3,000 p/exhibit	$1,500,000
Sponsors (500 exhibitions)		$120,000
Extended Learning		$10,000
Other		$5,000
Total Income		**$3,349,400**
Expenses		$1,881,438
Net Income		**$1,467,962**

The hotel budget will include meeting room rental, food and beverage, staff sleeping rooms, and service charges and gratuities. In creating the budget, Sue knows that she will have some negotiation opportunities based on the ASAA sleeping and meeting room usage ratios. The better that the ASAA's use of meeting rooms to sleeping rooms will match the hotel's ideal sleeping room to meeting room ratio, the better the rate that can be negotiated. To assist in managing the hotel blocks, Sue uses a housing bureau.

The convention center expenses will include the cost of space for meeting rooms, exhibit hall, electricity, Internet connection, garbage pickup, security, and staffing for coffee and food stations. To maximize dollars, Sue plans the majority of her educational events at the convention center. This not only enables her to use the daily rate for the rooms at the convention center but also is a selling point for the exhibitors who want attendees near the trade show.

Sue will need to identify a **general services contractor (GSC)** to provide decorations and to set up the trade show. She will also need to assess audiovisual needs for both the hotel and convention center. The GSC will provide staging for the reception, general session, trade show, and awards night, and the **audiovisual (AV) company** will provide sound and light. In order to provide an accurate quote, the GSC must be given information on carpeting requests, number of trade show booths, estimated freight use, and types of staging needed for the opening session, general session, and awards dinner. The AV company will need to know the sound and lighting needs for each venue and the type of production for the general session, opening reception, and awards dinner. The general session will be sent via Webcast to members who are unable to attend, so Sue lists this as a separate expense (see Table 15-2).

To budget transportation, Sue looks at past budgets to determine how many attendees used the shuttle service for airport transfers, but she knows this expense will vary greatly depending on the existing transportation options in a given city. At this point, she includes full shuttle service for each day of the conference, VIP transportation, and transportation to the off-site events and the golf tournament. In addition to ground transportation, Sue's transportation budget includes air transportation for staff and VIPs as well as freight shipping.

Table 15-2 Budget Expenses	
Budget	**Expenses**
Convention Center	$350,000
Host Hotel	$212,643
Decorations	$102,245
Signage	$80,000
Audiovisual Equipment	$125,000
Webcasting	$60,000
Pressroom	$50,000
Transportation	$18,250
Off-Site Venue	$50,000
Golf Event	$150,000
Marketing Committee	$185,000
Program Committee	$10,000
Speakers	$52,000
Entertainment	$17,000
Security	$180,000
Insurance	$100,000
Special Services	$5,000
News Delivery	$30,000
Temporary Staff	$67,200
Tote Bags	$30,000
Site Visits	$2,100
Other	$5,000
Total Expenses	**$1,881,438**

Reviewing the budget history is also a good starting place when Sue allocates funds for marketing. This year she will spend less on hard items like brochures and direct mail pieces and more electronic marketing and social media.

Of the speakers for the ASAA, 75% are members presenting research papers. To encourage members to make presentations, the ASAA offers presenters a 50% discount on the early registration fee. The majority of the money allocated for speakers actually is used for a keynote speaker and entertainment. To locate the keynote speaker and entertainment, Sue uses a speaker's bureau; the speaker's bureau's fee is included in this expense item.

In order to have a smooth meeting, Sue will need to hire temporary staff. This budget item includes the cost for registration personnel, staff for on-site assembly of attendee packets, room monitors, and staff to distribute evaluations and carry out other duties. Sue will need to bring in temporary staff one day prior to the meeting for training and will pay staff for their time.

Security is an ongoing expense that the ASAA must include in its budget. Because the ASAA is increasing its involvement in new research for small animals and this new research is both confidential and controversial, more security will be needed.

Insurance is another expense that is increasing. Sue includes insurance to cover attrition and loss of revenue due to acts of God, terrorism, and liability. The $18,000 budgeted represents 1% of the cost to host this meeting.

To cover expenses for attendees with special needs, Sue includes a special services item in the budget, which will be used for members who identify themselves as needing translators, written material to be published in Braille, sign language interpreters, special accommodations for Seeing Eye dogs, and so on.

When Sue creates the budgets, she contacts city officials where the meeting will be held. As a nonprofit organization, the ASAA is exempt from most city and state taxes, but she must file the documents to ensure the exemption. Furthermore, Sue will need to bring forms proving that the ASAA is a not-for-profit organization; the forms will also be filed with suppliers.

Sue includes some expenses in the budget even though she knows that these expenses will be picked up by sponsors. Each year, Sue has no problem finding a company to sponsor tote bags given to all attendees, the on-site newspaper, transportation, the meal for the opening reception, and the entertainment for the VIP dinner. It is important that Sue includes these items in the budget to document these expenses.

To allow for unexpected expenses, Sue creates an "Other" expense category, which is used to cover additional expenses that do not occur every year or that are not planned for. For example, if the cost of shipping increases, this contingency would be covered.

Income

The income (see Table 15-1) will offset the expenses for the meeting. Estimated expenses for this meeting are $1,881,438. To reach the financial objectives and make a profit, Sue must not only pay all expenses but also build in a profit.

In determining the income, Sue starts with income generated from the registration fees. She first takes the expected attendance of 3,000 and subtracts 500 exhibitors whose registration fee is included in the exhibitor fee and then subtracts the 100 speakers who will pay a reduced registration. The ASAA has three registration fee categories: members, nonmembers, and students. Convention history shows that 70% are members, 25% nonmembers, and 5% students. In order to reduce attrition fees, Sue creates an early registration fee and a late fee for members and nonmembers. Typically, 60% of the members and 50% of the nonmembers will register early. Sue estimates that if registration alone will cover expenses, she must charge $629 per person. With this in mind, Sue's registration fee structure is $600 for an early member, $700 for an early nonmember, $800 for a late member, and $900 for a late nonmember. Students only pay $100, thus encouraging them to join when they are employed in the field. Sue estimates her registration income to be $1,664,400.

Following the income generated from registration fees, the exhibitors are the largest single source of income for the ASAA. It will cost the ASAA approximately $10 per square foot to rent the convention space, GSC and audiovisual equipment. The ASAA will sell this trade show space for $30 per square foot. History shows a steady 10% increase in exhibitors per year; at the last conference, about 450 companies ordered booths. Sue estimates exhibitor income for this year to be $1,500,000 (500 exhibitors spending $3,000 each for a ten-foot by ten-foot booth).

Other sources of income that Sue will include in the budget are rebates generated from hotel rooms, the transportation company, and the GSC. Rather than accept commissions for these items, the ASAA negotiates a rebate per room night that becomes an income stream. There is a small amount of money raised by the sale of extended learning products, including DVDs, CDs, books, and audiotapes.

Income from the SAPDC is $100 per person, in addition to the registration. Last year, the ASAA charged $200 per person—the cost is low to encourage attendees to take classes toward certification.

REQUEST FOR PROPOSAL

Once the meeting objectives are laid out and a budget determined, Sue creates a **request for proposal (RFP)**. In creating the RFP, Sue wants to include accurate information to help hotels and cities submit good proposals. She includes meeting specifications on the ASAA and explains that the RFP is sent three years prior to the annual conference date. Sue collects proposals and reviews them with Dave Rogers, Executive Director, and Elizabeth Rice, a board member serving as the convention chair. Sue, Dave, and Elizabeth will choose two cities to visit in order to conduct an initial site inspection. After the initial site inspections to all selected cities are complete, a decision will be made, and Sue and Dave will conduct a second site inspection to the chosen city to begin contract negotiations. In order to avoid any bias, the ASAA will pick up the cost of the site inspection with the understanding that when a city is selected; the host city will rebate the cost of the site inspection.

The RFP will include a list of cities under consideration and the preferred dates. Although the dates may vary between the months of March and April, the days of the week must be Thursday to Sunday. The annual conference is held around the country, primarily in large cities near places where members of the board of directors reside.

Sue's RFP includes a detailed grid of her meeting room needs. She includes special requests; for example, her classroom sets require two chairs per six-foot table and a water station set in the back of the room. She also includes a food and beverage summary that notes special dietary needs of attendees. Her meeting room grid includes the event, number of attendees, and room set.

The ASAA prefers to use no more than five hotels in a given city. A grid is created requesting the number of suites, single rooms, and double rooms that the ASAA anticipates using at each hotel. In considering a city, Sue looks for downtown hotel properties that offer a wide range of room prices, but the hotels need to be in close proximity to each other. The host hotel must be willing to block a minimum of 900 rooms; in addition to the sleeping room block, the host hotel will be the site of the opening night reception and breakout rooms for special-interest groups.

A detailed history, in the form of a grid of the last three years, is included in the RFP. The history grid shows the peak room nights, meeting room block, sleeping room block, pickup for the host hotel and the room block, and pickup at each of the non-host hotels. She also includes a food and beverage section showing reported use. The ASAA reports a 10% increase in meeting attendees per year over the last two years and has an attrition rate of only 2%.

The final portion of the RFP is a two-page questionnaire for the hotel to complete and submit with the proposal. Questions include green initiatives, comp room policy, deposit policy, definition of "sold out," attrition policy, master accounts, split folios, shuttle service availability, tax rate, nonprofit tax policy, gratuity distribution, Internet connection, phone charges, and fitness facilities. Sue also includes questions about how the hotel handles "in conjunction with" (ICWs) and exhibitor room blocks and whether the hotel will work to create priority housing for members over nonmembers. Sue found that this form provides a quick way for her to compare hotels.

Using the RFP link on the destination marketing organization (DMO)/**convention and visitors bureau (CVB)** Web site, Sue enters meeting information and attaches a questionnaire for the DMO to complete. The questionnaire includes questions regarding state, local, and hotel room taxes as well as holidays, union contracts, special venues, DMO services, and citywide events or holidays that take place during the ASAA meeting dates.

FIRST SITE INSPECTION

Sue, Dave, and Elizabeth have reviewed the proposals and identified two cities with available dates to host the ASAA citywide: Chicago and Dallas. Sue calls the DMOs in those cities to arrange to spend three days in each city and explains to them that the team plans to conduct a detailed site inspection to look for hotels, off-site venues, and golf courses. She sends the site inspection form that the team will use to evaluate the city and properties, explaining that the team will stay at the hotels under consideration as host properties and will conduct short tours of non-host hotels under consideration. For the non-host properties, the team only needs to meet with the hotel sales contact, see a standard room, and tour the outlets.

Day One

Mark Tester, Vice President of sales, Chicago CVB, meets Sue, Dave, and Elizabeth at Chicago's O'Hare airport. On arrival, Mark gives a driving tour of downtown, passing by all the hotels under consideration. They have lunch at the Chicago Museum of Art, where they are joined by Kesha Evans, owner of Windy City, a **destination management company (DMC)**. Kesha explains the various services she can provide, including transportation and arrangements for off-site events, spouse tours, and private dining. Tom Delaney, Catering Manager at the Chicago Museum of Art, introduces himself and takes the group on a tour of the private function areas of the museum and recommends the best area for an off-site event. He gives Sue a sales packet with sample menus and pricing.

After lunch, Mark takes the inspection team to the Hyatt Regency McCormick Place to meet with its sales manager, Bob Taylor, and its general manager, Larry Rose. They tour the property, looking at sleeping rooms, suites, singles, and doubles as well as the meeting rooms and ballrooms for possible locations for the opening reception, special-interest group meetings, and available outlets. After the tour, they meet in one of the conference rooms to discuss available dates and rates.

Then Sue, Dave, and Elizabeth meet at 6:00 PM in the hotel restaurant for dinner. During dinner, they make observations, noting how the guests are treated, what the quality of the food is, the time food is served, and whether the wait staff are attentive. They order different entrées to sample the many types of food their attendees might order if they stay at this hotel. After dinner, Sue walks the meeting space, looking into the meeting rooms to see how the rooms are set.

Day Two

At 8:30 AM, Mark meets the team members who have already eaten breakfast and checked out of the hotel. Mark has arranged for a 9:00 AM meeting with Randy Moses, Senior Sales Manager of McCormick Place Convention Center. Randy gives a tour of the facility, taking time to show them what he sees as the best locations for their functions, loading docks, and shuttle drop-off and pickup, as well as the areas where sponsored items such as banners are allowed. Sue asks about available dates, food and beverage concession hours, taxes, union rules, and contract renewal dates. Randy provides this information and discusses the security and the medical and emergency procedure guidelines. Both Mark and Randy explain to Sue, Dave, and Elizabeth how the CVB and convention center work as a team to help market the Chicago meeting to attendees. They discuss marketing options, including pre-mailers and on-site promotions the year prior to coming to the host city.

For lunch, Mark takes the group to the Golden Princess, a luxury yacht owned by ABC Charters, a company that provides dinner tours of Lake Michigan. Rich Cunningham, General Manager of ABC Charters, meets with them. Today, they are having a special lunch for meeting planners to sample the menu and enjoy a mini-charter experience. The president of Chicago DMC Services, Deborah Adams, explains her services and has photos showing other off-site locations Sue may want to consider.

The afternoon is spent making contacts and touring the hotels under consideration. Mark arranges thirty-minute tours of each non-host hotel and explains to the hotel sales contact that they only want to see sleeping rooms and restaurant areas.

By 4:00 PM, Sue, Dave, and Elizabeth are ready to check into the Hyatt Regency Chicago, the second hotel under consideration as the headquarters hotel. Rachel Monroe introduces herself as the Association Sales Manager and begins the tour. She is excited about a new ballroom that was recently added and explains how the ballroom could be used for the opening reception. After the tour, Richard Moore, the General Manager, joins the group to look at available dates and rates.

Sue, Dave, and Elizabeth take an hour break and meet in the restaurant for dinner. During dinner, they review all notes from the past two days. After dinner, Sue takes her tour of the meeting rooms.

Day Three

The team checks out early and waits in the hotel lobby. They notice a line forming as people check out of the hotel. They take mental notes, observing how long the checkout time is and how courteous the employees are at the front desk and bell stand. Mark arrives at the hotel and takes the group to the first stop, Harborside International Golf Center, a four-star course only twelve miles from downtown Chicago. The group meets with the special events manager of the Harborside to discuss the optional golf outing that is part of the ASAA event. The tournament is held Thursday afternoon, prior to the opening reception. Mark takes the group to one more golf course and on two more hotel site inspections before they depart for the airport.

Sue, Dave, and Elizabeth thank Mark for his time and inform him that they will be touring Dallas next month and plan to make a decision in two months. After the Dallas site inspection, the ASAA will make its decision and will contact the bureau regarding that decision.

One month later, Sue, Dave, and Elizabeth go to Dallas for another three-day site inspection. Patty Towell, the Sales Manager of the Dallas CVB, arranges for the group to meet with staff from the hotels, the convention center, and the off-site locations. Patty points out all the changes in Dallas including the Omni Dallas Hotel that is attached to the Dallas Convention Center.

After both site inspections conclude, the inspection team reviews their notes. Due to the conflict of dates with other industry meetings, they decide to meet on St. Patrick's Day. In evaluating Chicago, they are concerned about room availability, the renewal dates for some union contracts, and the fact that the cost to hold the meeting in Chicago is 25% more than in Dallas. This increase in cost might be offset by the number of attendees who prefer to meet in Chicago over Dallas, but this meeting will attract more attendees seeking the SAPDC—thus location will not be as much of an issue. Dallas is selected for the annual conference. Sue calls Mark from the Chicago CVB, expresses their concerns, and explains why Dallas was selected. Sue reminds Mark that they have not held a meeting in Chicago in five years and would like to look there again in the future.

SECOND SITE INSPECTION

Day One

Sue sends Patty Towell, at the Dallas CVB, a letter of intent to hold the conference in Dallas and contacts her to help arrange a second site inspection. This second site inspection will include only Sue and Dave and will be for three days. The goal is to finalize non-host properties, select off-site venues and a golf course, select the DMC and transportation company, begin contract negotiations, and select an organization for CSR project. When Sue and Dave arrive in Dallas, they rent a car and take a self-guided tour of the city. They check in at the Omni Hotel Dallas, the location of the headquarters hotel for the meeting.

At the Omni Hotel Dallas in downtown Dallas, Sue and Dave meet with Erin Donohue, Global Director of Sales and Vicki Whitt, the **convention services manager (CSM)**. Once the contract is signed, Sue will work with the CSM for the remainder of the meeting. During this meeting, Sue and Erin will begin negotiations for sleeping rooms, meeting rooms, shuttle service, and so on.

After the meeting with the hotel staff, Sue meets Sonja Miller, Sales Manager of the Dallas Convention Center; Erika Bondy, CMP, Senior Event Coordinator; and Bill Baker, Director of Catering. Once the contract is signed, Sue will work with Erika on all her meeting details and with Bill on meeting food and beverage requirements. Today, Sue begins negotiating rates with the Dallas Convention Center; at the meeting, she will review her needs and see what is the best win–win situation for her attendees and the convention center.

Sue and Dave have lunch at the Dallas Museum of Art and meet with the Catering Sales Manager, Cindy Hartman, to review rates for having the VIP dinner in the restaurant. Carolyn Petty, president of EMC (a DMC), joins Sue and Dave for lunch to discuss what the DMC can provide for the ASAA meeting, including gift baskets and general transportation needs.

In the afternoon, Patty has arranged for Sue to meet with two of the non-host hotels under consideration in the city for sleeping room space; at each hotel, Sue meets the sales manager to negotiate the rates and amenities. For dinner, Patty takes Sue and Dave to a small Mexican restaurant that is a favorite of the locals. At dinner, Patty discusses the services the bureau can assist with, including registration personnel, marketing, slides, leads for suppliers, transportation, Internet services, and on-site brochures. She will staff a promotional booth at the meeting prior to the one in Dallas.

Day Two

The morning is spent touring and reestablishing contact with the remainder of hotels that will provide sleeping rooms. Sue and Dave have lunch at the Perot Museum of Science and History because they are looking for a fun site for the VIP meeting; they meet with Nicole Benson, Event Sales Manager, for a tour and a discussion of possible dining options. Although this is an option, it might be too casual for the group. Nicole brings a portfolio with pictures of events held at the museum, and Sue's concerns dissipate.

In the afternoon, Sue and Dave tour two golf courses. For each course, Sue makes contacts, has the event sales manager take them on a nine-hole tour, and begins discussing rates. Sue pays attention to where the group might meet before and after the tournament to determine if there is an area where the group might meet as they finish playing golf.

Day Three

Sue and Dave begin the day meeting the GSC contact, Jack Boyd, Account Executive for the Freeman Companies, the GSC and Mark Lee, Director of Sales, PSAV, Dallas, an AV company. Jack, Mark, Dave, and Sue meet first at the Dallas Convention Center and then at the Omni Dallas Hotel to discuss GSC and audiovisual equipment needs. They tour each venue, discussing specific staging, setup, and other needs for each event.

The last stop of the day is to the Dallas SPCA to meet with Iris Henderson, Volunteer Coordinator. In researching a site for the meeting CSR, Sue learned about the Dallas SPCA and their program for groups to donate time sanitizing the animal shelter.

MARKETING COMMITTEE

ASAA has both an in-house marketing department and an outside advertising agency, and they work together to create the marketing campaign for the annual conference. After Sue returns home from the second site inspection, she meets with George Day, the ASAA Director of Marketing, and Julie Love, the Account Manager for Idea Maker, Inc., an advertising company. George and Julie share the results of a member survey, which reported that members are using Facebook, LinkedIn, and Twitter. They explain to Sue the importance of increasing social media in the marketing plan. Sue discusses the convention location and the meeting objectives and also explains how important promoting the new SAPDC is for this conference.

After two weeks, Sue meets with George and Julie again. Julie brings theme ideas and visuals for the marketing pieces. After reviewing several themes, "Power of Prevention" is selected.

It is decided that three marketing tools will be used. A four-color, postcard-size mailer will be developed as a teaser and mailed to all past conference attendees and targeted to potential members; this teaser will also be used as an advertisement that will be placed in industry news-letters and magazines. The second piece will be an e-mail announcement sent to all association members with a link to the convention Web page that will include a convention agenda giving dates, times, and speakers; a program-at-a-glance grid; current sponsors; and convention and housing registration forms. The final approach is the social media campaign that will include post on Facebook, LinkedIn, and Twitter. Working with popular convention speakers, the marketing committee will post information on Facebook and LinkedIn and will tweet about the conference activities. In addition, YouTube videos will be added to the conference Web site to generate excitement and encourage early registration. In creating the meeting program to be given to attend-ees upon check-in, Sue meets with George and Dave to discuss content of the program. This year, in an effort to use less paper, only half the number of programs will be printed; attendees will be encouraged to download the electric program from the ASAA Web site or from the QR code that will be created and posted throughout the conference. Dave is concerned that attendees will take the wrong class because they will not understand the level of instruction. George assures Dave that each session will be color-coded to provide easy identification of the education level and that this color-coded scheme will be repeated in the both the printed and electronic programs both printed and electronic. Additionally the electronic program will include a search that will allow attendees to quickly find the session they want to attend. Among topics discussed are the size of sponsors' ads and the amount of copy for educational event descriptions. All agree that to sup-port the objective, the SAPDC should receive a full-page description in the front of the program and should have an electronic page.

During each conference, a new board of directors is introduced, awards are given, and important announcements must be made. Sue, George, and Dave meet to discuss the types of presentations that will be made and the scripts that George and his team will write. Sue is responsible for arranging rehearsal time for each presentation.

The marketing committee is responsible for creating press releases that will be sent to professional publications. For each conference, a new piece of research is featured, and the marketing committee works to promote this research to the public.

CREATION OF THE PROGRAM

When Sue returns from the Dallas site inspection, she meets with the program committee to begin creating the educational content of the meeting. Serving on the program committee is Doug Walker, Board Member and chair of the SAPDC; Dan Dearing, Chairman of the board of directors of the Program Committee for the Power of Prevention annual convention; and his appointed committee members Liz Stewart and Mark Collins, along with Donna Smith, ASAA Administrative Assistant. These five people and Sue will work together to create the content of the meeting.

Sue begins the meeting by giving each committee member an option to receive a hard copy or electronic notebook with responsibilities of the committee members, past convention notes, and the meeting theme, the "Power of Prevention." Sue wants to make sure that the committee members understand the objective of the meeting: to increase the number of member attendees taking the SAPDC by 10% by offering a four-day conference that is focused on education that will increase meeting profits by 5%.

The committee agrees to follow the same meeting agenda as in the past: opening reception, general session, awards dinner, and poster session (which runs at the same time as the trade show). The conference will include an ASAA VIP dinner, a golf tournament, and a total of 120 ninety-minute education sessions in two days. The one change in the schedule is to add 2 four-hour segments for the SAPDC class. The committee will locate speakers for SAPDC classes and all breakout sessions. ASAA members will present 100 of the 120 educational sessions. To help the program committee, a separate committee—called the paper review committee—is created that will issue the call for papers, grade and evaluate papers, and inform the program committee of its final selection for presentations and poster session. Sue will use a speaker's bureau for the opening reception, general session, awards dinner, ASAA VIP dinner, and all entertainment.

Sue reviews the time line with the committee. The paper review committee will begin the call for papers one year prior to the meeting; six months prior, the paper review committee will provide the program committee with the final selection, and the program committee will make initial contact with presenters and speakers. The committee will recommend speakers for all sessions. Once speakers and backup speakers have been identified, Sue will send out invitation letters, in which she will ask the speaker to sign a commitment sheet and will require the speaker to provide an abstract of the presentation and his or her biography.

The committee will be responsible for contacting all the speakers and following up with those not responding. There will also be a point person for all speaker questions. Once speakers have been selected, Sue's role is to collect information, assign time slots, and correspond with the speakers, including letters of acceptance and a reminder letter.

One key feature in the conference is the exhibitors. Jill Kochan, ASAA staff, is the ASAA trade show manager for the conference. Jill is responsible for all communications with the exhibitors and the GSC as they set up the trade show. Jill will work closely with Sue to communicate exhibitor needs and will meet with the GSC to create specifications for the exhibitor prospectus.

The newly formed CSR Committee will work with the Dallas SPCA on a program that will give attendees an opportunity to volunteer at the new shelter during the conference. In addition the committee will create a program for attendees to bring items that will be donated to the SPCA at the end of the conference. In return the SPCA will put on a "puppy pet" in the lobby on the first day of the conference.

PARTNERSHIPS

As Sue prepares for this meeting, she knows the importance of her meeting partners. Throughout the conference, Sue depends on many companies to provide excellent service and to create a memorable experience for the ASAA members. She reviews her contact list, looking at the many companies she will partner with for the upcoming conference.

Although most housing bureaus can provide a complete housing package, including hotel selection, negotiation, and contract, Sue prefers to work with the housing bureau after she has selected the hotels. Once the selections have been made, the housing bureau will manage the hotel room block. The housing bureau will create a Web link for attendees to book rooms online and a paper form for attendees to complete and fax. Once an attendee selects a hotel, the housing bureau will send a confirmation letter. One of the best aspects about Sue's partnership with the housing bureau is room block management: Rather than call all the hotels being used, Sue calls the housing bureau for monthly, weekly, and daily rooming reports as needed and depends on the housing bureau to manage the exhibitor room block.

Sue likes to partner with a local DMC for the annual conference. For this conference, Sue uses the DMC for arranging the airport transfers, VIP transportation, and shuttle service from hotels to the convention center. The DMC made all logistical arrangements for the VIP dinner, which allowed Sue to concentrate on VIP invitations and content of the event. Sue also appreciates the fact that a DMC normally has access to many motor coach suppliers because transportation is always an area of concern for Sue. Once, in Washington, DC, Sue contracted with a motor coach company, and one of the motor coaches broke down with all her attendees in it. The company had no backup motor coaches, so her attendees waited almost an hour to be rescued and taken to the event.

For key speakers and entertainment, Sue uses a speaker's bureau because she does not have the time to research the many speakers and entertainers who could speak to ASAA members. The speaker's bureau will make recommendations on the best speakers and entertainers; and once Sue makes her selection, the speaker's bureau will handle all arrangements. It will ensure that the speakers are at the meeting on time; and if something happens, the speaker's bureau can quickly arrange for a backup speaker.

Sue selects an online registration company to help with the many attendees who prefer this registration method. The designated registration company will accept registrations electronically, automatically send attendees a confirmation letter, and store the registrations for easy retrieval to create name badges at the meeting site.

Sponsors are important partners for the ASAA conference. Sue will work with all the sponsors to ensure that they receive exposure to members in exchange for their financial and/or in-kind support. Sue realizes that without annual conference sponsors, the ASAA would not reach its financial objectives for the convention.

The ASAA has always included meeting security for attendees' safety and exhibitor products, but for this conference Sue will increase security. An animal rights association contacted the ASAA and plans to protest a new test being conducted on laboratory rats. Sue realized that she must allow this group to protest, but she wants to ensure that they protest peacefully and do not disturb meeting attendees.

Key partners in making the conference a success are the GSC providing the decorations and the AV company supplying the electronic equipment. Sue considers the GSC as the partner that brings the theme to life, so the decorations must wow attendees visually. Sue recognizes the important role the GSC plays in keeping the exhibitors happy in addition to pleasing the conference attendees. This is important to the ASAA, as the exhibitors generate 44% of the revenue for the conference.

Sue loves to work with the AV company because this partner is crucial for every meeting event. Without proper projection and sound, the attendees would not be able to learn. Sue works closely with its staff during the meeting. One burned-out light bulb or malfunctioning microphone can ruin a breakout session.

In order to keep things running efficiently at the conference, Sue hires temporary staff and builds a partnership early with these people. They will be part of the team and will represent the ASAA during the conference.

Contracts

Sue has a contract for each convention partner and every service provider. Each contract specifies the exact services that are expected and the penalties if the expectations are not met. Early in Sue's career, she worked with an association that signed a contract that did not include a realistic attrition clause. The association did not meet its room block and paid the hotel over $10,000 for unused rooms. At least one year out, Sue reviews each contract carefully. Before the meeting begins, Sue will have contracts finalized with the host hotel, housing bureau, airlines, off-site venue, golf course, speaker's bureau, security, AV company, DMC, GSC, and many others.

ONE-YEAR TO SIX-MONTH COUNTDOWN

Sue looks at her **meeting time line** and realizes that she is eighteen months away from the Power of Prevention annual conference. She takes out her meeting resume and reviews all contracts. She meets with George and Julie from the marketing committee to review electronic and paper marketing pieces and the first draft of the program. If Sue and her team miss an educational session or a grammatical error, then that is the way it will be printed. If the mistake is important enough, the marketing piece will be reprinted and the expenses added to the cost of the conference. Fortunately, with the electronic pieces changes can quickly be made with minimal expense.

She arranges a meeting with Doug and Dan from the program committee to select the speakers for the convention. On selection, Sue sends out the acceptance letter to the speakers; in her letter, Sue requests that the speaker confirm his or her commitment by sending an electronic speaker biography, presentation abstract, and audiovisual needs form. Sue makes a point to contact the speaker's bureau to check the status of the motivational speaker and entertainment. She requests that all electronic equipment needs are identified one year prior to the meeting. By doing this, Sue is able to have a more accurate budget item for the equipment and can spot any potential fire hazards associated with its usage.

Sue secures ten sponsors for the meeting, including Small Vets Pluss, a company that supplies the vaccines for small animals, for the tote bags; Houver Pharmaceutical, a small-animal antibiotic producer, for transportation; LabSmlab, a provider of medical instruments used in animal surgery, for the opening night reception; Mix-a-vet, developer of special food for small animals, to sponsor the newspaper; and Smalco, a pet store featuring small-animal products. Small Vets Pluss will cosponsor the VIP entertainment and the awards dinner. Sue will contact each sponsor to confirm the commitment and sign the contract. In her conversation, Sue reminds sponsors that she needs to have them return a form with the exact spelling of their company name and the design of their signage or logo.

The trade show floor plan for the Dallas conference was created and approved fourteen months prior to the Dallas meeting. Exhibit space for the Power of Prevention conference was sold on-site at the ASAA conference prior to Dallas—the ASAA has an 87% exhibitor retention. Nine months out, the GSC updates the floor plan and mails exhibitor packets to potential exhibitors.

In addition to the trade show, Sue works with the GSC in finalizing the setup for the opening reception, general session, and awards dinner. She determines where the media center and the registration area will be located. Sue depends on the GSC to recommend the best location to place sponsor banners and signage. Most convention centers have strict rules regarding banner and signage placement, and GSCs that work with convention centers frequently know the rules and have great ideas on how sponsors can be recognized.

SIX MONTHS TO DAY OF THE MEETING

Fast forward to the six-month countdown for the Power of Prevention conference. The marketing committee writes and sends press releases. If timed correctly, the press releases will be published within a month of when the convention ads are scheduled to run and will be picked up by social media.

Early registration forms begin to arrive within weeks after being sent. In reviewing the registration forms, Sue notices that three of the attendees indicated that they have mobility disabilities and will need special accommodations. In compliance with the Americans with Disabilities Act (ADA), Sue will work with all meeting partners to ensure that these attendees are able to fully participate in the conference. She needs to arrange for handicapped rooms and notes that the meeting rooms will need to be set with aisles to accommodate these attendees.

Sue receives the menus from the hotel catering manager and selects the meals. She makes a special note informing catering that she will require five special meals for attendees with dietary needs.

She contacts the host hotel and convention center to get the names of the meeting rooms that will be used for the Power of Prevention conference. It is important for Sue to get the name of the location of the meeting rooms so that this information can be added to the convention program. Hotels and convention centers rarely want to give this information out early, as they do not want to commit to a particular meeting room that might be sold to another planner, so good communication and flexibility are important.

Sue works with the DMC to review the menu and with the GSC for the VIP dinner at the Perot Museum of Science and History. The dinner will be in a room that overlooks downtown Dallas and the evening will include a private tour of the museum and the opportunity to create a new virtual species of bird and test its ability to fly. Sue contacts Larry Grant, the Event Organizer at Tennyson Golf Course, to finalize tournament rules. It looks like this will be a great year for this event—ten people are already registered for this event. Sue gives Larry the names and handicaps.

During this time, Sue will also contact the DMC to finalize shuttle routes to all events, enabling her to begin ordering signage for transportation. Sue learns each year how even highly educated people get lost at meetings—it baffles her that veterinarians cannot read the location material in their program. Sue must clearly list all the events, their locations, and the shuttle service times. Signage is very important in the total conference experience.

Month Five

Five months prior to the meeting, Sue sends out reminders to all speakers, and she works with the marketing committee to finalize and send the marketing brochure and the e-mail announcement. After some quiet time to proofread the meeting program, she creates a detailed work schedule for staff, temporary employees, and volunteers. Sue orders meeting name badges and meeting supplies and then calls the security company to review her needs.

Months Four and Three

During the fourth and third months prior to the meeting, Sue monitors registration on a weekly basis. At the third month, Sue reviews registration and makes adjustments to her room block (she negotiated this option in her hotel contract as a way to control attrition).

Sue looks at her initial room block (see Table 15-3) and compares it with current hotel registrations. Convention history shows that 60% of the people register early, indicating that in a perfect world, the host property would have 600 rooms reserved and the remaining properties would have 300 each. In looking at the actual hotel registrations, Sue notices that all rooms have been filled at the Hyatt Regency Downtown Dallas, but she is unable to get additional rooms so will need to close reservations for the Hyatt Regency. The Hilton Anatole and W Hotel are right on schedule and will require no changes. The Holiday Inn is 200 rooms less than what it should be; Sue reduces the block by 40% and is now obligated for 300 rooms rather than 500. She has the opposite problem with the Omni Dallas Hotel, the host hotel—the host property is 100 rooms over what she expects, so she conservatively increases the block by 5% and is obligated for 1,050 rooms.

Hotel	Omni Hotel Dallas	Hyatt Regency Downtown Dallas	Hilton Anatole	W Hotel	Holiday Inn
Initial Room Block	1,000	500	500	500	500
90-Day Room Block Review	700	500	300	300	100
Room Block Adjustment	Over—will add + 50 rooms	No change	On schedule	On schedule	Under—will remove 200 rooms
New Room Block	1,050	500	500	500	300

Table 15-3 ASAA Hotel Room Blocks

In addition to the room block adjustments, she has received calls from the convention center to move the location of meeting rooms and calls from speakers needing to cancel. These changes affect the information in the program, so it must be revised. She sees this as a time of many changes, but these changes are all part of Sue's job. The work she did a year ago is paying off. A speaker cancels, so she contacts the program committee to see who they have planned as a backup.

Month Two

At two months out, Sue arranges another trip to Dallas. Patty, CSM of the Dallas CVB, arranges for Sue to meet with all the key contacts to make the Power of Prevention conference a success. Vicki, the Director of CSM at the Omni Hotel Dallas, meets with Sue to conduct a property walk-through, and he will introduce Sue to the catering manager to review the menu, the accounts receivable contract to explain the bill review process, the front desk manager to confirm pre-key guests and the check-in and checkout process, and the director of security and medical staff to review emergency procedures. The CSM explains that he is the hotel contact and will assist Sue in providing information needed from the hotel, from room pickup to bill review. Vicki and Sue will work closely together.

At the Dallas Convention Center, Sue will meet with Erika Bondy, Senior Event Coordinator, to conduct a walk-through and invites the GSC and the AV contacts to join her. By doing this, Sue has many eyes looking for potential problems that might occur. She will also spend time with the catering manager to review the menu for lunch and awards dinner.

Sue meets with the DMC representative to walk through hotel transportation routes and finalize menus, decorations, and entertainment for the VIP dinner at the Perot Museum of Science and History. Sue then meets with the event coordinator at the Tennison Golf Course to update the player list and review pairings.

When Sue returns from Dallas, she works with marketing to make final changes to the program and sends the paper program to the printer. She also ships materials to the convention site; works with the marketing committee on the final scripts; and reviews her staging guide that has all her contacts, the time line, contracts, menus, and notes for her to review.

Month One

One month prior to the meeting, Sue continues weekly monitoring of the registrations and sends reminder e-mail to all the speakers. She works with the advertising firm to approve press releases to announce research findings that will be presented at the Power of Prevention conference; she also works with the staff to finalize work schedules, marketing, scripts, and rehearsal times. Sue will create a checklist and pack her convention material. She is a good planner and has thought about backup plans for her activities; for example, if the golf tournament is rained out, the group will spend the morning on a sports tour of Dallas.

Sue likens the month before the meeting to a tennis match. Emergencies—which feel like five to ten tennis balls coming across the net at her at the same time—can hit her, so Sue knows she must be ready with her racket in hand to successfully hit those balls back over the net and be ready for the next barrage of balls.

Pre-meeting Activities

Three days prior to the meeting, Sue and her staff arrive in Dallas to set up the meeting headquarters. She is happy to see that all her convention material arrived safely. Sue meets all contacts to finalize meeting plans and arranges a walk-through of the host hotel and the convention center with her staff, temporary employees, and volunteers. The host hotel arranges a pre-con meeting where everyone working on the meeting will get together and review the meeting resume for any changes or concerns.

Sue monitors the setup of all meeting events and conducts on-site troubleshooting. Something always needs to be changed; it might be a sponsor sign with an error that needs to be redone by calling the GSC or a more complicated situation like the space for the registration being too small. This is a time of constant problem solving.

Sue joins George and the marketing staff as they rehearse for the general session, set up the pressroom, and conduct a press conference. George takes time to review the press list with Sue because she needs to know the names of press attendees to ensure that when they arrive, someone from the ASAA staff can quickly assist them. Good publicity can ensure the success of future conferences.

Meeting Day Activities

The meeting begins, and Sue is busy working with the staff to ensure all meeting rooms are set up properly and that all speaker materials and evaluations are ready. Her role is to work behind the scenes to make the attendees' experience perfect. She is the first one to arrive on-site and will be the last person to leave. The day is filled with questions that she must clarify or problems that need to be solved. This is the time that excites Sue—the time when she sees all her hard work become a reality. She uses the contacts she made to quickly solve problems. For example, the equipment in one of the rooms is not working, so she calls the AV company and the problem is quickly solved. At the beginning of each day, Sue meets with the hotel CSM and the accounts receivable department to conduct a bill review. She also checks with the housing bureau to follow up on a comparison of the ASAA registration with the in-house guest list to ensure that ASAA attendees are properly coded to the ASAA block, which helps with future event accommodations.

A special ASAA exhibitor headquarters office opens at the convention center. Jill, the ASAA's trade show manager, will remain in this office to handle any problems that might occur during the trade show and to accept exhibitor bookings for next year's ASAA conference.

AFTER THE MEETING

Immediate Post-meeting Activities

A tired Sue sips coffee and takes a moment to review the successes and the areas of opportunity of the Power of Prevention conference. Before leaving Dallas, Sue will facilitate a post-con meeting to evaluate this year's conference, where people who attended the pre-con meeting will be present to discuss the conference and answer questions: What were the problems? What could be done to improve this situation for future conventions? She will work with the hotel and vendors to reconcile registration numbers, review all pickups, and estimate ancillary business.

Planning a convention is a team event. Sue takes time to thank all speakers, sponsors, committee members, and facilitators for helping with the conference—she also rewards her staff by giving them a free day in Dallas to relax.

Since Sue works with small animals, she often jokes that her job is like "pulling a rabbit out of a hat." *Ruslan Olinchuk/Fotolia*

Two-Month Post-meeting Activities

After the statistics and evaluations have been reviewed, Sue begins her report to the executive director and to the board of directors regarding conference ROI. It is important after each conference that an evaluation is conducted. In creating this conference, Sue and her team set the convention objectives: to increase the number of attendees taking the SAPDC by 10% by offering a four-day conference that is focused on education and networking that will increase conference profits by 5%. What is the point of having a convention if the success is not measured? Part of the meeting planner's job is to demonstrate how a convention or meeting helps achieve organizational goals. By establishing objectives and reviewing ROI, a planner can show his or her role in supporting company objectives and the bottom line.

Sue is excited about the Power of Prevention convention. The industry press gave excellent pre-meeting coverage, with over $50,000 tracked as nonpaid advertising. Sue believes this third-party endorsement definitely increased attendance. The meeting objectives were met: 500 people took the classes for SAPDC (a 10% increase from the 454 who took SAPDC classes last year), and meeting profits grew from $1,393,297.60 to $1,462,962.50 (a 5% increase).

Sue finishes her report and takes a call from the Orlando Convention Center, the location for next year's annual conference. She is twelve months away from the conference and is receiving the names of the meeting rooms that will be used . . . and the meeting cycle continues.

Summary

In this chapter, you have learned about the process of creating a citywide meeting. This is a large task for one person and requires many partners to make the conference successful. Through this case study, you have been able to see a day in the life of a meeting planner on a site inspection and have looked at the many tasks leading up to the conference. The chapter began with creating conference objectives and budgets, and it ended with evaluating ROI to determine the success of the meeting.

Key Words and Terms

For definitions, see the Glossary, or http://glossary.conventionindustry.org

audiovisual (AV) company
convention services manager (CSM)
convention and visitor bureau (CVB)
corporate social responsibility (CSR)

destination management company (DMC)
general services contractor (GSC)
meeting time line
request for proposal (RFP)

return on investment (ROI)
sponsor

Review and Discussion Questions

1. Who is the group in this chapter? Why are they here?
2. Where else has the group met?
3. What are the steps Sue goes through to plan this meeting?
4. Whom does Sue work with on her staff?

5. Whom does Sue work with in the city where the meeting is being held? Which suppliers or vendors?
6. What does Sue do after the meeting is over?

About the Chapter Contributor

M. T. Hickman, CTP, CMP, is the head of the Travel, Exposition, and Meeting Management program at Richland College in Dallas, Texas. She began her career at the Irving, Texas, CVB, where she worked in many departments, including tourism sales, convention sales, and special events. Over the years, she has worked as director of marketing for the National Business Association and as a proposal writer for WorldTravel Partners. She is active in the meeting and exposition planning associations, including MPI, PCMA, and IAEM.

Previous Edition Chapter Contributors

David Gisler, Director of Sales and Training, Total Show University, Freeman Companies
Bitsy Burns, CMP, Director of Operations, Southwest Veterinary Symposium
Erin Donahue, Director Global Sales, Omni Hotel Dallas
Patty Towell, Sales Manager, Dallas Convention and Visitor Bureau

APPENDIX

This appendix includes a detailed example of a Site Selection Sample Request for Proposal (RFP). It is used with permission of the originator, Joan L. Eisenstodt.

FORMS FOR USE IN REQUESTING A PROPOSAL AND ON-SITE SELECTION

The sections that follow provide a number of forms, or frameworks, that are used by meeting professionals. Studying and reviewing these documents will help provide the reader with a better understanding of the myriad of details that a meeting professional must deal with.

Site Selection—Sample Request for Proposal (RFP)(v. 18b)

Group or Meeting Sponsor: Full name of organization (acronym in parentheses)

Contact Information: Name(s) including alternate contacts, title(s), address(es), communication numbers (phones, fax, e-mail, tdd/tty), and contact times and time zones

Organization: Provide brief organizational description—structure, mission, and purpose.

The Meeting: Provide brief description—purpose, goals and objectives, general format, and audience profile.

History: Provide up to 2 years of meeting history—dates, attendance, hotel(s) used, rooms blocked and picked up, and range of rates.

Schedule for Future Meetings; Future Years for Meeting

Considerations for This Meeting:

    Destination(s) and site(s)

    Dates (acceptable and unacceptable)

    Rates

    Special requirements/information (transportation, attractions/restaurants, quirks)

References: Request for meetings of similar size, focus/scope, held in last 6 to 12 months

Proposals Due/Decision Process: Provide date by which proposal must be received and what collateral materials should be included. Describe decision process and date by which decision is expected.

Meeting Specifications:

Sleeping Room Block: Describe day-by-day, including early arrivals/late departures; bed and room types; suites.

Meeting Space: Provide day-by-day description of the program, including meeting/conference office space, speaker ready room, lounges, and times needed.

Exhibit/Display Space: For literature tables, other displays or exhibits and the times the space is needed. Include move-in and move-out times.

Site Selection
Request for Proposal
Organization Name
Attachment A

If you plan to submit a proposal, please keyboard all information and upload these forms to (*e-mail address*).

Property name _____ *City/State* _____

Property contact name/title/e-mail and phone _____

Year property built _____   Last building inspection and results _____

Number of floors _____   Total number of rooms _____ suites _____

Single/one-bedded rooms _____   Double/two-bedded rooms _____

Number of nonsmoking rooms _____   Number of disability-accessible rooms _____

Year of last guest room renovation _____   Year of last public space renovation _____

Scope of Planned Renovation and Schedule:

Type of property

☐ *meeting/convention*   ☐ *resort*   ☐ *full service*   ☐ *limited service*
Market tier: ☐ *luxury*   ☐ *upscale*   ☐ *moderate*
Property location: ☐ *suburban*   ☐ *downtown/city center*

Property Ownership & Management

Chain owned? (Y/N) _____ If no, name of owners. _____

Management Company _____

Franchise? (Y/N) _____

Owner's company is at least 51% owned, controlled, and operated by an American citizen minority? (Y/N) _____

Owner's company is at least 51% owned, controlled, and operated by an American citizen nonminority woman? (Y/N) _____

Site Selection
Request for Proposal
Organization Name
Attachment A

If you plan to submit a proposal, please keyboard all information and upload these forms to (*e-mail address*).

Property name _____ *City/State* _____

Property contact name/title/e-mail and phone _____

Rating
AAA Diamonds   *1   2   3   4   5*   not rated
Mobil Stars   *1   2   3   4   5*   not rated

Other rating(s) (specify) _____

Outlets
Name _____ Location _____ Hours _____
Full or Ltd. Service _____ Nonsmoking?_____

Transportation and Parking

Airport One
Name   _____ 3-Letter code _____
Distance from property _____ miles
            Minutes/rush hour _____ Minutes/nonrush hour_____
Complimentary shuttle (Y/N) _____
Estimated taxi charge (each way) _____
Alternate mode of transportation _____ Cost each way _____
Driving directions (attach)

Airport Two
Name   _____ 3-Letter code _____
Distance from property _____ miles
            Minutes/rush hour _____ Minutes/nonrush hour _____
Complimentary shuttle (Y/N) _____
Estimated taxi charge (each way) _____
Alternate mode of transportation _____ Cost each way _____
Driving Directions (attach)

Number of parking spaces at property _____ Charge for self-park _____
Charge for valet park _____
Identify facility's parking capacity for large trucks, semitrailers, etc.: _____

Taxes, service, and/or gratuity charges
The current rooms tax is ____% plus $____ occupancy tax.
There is ___ is not ___ a ballot initiative in the next election to raise those taxes.
There is a ____ gratuity or a ____ service charge of ____% on group food and beverage.
This is taxed at ____%.

```
┌─────────────────────────────────────────────────────────┐
│                    Site Selection                        │
│                 Request for Proposal                     │
│                   Organization Name                      │
│                    Attachment A                          │
└─────────────────────────────────────────────────────────┘
```

If you plan to submit a proposal, please keyboard all information and upload these forms to (*e-mail address*).

Property name _____ *City/State* _____

Property contact name/title/e-mail and phone _____

Facilities/Services on Property (check all that apply)

☐ Cocktail lounge
☐ 24-hour room service OR
☐ Room service Start time _____ End time _____
☐ Safety deposit boxes/lobby area
☐ Express check in and out   ☐ Video review/check out
☐ Full business center   Hours _____ A.M. to _____ P.M.   Days of the week _____
☐ Gift/newsstand   Hours _____ A.M. to _____ P.M.   Days of the week: _____
☐ Full-service health club Hours _____ A.M. to _____ P.M.   Days of the week: _____
☐ Laundry/valet service (circle applicable responses)

Circle one: On property or *Sent out*

   Circle service: 5 days/week   *6 days/week*   *7 days/week*   *overnight service*
☐ Shoe shine service
☐ Indoor pool   ☐ Outdoor pool
☐ Airline desk(s)   (specify) _____, _____
☐ ATM (Current use fee is $ ____.____ .)
☐ Car rental desk(s)   (specify) _____, _____
☐ Evening turndown service   ☐ All guests   ☐ VIPs only
☐ Golf course
☐ Tennis court(s)
☐ Racquetball courts
☐ Other (specify) _____

Guest Rooms

☐ In-room safe   ☐ No charge   ☐ Charge to use ($_____/day)
☐ Working desks with outlets above floor
☐ Voice mail   ☐ Personalized voice mail
☐ 2 line phones/all rooms   ☐ 2-line phones/concierge/specialized rooms only
☐ Data ports on all phones   ☐ Digital or analog phone lines
☐ Phone in bathroom   ☐ Bathroom phone/concierge or specialty rooms only
☐ Access charge for local phone calls _____ ☐ Access charge for toll-free calls _____
☐ AM/FM radio   ☐ With cassette player   ☐ With CD player
☐ Color TV
☐ Remote control TV   ☐ Cable TV   ☐ Satellite TV
☐ All news cable channel   ☐ Weather channel
☐ Other special channels (specify) _____
☐ In-room movies on demand
☐ Closed-circuit television (CCTV)

Site Selection
Request for Proposal
Organization Name
Attachment A

If you plan to submit a proposal, please keyboard all information and upload these forms to (*e-mail address*).

Property name _____ *City/State* _____

Property contact name/title/e-mail and phone _____

Guest Rooms (cont.)

☐ In-room video players
☐ Iron/ironing board
☐ Mini-bar   ☐ Refrigerator on request
☐ Coffee/Tea maker   ☐ Daily complimentary coffee/tea
☐ Working desk/desk lamp
☐ Free **daily** paper delivered to room   ☐ Paper/**weekdays only**

Reservations and Check-in/out

☐ Reservations may be made through a toll-free number.
  ☐ That number is _____   ☐ Number is accessible throughout United States.
  ☐ A number that can be used for those residing in the state in which the reservations department is located:
  ☐ A reservation number for those outside the United States is ( ) _____.
  ☐ The TTY/TDD number is ( ) _____.
  ☐ The fax number for reservations is ( ) _____.
  ☐ Reservations may be made on line at http://www._____,
  ☐ or by email to _____.
☐ All rooms in a group's block are released to the toll-free number.
☐ The property has an in-house reservations department.
☐ The reservations department is located off-site.

☐ Check-in time is _____. Check-out time is _____.

☐ The facility will audit the room reservations using a group's registration list.

+--+
| <u>Site Selection</u> |
| <u>Request for Proposal</u> |
| *Organization Name* |
| *Attachment A* |
+--+

If you plan to submit a proposal, please keyboard all information and upload these forms to (*e-mail address*).

Property name _____ *City/State* _____

Property contact name/title/e-mail and phone _____

<u>Safety and Security (check all that apply)</u>
☐ Smoke detectors in all guest rooms   Hardwired?   Y/N _____
☐ Smoke detectors in hallways   Hardwired?   Y/N _____
☐ Smoke detectors in public areas   Hardwired?   Y/N _____
☐ Audible smoke detectors   ☐ Visual alarms for people with hearing impairments
☐ Sprinklers in all guest rooms   ☐ Sprinklers in hallways
☐ Sprinklers in public areas
☐ Fire extinguishers in hallways
☐ Automatic fire doors
☐ Auto link to fire station
☐ Auto recall elevators
☐ Ventilated stairwells
☐ Emergency maps in guest rooms/hallways
☐ Emergency information in all guest rooms
☐ Emergency lighting
☐ Safety chain on door   ☐ Doors with viewports ("peep holes")
☐ Deadbolts on all guest room doors
☐ Restricted access to guest floors
☐ Property has AEDs (automatic external defibrillators)
    ☐ Staff has been trained to use defibrillators   *Per shift* ____
☐ Staff trained in CPR   *Per shift* _____
☐ Staff trained in first aid   *Per shift* ____
☐ Secondary locks on guest room glass doors
☐ Room balconies accessible by adjoining rooms/balconies
☐ Primary guest room entrance accessible by interior corridor/atrium
☐ Guest room accessible by exterior entrance only
☐ Guest room windows open
☐ Uniformed security
☐ 24-hour security throughout facility   Number of staff ___
☐ Public address system
☐ Video surveillance in public areas/elevators
☐ Video surveillance at entrances
☐ Video surveillance in hallways
☐ Staff trained in issuance of duplicate keys/cards
☐ Emergency power source: _____
    ☐ SOPs for power outages _____

Food Safety:
Detail the frequency of inspection by county or city health inspectors and the results of the last three (3) inspections.

Site Selection
Request for Proposal
Organization Name
Attachment A

If you plan to submit a proposal, please keyboard all information and upload these forms to (*e-mail address*).

Property name _____ *City/State* _____

Property contact name/title/e-mail and phone _____

Emergency call response time (for fire, police, EMTs) in minutes to your property _____
Does property have an emergency evacuation plan? (Y/N) _____
How often does property conduct emergency evacuation drills? _____
Nearest police station (blocks/miles) _____ Nearest hospital (blocks/miles) _____
Does facility comply with all country/state/local fire laws? (Y/N) _____

Please describe

—The actions your facility took beginning 9/11/01 for the safety and comfort of your guests:

—Any change of policies governing safety/security instituted or reinstituted since 9/11/01.

—The communication tree among your property and local/state/federal emergency management officials.

—Any policies in effect that govern "containment" of guests in the property for issues of bioterrorism? Inability to travel because of airport closures?

"Oversold/Underdeparted" ("Walk") Policies or Guidelines
☐ Property will arrange accommodations at comparable or superior property within 10 minutes of this property.
☐ Property will pay directly for one room night and tax at comparable property.
☐ Traveler will be provided with transportation.
☐ Traveler will be reimbursed for (number) _____ of phone calls to home and/or office.
☐ Other (specify) _____

```
┌─────────────────────────────────────────────────────────────────┐
│                        Site Selection                             │
│                     Request for Proposal                          │
│                      Organization Name                            │
│                        Attachment A                               │
└─────────────────────────────────────────────────────────────────┘
```

If you plan to submit a proposal, please keyboard all information and upload these forms to (*e-mail address*).

Property name _____ *City/State* _____

Property contact name/title/e-mail and phone _____

Staff and Staffing

☐ Average length of employment at this property:
  Management staff _____ years   line staff _____ years
☐ Staff organized for the purpose of collective bargaining (List unions and staff positions, contract renewal dates on separate sheet.)

Policies and Miscellaneous Charges

☐ Credit cards are charged when reservation is made.
  ☐ If charged, is it for _____ first night _____ last night _____ all nights
☐ Guest may cancel guaranteed reservations without penalty/charge
  _____ to 4 P.M./day of arrival   _____ to 6 P.M./day of arrival   _____ 24 hours
  _____ 48 hours   _____ 72 hours   _____ other
☐ Guest substitutions are allowed, at any time, without penalty or charge to group and/or individual.
☐ Guest substitutions are not allowed without a charge to group and/or individual.
☐ Extended stays (based on availability) are allowed at no charge.
☐ Early checkouts incur a charge of $_____ if the front desk is not notified at check-in.
☐ The property charges $____/page for receipt of faxes.
☐ The property charges $___/page to send faxes.
☐ There is a charge of $_____ for receipt of packages.
☐ There is a charge of $_____ for property to send packages.
☐ There is a charge of $_____ to deliver packages to individual or group.

<u>Site Selection</u>
<u>Request for Proposal</u>
Organization Name
Attachment A

If you plan to submit a proposal, please keyboard all information and upload these forms to (*e-mail address*).

Property name _____ *City/State* _____

Property contact name/title/e-mail and phone _____

Policies and Miscellaneous Charges (cont.)

☐ Is a resort or hotel or other fee added to the room rate? Y/N _____
    ☐ If so, the current amount per room (or per guest) per night is $_____ which is/is not taxed.
        ☐ This covers:
            ☐ Contractual issues that must be included in our contract are attached to this document.

Energy Issues

☐ The property does charge an energy surcharge of $_____ per room per night. This charge is or is not taxed. (Is ____ Is not ____) If taxed, it is at _____%.
☐ The power supply for the property is from _____.
☐ Describe the property's backup power source(s):
☐ Describe the property's emergency procedures for brownouts and blackouts:
☐ Describe the property's backup systems for water and phones:
☐ Define any charges for use of electrical outlets for meetings and/or in public space and/or in guestrooms:

Environmental Issues

☐ Our property recycles the following materials:
       _____ paper   _____ plastic   _____ metal/tin/aluminum
☐ The method by which guests may recycle is:
☐ We ask guests to advise us by use of a card if they want their towels and/or bed linens changed every day.
☐ Other areas we protect the environment are:

Site Selection
Request for Proposal
Organization Name
Attachment A

If you plan to submit a proposal, please keyboard all information and upload these forms to (*e-mail address*).

Property name _____ City/State _____

Property contact name/title/e-mail and phone _____

Other Groups
During the group's preferred dates, the other events confirmed in the city, including conventions, festivals, other public and private events that are known to the bureau or the facility, are:

During the group's preferred dates, the other events confirmed in the facility are:

City/County Labor Issues
Note any groups organized for the purpose of collective bargaining in the city or county whose contract deadlines are 2 months on both side of preferred dates, and their history of labor actions:

Audio Visual Equipment
☐ The in-house or recommended company is _____.
☐ The facility has the ability to negotiate prices on behalf of the AV company. (Y/N) ____
☐ A discount of ____% off list prices can be offered for AV equipment for the meeting.
☐ The service charge is ____%. It is taxed at ____%. It is not taxed. ____
☐ If an outside AV company is brought in by our organization, there is ____ is not ____ a fee.
　☐ If there is a fee, it is _____.

Electricity Supply/Vendor
☐ Electricity (for exhibits and meeting space) is provided to the facility by ____ in-house or ____ external vendor. (If external, specify _____.)
☐ The facility has the ability to negotiate prices for meeting and exhibit electrical service.
　(Y/N) ____
☐ Electricity is available to the outdoor portions of the facility (for outside exhibits).
　(Y/N) _____
☐ A discount of ____% off list prices can be offered for meeting room and exhibit electricity for the meeting.

<u>Site Selection</u>
<u>Request for Proposal</u>
Organization Name
Attachment A

If you plan to submit a proposal, please keyboard all information and upload these forms to (*e-mail address*).

Property name _____ City/State _____

Property contact name/title/e-mail and phone _____

Operations and Technology
☐ Our sales/convention services staff use _____ word processing software, version _____.

☐ Sales and convention services personnel use e-mail. _____ yes _____ no
    E-mail addresses are:
        ☐ Sales _____
        ☐ Convention/Catering services _____
        ☐ Reservations _____
☐ Sales and convention services have Web access. ___ yes ___ no
☐ Reservations is fully automated and can respond by e-mail. ___ yes ___ no
☐ Our Web site address is _____.
☐ Group/Meeting reservations can be made on line.
        ☐ If reservations may be made on line, please specify information that must be included in any published URLs and any restrictions and/or policies.

NATIONAL SALES RESPONSE FORM
(Year/Meeting) Site Selection
Request for Proposal: (Name of Organization)

Please complete and return this form <u>after</u> reading the RFP. To allow us to track proposals, please advise to which properties in which cities you will send the RFP. **Please upload this to** (*e-mail address*), **or fax this form to** (*name, fax number*) **to be received by** (*day, date, time/time zone*).

Please print or type in black:

Company _____

Contact name/title _____

Direct phone no. _____

Direct fax no. _____

E-mail address _____

The RFP is being sent to the following properties:

_____/City _____

_____/City _____

_____/City _____

_____/City _____

_____/City _____

_____/City _____

Comments:

CVB RESPONSE FORM
(Year/Meeting) Site Selection
Request for Proposal: (Organization/Meeting Name)

Please complete and return this form <u>after</u> reading the RFP. To allow us to track proposals, please advise to which properties you will send the RFP, keeping in mind that it should only be sent to properties not represented by the companies noted in the cover note and only to those that meet the criteria. If responses are received by properties that do not meet the criteria, or by vendors for whom we do not need services, we will reject the proposals.

Please upload this to (*e-mail address*), **or fax this form to** (*name, fax number*) **by** (*day/date/time/time zone*).

Please print or type in black:

CVB _____

Contact name/Title _____

Direct phone no. _____

Direct fax no. _____

E-mail address _____

The RFP is being sent to the following properties:

                                      _____

                                      _____

                                      _____

                                      _____

                                      _____

                                      _____

Comments:

Property RESPONSE FORM
(Year/Meeting) Site Selection
Request for Proposal: (Organization/Meeting)

Please complete and return this form <u>after</u> reading the RFP but before sending a proposal. There is no need to send a follow-up letter or e-mail, or to call once this form has been sent. **Please upload this to (*e-mail address*), or fax to (*organization/fax number*) to be received by (*day/date/time/time zone*).**

Full proposals and collateral are due by (day/date/time/time zone).

Please complete and return this information <u>whether or not</u> a proposal is being submitted. If completing by hand, please use black ink.

Property name/City _____

Contact name/Title _____

Direct phone no. (_____)_____

Direct fax no. (_____)_____

E-mail address _____

URL *http://www.*_____

Check/complete all applicable responses:

_____ We will send proposal and collateral to be received by (*due date*).

_____ Dates noted on first option basis are being held for this group.

_____ Dates will *not* be held until a contract is signed.

Dates available/First option   **Dates available/Second option**

_____   _____

_____   _____

_____   _____

_____ We regret we are ***unable to send a proposal*** for the following reason(s):

  _____ None of preferred dates available.

  _____ Meeting space and/or sleeping rooms not appropriate for meeting.

  _____ Unable to meet rate parameters.

  _____ Other (specify):

     _____

     _____

Comments:

GLOSSARY

Definitions are taken from the chapters or from http://glossary.conventionindustry.org.

802.11: Engineering specification for the wireless standard. This defines how a wireless interface between clients and access points is constructed.

Accepted Practices Exchange (APEX): Initiative of the meetings, expositions, events, and conventions industry managed by the Convention Industry Council (CIC). APEX develops and manages the implementation of accepted practices (voluntary standards) for the industry.

Act of God: Extraordinary natural event such as extreme weather, flood, hurricane, tornado, earthquake, or similar natural disaster that cannot be reasonably foreseen or prevented and over which a contracting party has no reasonable control. It makes performance of the contract illegal, impracticable, or impossible; thus the parties have no legal responsibility to continue performance of the contract.

Action station: Place where chef prepares foods to order and serves them fresh to guests. Popular items for action stations include pasta, grilled meat or shrimp, carved meats, sushi, crepes, omelets, flaming desserts, Caesar salad, and so on. Also called performance stations or exhibition cooking.

ADMEI: Association of Destination Management Executives International

Agenda: List, outline, or plan of items to be done or considered at an event or during a specific time block and may include a time schedule.

Air lift: A city where the space limitations of the convention center, the hotels, or the air lift make the city more appropriate for smaller meetings and events.

Amenity: Complimentary item in sleeping rooms such as writing supplies, bathrobes, fruit baskets, shower caps, shampoo, and shoe shine mitts provided by the facility for guests.

American Forests' Meeting ReLeaf: A way for associations to offset carbon emissions from their major meetings, while also achieving significant additional environmental benefits. American Forests will plant a tree in honor of every attendee at your meeting in a carefully chosen forest restoration project in the United States.

American service: Serving style where guests are seated and served food that has been preportioned and plated in the kitchen.

American Society of Association Executives (ASAE): Membership organization and voice of the association profession. Founded in 1920, ASAE now has more than 22,000 association CEOs, staff professionals, industry partners, and consultant members.

American Society of Composers, Authors, and Publishers (ASCAP): Membership organization that represents individuals who hold the copyrights to music written in the United States and that grants licensing agreements for the performance of that music.

Americans with Disabilities Act (ADA): U.S. legislation passed in 1992 requiring public buildings (offices, hotels, restaurants, etc.) to make adjustments meeting minimum standards to make their facilities accessible to individuals with physical disabilities.

Amphitheater: Outdoor facility with a flat performance area surrounded by rising rows of seats or a grassy slope that allows the audience to view the performance. The seating area is usually a semicircular shape or adapted to the surrounding landscape.

Ancillary activity: Event-related support services within a facility that generate revenue.

Annual meeting: Meeting that takes place once a year.

APEX Initiative: Industrywide task force formed to begin a codification of definitions and standardized practices, policies, procedures, and terminology.

Arena: Facility featuring a large, flat main floor surrounded by fixed seats in a sloping oval or modified oval shape, much steeper than the typical theater. Some are arranged in two or more tiers. Sight lines are nearly always designed for events the size of a hockey floor, circus, ice show, or basketball court.

Association: Organized group of individuals and/or companies that band together to accomplish a common purpose, usually to provide for the needs of its members. It is usually a nonprofit organization.

Association professional liability (APL): Policy that protects the organization and its officers, directors, staff, and volunteers against personal liability arising from their official actions. This type of policy is broader than a traditional directors and officers (D&O) liability policy in that it covers the organization as an entity as well as individuals.

Attrition: Difference between the actual number of sleeping rooms picked up (or food and beverage covers or revenue projections) and the number or formula agreed to in the terms of the facility's contract. Usually there is an allowable shortfall before damages are assessed.

Audience response system (ARS): System in which the audience is outfitted with small keypads that allow them to answer questions quickly and have their data tallied immediately.

Audiovisual (AV) company: Supplier of technical staff and audiovisual equipment (e.g., projectors, screens, sound systems, video, and staging).

Auditorium style: Seating arrangement where chairs are arranged in rows facing head table, stage, or speaker. Variations are semicircular and V-shaped. See theater setup.

Augmented Reality: A live direct or indirect view of a physical, real-world environment whose elements are augmented, or supplemented, by computer-generated sensory input such as sound, video, graphics, or GPS data.

Ausstellung: German term for consumer show.

Awards ceremony: Event (usually formal) to honor outstanding performance.

B2B: An event at which products, services, or promotional materials are displayed to attendees visiting exhibits on the show floor. These events focus primarily on business-to-business (B2B) relationships.

B2C: An event at which products, services, or promotional materials are displayed to attendees visiting exhibits on the show floor. These events focus primarily on business-to-consumer (B2C) relationships.

Bandwidth: Amount of information that can pass through a communications line. As it relates to the Web, bandwidth comes in two basic flavors: dial-up and high speed.

Banquet Event Order (BEO): Form most often used by hotels to provide details to personnel concerned with a specific food and beverage function or event room setup.

Banquet French service: Serving style where platters of food are composed in the kitchen. Each food item is then served from the guests' left by the server from platters to individual plates. Any course can be "Frenched" by having the dressing put on the salad or having sauce added to an entrée or dessert after it has been placed in front of the guest.

Barback: Cabinets and work space behind a bar where alcoholic beverages are served.

Blogging: Online diary that is posted to the Web.

Bluetooth: Telecommunications standard that allows mobile devices to communicate a short distance with each other. Most devices are capable of utilizing Bluetooth at a distance of no more than 30 feet.

Board meeting: Meeting of the Board of Directors of an organization that is usually small in size.

Boardroom: Room set permanently with a fixed table and suitable seating.

Boardroom setup: Seating arrangement in which rectangle- or oval-shaped tables are set up with chairs on both sides and ends. It is often confused with hollow square setup.

Bonding: Purchase, for a premium, of a guarantee of protection for a supplier or a customer. In the hospitality industry, certain bonding programs are mandatory.

Break-even point: Figure calculated by the CIC manual as the total fixed cost divided by the contribution margin (the registration fee minus the variable cost).

Breakout room: Small function room set up for a group within an event as opposed to a plenary or general session.

Breakout session: Small-group session, panel, workshop, or presentation offered concurrently within the event, formed to focus on specific subjects. The event is separate from the general session but is held within the event format. The sessions can be arranged by basic, intermediate, and advanced levels or divided by interest areas or industry segments.

Broadcast Music, Inc. (BMI): Music licensing organization that represents individuals who hold the copyrights to music written in the United States. It grants licensing agreements for the performance of music.

Buffet: Assortment of foods offered on a table and self-served.

Butler service: (1) Style of service that offers a variety of both hot and cold hors d'oeuvres on platters to guests at receptions. (2) Style of table service where guests serve themselves from platters presented by the server. (3) Specialized in-room service offered by a hotel.

Call brand: Brand of liquor, distinguished from the house brands, selected by a customer according to personal preference. It is usually of a higher quality than house brands.

Carbon footprint calculator: Method for determining how many tons of carbon dioxide and other greenhouse gases are produced from the implementation of a meeting or event.

Carbon footprint: The total sets of greenhouse gas emissions caused by an organization, event, product, or person.

Carbon offset: A reduction in emissions of carbon dioxide or greenhouse gases made in order to compensate for or to offset an emission made elsewhere.

Carnet: Customs document permitting the holder to carry or send merchandise temporarily into certain foreign countries (for display, demonstration, or similar purposes) without paying duties or posting bonds. *Also called* trade show bond.

Cart French service: Style of service that involves use of serving pieces (usually silver); heating and garnishing of food tableside by a captain;

and serving of food on a heated plate, which is then served to the guest by a server. Plated entrées are usually served from the right, bread and butter and salad from the left, and beverages from the right. All are removed from the right.

Catered event: Event that generally has one host and one bill. Most attendees eat the same meal.

Center for Exhibition Industry Research (CEIR): Member of the Convention Industry Council (CIC).

Certificate in Sustainable Event Planning: Certificate program offered by the Green Meetings Industry Council (GMIC) where students will walk away with the knowledge, tools, and confidence to implement the highest quality of sustainable meetings and events.

Certification in Green Meetings & Events (CGME): Certification for planners and suppliers interested in greening their meetings offered through the Association for Green Meetings & Events.

Certified meeting professional (CMP): The foremost certification program of today's meetings, conventions, and exhibitions industry. The CMP program recognizes individuals who have achieved the industry's highest standard of professionalism.

Citywide: An event that requires the use of a convention center or event complex, as well as multiple hotels in the host city.

Citywide event: Event that requires the use of a convention center or event complex as well as multiple hotels in the host city.

Classroom style: A meeting room setup where participants sit at desks much like in a classroom.

Clear span tent: Tent that has a strong roof structure so it is possible to hang lighting from the beams by using special clamps.

Client project: This term is used when discussing DMCs and their services.

Community infrastructure: Those facilities and companies in a locale that support the MEEC industry.

Complete meeting package (CMP): All-inclusive plan offered by conference centers that includes lodging, all food and beverage, and support services, including audiovisual equipment, room rental, and so on.

Comprehensive general liability (CGL): Policy that is the commercial equivalent of a homeowner's policy. It protects the organization against personal injury claims and loss (including theft) or damage to the insured's property as well as the property of others. Although these policies are designed to cover "all risks," they frequently have exclusions, and it is important to carefully review what is not covered as well as what is included within the policy's scope.

Concessionaire: Person or company that operates the concessions.

Concessions: All-inclusive plan offered by conference centers that includes lodging, all meals, and support services.

Concurrent session: One of multiple sessions scheduled at the same time. Programs on different themes or subjects are offered simultaneously.

Conference: (1) Participatory meeting designed for discussion, fact-finding, problem solving, and consultation. (2) Event used by any organization to meet and exchange views, convey a message, open a debate, or give publicity to some area of opinion on a specific issue. No tradition, continuity, or periodicity is required to convene a conference. Although not generally limited in time, conferences are usually of short duration with specific objectives and are on a smaller scale than congresses.

Conference apps: Apps very much like one has on a smartphone but targeting at meeting the needs of conference planners and attendees.

Conference center: Facility that provides a dedicated environment for events, especially small events. It may be certified by the International Association of Conference Centers (IACC).

Congress: (1) Regular coming together of large groups of individuals, generally to discuss a particular subject. A congress will often last several days and have several simultaneous sessions. The length of time between congresses is usually established in advance of the implementation stage and can be either pluri-annual or annual. Most international or world congresses are of the former type, while national congresses are more frequently held annually. (2) Meeting of an association of delegates or representatives from constituent organizations. (3) European term for convention. *See* Conference and Convention.

Consideration: Cause, motive, price, or impelling influence that induces a contracting party to enter a contract.

Continuing education unit (CEU): Requirement of many professional groups by which members must certify participation in formal educational programs designed to maintain their level of ability beyond their original certification date. CEUs are nonacademic credit. One CEU is awarded for each 10 contact hours in an accredited program.

Continuing medical education (CME): Requirement for doctors to retain their medical license. They must take a certain amount of CME courses to keep current with innovations in health care.

Contract: Agreement between two or more parties that creates in each party a duty to do or not do something and a right to performance of the other's duty or a remedy for the breach of the other's duty.

Convention: Event where the primary activity of the attendees is to attend educational sessions, participate in meetings/discussions, socialize, or attend other organized events. There is a secondary exhibit component.

Convention and visitor bureau (CVB): Not-for-profit organization charged with representing a specific destination and helping the long-term development of communities through a travel and tourism strategy. CVBs are usually membership organizations bringing together businesses that rely on tourism and events for revenue. For visitors, CVBs are like a key to the city. As an unbiased resource, CVBs can serve as a broker or an official point of contact for convention and event planners, tour operators, and visitors; they assist planners with event preparation and encourage business travelers and visitors alike to visit local historic, cultural, and recreational sites.

Convention Industry Council (CIC): Federation of national and international organizations representing individuals, firms, or properties involved in the meetings, conventions, exhibitions, and travel and tourism industries. Formerly the Convention Liaison Council.

Convention services manager (CSM): Person whose job is to oversee and arrange every aspect of an event. The CSM can be an employee or hired ad hoc to plan, organize, implement, and control meetings, conventions, and other events.

Copyright: Federal law that allows for the ownership of intellectual property (writings, art, music). Copy-written material cannot be used without the owner's permission or the payment of royalty fees.

Corkage: Charge placed on beer, liquor, and wine brought into the facility but purchased elsewhere. The charge sometimes includes glassware, ice, and mixers.

Corporate meeting: Gathering of employees or representatives of a commercial organization. Usually, attendance is required and travel, room, and most meal expenses are paid for by the organization.

Corporate Social Responsibility (CSR): Corporate initiative to assess and take responsibility for the company's effects on the environment and impact on social welfare.

Corporation: A group of people who obtain a charter granting them (as a body) legal power, rights, privileges and liabilities of an individual but distinct from those individuals making up the group.

Crescent rounds: Seating at round tables with chairs placed at two-thirds to three-quarters of the table and no seating with backs to the speaker.

Cutoff date: Designated date when the facility will release a block of sleeping rooms to the general public. The date is typically three to four weeks before the event.

Dates, rates, and space: Words that begin the maxim "Dates, rates, and space–You can only have two," which is used by hoteliers to sum up meeting negotiations. The meaning is that the planner can get the dates and meeting space he or she wants for a meeting but may have to give on the rate.

Destination: City, area, or country that can be marketed to groups or individuals as a place to visit or hold an event.

Destination management company (DMC): Professional services company possessing extensive local knowledge, expertise, and resources and specializing in the design and implementation of events, activities, tours, transportation, and program logistics. Depending on the company and the staff specialists in the company, a DMC offers, but is not limited to, the following: creative proposals for special events within the meeting; guest tours; VIP amenities and transportation; shuttle services; staffing within convention centers and hotels; team building, golf outings, and other activities; entertainment, including sound and lighting; décor and theme development; ancillary meetings for management professionals; and advance meetings and on-site registration services and housing.

Destination Marketing Association International (DMAI): World's largest resource for official destination marketing organizations (DMOs) dedicated to improving the effectiveness of DMOs in more than 25 countries. DMAI provides members with educational resources, networking opportunities, and marketing benefits worldwide.

Destination marketing organization (DMO): *See* CVB.

Destinations showcase: Fast-paced and productive one-day exhibition and conference sponsored by the International Association of Convention and Visitor Bureaus (IACVB) where qualified meeting professionals attend valuable education sessions, network with industry leaders and peers, and explore a full range of destinations from throughout the world.

Disability: The consequence of an impairment that may be physical, cognitive, mental, sensory, emotional, developmental, or some combination of these.

DMAI online RFP: Service provided by the DMAI where the meeting professional can visit and select the cities he or she is interested in and either fill out the RFP form provided or attach an already prepared RFP.

Drayage: Delivery of exhibit materials from the dock to an assigned exhibit space, removal of empty crates, return of crates at the end of the event for recrating, and delivery of materials back to the dock for carrier loading.

Early bird rate: Lowered rate offered as an incentive for attendees to send in registration before a predefinite date. *Also called* early bird discount.

Education session: Time period during which information or instruction is presented.

empowerMINT.com: The Web site for "Empowermint," a resource provided by the Destination Marketing Association International. It is an industry-wide, collaborative marketing initiative whose mission is to connect planners to DMOs.

English service: Style of service where guests are seated and large serving platters and bowls of food are placed on the dining table by the servers. Guests pass the food around the table.

Event miles: The total number of miles traveled by all attendees at a meeting, convention, or event.

Exclusive: Agreement that limits who may provide specific products or services under certain conditions to only one party. A general service contractor, for instance, may have an exclusive in a particular facility, meaning that no other contractor is allowed to provide the same services or products in that facility.

Exclusive contract: Contract between a facility and a service provider designating that provider as the only provider of specific services or products in that facility.

Exclusive service: Service that is provided only by the official service contractor.

Exhibit hall: Area within a facility where the exhibition is located.

Exhibition: (1) Event at which products and services are displayed. The primary activity of attendees is visiting exhibits on the show floor. These events focus primarily on business-to-business (B2B) relationships. (2) Display of products or promotional materials for the purposes of public relations, sales, and/or marketing.

Exhibition management company (EMC): Company or individual who designs and/or builds exhibits. The EMC may also provide other services.

Exhibition service contractor (ESC): Organizer or promoter of an exhibition responsible for rental of space as well as financial control and management of the exhibition. Sometimes an agent can act in this capacity.

Exhibitor-appointed contractor (EAC): Company other than the designated "official" contractor providing a service to an exhibitor. EACs are a subset of service contractors that work for the exhibiting company and travel throughout the country setting up and dismantling their booths rather than working from one city or location.

Exhibitor service manual: Manual or kit, usually developed by the service contractor for an event, containing general event information, labor/service order forms, rules and regulations, and other information pertinent to an exhibitor's participation in an exhibition.

Expenditure Impact Study (ExPact): Study that updates the International Association of Convention and Visitor Bureaus (IACVB) delegate, exhibitor, and event organizer spending information for meetings, conventions, and trade shows. Additionally, ExPact provides an estimate for the economic impact that this industry has on the United States and Canada. Formerly known as the Convention Expenditure and Impact Study.

Experiential CSR: Corporate Social Responsibility activities that are active or "experiential" rather than passive.

Exposition: (1) Event at which products and services are displayed. The primary activity of attendees is visiting exhibits on the show floor. These events focus primarily on business-to-business (B2B) relationships. (2) Display of products or promotional material for the purposes of public relations, sales, and/or marketing.

Exposition management company (EMC): Company that is in the business of owning and managing trade shows and expositions. EMCs both develop and produce shows that profit their companies as well as produce events for a sponsoring corporation, association, or government client.

Exposition service contractor (ESC): *See* General Service Contractor (GSC).

Fair: (1) Enterprise principally devoted to the exhibition of products of agriculture or industry. Typically, fairs also provide entertainment activities such as rides, games, and food concessions. (2) Exhibition of products or services in a specific area of activity held with the objective of promoting business.

Fairs: (1) Event principally devoted to the exhibition of agricultural products or industrial products. Fairs may also provide entertainment activities. (2) Exhibition of products or services in a specific area of activity held with the objective of promoting business.

Fam trip: Familiarization trips. Method of promoting a destination or particular facility to a meeting planner. Fam trips are a no- or low-cost trip for planners to personally review sites for their suitability for a meeting. These trips may be arranged by a local community or by a hotel directly.

Festival: A special celebration usually involving a community.

Festivals and public events: Gatherings of people that focus on the community rather than sports, conventions, or business activities.

Field staff: Staff that are responsible for handling the installation and dismantling of freight, drayage, carpentry, electrical equipment, and plumbing and the oversight of iron workers, riggers, and maintenance crews.

First-tier city: City that is notoriously expensive based on the average year-round cost for one night—single room, corporate rate, plus three meals per day, and taxes—at a first-class hotel. *See* Second-tier City.

Fixed costs: Expenses incurred regardless of the number of attendees.

Food and beverage minimum: A lower limit or threshold above which a group agrees to spend on food and beverage during their event.

Force majeure: Event (e.g., war, labor strike, extreme weather, or other disruptive circumstances) or effect that cannot be reasonably anticipated or controlled. *Also called* fortuitous event. *See* Act of God.

Frame tent: Tent that is set up on the grass. It is one of the simplest of all meeting venues and requires little advance planning beyond making sure the tent rental people can get set up in time. *Also called* open-sided tent.

Function: (1) Organized occasion that contributes to a larger event. (2) Activity or role assigned to an event planner (or other industry professional).

Gamification: The use of game thinking and game mechanics in non-game contexts to engage users in solving problems. It is often incorporated into MEEC programming.

Gantt Charts: A type of bar chart, developed by Henry Gantt in the 1910s, that illustrates a project schedule.

General service contractor (GSC): Organization hired by the show manager to handle the general duties necessary to produce the show on-site, providing a wide range of services. *Also called* official show contractor. *See* Exposition Service Contractor (ESC).

General session: Meeting open to all those in attendance at an event. *See* Plenary Session.

Gesellschaft: German term for company or society.

GMBH: German term for a limited liability company.

Going Green: The action by an entity to incorporate sustainable practices.

Government agencies: Subdivisions of federal, state, or local government.

Green: *See* sustainability.

Green meeting: Incorporating sustainable practices.

Green Movement: The philosophical initiative to embrace sustainable practices.

Green sheen: The practice of companies disingenuously attempting to show that they are adopting practices beneficial to the environment.

Greenwashing: Refers to any misrepresentation by a company that leads the consumer to believe that their policies and products are environmentally responsible, when their claims are false, misleading, or cannot be verified. Greenwashing is also used to identify the practice of companies spending more money on the campaign to notify customers of their environmentally friendly efforts, than the efforts themselves.

Group history: Document that provides detailed information regarding previous events an entity has held.

Guarantee: Amount of food that the planner has instructed the facility to prepare and that will be paid for.

Hard data: *See* Quantitative Data.

History: Record of an event over time.

Hosted buyer: The business practice whereby a potential "buyer" of convention products or services has their travel expenses paid by exhibitors at a convention in return for agreeing to meet with exhibitors. The concept was originated by Ray Bloom of the IMEX group in the United Kingdom.

Hotel: A type of accommodation where one pays for the service.

House brand: Brand of wine or distilled spirits selected by a hotel or restaurant as its standard when no specific brand is specified. *Also called* well brand.

Housing bureau: Third-party outsourced company that handles all hotel arrangements for a fee (that may be paid by the local convention and visitor bureau).

Hybrid meeting: A meeting or convention that incorporates technological elements into their programming.

IACVB Resource Center: Online center that is a new and developing industry resource and that houses valuable information for CVB professionals. As the center continues to grow, a wealth of resources, such as sample bureau operations documents and bureau research statistics, will be provided. The IACVB Resource Center will also strive to act as a referral source for other industry-related information.

Incentive event: Reward event intended to showcase persons who meet or exceed sales or production goals. *Also called* incentive program.

Incentive trip: Travel reward given by companies to employees to stimulate productivity.

Incentive travel programs: A reward system for performance where travel rather than cash or products is given as the reward.

Indirect costs: Costs that are listed as overhead or administrative line items in a program budget. These are organizational expenses not directly related to the meeting, such as staff salaries, overhead, or equipment repair.

In-line exhibit: Exhibit space with exhibit booths on either side and back.

Interactive nametag: Radio frequency identification (RFID) either attached to a slim piece of paper behind a badge or made part of a slightly larger wearable nametag device. The RFID-based service offers better networking and interactivity between conference attendees as well as between attendees and vendors.

International Association of Conference Centers (IACC): Association in which member facilities must meet a list of over 30 criteria to be considered an approved conference center.

International Association of Convention and Visitor Bureaus (IACVB): Member of the Convention Industry Council (CIC). Now DMAI.

International Congress and Convention Association: Large international association.

Island booth: Booth/stand space with aisles on all four sides.

Keynote address: Session that opens or highlights the show, meeting, or event.

Kongress: The German spelling for a congress—a convention.

KSAs: Knowledge, Skills and Abilities.

Lead retrieval system: Process used to capture customer information. The process begins with the meeting organizer asking questions during the registration process that will identify information of importance to the exhibitor.

Level: (1) Level of audio volume. Level refers to the power magnitude in either electrical watt or acoustic watts but is often incorrectly used to denote voltage. (2) The relative depth of knowledge of attendees.

Local event: Event, such as a graduation ceremony or a local festival, that draws its audience primarily from the local market. Typically 80% of attendees reside within a 50-mile (80-km) radius of the event site. Local audiences typically do not require overnight accommodations.

Loss leader: Item offered by a retailer at cost or less than cost to attract customers. *Also called* price leader.

Material handling: Services performed by general service contractor (GSC) that include delivery of exhibit materials from the dock to assigned space, removal of empty crates, return of crates at the end of the event for recrating, and delivery of materials back to the dock for carrier loading. It is a two-way charge, incoming and outgoing. *See* Drayage.

MBECS: Meeting and Business Event Competency Standards.

MEEC: Meetings, Expositions, Events, and Conventions.

Meet and greet: System of deploying individuals at critical points of arrival for meeting or event attendees with the purpose of 'greeting' them and providing information.

Meeting: Event where the primary activity of the attendees is to attend educational sessions, participate in meetings/discussions, socialize, or attend other organized events. There is no exhibit component to this event.

Meeting event order (MEO): Specifications for each function that is part of the overall meeting or event.

Meeting event specification guide: Document used by a planner to communicate specific requirements for a function. It includes a general overview of the event, a timetable outlining all functions that compose the overall event, and specifications for each function that is part of the overall event.

Meeting Industry Network (MINT): Online information network tracking historical and future site/booking information. MINT is provided by the International Association of Convention and Visitor Bureaus (IACVB) to its members. Formerly the Convention Industry Network (CINET).

Meeting professional: Person whose job is to oversee and arrange every aspect of an event. This person can be an employee or hired ad hoc by large companies, professional associations, or trade associations to plan, organize, implement, and control meetings, conventions, and other events.

Meeting Professionals International (MPI): Member organization of the Convention Industry Council (CIC).

Meeting time line: Schedule that includes each task to be accomplished. It is the core of the program plan.

Messe: German term for trade fair.

Messegelande: German term for fair site.

Multilevel exhibit: System often used by large companies to expand their exhibit space without taking up more floor space. The upper floor may be used for special purposes, such as meeting areas, private demonstration areas, or hospitality stations.

Needs analysis: Planning tool used to determine the client's needs and expectations for a meeting.

Negotiation: Process by which a meeting planner and a hotel representative (or other supplier) reach an agreement on the terms and conditions that will govern their relationship before, during, and after a meeting, convention, exposition, or event.

Network: (1) Two or more computers or peripherals that are linked together for the purpose of sharing data. (2) Two or more people gathering in an informal setting.

NFC: The abbreviation for near field communication. It is a set of standards for smartphones and other mobile devices to establish radio communication with each other by touching them together or bringing them into close proximity, usually no more than a few centimeters.

Nonprofit association: Association whose members may not benefit financially from its net proceeds.

Not-for-profit: Organization that exists with the intention of providing a service for its members.

OfficialTravelGuide.com: Official Web site of the International Association of Convention and Visitor Bureaus (IACVB) that links consumers and meeting professionals directly to the CVBs and tourist boards. On this site, there is official information for 1,000+ destinations, including information on hotels, conference centers, convention centers, attractions, and activities.

Off-premises catering: Foods that are usually prepared in a central kitchen and transported for service to an off-site location.

Online meeting: Web-based service where participants meet virtually, using tools such as shared desktops, PowerPoint presentations, IM/chatting, and voice conferencing.

On-premises catering: Meals that are catered on-site during an event.

Opening ceremony: Formal general session at the beginning of a congress or convention.

Operations and production: Performance of the practical work of operating a program. It usually involves the in-house control and handling of all phases of the services, both with suppliers and with clients.

Outlet: Restaurant, lounge, or retail store within a facility.

Outsourcing: Hiring of an outside firm or individual to perform a task instead of using in-house staff or subcontracting of a task or responsibility to a third party.

Parol evidence: Evidence of an oral agreement that can be used in limited instances, especially where the plain meaning of words in the written document may be in doubt. A court will generally construe a contract most strongly against the party that prepared the written document; if there is a conflict between printed and handwritten words or phrases, the latter will prevail.

Peninsula booth: Exhibit with aisles on three sides.

Per diem rate: Rate paid per day. Some event attendees, such as government employees, have a limited amount of money (a daily allowance) they can spend per day on food, lodging, and other expenses.

Permit: License required by many local governments to use parks or even private property for special events. The police, the fire department, and (in many places) the building code officer must be notified when a permit is desired.

Personal digital assistant (PDA): Mobile communications device that provides individuals with most of their critical needs, such as calendars and contacts, in a handheld device.

Pickup: Of the hotel rooms set aside for a group, the number actually used by event participants or "picked up."

PLC: German term for public limited company.

Plenary session: General assembly for all participants.

Podcasting: Method of distributing multimedia files, such as audio or video programs, for playback on mobile devices and personal computers.

Pole tent: A temporary fabric-covered shelter that is supported by one or more poles in the middle of the area.

Portal: An electronic access point.

Postconvention meeting: Meeting held after an event to address any billing discrepancies, service failures, and other problems or to praise facility staff for a job well done.

Poster session: (1) Display of reports and papers, usually scientific, accompanied by authors or researchers. (2) Session dedicated to the discussion of the posters shown inside the meeting area. When this discussion is not held in a special session, it can take place directly between the person presenting the poster and interested delegate(s).

Pre-con: A pre-conference meeting at the primary facility at which an event will take place just prior to the event beginning. Attendees generally include the primary event organizer, representatives of the event organizer/host organization, department heads at the facility, other facility staff as appropriate, and contractors. The agenda focuses on reviewing the purpose and details of the event and making final adjustments as needed. Compare with post-con meeting.

Preconvention session: Meeting at the primary facility at which an event will take place just prior to the event beginning. Attendees generally include the primary event organizer and/or representatives of the final adjustments as needed. *Also called* pre-con meeting.

Prefunction space: Area adjacent to the main event location often used for receptions prior to a meal or coffee breaks during an event.

Premium brand: Higher-quality, higher-priced spirits (hard liquor).

Preregistration: Process of registering attendees weeks or months in advance of an event. This benefits the planner in several ways.

Presenter contract: Contract for the person explaining a given topic in an informational session.

Preset service: Style of service that puts plated foods on banquet tables prior to seating guests.

Profile: Detailed information about a traveler and/or a company kept on file by a travel management company.

Program: Schedule of events that gives details of times and places.

Promotional mix model: Mix that includes four elements: advertising, sales promotion, publicity and/or public relations, and personal selling. However, this author views direct marketing as well as interactive media as additional major elements in a promotional mix model.

Proposal: (1) Plan put forth for consideration or acceptance and (2) communication sent by a supplier to a potential customer detailing the supplier's offerings and prices.

Public show: Exhibition that is open to the public, usually requiring an entrance fee. The attendees are basically defined by their interests and geographic proximity to the show location.

Qualitative data: Descriptive information that is a record of what is observed, presented in narrative by the respondent. *Also called* soft data.

Quantitative data: Information that is represented numerically, that can be assigned ranks or scores, and that can be used to determine averages and frequencies. *Also called* hard data.

Rack rate: Facility's standard preestablished guest room rates.

Radio frequency identification device (RFID): Tag attached to a product or device that emits a short-distance signal that allows the user to accurately track information.

Really simple syndication (RSS): Tool by which a Web site creates or gathers a feed of information about a specific topic and publishes it as an RSS feed. This information is updated continuously.

Request for proposal (RFP): Document that stipulates what services the organization wants from an outside contractor and requests a bid to perform such services.

Return on investment (ROI): Net profit divided by net worth. This financial ratio indicates the degree of profitability.

Risk: The potential of losing something of value.

Risk management: Recognition of and plan for the possibility of injury, damage, or loss as well as the means to prevent it or provide insurance.

Room block: Number of rooms guaranteed by the event planner. These rooms are subtracted from the hotel inventory as attendees make reservations.

Room design software: Computer-aided design (CAD) that is applicable to room design. This software is used to enhance communications between the venue, the meeting planner, and the client.

Room list: Listing that is compiled as attendees reserve rooms with their organization and then given to the hotel. In the case of a small high-profile event, the room list includes the type of room and special requests.

Room setup: Physical arrangement of a room, including the layout of tables, chairs, and other furniture.

Rooming list: A list, whether printed or electronic, by which an event organizer and/or their designates (e.g., a housing bureau) delivers multiple reservations to a hotel or other housing facility. Often the information contained in a rooming list is originally gathered through attendees' completed Housing Forms.

Roundtable session: Group of experts who meet on an equal basis to review and discuss specialized professional matters, either in closed session or (more frequently) before an audience.

Russian service: Style of service where foods are cooked tableside on a réchaud (portable cooking stove) that is on a gueridon (tableside cart with wheels). Servers place the food on platters and then pass the platters at tableside. Guests help themselves from the platters.

Sales and marketing: Process of identifying human wants and needs and developing a plan to meet those wants and needs. It encompasses everything involved with convincing an attendee to come to the event and also refers to providing information to support the exhibit sales function.

Schedule: Listing of times and locations for all functions related to an event. This information should be included in the specifications guide for an event.

Schedule of events: Timetable that outlines all functions that compose the overall meeting or event.

Seasonality: Period of time when the demand for a certain supplier's product or service is usually high, low, or neither. For example, winter in Florida is high season, while summer is low season.

Second-tier city: Destination city that is often more affordable than major cities. It is more likely to negotiate the best prices for accommodations and services. *See* First-tier City.

Service contractor: Outside company used by clients to provide specific products or services (e.g., pipe and drape, exhibitor manuals, floor plans, dance floors, or flags).

Set Over Guarantee: The number of seats or places a facility sets up over and above the minimum number assured by the host.

Shoulder: Beginning and ending days of a room block when fewer rooms are contracted.

Shoulder season: Period when the demand for a supplier's product or service is neither high nor low.

Showcase: Event to preview/highlight someone or something.

Signing authority: Person from the sponsoring organization who has the authority to make additions or changes to what has been ordered.

Site inspection: In-person on-site review and evaluation of a venue or location for an event. *See* Fam Trip.

Site selection: Process of deciding the physical location for the event, the type of facility to use, the transportation options, and many other meeting components.

SMART: Acronym for the critical components of a well-written objective: Specific, Measurable, Achievable, Relevant, Time.

Smartphone: 3G phone that supports not only voice but high-speed data transmission. This allows the smartphone to be used for services such as Web browsing, e-mail access, and audio/video streaming.

SMERF: Acronym for certain categories of meeting market segments: Social, Military, Educational, Religious, and Fraternal.

Social event: (1) Event with the purpose of facilitating pleasant companionship among attendees or (2) life cycle celebration (e.g., wedding, bar/bat mitzvah, anniversary, birthday).

Social media: The social interaction among people in which they create, share, or exchange information and ideas in virtual communities and networks.

Soft data: *See* Qualitative Data.

Sourcing: Refers to a number of procurement practices aimed at finding, evaluating, and engaging suppliers of goods and services.

Speaker bureau: Professional talent broker who can help find the perfect speaker to match the event objectives as well as the budget.

Speaker guidelines: (1) Instructions regarding the specific expectations for a speaker at an event. Usually outlined is the required format for presentations, AV request procedures, travel and accommodations instructions, and so on. (2) Instructions regarding the required format to be used for the written preparation of a speech.

Speaker ready room: Area set aside for speakers to meet, relax, test audiovisual equipment, or prepare prior to or between speeches. *Also called* ready room and try-out room.

Special event: Onetime event staged for the purpose of celebration; unique activity.

Specialty service contractor: Supplier that deals with a specific area of show production or event service, such as photography, furniture rental, audiovisual equipment, or floral decoration.

Specification Guide: Spec Guide. The industry preferred term for a comprehensive document that outlines the complete requirements and instructions for an event. This document is typically authored by the event planner and is shared with all appropriate vendors as a vehicle to communicate the expectations of services for a project. *Sometimes called* Staging Guide, Résumé, Bible.

Sponsor: (1) Person or company underwriting all or part of the costs of an event. Sponsors may or may not participate in any of the profit from the event. (2) Individual who assumes all or part of the financial responsibility for an event or commercial sponsor that provides financial backing for an aspect of an event and in return receives visibility, advertising, or other remuneration in lieu of cash.

Sporting event: Event where athletes compete and spectators view the athletic activities and ceremonies.

Sports facilities: Venues in which sporting events are held.

Stadium: Facility that is usually designed for baseball or football as a primary function and that may be domed or open. It is sometimes difficult to distinguish a stadium from a large arena.

Stand: European term for booth or exhibit. *See* Standard Booth.

Standard booth: One or more standard units of exhibit space. In the United States, a standard unit is generally known to be a 10-foot by 10-foot space (one standard booth/stand unit equals 100 square feet). However, if an exhibitor purchases multiple units side by side or back to back, the combined space is also still referred to as a booth or a stand. It is a specific area assigned by management to an exhibitor under contractual agreement. *See* Stand.

Subject matter expert: A person with in-depth knowledge of a particular topic.

Sustainability: Practices and development that can continue indefinitely without degrading the environment.

Tablescapes: Décor and decoration places on top of tables such as flower arrangements.

Theater: Facility with fixed seats, usually on a sloped floor, with sight lines focused on a permanent stage. Typically, a stage box is located behind the proscenium, which contains the performance area and the fly loft.

Theme party: Event at which all foods, beverages, decorations, and entertainment relate to a single theme.

Third Parties: Intermediaries in the sales process such as Hotels.com for hotel rooms or Experient for meeting and convention venues.

Track: Separation of programming into specific genres, such as computer skills, professional development, marketing, personal growth, legal issues, certification courses, and financial issues.

Trade exhibition: *See* Trade Show.

Trade fair: International term for an exhibition.

Trade fair bond: When exhibiting tangible products outside the home country of the organization, a Temporary Importation Bond (TIB) or Carnet must be posted. This is usually equivalent to the sales tax of VAT generated by that product and is meant to ensure that the product is "exported" after the trade show or exhibition.

Trade Fair Certification Program: Program developed by the U.S. Department of Commerce to promote exports of U.S. products and services abroad. The Trade Fair Certification Program endorses independent and association show organizers who manage and organize overseas events. The certification helps trade fairs attract more exhibitors, provides additional support and value-added services for exhibitors, and promotes the event through a variety of publications and sources.

Trade show: Exhibition of products and/or services held for members of a common or related industry that is not open to the general public.

Trade show bond: Method used so that goods can be temporarily imported to an international show site without having to pay duties or taxes. *See* Carnet.

Twitter: An online social networking service that enables users to send and read short 140-character messages called "tweets."

U.S. Department of Commerce: Cabinet department of the U.S. government concerned with promoting economic growth.

Variable costs: Expenses that vary based on the number of attendees.

Venue: (1) Site or destination of meeting, event, or show. (2) Location of a performance, such as a hall, a ballroom, or an auditorium.

Videoconference: Conference that uses video (and typically audio) to send content to and from facilities. Traditionally, videoconferencing is not Web-based; it uses production facilities to both upload and download the information.

VIP services: Services provided to a very important person who has a special function at the event (speaker, dignitary, etc.) and who should be treated with special care and attention.

Virtual tour: Technology tool that is ideal for remote site inspections but that can also be used in tandem with a traditional site visit (perhaps used with a laptop or personal computer), where a planner can call up alternate room setups and capacity information at a single click.

Virtual trade show: Attendee-based trade show that is an online experience where the individual can "walk the floor" and "visit booths" without leaving his or her home or office. Varying styles of interactivity and graphics are used in this approach.

Voice over Internet protocol (VoIP): Digital telephone that is used with a high-speed Internet connection to make and receive phone calls.

VoIP: Abbreviation for voice over internet protocol that enables telephone-like conversations to be carried over the internet. Skype is an example.

Web casting: Streaming audio and video, using the Web as the delivery tool to deliver content to individuals.

Web conferencing: Catch-all term to describe the various types of e-learning options available to the planner and attendee.

Webinar: A service that allows conferencing events to be shared with remote locations.

Well brand: Brand of wine or distilled spirits selected by a hotel or restaurant as its standard when no specific brand is specified. *Also called* house brand.

Workshop: (1) Meeting of several persons for intensive discussion. The workshop concept has been developed to compensate for diverging views in a particular discipline or on a particular subject. (2) Informal and public session of free discussion organized to take place between formal plenary sessions or commissions of a congress or of a conference, either on a subject chosen by the participants themselves or on a special problem suggested by the organizers. (3) Training session in which participants, often through exercises, develop skills and knowledge in a given field.

World Trade Centers Association: Association created in 1970 as an apolitical not-for-profit organization to promote the concept of world trade centers worldwide and to encourage reciprocal programs among all of its members. Today, there are more than 300 world trade centers in 91 countries servicing more than 750,000 international businesses.

Yield management: Computer program that uses variable pricing models to maximize the return on a fixed (perishable) inventory, such as hotel rooms, based on supply-and-demand theory.

INDEX